THE STORY
OF MY LIFE

THE STORY OF MY LIFE

Benno Gitter

*Translated from
the Hebrew by
David and Leah Zinder*

Weidenfeld & Nicolson
LONDON

First published in Great Britain in 1999
by Weidenfeld & Nicolson

First published in Hebrew in 1997 by Schocken Publishing House Ltd, Tel Aviv
Hebrew edition published with the help of Yehudit Rotem.

A CIP catalogue record for this book
is available from the British Library.

ISBN 0 297 64371 1

Filmset by Selwood Systems, Midsomer Norton
Printed in Great Britain by
Butler & Tanner Ltd, Frome and London

Weidenfeld & Nicolson
The Orion Publishing Group Ltd
Orion House
5 Upper Saint Martin's Lane
London, WC2H 9EA

To my grandchildren
Yifat, Sharon, Boaz, Ariela and Dafna
that they will know my family – their family.

CONTENTS

INTRODUCTION

Most people have one homeland, just as they have only one mother, but in my life I have had the good fortune to be able to call three different countries home. Holland is where I was born and educated and where I spent my formative years; Argentina gave me and my entire family a safe haven when we fled the horrors of Nazi persecution; and Israel, the land of my childhood dreams, is now my country, the land where I live my life. To each of these three homelands I owe a profound debt of gratitude. I love all three, and am deeply attached to them all. They are the threads out of which the fabric of my life has been woven, and each has made its own unique contribution to what I am today.

I emigrated to Israel with my wife, Alice, and my daughters, Beatriz and Judith, in 1954. My daughters, nicknamed Bixie and Judy, have given me five wonderful grandchildren, in whose bright eyes I now see reflected the future of my family. Bixie has worked for over twenty years in one of the banks I helped establish in Israel, and has one daughter, Yif'at. In August 1998, as I was preparing this English version of this book, Yif'at married Ran Kivetz, who is now completing his studies at Stanford University in the United States, and she will soon be continuing her studies there herself. Judy and her husband, Yitzhak Shweiger, both lawyers, have four children: Sharon, Boaz, Ariela and Dafna. Three of my five grandchildren have already completed their army service, while the two younger ones are still in high school.

Apart from those I love whose presence enriches my life today, including my immediate family, my brothers, Shimon and Ya'akov and their families, my beloved companion, Ilana, and many friends and relatives, deep in my heart I also cherish the memory of those who are no longer with me: my wife Alice, my daughter Ariela, and my parents, Natan and Jenny Gitter. People are always deeply attached to the places where they feel closest to their loved ones, both those who have passed

I

away and those who are still alive. For me, from every possible point of view, Israel is that place: Israel is home.

My commitment to public service, as strong today as it ever was, has been one of the most characteristic pathways of my life. I consider it among my greatest achievements. Not long after my Bar Mitzvah, I was already actively involved in a religious-Zionist youth movement in Amsterdam known as Zichron Jacob. Decades have passed since then. As a rule, I don't enjoy passing judgement on people or events, but there are times today when I feel that Zionist values are no longer as widely respected as in the past. The 'New Historians' are very critical of the Zionist movement, and generally seek to highlight its defects. I myself am not a historian of any kind – either radical or conservative – but I certainly do not count myself among the critics or the iconoclasts. This story is about my own 'Zionist connection'. Although I feel uncomfortable with hyperbole, one thing is certain: I have had the great privilege of being involved in several momentous and dramatic events in the years leading up to the creation of the state and immediately afterwards. Basically I am a man of action, and therefore to this very day I am still working hard and trying to do some good.

Writing an autobiography almost invariably raises questions among the sceptics, such as 'Why?' or 'What for?' As I go on writing, I, too, continually ask myself: why and for whom am I making this effort? While I have never been prone to any form of self-revelation, it was my late, beloved daughter, Ariela, who committed me to this unusual task when she requested, or rather commanded: 'Abba, write your memoirs, if for no other reason than for your children.' She was fourteen years old at the time, a short time before her tragic, unexpected death. Her bright, innocent and shining wisdom has guided me ever since, giving me the strength to carry on with the challenge of writing, even though it is a task that is both new and daunting for me.

In this book I shall try to present the events of my life as I have witnessed them, although, naturally, some of my experiences and private thoughts will, of necessity, be kept safely locked away until after my death. I will not try to touch up any events in order to portray them in a more favourable light. I am totally committed to bringing the truth – my own truth – to light. Some of the experiences I have been through have caused me pain and disappointment; but anyone who has lived as long as I have eventually learns that life is an endless play of light and shadow, and sometimes the shadows gather and obscure the light. Despite the pain I have suffered in my lifetime, I count optimism among my more prominent qualities. At this point in my life, when I put all the good and the bad in the balance and weigh them against each other, as I have done so often in the past, I still find that despite all the tragedies, the anguish and the disappointments the good invariably far outweighs the bad.

This is not the first time I have tried my hand at writing. I have attempted, on a number of occasions, to set down in writing some chapters of my autobiography. And each time I have discovered once again how right the Chief Rabbi of Amsterdam, Rabbi Sarlouis, was, when he jokingly inverted the meaning of the Biblical injunction 'Hishamer lekha pen . . .' ('Beware lest . . .') to mean 'Beware of the pen'. And indeed, more than seventy years ago my elementary school teachers already noticed my limited prowess with the pen, as opposed to my much greater success in public speaking and conversation. Over many decades I have proven my ability to win over listeners to my point of view, and successfully promote business or personal interests through public speaking, private conversation, or meetings with individuals or groups. Now I have set myself a new challenge: to prove myself in a different medium. It is a new and intriguing task, and throughout my life I have always enjoyed taking on challenges.

My previous inability to complete the task of turning my life story into a book has not weakened my resolve. A deep, inner conviction, springing from an ongoing process of soul-searching, assured me that this is a story that deserved to outlive its author. I have played a part in many of the epoch-making events that shaped the present era in the history of the Jewish people, an era that has been one of the most dramatic in the annals of our nation. And it is for this reason, more than any other, that I feel that I cannot allow my story to disappear after me into the grave. Although it is a story that begins with my childhood in Holland before the war, I have no intention of turning the Holocaust into the main issue of this book. At the same time, it is vitally important to me to describe my own part, and that of my family and my community, in that terrible experience. We were incredibly lucky, and managed to survive, but we were not spared the trauma, whose aftershocks still reverberate through everything I have done during sixty years of ceaseless endeavour that has touched upon the fate of countries and individuals in three continents, and shaped my Zionist convictions and deepest personal feelings.

I have made many decisions in my lifetime, and today, as I look back on the past, and inward into my soul, I am fascinated by the process of decision-making – my own and others'. In fact, I believe that whenever we weigh the pros and cons of alternative courses of action, they are never absolutely evenly balanced. Every decision, or lack of a decision (and deciding not to decide is, after all, also a decision), is usually the only option possible at a particular moment in time, even though in retrospect one may eventually conclude that it was not, after all, the wisest choice. I realize that this sounds like an apology before the fact, but people do indulge in soul-searching once in a while – certainly when they reach my age and decide to write their autobiography.

And so I am about to embark on my journey into the world of writing. More than anything else, it will be a journey inwards, an attempt to sum up my life until this moment in time. Despite the relatively public nature of this soul-searching, for me it has been a very personal, very intimate process. I am about to take my readers with me into my story of escape and salvation, healing and building, of ends and beginnings, difficulties, failures and successes. This is a story of tragic personal loss, but also of friendships and deep personal bonds whose glowing memory warms my heart with the undying flame of comradeship. Quite possibly, my writing may occasionally wander, focusing, through flashes of unexpected associations, on minor details that relate only obliquely to the main stream of the story. Please bear with me, and if, dear reader, from time to time a smile lights up your face, I will feel that my efforts will not have been in vain.

Tel Aviv
Autumn 1998

PART I

HOLLAND

1

A NEW HOMELAND

I was born Mozes Bernhard Gitter in Amsterdam, the capital of Holland, on 8 May 1919. My nickname – Benno – the name by which I have been known for most of my life, was derived from Bernhard. My parents, Jenny Fischler and Natan, son of Shimshon Gitter, were married in Vienna at the beginning of 1915, but soon after their marriage, in the spring of the same year, they moved to Holland. At that time, with the First World War raging in Europe, they were afraid that my father would be drafted into the Austrian army. Apart from his reluctance to risk his life in a senseless war, my father also objected in principle to serving in an army that was notorious for its anti-Semitism and the humiliating treatment of its Jewish conscripts. My father's fateful decision on this matter eventually became a model that our family emulated at other critical moments in our lives. It was as though he had intuitively foreseen our escape from Holland, our change of nationality, of home and of fortunes. In moving his new family away from Vienna he set an example for us in the years that followed: 'We do not wait until danger shows up on our doorstep.'

The move was no easy matter. My mother was nineteen years old and already pregnant with my elder brother Shimon ('Zigi' as he would be known in the family), and my father was twenty-six. Their characters had been moulded in the predominantly Jewish towns of their birth in Eastern Europe, and there was no one waiting for them in Holland to ease them into a new life in the strange land that was to become their adopted homeland. For both my parents, Holland was totally foreign, in its language, its manners, and the customs of the local Jewish community. Nevertheless, they looked forward to the future with high hopes. Unlike many Jewish immigrants, who moved into the Scheveningen suburb of The Hague, bringing with them the lifestyle they had been accustomed to in their home towns, my parents chose to live in the city itself, and it was there that my brother Shimon was born.

As soon as they began to feel more confident about their new surroundings and new nationality, they moved to Amsterdam.

My father, the youngest of eight children, was born in a small town
called Horodenka with a total population of 12,000 inhabitants, two-
thirds of whom were Jewish. The town was situated in a contested
region of Europe that changed hands a number of times during the
early part of the twentieth century. Initially a part of Austria, it was
annexed first by the Ukraine at the end of the First World War, then
by Poland, and later by Russia. Finally, after the collapse of the Soviet
Union, Horodenka once again became Ukrainian territory. I know very
little about my father's doings from the time he left his parents' home
at the age of fourteen, following the early death of his father, until the
time he settled with my mother in Amsterdam. From the little I do
know, I gather that it was during those years that he acquired his
knowledge of the tanning trade, and the technology and marketing
strategies that went with it. I can only assume that he acquired the
greater part of his training as an apprentice in a tannery. The eldest of his
brothers-in-law, his sister Tzirel's husband, was in the leather business, as
were other members of their family, and my father must have inhaled
the aroma of leather being treated in the workshop in the backyard,
along with all the other scents of his childhood. An equally important
part of his training came from his own observations, ideas and inven-
tiveness. My father was, in fact, a self-taught man. He never had the
opportunity to sit and study in an orderly fashion, but what began as
a necessity soon became his second nature. Throughout his life, his
achievements in business, or in cultural and intellectual pursuits, were
those of a self-made man. To the end of his days he was a man of lively
curiosity in many varied fields, and always seeking ways to broaden his
horizons through his own efforts. Natan Gitter was one of the most
influential people in my life, if not *the* most influential. He laid the
foundation upon which I later built my own life. If, in the course of
this narrative, I speak of him again and again, it is not only because of
my love and admiration for him, but also because our lives intertwined
and intersected on so many levels for many years. In his lifetime and
after his passing, he was one of the most powerful motivating forces in
my life story.

My mother was born in Stanislawow, a provincial capital in East

Galicia, some forty kilometres from Horodenka. Conceivably, when my father first began journeying beyond the limits of his own town to the 'world at large', Stanislawow must have seemed to him to be a major metropolitan centre. It was there that he met my mother, though I never learned the exact details of their first encounter. My mother was a beautiful woman, cultured and warm-hearted, a true *Yiddische Mamme*. She was the second of six children in a well-to-do family.

I met my maternal grandfather, Alter (Yisrael) Fischler, only once, during a two-week trip we took to the 'old country' of Galicia in 1926. I was very impressed by his Hassidic bearing: his large beard and side-locks, his beribboned *shtreimel* (fur-trimmed hat) and silk *kapota* (traditional long coat of the orthodox Jews). The visit was not an altogether harmonious one, at least not as far as I remember it. I was bitterly jealous of my cousin, Aunt Toncia's son, whose name was the same as mine (and, like me, was nicknamed Benno). The entire family regarded him as a model child, and my grandfather never missed an opportunity to sing his praises to me. I, in turn, never missed an opportunity to make my poor cousin's life a misery. Once I locked him in the toilet in the courtyard, where he spent a good few hours in captivity before being released. My grandfather sternly reprimanded me for my mischief, and I well remember the bitterness I felt at the time: after all, I reasoned, this Benno was close to our grandfather all the time, and he could love him at any time, even after I was gone. Grandpa showed little understanding for my point of view, and in retaliation I cut the fur trim of the *shtreimel* that he left on the table after the Saturday evening *Havdalah* prayers.

I remember the sorrowful look in my grandfather's eyes as he accompanied us to the railway station. Like many other railway stations in the Austro-Hungarian Empire, this one had a very high ceiling to allow the smoke from the locomotives to dissipate. The people in the station were dressed in light summer clothes, and it was a warm and very pleasant day, but the look in my grandfather's eyes was dark and sombre. Without the *streimel* and the *kapota* he looked like any other old man, and was no longer as awe-inspiring as he had been in his home. I, too, suddenly became very sad. My mother leaned over and whispered to me: 'Give Grandpa a kiss, and take a good look at him; you may not see him again.' Her voice was choked with tears. I brushed my face against his with some indifference. The bustle of the locomotives and the coaches in the station was far more intriguing than the prolonged leave-taking. I never saw him again. Shortly after our visit he died of cancer. For years I was convinced that my mischief and disrespect on that visit had had something to do with his death, and it took me a long time to overcome my feelings of guilt over the anguish I caused him during our stay.

From the perspective of modern Jewish Amsterdam, and from my own personal point of view, my grandfather was a representative of the Old World. And yet, judged by the standards of those days, my mother was very fortunate in having the opportunity to enjoy the best of both worlds: the deeply rooted Hassidic tradition on the one hand, and on the other a general education that not too many women her age acquired. Listening to her talk of her past, one could sense her pride in the special privilege she had enjoyed. For a young girl from a Hassidic household to study in a Hebrew *Gymnasium* (high school) and to receive a Zionist education was very rare indeed. But Grandfather allowed her to study and broaden her intellectual horizons. She often recounted the story of that sad day in 1904 when Theodor Herzl, the founder of modern Zionism, died. She was ten years old at the time, and clearly recalled that instead of the flower she habitually wore to soften the severity of her school uniform, on that day she pinned a black ribbon on her lapel as a sign of her grief over his passing.

In Austrian Galicia of that time an academic education was both a cherished goal and a status symbol. Many sons and daughters of upper-class Jewish families travelled to Vienna to study in the city's universities to earn a degree and learn a profession. Some of them became lawyers, doctors, economists and scientists, and made important contributions in their chosen fields to their adopted countries, and, eventually, to Israel as well. My mother's higher education was cut short by the First World War, but she never felt any frustration at not having realized her academic ambitions. From the time she married my father and became his helpmeet, she focused on her duties as wife, mother and head of the household. Enjoying life to the full, not in the sense of light-headed pleasure-seeking, but rather as an expression of her natural *joie de vivre*, and her love of everything that was good and beautiful in the world were major mainsprings of her life. As she understood it, this meant maintaining a busy social life, helping others in need, and an unbounded spirit of volunteerism that remained with her well into old age.

We, the children, adored our mother, and consequently accepted all the rules she laid down for us without question. We were still very young when she said: 'My Zigi is an outstanding student. I will send him to study and become a professor of medicine.' Given my mediocre performance at school, her plans for my future were quite different: 'Benno will become Natan's partner. He has a head for business, not for studies.' My brother and I often heard her repeat this in conversations with friends of the family. At the ripe old age of seven I was quite offended to learn that I was not cut out to be a professor like my brother, even though at the time I did not really understand the meaning of the word 'professor'. But why, I wanted to know, was something that was good enough for my brother not good for me? When I asked someone what the difference was between a doctor and a professor, I was told that a doctor made two and a half gulden for each house call, whereas a professor made ten. This really infuriated me: was I destined for ever to earn less than my brother?

In time, my mother's prediction concerning our respective futures proved to be accurate. My brother did indeed become a well-known physician, while I, after a period of apprenticeship with my father, eventually took off on my own, and built up an independent career in business.

But I am running ahead of my story. As I mentioned earlier, my father learned the leather trade as a youth, in his sister's home. The tanning business is not for the faint-hearted: just think of the smells, the messy business of rinsing the fetid animal hides, stained with blood and excrement, soaking them in salts and chemicals, removing hair and flesh, not to mention the splitting and tanning. It is no wonder that Gentiles shied away from the trade. Jews, however, could not afford the luxury of turning down any promising business opportunity. Over the years it became clear that the Jews were actually fortunate that the Gentiles preferred leaving this trade to them, since it eventually became a predominantly Jewish industry. As a cottage industry, tanning was one of only a few industries open to Jews. Slaughtering cattle, which was also looked down on as a profession and left mostly to the Jews, was a springboard into the burgeoning tanning trade. Jews who worked in the slaughterhouses removed the hides, rinsed, cleaned and scrubbed them clean of blood and hair, and from there it was but a step to the setting up of small, rudimentary tanneries behind the butcher shops. Many modern tanning firms grew out of these small tanneries and backyard workshops, where youngsters began their careers first as apprentices, then as professionals, as small family businesses turned into large-scale tanneries. Leatherwork provided a good income for those who plied the trade, and there was plenty of scope for financial and marketing initiatives. By the end of the last century there were a number of tanners in Central and Eastern Europe who had become well-known industrialists, such as Adler and Oppenheimer, and wealthy traders – Chilewich, Kaufmann, Hollander and others. They traded with Russia, Poland, Germany, Hungary, Czechoslovakia and Western Europe, and even as far afield as Great Britain and across the seas to both North and South America, as well as Africa and Australia.

These are stories that I heard at first hand from my wife's family, which had a leading reputation in the hide and leather business. It all began with the inspired initiative of my wife's great-grandmother, Mrs Amalia Kaufmann. She was a woman of far-reaching social and financial aspirations, but had married a man, a butcher by trade, who was incapable of realizing her dreams. One day she had an idea: she asked her sons to collect the hides discarded by the family butcher shop, and by other butchers in the area, and bring them to a local tannery for treatment. When this first effort proved profitable, she bought a small, dog-drawn cart, and her sons would make the rounds, collecting hides from a number of butcher shops in the area to deliver them to the tanneries. Slowly, Mrs Kaufmann and her sons expanded their business, developing it from the initial stages of gathering hides in the slaughterhouses to tanning, production and marketing of finished leather. In time, they gained a monopoly on the hide trade in their city and throughout the entire region, and the Kaufmann family emerged from poverty into substantial financial security.

My father, who entered the business at the ground floor, eventually mastered all aspects of the leather trade. Professionally speaking, he was a true master craftsman. His professional talents, his dedication and gentle manner, coupled with a fierce determination – all these paved the way for his success. He was proud of the wealth and financial security he managed to provide for his family. It was difficult and very demanding work, but my father loved his trade, loved to work and, even more, loved to succeed. In Holland he became an entrepreneur, expanding his business into the international market-place. He knew where and from whom to buy hides at the best prices, and where to market his finished products for the highest profit. Trading on its own never completely satisfied him, and he was constantly seeking to develop the business by introducing inventions and technological innovations, which eventually propelled the business out of its primitive state of the past into the modern world.

F. H. Helt, a small leather trading company, recognized my father's talents, and took him on during his early years in Amsterdam. With his boundless professional ambition and tireless capacity for work, he was a true asset to his partners. His reputation in the trade grew rapidly. After making his mark in a small firm, he soon became a partner in the M. Levenbach company, one of the largest in Holland. From there, it was but a small step to marketing, importing and exporting leather on a large international scale.

All my life, I have never ceased to be amazed by my father's achievements, yet one question has always puzzled me: why was it that despite his extraordinary enterprise and daring, he never aspired to own his own business? We were not in the habit of conducting heart-to-heart conversations, and as a result I never truly understood his thoughts on this subject. Why did he feel the need to create partnerships for his businesses? Did he enjoy the support he received from his partners, or were there practical and business considerations behind this decision? Was he perhaps wary of unnecessary risks? Or was it because he did not want to put all his eggs in one basket, since he began his business from nothing and could not afford to lose it? To this day I can't really answer these questions. Whatever his reasons, my father's tendency to form partnerships was one of the most characteristic traits of his business life. He changed partners from time to time, and a new partnership usually signalled a step up in his professional standing, or else was the consequence of a fundamental change in his life (such as his inability to return to Holland from Argentina during the Second World War).

But why should this bother me in the first place? After all, I am exactly like him in this respect! I have never enjoyed working as a lone wolf, and have always preferred to share my successes with partners. However, whereas in my case some of my partners sapped both my strength and my finances, my father was far more fortunate. His partnerships were much more relaxed and peaceful than mine, and with their help he achieved many great successes.

To illustrate my father's unbounded loyalty to his partners, I will jump ahead some twenty-five years in this narrative. One day, returning to Argentina from a trip to Israel, I reported to my father on the success of a major deal. This had been one of my first visits to Israel, and it took place shortly after the period of austerity that marked the first difficult years of the Jewish state. At that time I was employed by an Argentine company in which my father was a partner, and my position in the business was somewhat vague. It was not altogether clear to me whether I was my father's partner or his employee, whether I was accountable only to him or to his partners as well, or, indeed, if I was free to establish my own independent business contacts. I must confess I was very anxious to reap the profits of that quick and highly successful deal, which I had initiated and pushed through completely on my own. The entire venture had not required any financing, nor did it place at risk either my own money or anybody else's. All I had done was to arrange the transfer of some goods from one party to another, and I could easily have chosen not to report it to my father's partners. When I returned to Buenos Aires, ecstatic over my success, my father, in his inimitable style, did not tell me what to do or what not to do. He looked at me with that wise expression of his and said: 'Just imagine how happy our partner, Mr Van Waveren, will be when you tell him of your success!' As usual, I followed his advice.

THE HOUSE BY THE CANAL

My parents' first few years in Holland were dominated by the struggle to find their feet in their new homeland. After overcoming the initial difficulties, which plague immigrants everywhere, the family moved to a house on Jan Steen Street, in a lower-middle-class neighbourhood of Amsterdam. As soon as my parents' financial and social situation improved, we moved into a lovely house on Stadhouderskade, near the pier on one of the Amstel River canals. Our new home was not in the Jewish neighbourhood, but rather on one of the curves of the river on the opposite bank, near the place where the Amstel narrows into a canal. It was a large and very comfortable house, filled with beautiful pieces of furniture designed by a master architect. It had one more advantage: its proximity to the Jewish quarter of the city. As a child I used to skip all the way to the synagogue, a matter of twenty minutes or so. As I grew up, the distance between our house and the synagogue naturally seemed even shorter. On rainy Saturdays – a very common occurrence in Holland – we regretted the fact that the nearby bridge over the canal had not been built a little closer to our house, as that would have afforded us a more sheltered walk to the synagogue. Today whenever I pass this area I feel a twinge of regret because now the bridge is indeed right there where we always wished it to be. The synagogue, however, was destroyed, and its worshippers are no longer among the living.

Our house enjoyed an excellent location: from the opposite bank of the canal – the large canal on the Amstel side – we could see the Amstel Hotel topped by its shining crown. The Amstel River itself was an endless source of entertainment and fun. Not being great athletes ourselves, from our balcony we would watch the festive boat races that were run frequently on the canal. The sole drawback of the house, particularly in the morning and afternoon, was the noise made by the beer carts, drawn by pairs of massive Belgian draught horses, as they crossed the nearby stone bridge. Piled high with beer barrels from the Amstel brewery opposite the canal, these carts made a loud noise as they clattered over the cobbled street, and when they were empty the din was even louder. My father turned this daily nuisance into a private superstition that helped him start his day. Every morning, before leaving the house, he would listen to the sound of the approaching beer carts; if they were particularly noisy, in other words, empty, he would linger in the house a little while longer to avoid an unsuccessful – or empty – day; if the carts made less racket, he would announce: '*Mit fillem*', meaning 'packed full', and immediately leave the house in high spirits, buoyed by hopes for a fruitful business day.

My father's business connections often took him to the small resort town of Koenigstein near Frankfurt in the Taunus Mountains in Germany. We used to take our vacations there together with families of my father's friends, religious Jewish families of German origin. Among them I particularly remember Yitschak Breuer, the grandson of Rabbi Samson Raphael Hirsch, who was known by the acronym of his name – an indication of his scholarly repute: 'Ha-Rashar'. These were magical vacations. We made friends with the children of the other families, breathed the clear mountain air, lived in a luxurious villa, and enjoyed the company of people who, apart from their business acumen, were also cultured and well-read. My parents wanted us to be exposed to Jewish influence, but at the same time tried to spare us any form of dogmatism. These summertime idylls came to an abrupt end in 1933 with Adolf Hitler's rise to power.

Sometimes we would spend our summer vacations in Holland, in Scheveningen near The Hague. My father, however, preferred to take his vacations outside Holland, in the Ardennes in Belgium, or the spas at Marienbad (Marijenska Lazna) and Carlsbad (Karlovy Vary) in what was then Czechoslovakia. He was particularly fond of these two resorts, because there he could meet renowned Hassidic rabbis who came to the famous spas to take the waters with their followers. As a descendant of a Hassidic family himself, he had a soft spot in his heart for Hassidism and its rabbis.

I still remember one trip to Marienbad when I was six years old. My father began making the rounds, paying his respects to the rabbis who had come to take the cure in this charming town. Our first visit was with the Rabbi of Belz. I remember our amazement at the dreadful disorder in his house. My father felt obliged to apologize on the rabbi's behalf, explaining to us that this was the custom at that particular time of the year – the nine days before Tish 'a Be-Av (the ninth of the Hebrew month of Av, the date of the destruction of both the First and Second Temples). During this time, as a sign of mourning, Hassidim traditionally refrained from changing their clothes or bed linen. On the other hand, at the 'court' of the Rabbi of Czordkow, my father's rabbi, this was not the case. This rabbi, who preferred receiving his visitors privately, was not surrounded by hundreds of followers, and the situation in his house, therefore, was very different.

We made our way, then, to the family *Rebbe*, our grandfather's rabbi, whom my father respected and perhaps even venerated. And indeed, the rabbi seemed very dignified and important, and was pleased to receive in his clean and tidy house. The conversation between the *Rebbe* and my father, in which they both used the familiar '*du*', centred on the issue of the quality of Jewish life among the *goyim*, in other words in Holland. As far as the rabbi was concerned, Dutch Jews were not real Jews at all, since, after all, they were not '*fun unser*' – 'our own'.

Then the rabbi put me on his knees and asked me my name. My father paled, and I could see from the look in his eyes that he was afraid I would answer 'Benno' – a *goyische*, Gentile name. I stood up, looked directly into the rabbi's eyes and said: 'Moishe-Baer', the Yiddish version of my Hebrew name, Moshe-Dov, which was given to me in memory of my great-grandfather whom the rabbi knew well. 'Well done, Moish-aleh,' the rabbi praised me. 'I see that you know where you come from.' I could almost hear the great sigh of relief that welled up deep in my father's heart when he heard my answer. And yet, as we left the house, I could sense that he was unhappy. That visit was the last we paid to any great rabbi.

Our home was religious, not Zionist, and we observed the basic tenets of our religion. My father, who inclined politically towards the Agudat Yisrael sector of religious Jewry (so much more enlightened then than its present-day version), did not oblige us to wear a skullcap except in the house or, naturally, in the synagogue and during certain religious ceremonies. Nevertheless, the house was strictly kosher, and we all observed the Sabbath and prayers, went regularly to the synagogue and upheld the precepts of social behaviour as laid out in Jewish law and thought.

Throughout their lives, both my father and my mother steadfastly practised charity and good works. My father, who was respected and beloved by the community, often risked his social standing by undertaking charitable deeds that were frowned upon. The Dutch Jewish community was characterized primarily by a kind of dry, stolidly bureaucratic mindset. For example, generally speaking, no one was expected to make personal gifts of charity, and helping the needy was the sole province of community bodies. While the underlying intention was a good one – to ensure that charity would be provided in an orderly and equitable fashion through the community institutions so that all those in need would indeed receive help – in the eyes of an Eastern European Jewish philanthropist like my father, it seemed an arbitrary and superfluous limitation. That being the case, he set up a personal benevolent fund for the needy and arranged meals for Jewish immigrants in the homes of members of the community. Before services ended in the synagogue, he would ask each new immigrant if he had been invited for a meal, and then gave out vouchers for a full meal in a kosher restaurant to all those who hadn't. The leaders of the community disapproved of my father's charitable initiatives, and one of them even publicly reprimanded him, charging that his actions might encourage 'schnorr' – unseemly solicitation for money. My father took no notice of the criticism levelled against him, and continued to do what he thought was right.

On the face of it, it would have been only natural for two boys born and raised in a house like ours (our youngest brother was born only many years later) to be sent to Jewish day schools where the daily practices of Jewish life were strictly observed. However, our parents, true to their unconventional way of thinking, preferred that we should receive a general education at the local school, which they believed was on a higher scholastic level than the Jewish school. At the same time, they spared no expense in supplementing our Jewish education with the help of private tutors who taught us at home and made up for everything we lacked in this respect at school. These teachers were a permanent part of the household, and often spent the night at our home. Their mission was to reduce our free time to a minimum, and to teach us Torah, Talmud, and Hebrew. You can probably well imagine what ingenuity I had to exercise in order to evade the constant educational presence in our house. However, today, from the perspective of my advanced years, I cannot but be grateful to my parents: everything I learned during that period of my life eventually stood me in good stead. Learning Hebrew at an early age was to give me a tremendous advantage, easing my entry into Israeli business and society, and giving me the sense of a national home even before I came to this country. The same held true for my brother Shimon as well.

One of the most unforgettable characters in our lives, who left a profound imprint on our souls, was Rabbi Yisroel Aronson; a *talmid hacham* (Talmudic scholar), childless and ascetic, and profoundly knowledgeable. He came to Amsterdam from Vilna before my family did, but his young wife died soon after her arrival, and the great hopes that had accompanied their move to Holland turned into a tragedy. My mother, for ever seeking ways to help those in need, lavished familial kindness on him, sending him home-cooked food every day. My father, who had great respect for Jewish scholars, asked him to bestow some of his spiritual riches on us, for which he would, of course, be paid. At first Rabbi Yisroel refused, claiming that he did not wish to turn the Torah into a tool to be used for mundane purposes. My father, however, insisted on remunerating him, and in the end they reached a compromise. Rabbi Yisroel, a diamond polisher by trade, was hired by my father to teach us the secrets of his craft, and, in addition, to lead us – *gratis* – through the complex and erudite arguments of the great Talmudic rabbis Abbayei and Rabba, and the intricacies of the *pshatt* (superficial commentary) and *drash* (the hidden subtext) of the Talmud. His wages, then, were not given to him for teaching us Jewish studies, but rather for initiating us into the art of diamond polishing. In this manner both Rabbi Yisroel and my father were able to ease their troubled consciences. I no longer possess the skill to take on the thrust and parry of a Talmudic discussion, but at the same time I am not a total stranger to this world either. I still have a vivid memory of some of the interpretations of the Scriptures by the great commentator Rashi. But, perhaps more importantly, I know that in case of need, I always have another profession to fall back on – diamond polishing...

It is somewhat bizarre, and indeed even acutely embarrassing, to describe the profound influence German culture had on our home life. Nevertheless, that was indeed the case in those early years. Despite Germany's defeat in the First World War, German culture had lost none of its lustre and prestige. The *Zeitgeist* of that era emanated powerfully from German-speaking countries, and knowledge of the language was regarded as a vitally necessary cultural tool for every self-respecting European. Any Jew intent on fitting in with the European way of life strove to expand his knowledge of the language and fine-tune his pronunciation in an effort to erase all traces of the sing-song Yiddish intonation of his mother tongue. Families that cared about the proper upbringing of their children understood that education begins from the cradle. Consequently, *petit bourgeois* Jewish mothers tried to fulfil their social and maternal aspirations by employing young German girls (from among the many then seeking employment outside war-ravaged Germany) as nannies in their homes. My mother was no exception in this respect, and employed several such girls during our childhood to teach us German language and manners.

At that time, my father used to set out every Saturday evening on his weekly business trips, crisscrossing Europe in overnight trains. In order to take best advantage of the two days of the week when he worked from his office at home, he hired a secretary, a German-speaking Jewish woman who helped him with his office work, and slept over at our house. These secretaries were replaced from time to time, usually after they married, but they all shared a few common characteristics: a German-Jewish background, strikingly unattractive appearance, and devout religious observance. All this was conceivably an attempt to ensure my mother's peace of mind, although I have no idea which one of my parents set down these rules for their employment or how they did so. During my father's absences from home, the secretary was pressed into service to help my mother in the running of the household. The result, at least as far as we boys were concerned, was that German became our second language. The Dutch language commonly used by my parents and the rest of the household had to make room for German. Although German took over an increasing portion of our daily conversations, Hebrew retained its pre-eminence as our language of the soul.

If the reader is, by now, under the impression that our house was strictly disciplinarian, and that our father kept us to a harsh and demanding daily regimen, I must take a moment to correct this impression. The atmosphere in our house was actually very easy-going. My father was a great optimist, always in good spirits and somewhat naïve, who never believed, even in the most difficult circumstances, that any harm could possibly come either to him or to those dearest to him. My mother, too, always looked for the positive and pleasant aspects of her surroundings. And, just like most children since time began, out of sight of our parents' caring eyes, we led a fascinating life of adventure. Not far from our hose, along the road Zigi and I walked every day on our way to elementary school, there was a wall which surrounded an imposing building: the Paleis voor Volksvlijt, a theatre built by the Socialist municipality for the benefit of Amsterdam's working class. One night, in 1927, a fire swept through the building, burning it to the ground. The flames were so fierce that residents of the neighbouring houses had to be evacuated, and only a fortuitous change in the direction of the wind that night prevented the fire from spreading and causing even more serious damage. The charred remains of the building, which to passers-by must have looked like a forbidding and abandoned ruin, became for us children a magical kingdom. The burned-out shell of the building made it possible for us to vanish out of sight right in the middle of town, to play, to go wild and fight, one children's gang against another. As far as we were concerned, far from being a disaster, the great fire that destroyed the building was a huge blessing, since it provided us with two or three wonderful years of exciting fun and games in the enchanting playground of the ruined theatre. Even now, whenever I pass the site, I am filled with fond memories of those days. No new theatre was ever built to replace the one that was burned down, and eventually, when the ruins were cleared, the Central Bank of Holland erected its impressive headquarters on the site.

We maintained a strict division between the religious nature of our home life and our experiences in school. At the elementary school we absorbed fundamental Dutch values of liberalism and tolerance. Our teachers were progressive, liberal-minded Socialists, and they had little use for traditional values such as religion and the monarchy. We were brought up to accept the individual's inalienable right to live freely in accordance with his own beliefs, tradition and religious persuasion. Every religion was equally respected in our school, but none dominated or had its precepts enforced on us in any way. I will be for ever grateful to our parents for endowing us with such an enlightened education, which, as a matter of principle, separated religion from state. Their decisions on this aspect of my upbringing shaped my attitude to religion along the lines of the Dutch paradigm: profound respect for religion on the one hand; while on the other an independence of thought that has been a fundamental part of my character since childhood. Religion has never governed any aspect of my way of life.

My Bar Mitzvah, which took place in May 1932, on the Sabbath of the *Emor* portion (Leviticus 21–24), was a very pleasant affair. My father, the *gabbai* (lay leader) of the synagogue, and one of the pillars of the community, held a festive *Kid-dush* (traditional Sabbath reception) for friends and relatives. In the evening, family and close friends gathered at our home to celebrate the occasion. At the height of the event, of which I was the centrepiece, one of our family friends hinted that after this *simcha* (joyous occasion) our family was about to experience another no less joyous event. That was how I learned, in a totally unexpected manner and with no little shock, of the imminent birth of a new sibling. And indeed, two months later, my younger brother, Ya'akov, was born.

As is customary in Jewish tradition, following my Bar Mitzvah I began observing the *mitzvah* of laying *tefillin* (phylacteries). As far as I was concerned, neither the observance of the practice, nor the fact that I eventually ceased to do so, were in any way a religious (or, for that matter, anti-religious) statement. For years I carried my *tefillin* with me everywhere I went, as a sign of my affiliation, my identity and my commitment to my spiritual home.

A Bar Mitzvah is an important initiation ceremony, and at the time I was acutely aware of my transition from childhood into maturity. Immediately following my Bar Mitzvah, I felt that the process of my growing up had suddenly accelerated, as though I had been put into a pressure cooker. However, this rapid progression from childhood to manhood was not only the result of my character and personality. Like all my peers, I was caught up in the events of the times, and conceivably it was because I was studying at a non-religious school that I felt a special need to bolster my Jewish identity. Unconsciously, perhaps, I sought a goal, a model to emulate, an ideal to espouse and, as I was soon to discover, it was right there, within easy reach, all the time: the religious Zionist youth movement known as Zichron Jacob, which was to have a profound influence on my youth and my later life as well. This youth movement suited my needs perfectly: it challenged the establishment, and upheld just and enlightened values. By joining the movement, the youthful vigour coursing through my veins had found a worthy outlet.

By that time, things had begun changing in Europe. From 1931 onwards, the influence of German National Socialism spread rapidly. Holland seemed very far removed from all this, or so most people thought. Not so my father and some of his friends. They decided to respond to these developments by stressing their Jewishness and intensifying the Jewish education they provided for their children. It was during this time that I 'came of age'. Up until then I had been studying in elementary school, while my elder brother had already begun attending the *Gymnasium*, where he was studying Greek and Latin in preparation for his career in medicine (from as early as he could remember he had always known that he would study medicine). My father registered me at the regular Jewish High School, which had been opened two years earlier, and which, at that time, had only three classes and a single study track in the humanities. As the years went by, more and more classes were added, more tracks opened, and the school grew and prospered. The school still exists to this day, and after the war was renamed Maimonides Lyceum after the great Jewish sage. Immediately after the Second World War I returned to Amsterdam and, among other places, visited the school to see how it had weathered the war. The veteran teachers, those few who had survived, received me warmly, even though I couldn't recall ever having given them any pleasure during my studies there. I could easily identify with the profound pain I saw etched in their faces: so few of their students and colleagues had survived the Holocaust.

At the age of sixteen, three years after entering the school, I was transferred to the high school (HBS), this time for purely practical reasons: the Jewish school's focus on the humanities was simply not enough for me. I wanted to study science and economics, and the only place I could pursue this was at the local school. Eventually, as I grew up, this proved to be a wise choice in every way, but at the time it was not easy for me to leave the Jewish school. Among my teachers there were many wonderful, unforgettable people whom I truly admired, and who had a powerful influence on my life. As for my classmates, I didn't really have to part from them, because I remained active in the Zionist youth movement, perhaps with even more dedication than before.

2

MY AMSTERDAM

Amsterdam, the city of my birth, played an important role in the shaping of my childhood. My attempt to describe the city here is a debt of honour for me, since I cannot imagine a childhood, youth, or coming of age other than my own as I experienced it in that city. I was deeply influenced by many things, great and small. The houses we lived in, the familiar streets, 'our' synagogue, the other synagogues we passed by respectfully, the schools where my brother and I studied, the stores we frequented, the people we met and those we knew well – all these marked my life indelibly, enriching me, and turning me into the person I am today.

Jews have lived in Amsterdam for 400 years. The first to arrive were survivors of persecution. The great expulsions from Spain and Portugal, the pogroms, the persecution and suffering – all these caused thousands of Jews from all over Europe to seek refuge in the Netherlands. While in other parts of Europe Jews suffered discrimination and deprivation because of their religion, in Holland they were received with a matter-of-factness which, in typical Dutch manner, was somewhat phlegmatic but nevertheless completely unquestioned. I recall the Dutch as a very open people, both warm and humane. Despite the shifts of fate and the changes wrought on people by the passage of time, I believe to this day that the Dutch, as a people, deserve both our gratitude and respect.

More Jews from Eastern and Central Europe began arriving in Amsterdam at the beginning of the twentieth century. During the First World War they were joined by Jews from Belgium as well. As I mentioned earlier, I was born a few months after the end of the First World War. During the years of my childhood and youth, some eighty thousand Jews lived in Amsterdam, out of a total population of over seven hundred thousand. This relatively high proportion of Jews among the population – over eleven per cent – left its mark everywhere on the Jewish and non-Jewish residents of the city, affecting their social and economic situation and their way of life. The influence of the Jewish community on the life of the city was so pervasive that some Hebraisms even crept into the local Dutch language, albeit in a somewhat distorted fashion. For example, when it rains, people in Amsterdam say: '*Het majimt*', from the Hebrew *mayyim*, water; and alcoholic drinks are known locally as *Jajim*, from the Hebrew *yayyin* for wine. I even once heard a non-Jewish driver giving instructions to another driver by telling him: 'Now do an *oisseh sholem*,' meaning 'reverse a little', after the traditional three steps back executed at the end of the *Shmoneh-essreh* prayer on the words: '*Osseh shalom bimromav*' ('He who makes peace on high', '*Oisseh Sholem*' in the Yiddish pronunciation).

The two Jewish communities in Amsterdam, the Ashkenazi community from Eastern and Central Europe, and the Sephardi Portuguese community (descendants of the Jews expelled from the Iberian peninsula), lived side by side in the city. For hundreds of years the Portuguese Jews enjoyed special standing as the 'first-comers' – the *Mayflower* pilgrims of Dutch Jewry. Their synagogues, chiefly the famed 'Esnoga', contained priceless items of Judaica. In the aristocratic households and in their synagogues, Portuguese remained the language of choice among the Sephardi Jews, and it was used exclusively for all the instructions in their prayer books and their announcements of prayer times.

With the passing of the generations, the Dutch Jewish community gradually underwent profound changes as the influence of the Portuguese community – though not its prestige – waned. Intermarriage, the lack of new blood, and the loss of their taste for leadership, drained the vital spirit of this ancient, aristocratic community. The Ashkenazi community, on the other hand, grew steadily in numbers and in strength. They developed their own brand of Dutch-Yiddish, which was very different from its Eastern European counterparts. They made great efforts to integrate into Dutch society at large and into the greater Jewish community in particular, to become honest, law-abiding citizens, and to inculcate in their children both traditional Jewish values and respect and appreciation for their Dutch citizenship.

As a Jewish boy in Amsterdam, I was born into a tolerant social milieu. Only someone who was fortunate enough not to have encountered any form of aggressive anti-Semitism could have believed, as I did, that religious tolerance was as natural as sunshine. In its time, Amsterdam set a rare example: its Jewish citizens enjoyed complete equality and were imbued with an unshakable feeling of '*lokal-patriotism*' and devoted citizenship. The city was not altogether free of discrimination, and here and there one did encounter open hostility, but in many cases native: it was Dutchmen of opposing faiths, either Catholic or Protestant, who directed this hostility the one against the other. This was the reason why we never attributed purely anti-Semitic motives to any of the unpleasant incidents that we occasionally encountered. There were a number of businesses, including the well-known Brennickmeier company (owners of the C&A chain) who maintained a policy of employing only Catholics in their stores. We consoled ourselves with the observation that the owners refused to employ Protestants as well. In much the same way, certain Protestant businesses refused to employ Jews or Catholics. I cannot, however, recall a single Jewish firm that refused to employ non-Jews, whatever their denomination.

In general, we tried to overcome these less pleasant aspects of our lives with a healthy sense of humour. There was, for instance, the following joke about Brennickmeier that made the rounds in town. Brennickmeier, as I have mentioned, was a devout Catholic and did not allow Jews to work in his company. One day a Catholic priest who was friendly with Brennickmeier came to his office and complained bitterly: 'How is it possible that your company employs a Jew in the furniture department?'

'Ah, yes,' Brennickmeier replied, 'he's the manager of the department. He's an excellent worker, and I can't begin to tell you how much he has done for his department and for the company in general.'

'That may be,' the priest responded angrily, 'but he is a Jew and we do have rules! Have any of you tried to convert him?'

'Ah, my dear Father,' Brennickmeier sighed, 'how can we? He might be offended!'

'All right,' the priest said, 'I see I have no alternative. I'll go to him and see if I can persuade him.'

An hour passed, two hours, and then, a few hours later, the priest finally came out and left the store without saying a word.

Brennickmeier went over to his Jewish employee and asked him:

'Well, did the priest manage to convince you of the error of your ways?'

'No,' answered the Jew. 'But, on the other hand, I convinced *him* to buy a double bed.'

Dutch egalitarianism was very much in evidence in Amsterdam's schools. On Fridays and the eve of Jewish holidays, Jewish children were released earlier than usual from school to enable them to get home before the beginning of the holy days. The community itself provided comprehensive and varied opportunities for Jewish education: there were several elementary schools, and the Jewish High School. The Jewish community of Amsterdam was extremely well organized, having absorbed and internalized typically Dutch traits, the most prominent of which were diligence, modesty and a high degree of organization. Institutions were established to provide assistance for the needy so that all the members of the community could live a decent life. Concern for the physical welfare of the community was uppermost in the minds of its leaders, and the city boasted three Jewish hospitals: the NIZ, a well-equipped Dutch-Jewish general hospital; the CIZ, the main Jewish hospital devoted to special cases and private clinics; and PIZ, the Portuguese-Jewish hospital for the wealthy members of the community. The latter institution was founded by the Portuguese community, and the last names of its staff and patients, all of Iberian origin, sounded quite exotic to us. This was one of the ways the Portuguese community tried to maintain the trappings of its past, choosing to ignore the fact that over three hundred and fifty years had passed since their ships first dropped anchor in Dutch harbours.

My parents, too, had their own status symbol when it came to medical care: the highly regarded PIZ hospital. This was where I was born. When I was about to make my entry into the world, my parents chose the most prestigious hospital for the event, a fact that lends some credence to my belief that by the time I came into the world, the Gitters' acclimatization into Dutch-Jewish society was complete.

Whatever social, political, medical, or religious institutions Jews might require – synagogues, schools, hospitals, public institutions and social organizations – were all available within the Jewish quarter, which covered a two-square-kilometre section of the city. This quarter was never regarded as a 'ghetto', and indeed had none of the depressing characteristics of a ghetto, and many of the Jewish inhabitants of the city chose to live either in the area itself or very close.

Before the war, most of the synagogues were built around the Jonas Daniel Meier Square. Some of the smaller ones had been built a bit further away. Among the more important synagogues, the imposing Portuguese synagogue – the Esnoga – was the oldest and best known; in fact, it was one of the most renowned synagogues in the world. It contained a superb collection of Judaica which had been brought over from Portugal by the first Jewish immigrants, and items from the collection were proudly displayed on important festivals such as Simhat Torah and Hoshannah Rabba. One of the halls in the building contained the Etz Haim library, one of the oldest, richest and most important Jewish libraries in the world. It contained priceless ancient manuscripts, manuscripts by the philosophers Baruch Spinoza and Uriel d'Acosta (both controversial Jewish philosophers who were expelled from the community), Torah scrolls and manuscripts of many of the great commentators.

Did the Ashkenazi Jews in the community feel that the Esnoga Synagogue overshadowed the prestige and honour of their own synagogues? I truly believe that this ancient synagogue was loved and admired equally by all the Jews of Amsterdam, regardless of their background. For the Sephardi community, the Esnoga was a symbol of their illustrious past as well as their long-standing residence in Holland. Guests and tourists from Holland and from all over the world came to see the splendours of the main hall and the glorious treasures it contained. Since electric lighting was regarded as a form of blasphemy or a capitulation to modernity, the main hall was lit by candles – 613 of them, representing the traditional number of *mitzvot* (religious obligations) found in the Torah. The ancient, stunningly beautiful furniture had been wonderfully preserved over the generations, and had not suffered either from the ravages of time or of the climate. There was great irony – and great good fortune too – in the fact that even during the time of the Nazi conquest and Occupation of the city during the Second World War, the Esnoga was regarded as a rare historical monument, and was included in the official international list of protected buildings. It was this reverence for the unique Esnoga Synagogue that saved it from destruction at the hands of the Nazis, leaving it intact as a living testimony to the glorious Jewish past in the city.

The two large Ashkenazi synagogues were known as the Great Synagogue, and the New Synagogue, even though they were both virtually identical in size and importance. During the week, worshippers tended to pray in smaller and simpler *shuls*, annexes that were built adjacent to the larger synagogues. The large halls were generally opened only on the Sabbath and on major religious festivals.

Apart from the main synagogues, there were many *minyanim* (a *minyan* – the ten-man quorum required for Jewish prayer services) and *shtibel* (small, makeshift synagogue halls) in which prayers were held. As the Eastern European Jewish population grew, many of these places of worship developed into full-fledged synagogues, such as the popular Polish Synagogue in Nieuwe Kerk Street, with its unique Hassidic atmosphere. The communities of Hassidim and Misnagdim (those opposed to Hassidism), remained fiercely loyal to 'their' synagogues, just as Jews of all persuasions do all over the world to this day.

My family generally attended the Kehillat Ya'akov Synagogue in Swammerdam Street, popularly known as the Russische shul – the Russian Synagogue. Many Hassidim and scholars prayed together in perfect harmony in our synagogue. To this day I remember my first visit to the synagogue when I was five or six years old. My father was deep in conversation with two impressive-looking gentlemen with flowing white beards and striking top hats. I tugged at my father's sleeve and said, 'Look, Daddy! Two Santa Clauses!' One of the two gentlemen, who appeared to me to be ancient, was the father of the Zionist leader Abel J. Herzberg, a well-known writer and lawyer. The other was the head of the Bavli family, known for its devotion to Zionist causes. I recall several Sabbath mornings when my father told my mother that he would be home from the synagogue a little late because of a toast marking the departure of yet another one of the Bavli children for Palestine. One Shabbat my father asked my mother to join him for the traditional *Kiddush* (the prayer said on the Sabbath either after prayers or just before the midday meal), this time to mark the *aliya* of the Bavli parents themselves to Israel.

Very few of the Dutch Jewish families of my generation remained intact after the Second World War. The elder Bavli parents, together with their children and grandchildren, did manage to escape the devastation of the Holocaust, and lived to see the birth of their great-grandchildren. In time, one of the Bavli grandchildren, Michael Bavli, returned to Holland as Israel's ambassador to the Netherlands. This could be seen as the closing of a circle, but I prefer to regard it as 'the Forefathers' legacy', since it was only due to their parents' decision to emigrate to Palestine that the Bavli family managed to survive.

The community in Amsterdam was a heterogeneous, highly diversified Jewish society, which embraced people of many different points of view, some of them highly controversial and eccentric. One of the more extreme examples of this diversity was Shmuel Halperin, a uniquely idiosyncratic person, and a distant relative of ours, who used to pray in our synagogue. The older he grew, the more extreme he became in his views. In a manner reminiscent of Naturei Karta, the extremist, ultra-orthodox Jews in Jerusalem, he rejected both the religious and the civil authority of the rabbis of the community, refusing to avail himself of their services, and pressuring his students to follow his example. The Jews of the city, as citizens with full civic rights, were very much involved in municipal politics. The majority of them belonged to the working classes. Many of them were diamond polishers, and belonged to the trade unions and the Socialist movement. Middle-class and well-to-do Jews generally belonged to the Liberal Party. As such, Jews of all political persuasions played a prominent role in the various parties, many of them even rising to positions of leadership. These activists were not all devoutly observant, but, at the same time, they were certainly identified, without a hint of discrimination, as Jews. Halperin tried to persuade his followers not to support either one of these parties, but to give their votes to the Catholic Party, which had never once put forward a Jewish candidate for public office. According to Halperin, it was preferable to vote for a Catholic *goy* than for a Jew who did not observe even the least important of the Jewish religious obligations. In time, Halperin was formally accused by the local rabbinate of undermining its authority, but, in keeping with his radical nature, he took advantage of the publicity afforded him during his trial to display once again his profound contempt for the rabbis whom he accused of compromising their beliefs. He was regarded by all as a strange bird, though no one believed he was really dangerous in any way. Eventually, the Halperin family went on *aliya* to Israel and settled in the ultra-orthodox town of Bnei Brak.

This vibrant human panorama was completely eradicated and is gone for ever. The Jewish synagogues of Amsterdam were torn down during the 'Hunger Winter' of 1944–5, when the starving and freezing non-Jewish residents of the city stripped the main Ashkenazi synagogues and their annexes of all their wooden sections and furniture to use for heating. There is some comfort in the thought it was not sheer vandalism or hatred for the Jews that caused these people to destroy the beautiful interiors of the synagogues, but rather a very basic urge for survival.

EXCUSED FROM THE ENGAGEMENT PARTY

As I mentioned before, Holland was not altogether free of the dark undertones of anti-Semitism. While I personally never encountered any anti-Semitism as such, we all knew about some ugly and worrisome manifestations of the phenomenon. We did not ignore these incidents, or try to close our ears to the disturbing sounds; nevertheless, in all the years we lived in Amsterdam, I cannot recall a single family discussion on the issue, or even the slightest complaint about any of its manifestations, such as they were. It was very tempting for us – and all too easy – to disregard this troublesome phenomenon. In fact, compared to the bitter experiences some Jews underwent in their home countries before coming to Holland, we had little reason to be overly concerned about our trivial incidents. There were occasional manifestations of anti-Semitism, but within the broader context of life among the Gentiles over hundreds of years, the tendency of Dutch Jews to overlook such incidents – however minor or serious – was understandable.

At this point it is also important to mention one more thing: for everything that Holland gave to the Jews, it received no less from them in return. The Jewish minority in Holland was cultured, well-disciplined, patriotic, appreciative, diligent and highly gifted. The Jews of Holland knew their place and made every effort to downplay their considerable achievements. They blended discreetly into their surroundings without conceding any of their vitality and distinction, and for a while it seemed as though this uniquely profitable intertwining of destinies between Holland and its Jewish community was destined to continue to grow for centuries to come.

Such was the peaceful nature of the time I spent in the high school. I enjoyed the opportunity I was given to get to know and befriend non-Jewish Dutch youngsters of my age. I have no recollection of any unpleasant or untoward incidents from this time. Slowly – perhaps because of a heightened Jewish awareness that developed in me along with the beginning of my activities in the youth movement – I began to notice the slight, but nevertheless perceptible, changes in the wind. Reports began filtering back about attacks on Jews in other countries, though there were no such incidents in Holland itself. Once again immigrants from Germany and Eastern Europe poured into the Netherlands, and the Dutch received them with their customary propriety. Nevertheless, I believe that when certain communities are attacked in one part of the world it always affects the way similar communities in other places are treated as well: first beneath the surface, and then openly. The humiliations and deportations endured by the Jews of Germany appeared to encourage similar acts almost everywhere, and the knowledge that Jewish property and lives were easy game slowly percolated into our systems, gradually preparing us for what would happen in the years to come.

If one listened carefully to the sounds and did not attempt to evade or suppress the issue, one could now hear new and ominous music. Even in the high school there was a small and marginal – but none the less highly visible – group of supporters of National Socialism. On certain festive occasions, following Hitler's rise to power, there were public readings of poems containing formerly unknown motifs such as *bloed* (blood) and *vaderland*. Some people in Holland did not think that the Nazi rule in Germany was as despicable as did others. Thus the meeting between the German armed forces and the local Dutch populace during the Nazi invasion of Holland took place on fertile soil, and many Dutch people – too many by far – received the occupying Nazi forces with enthusiasm.

At that time, while I was still at school, the engagement was announced of Dutch Crown Princess Juliana. In anticipation of the marriage, her German-borne fiancé, Prince Bernhard, renounced his

German citizenship and became a bona fide citizen of Holland, but many of us young Zionists were deeply concerned about this connection between the Dutch royal family and the German nation. I recall how I approached the principal of the high school, and, speaking out on my own behalf and that of some of my friends, I asked him to excuse us from the planned celebrations in honour of the royal engagement. I presented our case to him in a forthright and very determined manner, and felt rather proud of the way I handled the issue.

'I understand,' the principal sighed. 'I wish I could do the same, but what can we do? In my position things are different. Enjoy yourselves, my friends,' he added without any rancour, and dismissed us.

The extent to which our protest, the protest of impressionable youngsters, was justified was brought home to us very clearly soon afterwards, when it was announced that the princess and her fiancé had paid a courtesy call to the head of the German state, *der Führer* Adolf Hitler. Knowing as I do the feelings of the Dutch royal family about that period of their history, I believe that the royal couple's meeting was a very sad mistake, the result of human, ethical and political short-sightedness. Just a few years later Holland was overrun by the Nazis, and the royal family went into voluntary exile.

It was during this period that my Zionist consciousness gained in strength and conviction. It is difficult to put my finger on what impelled me so forcibly and unambiguously towards Zionism, but there can be no question about the fact that the youth movement was a major influence. I often look back with some incredulity at my activities in the Zichron Jacob movement at the tender age of fourteen, but the momentous and rapidly evolving events of those days forced me to grow up rather quickly. For two years I served as leader of the youth movement's branch in the southern part of the city – a new group made up primarily of children of German-Jewish refugees – that I had built up from scratch. This was the first of many public duties I would undertake in my lifetime, and it provided me with my first practical lessons in leadership, management and organization. Naturally, it was very flattering for me to be chosen as a branch leader. Within a very short time the movement became the centre of my universe. I loved my group leaders, my fellow counsellors and the younger children in the group I led. But above all, I was completely caught up in the movement's social and political vision and my own powerful sense of identification with it.

There were certainly enough rational and practical reasons to take up the cause of Zionism, but in these matters nothing is ever quite as convincing as a traumatic experience, and it was just such a devastating personal ordeal that profoundly affected my Zionist convictions. It was in 1933, the year the Nazis came to power in Germany. The situation in Holland was still bearable. The generous and liberal-minded Dutch nation once again opened its gates to refugees, providing them with temporary shelter and *laissez-passez*, and offering them – if they so wished – a permanent haven. At the time no one could have imagined that within a few short years Holland would seal its borders to Jewish refugees. Clearly there was no way we could have foreseen – even in our darkest dreams – that Holland would turn from a haven into a death-trap for its own Jewish citizens and for those who had come there to escape persecution in other countries.

I was all of fourteen years old when I waited at the railway station in Amsterdam for a group of Jewish refugees from Germany. My friends and I from the Zichron Jacob movement wanted to give them a feeling that someone was expecting them, someone who would invite them home and see to their needs during their first few days in their new country. I will never forget the sight of the group of people who stepped off the train: they seemed so lost, so helpless! True representatives of the Jewish tragedy. I felt in no way superior to these people. After all, the fate of the Jewish people made no distinctions between its victims. What was happening in Germany today could easily happen next to the Jews of Holland. At that moment, as I looked at these people on the platform, I experienced a profound illumination: I suddenly realized, for the first time, that Holland was only a temporary home, and that in the entire world there wasn't a single country I could truly call my own – except Palestine. For the briefest moment, in a flash, my future was revealed to me, and then, just as suddenly, the vision faded and disappeared once again into the darkness.

That first encounter with refugees at the station was not the last one. The plight of the refugees was taken up not only by the youth movements, but by the adults of the community as well. My father continued to prepare lists of worshippers who volunteered to take in needy refugees on the Sabbath. A few years later, while travelling by train from Budapest to Warsaw, I struck up a conversation with a wealthy Jew in my compartment, and when I told him my father's name, tears welled up in his eyes and he said, 'You're Natan Gitter's son? I owe him my life! Whatever I have achieved in my life is thanks to him!'

Events had begun to close in on us, but the Jews of Holland simply refused to believe that disaster would ever touch their lives. 'It will never happen here,' was the popular motto of the time. The more pragmatic among us saw it only slightly differently: 'If anything does happen, it will only be temporary, short-lived.' It was only the Zionist movements who saw things otherwise. They provoked unprecedented anger in the Jewish community of Holland when they refused to participate in a demonstration organized under the slogan: 'We are one nation, with one past and one future.' As far as the Zionist youth movements were concerned there could be only one motto: Eretz-Yisrael is the only future!

The leaders of the community, especially the religious ones among them, rejected the Zionist solution out of hand. They regarded the young Zionists as dangerous elements whose activities only served to fan the flames of anti-Semitism, and possibly even brought about its emergence in the first place. One well-known gentleman angrily and haughtily dismissed us by saying, 'Those Zionist kids – what they really deserve is a spanking.' He himself eventually managed to save his family by escaping to the United States at the eleventh hour, two days before the German invasion of Holland. Many years later his children, who lived in the USA, became well known for their donations to the state of Israel, and their fundraising efforts on its behalf.

Despite strong internal opposition, the influence of Zionist ideologies on the Jewish community in Holland continued to grow. The movements involved were the General Zionists, the Socialist Zionists, and the religious Mizrahi Zionists. Each of them had its own youth movement with branches outside Amsterdam as well, some of them in small and fairly remote locations. My own movement, Zichron Jacob, was named after the founder of the Mizrahi, Rabbi Jacob Reines, and resembled the current religious Zionist movement, B'nei Akiva, but with none of the messianic and nationalistic overtones that have distorted the nature of this movement in its present-day version. As a Zionist movement, Zichron Jacob was very close to the non-religious youth movements, and shared their understanding of the central importance of *aliya* – emigration – to Eretz Yisrael. The Hakhsharot (groups that underwent preparations – mostly agricultural training – for *aliya* and life in Palestine) set up by the movement at that time were designed for religious *Halutzim* (pioneers), and functioned as 'kibbutzim-in-the-making', based on the model of a religious kibbutz where kosher food, prayers and the Sabbath were strictly observed. The non-religious *Halutzim*, by comparison, devoted all their time to agricultural training on Dutch farms. The word *Hakhsharah* means both study and preparation. Perhaps, somehow unwittingly, the additional, religious, meaning of the word in Hebrew – making things kosher – also became attached to it, and indeed one of the reasons for the establishment of the religious Hakhsharot was the need to provide the religious *Halutzim* with kosher food.

There were a number of ideological and practical differences of opinion that even then divided the none-too-large Zionist community in Holland. Among the Dutch Zionists there were those who belonged to the 'Nein sagers' (the 'nay sayers' who opposed the UN-proposed Partition Plan for Palestine), and others who belonged to the 'Ja sagers' (the 'yea sayers' who favoured it as the only way of ensuring the creation of the Jewish state). I do not identify with either faction. I was primarily influenced by the views of our leaders, Peretz Bernstein, and Nehemia de Lima. According to their doctrine, which became known as 'Unconditional Zionism', we were meant to forgo all other ideals and go on *aliya* to Palestine. It would be many years before I finally managed to put into practice this very clear call for Zionist action.

PRAYING WITH A SEPHARDI PRONUNCIATION

The official Zionist institutions in Holland treated the practical and resolute Zionism of the youth movements with circumspection. At that time there was no necessary connection between Zionism and *aliya*, even though the National Committee of the Zionist Movement in the country had passed a resolution promising aid to anyone going on *aliya* to Palestine. None the less, no comprehensive, practical ideology had been established to turn the theory into practice and swell the ranks of the *olim* (emigrants) to Palestine.

The youth movements were up in arms against both the indifference and the outright opposition to their brand of practical Zionism. For them only two ideals mattered: *aliya* and *hagshama* (realizing the Zionist ideal of emigrating to Palestine and settling the land). On this issue there was total agreement among the various youth movements. If one belonged to a youth movement, one was committed to going to Palestine, if not immediately, then in the near or more distant future.

Our religious Zionist youth movement, Zichron Jacob, found itself in a somewhat more delicate position than the other movements. They, like us, received neither support nor backing from the official parties in the community. But we, in the religious movement, had been brought up to treat the community leaders and the authority of the rabbis with great respect. Defying their authority might undermine the religious and moral basis of our way of life, and in extreme cases might result in severe social sanctions. Despite our apprehensions about the inevitable head-on collision, we held our ground. On the surface, the dispute appeared to involve a minor issue: in the separate *minyan* (prayer service) that we had established – in itself a daring and insolent act – we chose to use the Sephardi pronunciation of the Hebrew language rather than the Ashkenazi. In so doing we followed the example of the Jewish Yishuv in Palestine, where the Sephardi pronunciation signified a Zionist break with long-held Diasporic traditions. It is difficult to describe the anger we aroused in the community by this act, which was construed as an outright declaration of support for Zionism. The rabbinate took the orthodox position, summed up in the words of the sages: 'Innovation is prohibited by the Torah.' The *halachic* demand to toe the line was waved in our faces with all the authority the rabbis could muster. I myself did not flinch under the attack, but the young teachers and rabbis among us who had been ordained in the Rabbinical Seminary wavered. The older rabbis warned them, in no uncertain terms, that if they refused to retract their wayward decision, their chances of finding clerical employment would be seriously diminished. Nevertheless, in the end and despite the threats, we stood our ground – *hutzpah* of epic proportions.

This was one in a series of confrontations we had with the rabbinical establishment, and our most serious one up to that time. We were convinced that the Zionist religious course we were committed to was the right one. In 1939 I was invited to represent our movement at a B'nei Akiva conference in Poland, and there I met Zerah Warhaftig, who was to become one of the leaders of the Mizrahi movement in Israel and eventually Minister of Religious Affairs. To my surprise, he was familiar with the details of our clash with the official religious leadership in Amsterdam, and to my astonishment he opposed our stand on the issue. This was three months before the outbreak of the Second World War.

That was the Amsterdam I knew. Soon after the end of the Second World War I came back on a visit. I found a city that had been virtually emptied of its Jewish population. The faces I passed in the street had an aura of strangeness, even though I did recognize a few of them. Where were all 'our' people, the people I had loved, all those who had been a part of my childhood? Throughout the week I tried to convince myself that things were back to normal, but on the Sabbath I could no longer suppress my sense of devastation over what had occurred. I was overwhelmed with pain, loneliness and a deep yearning, the likes of which I had never felt before. Outside the hotel, which faced part of the Jewish section of town, cars and trams filled the streets. This was a totally unfamiliar experience for me. Like most of my fellow Jews, I had never crossed over from the Jewish quarter to the busy city on the Sabbath. From my hotel window I could see the neighbourhood where I had spent my childhood and my youth. On the wall surrounding our former house I could still make out the words 'Zigi is gek' ('Zigi is crazy') that I had scratched on to one of the stones when I was a mischievous youngster. Everything else was gone.

3

MY EARLY CAREER

Throughout the turmoil of 1937, life went on as usual. There were many personal decisions to be made, such as whether to continue my studies or to choose a profession. Since it was clear to me that I belonged in Palestine, and since I had studied economics in high school, I applied to the Department of Economics at the Hebrew University in Jerusalem. With great pride I showed my mother the reply I received from the university authorities, bearing a stamp with the portrait of King George V. I had been accepted! Perhaps I would become a professor, like Zigi, after all, or at least a doctor? This was my last opportunity, and the closest I ever came to realizing my dream. But my hopes were soon dashed: the political situation made it impossible for me to acquire the hoped-for immigration 'certificate' that would enable me to buy a boat ticket to Palestine and give me official access to the Promised Land as an immigrant. Thousands of refugees were waiting impatiently in Holland for immigration permits to Palestine, and the Jewish Agency, which was in charge of issuing the certificates, quite rightly gave priority to refugees from Eastern and Central Europe bent on making *aliya*. I was told that I would have to bide my time on the waiting list for at least three years before my turn came for a student's certificate – an eternity for a youngster like myself.

What was I to do? At that time no one was considering extreme solutions to the problem, such as illegal emigration to Palestine. The spirit of Dutch discipline had thoroughly permeated the Jewish community of Holland, and the idea of doing anything illegal or of circumventing the law in any way was still unthinkable.

In the meanwhile I had to keep myself busy. My parents did not object to my plans of going out on *Hakhsharah*, but my father, true to his pragmatic nature, advised me not to make any long-term commitments. And so, instead of joining a *Hakhsharah* group for agricultural training, I went to a village where I found work with a local farmer. Blithely ignoring the heavy rain, I cheerfully set out on my bicycle and made my way to the farm. I arrived at four in the afternoon, in total darkness, and the Boer (Dutch farmer) showed me to my room, where I went straight to sleep. At three in the morning I was unceremoniously shaken out of bed and taken to the barn. I shuffled through the mud in the heavy darkness, and then was given a stool and a few basic pointers on how to milk a cow. With my head pushed up against the teats of the docile animal, my future seemed less than brilliant, and milking turned out to be a thoroughly unenjoyable task. If only my father could have seen his son recoiling in disgust, guarding his life and soul from the very beast whose hide provided him with his daily bread! At sunrise, I cycled back to town. The sight of Amsterdam at first light filled me with an unforgettable wave of happiness.

What was I to do now? I had failed miserably as a *Halutz*, but, fortunately, my father needed me in his business, and so, until the arrival of the hoped-for Certificate of Immigration, I could at least help him out at work. I believe that my short-lived encounter with farming gave my father some cause for concern. He had always loved everything to do with farm work, and now had no choice but to acknowledge that at least in this respect I was not going to follow in his footsteps. And what if it turned out that I was not as diligent, patient or hardworking as he was? For didactic reasons, and in an attempt to prepare me for life, he decided to bring me into his business without delay, so that I would at least not remain unemployed! Even if I decided eventually not to go into the family leather business, he said, at least I would learn a trade. And if I wished I could start from the ground floor and work my way up, just as he had done. After checking with some of his contacts, he chose Hungary as the best place for me to begin my apprenticeship. There was a thriving tanning trade there, and he had excellent connections with some of the largest Hungarian suppliers and manufacturers, all of whom were professional experts and important merchants, with a wealth of experience in the field. He was convinced that I could learn the secrets of the trade from all of them, perfect my understanding of it, and eventually make my own way in the business. My father also felt that my stay in Hungary would be interesting and beneficial both for me personally and for his company.

MY 101 SURVIVORS

It was 1938. Austria was about to be annexed by Germany in the *Anschluss*. I left Holland, where everything seemed perfectly normal, for Hungary, where the situation was more or less the same as in Austria. I remained there for nearly a year and to this day I have nothing but pleasant memories of my stay. It was a very special time for me. I had left home and was on my own for the first time in my life. It was my golden opportunity to learn about life, make my own decisions, and shape my character far from my parents' sheltering wings. This is the way a young man in Israel must feel when, for example, he goes into the army or goes abroad to see the world. Independence was a heady brew for me. Consciously or not, my father once again proved the depth of his wisdom when he released me for a while from his protective shadow. I gained a profession and many new friends, and I was never lonely.

There was one person who, more than anyone else, helped me to overcome the initial difficulties of life in a strange country, and that was my mother's youngest and favourite brother, Uncle Lonek (Aryeh) Fischler. Lonek, who had been born in 1904, had married Edith Feigl, the local rabbi's daughter, and lived comfortably with his wife and two children in a large community of some twenty thousand Jews in a small town of about eighty thousand inhabitants, called Gyongos. How did my Uncle Lonek find his way to this town which was renowned for its excellent fruit, physical beauty, and large Jewish community? In order to answer that question, I have to digress briefly from the main line of my story.

Whenever I think of my uncle's life story, I feel that it is the embodiment of Jewish destiny. In 1917, at the height of the First World War, a gang of Ukrainians entered my mother's and Lonek's home town of Stanislawow, which had already changed hands several times. The rioters were followers of Petlyura, a new and particularly savage reincarnation of the infamous anti-Semite Bogdan Chmelnitzky and his army. As they swept through the town, they took a random group of Jews hostage. Lonek was among them. The Ukrainians were desperately hungry, and so they left their prisoners tied up at the side of the road and went to look for food. 'When we come back, we'll kill you one by one,' their commander threatened. Fortunately, passers-by released all the hostages before the Ukrainians returned. This happened a short time after Lonek's Bar Mitzvah, by which time my mother had already moved to Holland with my father.

I don't exactly recall how my parents maintained contact with their former homeland – by letter or by telegram. At any rate, when my mother heard of the trauma her younger brother had experienced, she was deeply distressed. And it was then that my parents both agreed that the young boy would best be able to recuperate if he were to come to stay with us in Holland. The result was that Lonek came to live with us and soon became a part of the family. Since he was only ten years older than Zigi, we both regarded him as more of a beloved older brother than an uncle. My father was very fond of him, and when Lonek grew older, my father often took him along on his business trips. A few typical 'Gitter-jokes' have remained engraved in my memory from this period in our lives. One of them went like this: my father loved to travel overnight in the luxurious *wagons-lit* of the European trains. But these carriages were very expensive. So he would go into one of these first-class coaches, put down his things, place Lonek at the entrance and say to him in Yiddish: '*Lonek, mach dich meshiggeh*' ('Lonek, make yourself crazy'). Lonek would then fake an attack of epilepsy, and if anyone had been considering sharing that compartment with them, they invariably turned tail and fled at the sight. To this day, when my brother and I hear the words '*Lonek, mach dich meshiggeh*', we burst out laughing, a laughter tinged with sadness and nostalgia for a world long gone.

Lonek was very talented and was successful in almost everything he set his mind to. This was particularly true with respect to his grasp of foreign languages. I believe I inherited my own facility with languages from him. In 1928 Holland hosted the Olympic Games, and my brother and I – all of nine years old at the time – were very proud of our uncle who had been chosen as an official translator for the soccer matches. He translated in all the languages in which he was fluent: German, Polish and Dutch. With his help I managed to get in to see the most important matches of the Games, and I particularly remember Uruguay's historic victory over Argentina in the final. How could I have known then just how important those two countries were to become in my future? When I arrived in Montevideo at the height of the war, after a harrowing odyssey, I remember noticing the sign 'Amsterdam' on top of the local stadium, in memory of Uruguay's unforgettable 1:0 victory over Argentina.

Lonek wanted to go into business for himself, and soon left my father's company to enter the coffee trade. My father encouraged him to go his own way. Lonek went to Germany, and, in 1933, after having made a small fortune there, he finally settled in Hungary and set up a fruit exporting business. Years later, when the Nazi noose tightened around the Jews of Hungary, I went to see him again to try and persuade him to go to Palestine or at least to leave Hungary without delay. With great difficulty, I managed to salvage some of his fortune and transfer it to Holland, but his wife adamantly refused to emigrate to 'that hot country where camels wander around in the streets'. All my efforts to persuade him to leave failed. When the Nazis invaded Hungary, Lonek, the Polish Jew, was forced to return to his native country – Poland. Lonek and his family moved into the ghetto, setting up house in my father's sister's tiny two-and-a-half-room apartment, which they shared with forty other relatives. Eventually, they were all murdered by the Nazis and buried in mass graves, and that was how my young, gifted and high-spirited uncle's life came to an untimely end, murdered by the Nazis with the help of the same merciless Ukrainians who had failed to do so twenty-five years earlier.

But let us return to Budapest – one of the most beautiful cities of the world, with its two parts: ancient Buda, with hills, castles and ruins, and modern Pest, with numerous parks, bridges and lovely avenues. Modern Budapest was designed by Haussmann, the same architect who re-designed Paris in the nineteenth century. I loved the streets leading out of the city to the pastoral vistas, the 'Duna' (the Danube) as it was known by the Hungarians, which split the city in two like a silver ribbon, and the lights sparkling over the bridges at night like diamonds. I enjoyed eating at old man Stern Baczi's ('Uncle Stern's' in Hungarian) kosher restaurant, and attending services at the Rombach Utca (Rombach Street) synagogue, where the cantor Tekacz intoned the prayers so beautifully. Even the orthodox worshippers from the Kasinskzi Street synagogue and the Neologues (Reform Jews), from the Dohany Street synagogue came to listen to his *niggunim* (cantorial melodies).

The Jewish community in the city was sharply divided, and feelings ran high between the orthodox Jews and the liberals – except on one issue: they all fervently believed that they would survive the turmoil of the times. Even when they learned that the government set up by the extreme right-wing, practically Fascist, regent, Horthi, was nothing more than a puppet régime; even when Nazi laws were enforced in the country – they all remained convinced that 'it will never happen to us.' Just like their brethren in Amsterdam, the Jews of Budapest were dutiful, obedient citizens. Most of them did not consider *aliya* to Palestine as a possible solution for their predicament until it was too late – much too late.

I was caught up in this easygoing, even frivolous atmosphere. The Hungarians whom I met, Jews and non-Jews alike, were a happy breed, full of *joie de vivre*, openly and unabashedly warm and affectionate. Having been accustomed all my life to the typically dry Dutch temperament, the Hungarian girls had an electrifying effect on me. For a young man my age, Budapest was the perfect place to be at that time. Lonek, who was fluent in Hungarian, frequently took time off under the pretext that he had to take care of 'the boy' (I actually saw very little of him on those occasions ...). He found me a one-room apartment on Paulay Ede Street, in the leather trade sector of the city, which turned into an entertainment area at night. Women frequently approached me at the entrance to my flat, mumbling words I could not understand. Lonek solved the problem for me: 'Tell them *tiz filer* [ten filer, a tiny sum], and they won't bother you any more.' And indeed, his magic formula worked.

I worked with Hungarian tanners, and thoroughly enjoyed my new-found freedom and the feeling that I was learning something new and important every day. One event from this period of my life that I particularly remember was a party given in honour of the birth of Dutch Crown Princess Beatrix, to which I, as a Dutchman residing in the Hungarian capital, was invited. I rented a tuxedo for the first time in my life, and set off with high expectations for an exciting evening. The party was a rousing success. It was a winning formula that could not be beaten: a mixture of Dutch decorum and Hungarian-style fun and games. When the party was over, a group of us – young, vibrantly alive Dutch and Hungarian men and women – made the rounds of a series of pubs and bars, ending up at last by the pool of the elegant Gellert Hotel, where I soon found myself in the water. When I emerged I found that someone had taken a fancy to my tuxedo trousers. I was relieved to discover that no potential clothes' fancier had been similarly attracted to the elegant jacket. But on the following day, when I finally plucked up the courage to go back to the rental agency with only the top half of the tuxedo, they were singularly unimpressed by my story, and I was forced to reimburse them for the entire suit. Luckily for me, Hungary was in the throes of high inflation, and the allowance my father was sending me in the stable Dutch currency, irrespective of the monetary fluctuations in Hungary, allowed me to maintain a high standard of living, so that the unexpected expense did not set me back too much.

However, the most significant memory I have of that period touches, once again, on the Jewish issue. Although we kept our distance from Germany, where my father had extensive business interests up until 1933, Vienna was a different story altogether. From Hungary, I went on a brief visit to the Austrian capital to try to help my relatives leave that country before it was too late. Protected by my Dutch passport, I travelled without the least sense of any personal danger. But I soon learned that it was impossible for me to be of any help to anyone else. Naturally, I had no way of knowing that when I set out. Nevertheless, when I look back on this trip, I am convinced that it was not totally in vain. My visit to Austria, which had been annexed to Germany just a few weeks earlier in the *Anschluss,* brought home to me the true danger inherent in the rise of Nazism. The preparations the Austrian masses were making to join the ranks of their Nazi patrons-conquerors were blatantly evident everywhere. The heated demonstrations of the youth, the Nazi slogans, the sights and the fevered emotions, all these were seared into my soul. I never forgot the lesson I learned in Vienna, and it served as the basis for many important decisions I was to make later on.

On my return to Hungary, I re-established and deepened my ties with the centre for *Hakhsharah* in Holland, and asked them to send me work permits for young Zionists from Budapest. I based my request on the stated desire of these youngsters – some of them refugees from Eastern Europe – to acquire Zionist agricultural training in a

Hakhsharah group prior to their emigration to Palestine. I hoped that the Dutch government would consider these requests on a humanitarian basis, and that, since they were aware of the gathering clouds in Austria, the Dutch authorities would grant entry permits to as many of these youths as possible. And indeed, within a short time, I was notified that one hundred permits had been approved and were on their way. I was also told that in order to avoid any possible confrontations with either Germany or Hungary, no more permits would be issued. I was distressed to hear that, because I knew how many thousands needed to be saved, but at the same time I was grateful that my efforts had been at least partially successful.

The list of fortunate recipients of the entry permits was drawn up after a strict selection process that had been supervised by a Dutch official and a representative of the Jewish organization in Budapest. I was asked to teach the would-be émigrés the fundamentals of the Dutch language, a request to which I gladly agreed. Twice a week, for two hours each time, I taught Dutch in the offices of the Supreme Zionist Organization on Andraszy Street. I have no way of judging whether or not I was a successful teacher or whether I managed to teach my students anything at all about the Dutch language. I myself managed to pick up some Hungarian from them, and, to my amazement, I still remember the language rather well to this day.

A few short weeks after my return to Holland, I stood on the platform at the Amsterdam railway station waiting for 'my' *Halutzim* to arrive. Surprisingly, instead of a hundred, 101 huddled together on the platform. The extra *Halutz* was a friend of mine, a religious boy, who had been refused entry into the group because he had demanded kosher food. Somehow, in the end, I managed to persuade the selection committee to accept him; and he made it to Holland with all the others.

The arrival of the immigrants in Holland did not solve all the problems. Whereas up to that time the Dutch border police had not distinguished between Jews and non-Jews, immigration regulations relating to Jews were suddenly tightened up. In fact, everyone was affected, even veteran members of the Jewish community in Holland. Anyone who, like me, wanted to go to Palestine, had to sign up and wait anywhere between three and five years. Some priority was given to refugees from Eastern Europe. About a year after their arrival in

Holland, many of 'my' refugees asked me to help speed up their process of emigration. At that time, illegal immigration operations into Palestine – known as *Aliya Bet* – had begun, in an attempt to circumvent the British White Paper of 1936, and the severe limitations it had set on the number of Jews allowed into Palestine. A ship named *Doria* was chartered for this purpose, and I remember being very excited when I helped sign up the members of my group for the voyage to Eretz Yisrael. When the list was complete, my friend from the Hungarian pioneer group – number 101 – approached me again, complaining bitterly of discrimination. I intervened on his behalf, and, for the second time, managed to get him included in the list. Although I did not stay in touch with the members of the group, I was deeply conscious of being a *shaliach mitzvah* – the executor of a *mitzvah* (religious obligation) – by virtue of being privileged to help save 101 young men and women from certain death.

When I look back on the time I spent in Hungary, I recall a wonderful period of my life, one that had a distinctive flavour all its own. I enjoyed meeting so many different people: businessmen, Gentiles, Jews, Zionists and non-Zionists. All of them taught me something important in one area or another of my life. I enjoyed their hospitality, their *joie de vivre*, and the friendship showered on me by my friends, men and women alike. I left Hungary and the Hungarians with fond memories of my stay. To this day I don't recall if I left any broken hearts behind me.

It is very likely that my father never imagined that my apprenticeship with the Hungarian tanners would become such an important turning-point in my life, and give me so much. I developed a great deal of self-assurance, and was confident that I could deal with problems and take on tasks that others might find it impossible to accomplish – assuming they would ever consider undertaking such tasks in the first place. And the years that followed proved this beyond a doubt: at critical moments in my life I accepted responsibility and achieved the goals I set for myself. I was not yet twenty, an age when we feel we can overcome all odds, and only the sky is the limit. And, as I was soon to find out, confidence and daring would indeed be required of me. The future that awaited me – that awaited all of us – was just around the corner. It did not in any way resemble our predictable, complacent past.

A LAST VISIT TO THE FAMILY IN POLAND

A family portrait, photographed in 1935, reveals something of the special nature of my father's family: one sister was known as 'the Pole', my father was 'the Dutchman', there was an aunt who lived in Romania, another who had made her way to Italy, and there was Zelig 'the Austrian', and – my favourite – Uncle Shlomo, 'the German'. Uncle Shlomo was an enormously warm-hearted and generous man. The gifts he brought for me when he came to live with us for a number of months gave me more happiness than any other presents I ever received. I remember that he took me to my very first cabaret performance. He was, without a doubt, a man who enjoyed life. Shlomo-Solomon was also an exception in our family: he was not religious, and carried the stigma of a divorce. At the end of his extended stay with us, and despite our entreaties and warnings, he returned to Germany. In 1938 we learned that he had been arrested in Hamburg, tried and sentenced to five years with hard labour. His German girlfriend's brother had informed on him. According to the Nazi Race Laws of Nuremberg, romantic relations between Aryans and Jews were a very serious crime.

From the time of his sentencing, our family stood by my uncle, prepared to raise heaven and earth to deliver him from the terrible punishment that awaited him. My father hired an excellent lawyer by the name of Van Haastert to take on his defence. After an exhaustive investigation and in consultation with his colleagues, the lawyer finally found a loophole: my uncle's Polish nationality. As soon as this could be officially confirmed, Uncle Shlomo would be sent back to Poland. But here was the catch: what was his true nationality? At that time the town of his birth was considered Polish territory, but when he was born it had been part of the Austro-Hungarian Empire, and later became part of Romania. My father found out that there was only one person who could help: a brilliant lawyer by the name of Chmurski, a member of the Polish Siem (parliament). He had a reputation as a notorious anti-Semite, but we decided to overlook that fact if only he could help us. After our own lawyer made the initial contact, I was chosen to go to Warsaw to find Chmurski and try to persuade him to take on the case.

On 8 May 1939, my twentieth birthday, I arrived in Warsaw to

conduct the negotiations with the Polish lawyer. I only had his telephone number, and I was tired and hungry after ten hours on the train.
Actually, I was more hungry than tired, and shortly after I arrived, I
left my hotel to look for a kosher restaurant I had heard of. It was
almost ten p.m., and I could not find either that kosher restaurant or
any other from the list I had been given; it was as though they had all
disappeared off the face of the earth. It was only on the following day
that I discovered that the Polish authorities had ordered that all signs
in Yiddish or Hebrew be removed from Jewish businesses, thus making
it impossible for me to locate any of the restaurants I was looking for.
Hungry and frustrated I returned to my hotel. I asked the concierge to
wake me at eight in the morning, so as to begin my day as early as
possible. I went to sleep, and a phone call woke me up. It was not the
wake-up call but rather my relatives from Stanislawow who were on
the line, inviting me to come and spend the weekend with them. I
gladly accepted their offer and then immediately called the lawyer,
Chmurski. We arranged a time to meet later in the day, and I got
dressed and went out to look for some breakfast. The hotel restaurant
was closed. I'm late again, I thought gloomily. But when I reached the
street, I suddenly realized that my watch had stopped. Daylight comes
early in Poland at that time of year, and I was certain it was already
mid-morning – whereas in fact it was four o'clock in the morning. It
was only then that it dawned on me that the phone call from Stanislawow had come through in the middle of the night, and not in the
morning as I had thought. When I met the lawyer later that day, I apologized for having woken him up at such a strange hour. 'Never mind,' he
said, waving away my apologies, 'in this country lawyers – like doctors –
are used to receiving phone calls at all hours, day or night.'

The lawyer agreed to take the case for a considerable fee. But the
wheels of justice turned very slowly. After some time Chmurski told us
that he was on the verge of a successful conclusion of the case, and was
just waiting for the official documents. Informally, the Polish authorities
had already recognized my uncle's Polish citizenship. The months
dragged on, and then, on 1 September 1939, before anything had been
settled in the case, the war broke out. Poland was overrun by the Nazis,
and everything we had worked so carefully to achieve vanished into
oblivion. From that point on, we lost contact with my uncle. I sub-

sequently learned that he served out his entire five-year sentence of hard labour in Germany, and in 1944 was released from prison. One day after his release, he was sent to Poland – straight to his death in the concentration camps.

I often wonder how short-sighted we are, and just how our fate manipulates us like marionettes. At times I toy with the totally futile thoughts of 'what if': if my uncle had been sentenced to seven years instead of five, he might have remained alive and survived the war. In retrospect, the sentence of five years of hard labour, which at the time my father regarded as a terrible disaster, could in fact have been Uncle Shlomo's salvation, had it only been extended for a short while longer. How pathetic all our efforts to secure Uncle Shlomo's release seem to us now!

My trip to Poland was totally devoted to family. I visited my relatives in Stanislawow who welcomed me with open arms. I begged them to flee Poland, but my efforts to open their eyes to the seriousness of their situation came to naught. I took comfort in the fact that at least I had been given the opportunity to get to know them a little better. After my trip to Galicia, I also visited Lodz. Everywhere I went the predicament of the Jews seemed intolerable, and the way in which they had been herded into ghettoes was deeply distressing. I wanted to say to all of them: 'Jews, get out of here before it's too late!' But a tragic short-sightedness had overtaken them all. Very few immigration permits to the United States and to South America were available, and no one even considered fleeing to safety across the borders.

4

THE OCCUPATION

In April 1940, six months after the outbreak of the Second World War, we saw my father off on a trip. Our leave-taking this time was particularly emotional. All of us pretended to be happy, especially Father, who promised to return home soon. This was not a pleasure trip or a vacation, but a business trip, to buy leather in Argentina. Nevertheless, the name Argentina sounded highly exotic to all of us. I knew very little about that country, only that it was very far away, across the ocean, in the Southern Hemisphere; that the seasons were the opposite of our own, as was the case in its neighbours, Brazil and Uruguay and all the other enchanted countries of South America; that it was rich in natural resources, and full of jungles and rivers. Our father intended to make his base in Buenos Aires, the beautiful capital of the country. We thought he would be away for four months at the most: two weeks at sea en route, two to three months of work, and then another two-week trip by boat back to Holland.

To use a jaded but absolutely fitting metaphor of our behaviour at the time, we buried our heads in the sand like ostriches, and refused to see things as they really were. And I include myself in this indictment, at least in the initial stages of the chain of events that were to follow. This was a pattern of behaviour that was typical of Jewish communities everywhere at that time. Just like the Jews of Hungary, who refused to see the unmistakably clear writing on the wall, or the Jews of neighbouring Belgium, we simply did not believe that the relative calm was in fact the precursor of a violent storm, and that these were the final days of grace before the great darkness that descended on Europe. In those days, refugees from occupied Eastern Europe found their way to Holland in very small numbers, but we did not want to know what was happening outside our country. We were not emotionally prepared to deal with the unimaginable reality. Until the wave of annihilation actually reached our doorstep, we continued to bask in our complacency. Who could have imagined that Germany would regard Holland as an Aryan province, ripe for annexation? In our boundless naïveté, we believed that, just like in the First World War, Holland would stick to its role of a 'neutral' country and remain outside the main events of the times.

And so it was, then, that my father set sail for Argentina. Less than a month after he left, at the beginning of May 1940, the German army invaded Holland, and turned our entire world upside down. Holland became a German-occupied country, with the terrifying ramifications of such an event. Germany fought the Allies on the sea, on land and in the air. Vast expanses of the ocean turned into hostile territory, ports were closed, and warships and submarines patrolled the seas, both above and below the waters. The sea routes from Argentina to Holland were closed, and a vast and hazardous ocean now separated my father from our home. My father would certainly not have left the country had he known that the sea lanes would be closed. At the same time, it is absolutely clear to me now that if my father had remained in Holland, we would have never survived the Holocaust. The knowledge that he was there, waiting for us across the ocean, gave us the strength to go on. Father's trip was our great good fortune, and I have little doubt that if he had stayed in Holland, we would all have been swallowed up for ever behind the gates of the Westerbork transit camp and then deported to the death camps in the East.

My twenty-first birthday, 8 May 1940, is engraved in my memory. In Holland, as in many countries, this is the age when a young man or woman is first considered a mature and independent adult. It is, there-fore, a birthday with both formal and legal significance. To celebrate the event, I invited some friends over to our house. I told them that my father had written begging us to come and join him in Argentina, but that we had decided not to respond to his entreaties. My older brother was about to complete his medical studies, and I was awaiting my immigration certificate for Palestine. My mother did not want to leave us alone in Holland, and my brother Ya'akov was too young to have an opinion on the issue. We talked about the future, which was now more uncertain than ever before, and as usual, opinions were divided between the optimists, who believed that Holland would manage once again to remain neutral, as it had in the past, and the pessimists, who predicted disaster ahead. We parted none the wiser or stronger, trying valiantly to suppress our fears.

On the following day, 9 May, the die was cast. That morning, I left Amsterdam and headed east to the city of Arnhem on the German border, not suspecting anything untoward. One of our main suppliers had a tannery there. In the evening, as I got into my car to drive back home, one of my friend's neighbours called out to me: 'The Germans are crossing the border,' but I took little notice of what he had said. It was only on the following day that I heard on the radio that low-flying German bombers had invaded Dutch air space and had been sighted over Holland's major cities.

For five days the Dutch attempted to prevent the Germans from invading their country. But defeat was a foregone conclusion. What chance did a small nation have against the vastly superior military force of Nazi Germany? However, it was not only the differences in size between the two countries that precipitated Holland's surrender: as we learned later, Dutch border defences collapsed almost immediately, apparently the result of acts of treason on the part of some Dutch army personnel.

More than anything else, it was the news that Queen Wilhelmina, together with her family and closest retinue – including members of the government – had fled the country and sought asylum in England that brought home to us the gravity of the situation. Many Dutch citizens were furious with the Queen for doing so. 'We are ashamed of our Dutch nationality,' I heard non-Jewish Dutch people say angrily.

Now we were absolutely convinced that we had to escape without delay, to leave everything behind and not look back. We piled our company car up with everything it could carry, and set out. The only port that had not been bombed or mined was a small fishing harbour called Ijmuiden, twenty kilometres from Amsterdam. We hoped to find a boat or ship that would take us to England. With a heavy heart we parted from everything we had loved and nurtured over the years. We did not abandon our home. We asked cousins of ours, Dino Jarach and his wife, to live in the house in our absence. Dino had recently been appointed head of the International Government Office for Tax Documentation on behalf of the International Court of Justice in The Hague.

We hoped that they would feel comfortable in our house, and that their Italian citizenship would protect them from any harm.

After a slow and nerve-racking drive, we arrived at Ijmuiden around three in the afternoon. Hundreds of cars were slowly making their way towards the harbour. Thousands of people had entertained exactly the same thoughts we had, and hoped to find a place on any merchant ship leaving Dutch shores for any destination. There were only two ships in the harbour, one of which was plainly visible, but the harbour itself seemed totally paralyzed: nothing was happening and no one was moving about. We remained in the car, occasionally getting out to stretch our limbs and talk to our fellow travellers. All through the night rumours raced back and forth among the potential travellers, and finally, at dawn, we were officially notified that the harbour was closed due to an unexploded bomb that had fallen nearby.

Slowly, in an agonizing bumper-to-bumper drive, we returned home, totally depressed and at a loss as to what to do next. As we entered the house, we were greeted by a strong smell of alcohol. I quickly ran down to the cellar to try and find out what had happened, and was appalled by what I saw there: in our absence Dino and his wife had smashed to bits the hundreds of bottles of fine wines and spirits that had been my father's pride and joy. Trying to explain his strange behaviour, Dino told us that official instructions had been issued over the radio concerning measures that should be taken in case of an enemy invasion. Among other things, citizens were requested to remove all alcoholic drinks from their homes to prevent them from falling into German hands. Dino and his wife took this to mean wines as well and proceeded to destroy the contents of our cellar. Conceivably, they also felt that they should prevent the Germans from taking pleasure in such a wealth of spirits. To this day it pains me to think of that wanton destruction of my father's superb collection of fine wines. We weren't sure if we should laugh or cry over the naïveté of the couple's absurdly strict compliance with the instructions they had heard on the radio. In the event, fatigue got the better of all of us, and we simply threw ourselves into the beds we thought we had left behind for ever, and fell into a deep sleep. With tragically ironic timing, the day after the onset of the German Occupation of Holland, I finally received my long-awaited Certificate of Immigration to Palestine. The dream that I had nurtured for three years – ever since 1937 – was no longer worth the paper it was written on.

Fear spread like wildfire through the Jewish community. We were all convinced that our lives were about to turn into sheer hell. We were all too familiar with the Germans' treatment of the Jews in 1933, and prepared ourselves for the worst: pogroms, closing down of Jewish businesses, deportation to camps, and endless edicts limiting our basic freedom. The manner of the Germans' entrance into the capital multiplied our fears tenfold: masses of troops surrounded the city, encircling it two or three times around. Later we learned that the terrifying tactics employed by the occupying forces had been a carefully orchestrated show of strength aimed at warning us against attempting any kind of resistance.

In the days that followed, ominous rumours made the rounds in the community. Some of our closest friends refused to reconcile themselves to the idea of living under German rule, and took their own lives. Among them were young couples with children. First they killed their children and then they committed suicide. Among them was Mr E. Boekman, a Jewish deputy mayor of Amsterdam.

During the first few days of the Occupation, having rolled through Holland virtually unopposed, the Germans appeared to be totally uninterested in the local inhabitants. Soldiers passed by with expressionless faces, seemingly oblivious to our existence. It was not surprising, then, that some of the more optimistic among us jumped to typical conclusions: 'It's been over a week now, and they haven't done a thing to us. You see? This isn't Germany. They have no intention of doing us any harm; they're only out to get their own Jews.' Many of us were amazed at the courteous behaviour of German officers, who politely greeted obviously Jewish-looking people as they passed them in the street. Stories like this were eagerly repeated during those early days, perhaps as a desperately needed form of reassurance.

Looking back on all these events from a distance of many years, it seems very clear that the Germans' behaviour was part of a carefully thought-out and devilishly premeditated plan. I actually believe that they developed psychological guidelines for dealing with the inhabitants of occupied countries, in order to reap the greatest benefit for themselves from the Occupation. By the time the Germans invaded Holland they had already gained a wealth of experience in these matters in Poland and elsewhere, and adjusted the theory to suit the particular nature of each country they occupied. Among their discoveries was that over a period of time most people will get used to almost any deterioration in their standard of living. This was the key to the Nazis' method of 'gradation': strictures were never imposed all at once, but rather at irregular intervals through the sporadic announcement of new restrictions of varying degrees of severity. At one point they would announce a particularly harsh new edict and enforce it immediately and very strictly, and later they would announce another, rather trivial regulation, and make a point of enforcing it in a half-hearted manner. I often thought of them as the Pied Piper of Hamelin: they played their soothing tunes, and we blindly followed the music.

New edicts were issued with ever-increasing frequency: one day Jews were forbidden to sit on public benches; then the newspapers and public notice-boards in town carried announcements that Jews would no longer be permitted to attend public events such as concerts, plays, lectures etc. These bitter pills were dipped in a deceptively sweet coating: Jews would be allowed to produce their own performances, set up theatre companies or orchestras exclusively for their own purposes. Once again the optimists among us found some consolation: 'We told you so! They don't really want to hurt us. These are harmless, temporary regulations – just until the war is over.' We continued for some time to play this game of self-delusion, until finally the true, grim reality of our situation began to dawn on us. More draconian decrees soon appeared, as strict limits were set on the use of private cars, and petrol purchases were prohibited. Throughout most of 1941, for as long as we were still allowed to travel by train or tram, I used public transport – particularly trains – for my business trips outside Amsterdam. But by 1942 a special permit issued by the Jewish Council was required if anyone travelled by train beyond the city limits. These permits were hard to come by, and were normally issued only in cases of emergency or for people working at the Westerbork detention camp. Soon even these special permits were revoked, and from that time on I maintained my business contacts by bicycle. Since bicycle tyres were in severely short supply, I often had to do without them, toiling along the roads on the metal wheel rims. Occasionally, when my affairs required a trip of twenty kilometres or so in each direction, I stayed over with my clients or suppliers, sometimes even for a number of days, and found this an unexpected way of strengthening my ties with them.

LEADERS IN A QUANDARY

The actual invasion of Holland was carried out by the German Wehrmacht, but almost immediately after the occupation was completed, the combat soldiers departed, leaving the daily administration of the country to the Gestapo. The occupying forces quickly enlisted the help of the German Military ('Green') Police and the local police force. This was a devastating combination, as the Germans took complete control of every aspect of our daily lives. And even though there were still a few good people to be found in these organizations – like islands of sanity and decency in a rough sea of cruelty – there was nothing they could do to change the overall picture. The Germans soon proved how adept they were at exploiting the rotten elements of Dutch society. They dissolved the elected municipality of Amsterdam and reconstituted it to suit their needs, installing the well-known anti-Semite Voute as the new mayor. Collaborators, opportunists, unscrupulous elements and closet anti-Semites now came out of the woodwork, and soon figured prominently in the police force. In fact, the Germans needn't have taken such great pains to win over the Dutch police: a good number of those who served in the force under the Occupation needed no prompting and displayed a natural, and even willing, propensity for anti-Semitism.

In retrospect, this shift in the attitude of many Dutch people towards the Jews was not altogether surprising in view of the fact that, from 1933 on, the rise of Nazism in Germany had had a marked influence on Holland as well. The rapidly growing power of the large German neighbour, and the possibility that the German Reich would indeed last a thousand years as promised, was cause for deep concern among many Dutch government officials. As Nazi strength in Germany increased, so fear of its possible consequences percolated deeper into the lower levels of the Dutch population. This was the main reason for the policy of appeasement pursued by Holland in an effort to head off any possible confrontation with the German giant next door. The police played a major role in this process, subjecting refugees from the Nazi régime to harsh treatment, and imposing strict limitations on the activities of leftist movements.

On the face of it, the police appeared to be adhering to a policy of strict neutrality, but I have learned, over many years of observing human behaviour, that neutrality, as practised by people, countries, or organizations, is really a polite way of taking a stand. In most cases, the neutral party manages to deceive its surroundings, and to disguise its clear support for one of the sides to a conflict under a cover of 'neutrality'. The first seven years of Nazi rule in Germany, from 1933 to 1940, were time enough to prepare the policemen of Holland for the task at hand. The Occupation caused many of them to regard any German in uniform, even their equal in rank, as their superior and commander. There were many small-minded, highly disciplined people in the police force, who were entirely in the thrall of power, uniforms and high military ranking. A small number of Dutch police personnel outdid themselves in their displays of inhumanity, cruelty, and indifference to suffering. These were the members of the NSB, a Dutch Nazi organization. In fact, it was the NSB that established the WA – the Dutch arm of the SS – which attracted those simple-minded policemen who were notorious for their cruelty, and who were intoxicated by the trappings of power and the possibilities of intimidation that came with them. These were men whose inhumanity knew no bounds. At the same time, during the two years and two months that I lived under Nazi rule in Holland, I also encountered Dutch policemen who, despite the situation in the country, treated us decently, never engaging in the mindless cruelty displayed by some of their colleagues.

Among the ordinary citizens of Holland it was difficult to discern a clearly unified stand. One mustn't overlook the fact that during the first three years of the war Germany's overwhelming victories on the battlefield sent a powerful message to the people of Holland – and to the rest of Europe as well. The inevitable result was that everyone took pains not to run foul of the German monster in any way. What is more, some Dutch people were driven by purely opportunistic desires to take advantage of the Nazi tidal wave, and join in its triumphant sweep through Europe, rather than try to resist it in any way. As they saw it, if they could derive personal gain and make a profit, or acquire some position of authority in the government bureaucracy, so much the better. Among the Jews, too, there were many who feared the Germans, and believed that a policy of non-resistance (a euphemism for the shameful term 'collaboration') would afford them a better chance for survival. This was the way things stood for at least as long as I had first-hand knowledge of events in Holland; in other words, up to the middle of 1942.

But we must review the facts of the situation as honestly as possible. Under no circumstances do I mean to give the impression that the Dutch nation as a whole was a collection of opportunists and cowards. Many Dutch men and women risked their lives in a relentless struggle against the Nazis. At the very same time as the shameful policy of appeasement reared its head in Dutch society, a number of underground groups – made up of both Jews and non-Jews – maintained an active resistance. And among my friends in the underground there were a number of true heroes, like, for example, the Meyers brothers, Max and Bernard. One was a pharmacist, and the other, my brother's friend, was a doctor. Initially, Bernard Meyers, like so many others, did not regard Nazism as an extreme threat to our existence. He even had a copy of a lithograph of a swastika combined with a *Magen David* (six-pointed Star of David) in his notebook, as though it were some kind of joke. It was only later that he understood the cruelly racist nature of the movement, and became a fierce opponent of the Nazi Occupation. Towards the end of 1941 the Meyers brothers proposed that I join them in an attempt to escape Holland to England by sea. I told them I would, and waited for them to notify me of the exact date of the planned operation. We decided to hold a full 'dress rehearsal' with the entire group in order to become familiar with the boat we intended to use. Due to so-called weather conditions the rehearsal was postponed, which made me doubtful, and so my life was saved, as I shall revert to later. The police discovered the plan, apparently with the help of an informer inside the group, and imprisoned them all. There was a mockery of a trial, and all but one of the participants were sentenced to death. Among others who were captured by the Germans in similar operations was Henk Hart, the son of friends of our family. Henk's brother Fritz was already in Argentina at the time, and one of the first, and most difficult, tasks I had to attend to when I eventually arrived there was to notify him and his parents of Henk's death. The fact that I had barely known Henk himself didn't make this any easier.

A couple whom I knew well, Betty and Philip De Leeuw, were particularly daring members of one of the underground groups. Betty had been a childhood friend of mine. To this day I have fond memories of a joint birthday party we celebrated when we were both seven years old. In fact, she was the first love of my life, but I hesitated to reveal my feelings for her, and, some time after her nineteenth birthday, she married Philip De Leeuw, a good friend of mine who was somewhat older than both of us. At the time of their wedding, Philip was an officer in the Dutch army. Later, they both joined the Zionist *Hakhsharah*, and in time also joined the underground. In 1944 they were arrested separately, after a failed attempt to blow up a German troop train. Philip, who was carrying arms at the time of his arrest, was tortured by the Gestapo, but refused to reveal the names of his colleagues in the underground. He even managed somehow to get important information through to his wife. A few days later he was executed in Utrecht prison. The Dutch guards at Betty's prison, who did not know that they were a married couple, helped her survive this harrowing ordeal, and in the end, surprisingly, the Gestapo let her go. It was in the maximum-security prison in Scheveningen, nicknamed the 'the Orange Prison' after the Dutch royal family, that many of the heroes of the Dutch resistance went to their deaths. Whenever I go to Holland I make a point of going past the ancient fortress, as though to seek out the ghosts of my brave friends from those days.

After the war, Betty began a new chapter in her life. She became a well-known public figure, and saw to her husband's reinterment in a section of the cemetery near the Dutch village of Loenen set aside for Heroes of the Nation. Today, Betty divides her time between her homes in The Hague and in Eilat (the Red Sea resort town in Israel), and is well known for her work on behalf of many public causes. I am very proud that Betty and I continue to this day to share a friendship that has spanned seven decades.

At the end of the war, when it became clear that the ultimate defeat of Nazi Germany was only a matter of time, a few former collaborators and NSB personnel joined the underground – some out of genuine remorse and sorrow, others in a calculated move to save their skins in the rapidly approaching time of reckoning. While this is not information that I can vouch for myself, a number of people who had first-hand knowledge of these things told me so.

All this, of course, relates to events that occurred long after the war. At the time, the shocking realities of the Nazi Occupation and the edicts imposed on us by their occupying forces forced the Jewish community to regroup. In 1933, seven years before the Occupation, the community had set up a supreme representative body, which served as an umbrella for all the institutions within the community. Among these was a central council for Jewish refugees from Germany, headed by the historian Professor Cohen, a long-time Zionist leader, and by Abraham Ascher, a world-renowned diamond manufacturer and prominent businessman, well known for his liberal views. These two leaders were greatly respected in Holland, and became famous for their efforts on behalf of the refugees from Germany. It was only natural that the members of the community felt they should continue their endeavours during the Occupation. During their initial term of office they had gained a great deal of experience, and had created an extensive network of contacts through their work for the community and their dealings with the authorities.

No one could have imagined that they, the acknowledged leaders of the community, would become so subservient to the German Occupation forces, becoming, to all intents and purposes, both their lackeys and their hostages. There was no middle way. Total obedience to Nazi dictates was a cast-iron condition for retaining any positions of influence. Refusal to comply with the German authorities, or any attempts at independent policies, or the merest hint of subversion on their part, could have cost them their lives and the lives of their families. It is exceedingly difficult to judge them for their actions. Theirs was an extremely complicated and unenviable position, to say the least. On the face of it, they were the representatives of the Jews *vis-à-vis* the Jewish community. It was certainly not a role they undertook willingly or for any personal gain. Nevertheless, there are those who claim to this day that these representatives of the community acquiesced more readily and willingly to German demands than was absolutely necessary. Can we blame them? Can we understand them?

One important event that occurred some time in 1941 should have served to these Jewish leaders as a very clear warning of things to come. As I mentioned, beginning in September 1940, the Germans began imposing severe restrictions on the Jewish community. The following autumn, that of 1941, was especially depressing after two particularly harsh edicts were issued, one requiring all Jews to wear the yellow identity badge on their clothes, and the other imposing a curfew on Jews from eight in the evening until eight in the morning. Unlike the ghettoes of Eastern Europe no physical barriers had yet been erected around the Jewish area of Amsterdam. Nevertheless, the borders of the community were clearly delineated. The mood in town was sombre and tense. And yet, although the Jews were confused and lived in constant fear, still no one drew any practical conclusions from the situation. One evening, the members of the community council were called in to meet two distinguished guests: Dr Edelstein from Prague, and Dr Friedman from Vienna, leaders of Jewish communities in their own countries, which had already been occupied by the Nazis, Austria in 1938 and Czechoslovakia in 1939. After introducing themselves, they informed us that the object of their visit was to try and establish some form of cooperation between the *Judenrats* (Jewish Councils) of the three cities. They described to their Dutch hosts the situation in their own cities. There was no doubt, they said, that the Germans would ultimately be defeated, but until such time Germany was still very powerful, and attempting to oppose it was tantamount to butting one's head against a brick wall. As they saw it, we were facing even more difficult years ahead, and the only way to ensure our survival was through cooperation.

Although it was never said openly in any way, the real aim of their visit began to emerge. It gradually became clear to us that these two gentlemen were in fact seeking to obtain our cooperation in reorganizing shipments of Jewish labourers to work camps that were being set up deep inside Poland. Edelstein and Friedman described these camps in seemingly realistic terms. They did not describe them as fun-filled summer camps, but at the same time they gave no intimation that they would eventually turn into sinister death camps. They made it clear that the forced labour in these camps would be hard, but then went on to promise that the chances for survival there were good. They explained at some length what was already being done in this respect in Prague and Vienna, and what we, the Jews of Holland, would be required to do.

We all experienced a growing sense of discomfort. For our part, the Jewish citizens of Amsterdam, a city famed for its liberal tolerance, were now forced to live under harsh civil restrictions, forbidden to use any form of public transport, and allowed to travel only by bicycle or on foot. Even in order to meet these two Jewish officials one had to request a special permit, while they, our guests, seemed not to have a care in the world. We could not help regarding their apparent freedom to come and visit us with a mixture of suspicion and envy (it later transpired that they had travelled to Amsterdam by sleeper train with the Germans' blessings). Could it be, we thought, that the Germans had orchestrated this entire visit? I do not blame these two men. It is entirely possible that under the circumstances they had no choice but to do what they did. Perhaps they actually believed that within the terrible context of those days they were even doing us some good and providing a measure of relief from the suffering.

One way or another, their visit served as a catalyst for a violent dispute that soon rocked our community, and led to the resignation of a few council members. The Zionist-oriented physicians who served the community notified the council that they would refuse to have anything to do with the 'selections' for deportations, where their medical opinions would be used to determine people's fate to life or death. I must emphasize, however, that at that time no one in the community had any first-hand knowledge of the fact that what awaited us at the other end of the deportations would almost always be death.

That was the last chance for Messrs Ascher and Cohen, the leaders of the Jewish community of Amsterdam, to resign from their posts with any measure of self-respect. They chose, however, not to do so, and instead announced that they would hold the recalcitrant physicians responsible if people unfit for work reached the camps. The greater part of the community sided with its leaders, and no serious challenge was ever posed to their authority. The Jews living in Holland, like the people in whose country they resided, were profoundly committed to law and order, and were reluctant to engage in radical changes of any kind. Most of them preferred to keep their heads down and wait for the storm to pass.

Perhaps the only way we can grasp the true complexity of the situation these leaders faced is by comparing their decisions to those made by members of *Judenrats* elsewhere in Europe and in other cities in Holland itself. The fact is that the Dutch Jewish officials, almost invariably, became tools in the hands of their German masters, and as such played a crucial role in the annihilation of Dutch Jewry.

Despite the dark atmosphere that prevailed in the Jewish community at the time, every so often the inbred Jewish propensity for irony created jokes which, however briefly, alleviated the suffering. One example of a joke that made the rounds then is the following. Two Jews are sentenced to death by firing squad. When they arrive at the designated place of execution, the executioners inform them that their sentences have been commuted – to death by hanging. Says one Jew to the other, 'You see? It's a good sign! That means they don't have any more ammunition.'

FIRST THERE WERE POSTCARDS

In 1941 the Jewish quarter in Amsterdam was rocked by the following tragic incident. A number of Dutch WA men – members of the Dutch version of the SS – were strutting through the quarter when they encountered a group of young Jews. Words were exchanged and then blows, and by the time the dust had settled, one of the Dutch WA men lay dead on the ground, having been beaten to death by the Jewish youths. In retaliation the WA, together with a number of policemen, took into custody all the young Jews formerly belonging to the Hakh-sharot. These, we should recall, were a few hundred youngsters from Eastern Europe who had emigrated to Holland and joined the Zionist Hakhsharot. Some of these Hakhsharot were in Wieringen, near the coast. After the Germans invaded Holland, the Hakhsharot were disbanded, and the Zionist organizations placed these youngsters in the homes of Jewish families. Not all of these families were affiliated with the Zionist movement, but nevertheless they received the young people with open arms. The police had no difficulty in locating them: every single one of them appeared on the lists the community had given the police as a token of good citizenship. The next step was a punitive *aktion*: taking full advantage of the repercussions of the beating incident, the police now went from house to house arresting not only all the *Hakhsharah* youngsters, but also all the male members of the host families as well. This *aktion* led to the deportation of over four hundred young people to the Mauthausen death camp.

My own reaction, and that of all of my friends and relatives immediately following this tragedy, clearly illustrates just how profoundly incapable we all were of dealing with the situation head-on, preferring rather to live in a fools' paradise. It never even crossed our minds that these young people would probably never return from Mauthausen. On that terrible day the Germans closed off the Jewish quarter and raised all the canal bridges, making it impossible for anyone to enter or leave the area. Within half an hour everyone knew what had happened. We got together – my brother Shimon and his wife Leah, Felix Levenbach, my father's partner's son, his young wife Irma, and me – got on our bicycles and boarded a train. At noon we arrived at a resort hotel, the Bilderberg, to this day one of the most beautiful and elegant in the country. We were all somewhat light-headed, and when the waiter asked us if we would like German wine with our meal, I replied jokingly, 'Yes, but only from a pre-1933 vintage.' We all burst into wild laughter over my witticism.

We returned home the following day. I don't recall if we actually realized that we were on the brink of a new era, which was to be more overtly cruel than anything that had preceded it. We may have been somewhat encouraged by the general strike that had been declared by the workers of Amsterdam as a sign of solidarity with the Jews, a show of resistance the like of which had never been seen in any of the occupied countries up to that time. 'Don't Touch Them!' one of the posters proclaimed, while another stated 'Even If They Are Dirty Jews – They Are Our Jews!' But the workers' demands for the release of the prisoners made no impression whatsoever on the Germans. In retaliation for the strike, the Germans slapped a collective punishment on all the participants: a fine in the form of a double payment of income tax. And everyone – ourselves included – paid up without a word.

Little by little, information filtered back to us about what had really happened to the young prisoners. First there were postcards. Even though the youngsters initially tried to give us hope, the ominous undertones we could discern between the lines were unmistakable: 'Don't worry about me! Keep your heads high!' Later, pointed hints appeared in the postcards which left little room for doubt: 'Fritz has gone to meet Grandma' (Grandma having been dead for a number of years). Eventually, the Germans notified the heads of the community of the death of all the youngsters involved. Rabbi Philip Frank, one of the younger and most beloved rabbis of the community, went from house to house informing the families of the terrible fate of their loved ones. He carried out his dreadful mission heroically, comforting and consoling each of the families in turn. A short while later, he himself met his death at the hands of the Germans in no less cruel a manner.

The newspapers that appeared in the days that followed were filled with black-framed death notices, breaking everyone's hearts. Soon afterwards, the Germans decided to sever all means of communication between the families and their loved ones in the camps, needless to say not out of any humanitarian concern for the families' wellbeing. The result was that many families, who had not heard anything certain about the fate of their dear ones, continued to be buffeted between hope, uncertainty and despair.

Even though by this stage there were more than ample signs of the impending catastrophe, very few of us considered the alternative of escape. Most of the daring attempts – like that of my ill-fated companions – to flee Holland by way of the North Sea to England, ended in disaster. Potential escapees were routinely caught and sentenced to death. In those cases where the escape attempt was discovered through informers, the Occupation forces maintained a semblance of 'due process'. This was the way my friends – the Meyers and the others – were murdered. To this very day the Germans' insane logic never ceases to amaze me: throughout the war they murdered millions of people in cold blood without batting an eyelid, yet in Holland, for some reason, they made an effort to keep up a pretence of 'decency', wasting time, money and effort on extravagant – and totally unnecessary – mock trials.

Very few people in the community considered the possibility of fleeing to a neutral country, such as Switzerland or Spain. The prospect of such an attempt was simply too terrifying for ordinary citizens who had always had a profound respect for law, order, and accepted social mores, and lived their lives accordingly. As they saw it, fleeing the country would mean embarking on an odyssey fraught with dangers, obstacles, informers, and hazardous border crossings: from Holland to Belgium, to Vichy France, to the narrow, constantly shifting strip of land that constituted Free France, or even ranging as far as Switzerland. Despite its official stance of non-intervention and neutrality, Switzerland had a bad reputation among the Jews. Hair-raising stories made the rounds by word of mouth about so-called 'neutral' Swiss officials who had forced Jewish immigrants back across the border into the hands of Nazi policemen on the French border near Geneva.

THE EXECUTIONS OF MAX AND BERNARD MEYERS

A small group of Dutch ex-officers and civilians had decided to escape rather than to wait and be killed by the Nazis. Being a friend of the Dutch ex-officers, Max and Bernard Meyers, Frederick Spitz was offered the chance to join the group. He cancelled at the last moment, fearing the perils and dangers involved and thus survived. After the war Spitz lived in Israel. In a long letter to the Meyers' parents, who were at that time in the US, he described the account of the attempt to flee to freedom. Here follow some quotations from his letter:

After many meetings, long deliberations and verification of the good faith and brinkmanship of the organizers we decided to flee to England during the first days of January 1942. However, a severe cold spell, causing ice and dangerous conditions, dictated a change in the date of departure. Due to the tides and moon condition the departure had to be delayed by at least one month. On 1 February it was decided that since the road conditions had not improved the departure would be set for 21 March 1942.

Needless to say that since I had decided not to participate on account of the danger, I told Max and Bernard about my reasons and suggested that they should follow my advice. On that occasion we spoke for hours but they were adamant and in spite of the possible dangers ahead, they decided to try to escape.

On Saturday, 21 March the members of the group left Amsterdam for Rotterdam by train. Although Jews were not allowed to travel by train it was still easy to get permits since the Yellow Star had not yet been imposed. We bought first-class seats after Bernard's statement: We will either be in England tomorrow or in prison tonight but now – we are going to travel first class. Max took along his last cigars from before the war. The mood of the group members altered frequently from elation and anticipation of freedom, to fear and nervousness.

The meeting point in Rotterdam was the home of one of the members of the group. We arrived there in small groups through various routes and entrances, trying not to attract attention. To reduce the excitement of farewell I took leave of my friends, promising to wait a safe distance away to ensure that the plan was precisely executed or, alternatively to take measures to rescue them.

At five o'clock the grey 'Wehrmacht' car arrived and stopped at the agreed place. The group went in and soon disappeared from sight. I am not able to describe the feeling I had, standing on top of the River Maas's dyke watching them disappear. Was it the unconscious knowledge that this was the last time I was to see my good friends or was it the feeling of a missed opportunity and having taken the wrong decision?

The details of the flight were reconstructed later from information I received from the survivors.

The boat anchored in one of the islands of the Province of South Holland, set to sail after dark. Since the area was a military zone, only authorized Germans were permitted to enter. The group, driving a German car and holding false papers, reached their destination, a farm near the beach, with no difficulties. In the evening they loaded the luggage and other necessities into the boat which was about a hundred metres ahead of them, in the water. They waited in the farm for complete darkness and for the right tide to start their escape and then they heard the engine of a boat in the distance. The sound was disturbing since there was no nautical traffic on that closed part of south Holland. Soon those sitting near the window saw armed German soldiers approaching and immediately thereafter heard from loudspeakers that they were surrounded. The members of the group could not run or hide. Only one, a Czech professor, managed to crawl into a potato crate and hide successfully to live and to retell the story.

The group members were taken to the Gestapo headquarters in Rotterdam for initial investigation and then to the police jail where they were held till their sentencing.

Friends and your brother and his wife tried to contact them through the underground and to provide them with legal representation. No lawyer, whether Jew, Christian or German, was ready to defend the group. We tried to bribe the guards to give them better treatment but in vain. The only benefit of our efforts was that they were not tortured and that they were tried in a military court in Amsterdam. They were sentenced to death, pleaded for a pardon but were rejected.

On 25 August 1942 the uncle of Max and Bernard Meyers, in Amsterdam, received a letter notifying him that both their executions had taken place ten days earlier.

The person who informed the Nazis about the plan to escape stood trial in April 1946. It was revealed that the driver who took them from Rotterdam to the farm was the informer and betrayed their trust for a large sum of money. He was sentenced to death but a year later Queen Wilhelmina reduced his sentence to life in prison.

On 8 February 1960 Queen Juliana again reduced his sentence to twenty-five years and from 1970 this criminal murderer who had betrayed his country, deceived his fellow citizens and was responsible for the death of the group was free to leave the prison.

I blame neither Queen Wilhelmina nor Queen Juliana. After all, they had not been in the country during the terrible war and have perhaps not understood the plight of 110,000 of their fellow countrymen who were descendants of honourable citizens of Holland for more than three hundred years. Although the blame rests entirely on the German Nazis and their Dutch collaborators it is still sad that such a royal 'grace' has been spilled on a notorious traitor. I hold the corresponding Prime Ministers and Justice Ministers responsible for their ill advice to both Queens.

THE CARPET HE KEPT FOR HIMSELF

The general strike was a wonderful example of the Dutch spirit at its best, but it also served to sharpen the ambivalence I still feel towards the Dutch people as a whole. As a nation, the Dutch did not display any true generosity or loyalty towards the Jewish minority that had lived in their midst for hundreds of years. The majority of the Dutch people acquiesced meekly to German dictates, with subservience that at times bordered on enthusiasm. The facts speak for themselves: four years after the beginning of the German Occupation only ten per cent of the Jewish population of Holland was left alive.

This ambivalence I feel towards the Dutch derives, in part, from the wonderful memories I have of my childhood and youth in that country. I am keenly aware of the common history of these two peoples, and am profoundly grateful for its better sides, but I cannot erase from my memory those two years under the Nazi Occupation. Dutch collaboration with the Nazis was an indisputable fact, and as such has been indelibly engraved in my memory. No one forced the Dutch to collaborate, and those among them who did so acted quite of their own free will – voluntarily, willingly, and, not infrequently, out of petty greed: for every Jew handed over to the German authorities they received seven gulden – a truly negligible sum. I am not implying that these avaricious informers really knew where the Jews were being sent, or that they would never be seen alive again, but I have no doubt that a number of Dutch people were quite willing to embrace the despicable German principle of *Judenrein* ('a Jew-less country').

Why was that? Is it possible that we, unknowingly, aroused envy or a fear of competition among the Dutch? The answer is perhaps to be found in the many studies that have been carried out on the phenomenon of anti-Semitism, among them a book by my mentor, Peretz Bernstein. Anti-Semitism does not appear to have been a universal phenomenon in Holland. Nevertheless, various episodes in our lives, even after the war, tell us something about the depth of the anti-Semitic feelings found in the collective psyche of the Dutch. One such story involves a family friend of ours, a very likable person who worked in my father's company. Just before we fled Holland, we entrusted him with a valuable carpet and a silver *Kiddush* cup that had been given to me by the synagogue for my Bar Mitzvah, and was very precious to me. When I returned to Holland after the war, I looked the man up and asked him for the cup and the carpet that we had left in his care. Without hesitation, or even the slightest hint of embarrassment, he replied, 'The carpet is going to be a problem: all my friends and relatives know that it's mine. How will I explain to them that it's gone?' I suggested several solutions to his problem, but he stood his ground. 'Keep the carpet,' I finally hissed between clenched teeth. He had little use for the *Kiddush* cup with its telltale Hebrew inscription, and was only too glad to be rid of it. It was this same *Kiddush* cup that I held tightly in both hands on my seventy-fifth birthday as I drank the wine and said the prayer '*Shehechianu*' (Thanks be to God for keeping us alive).

Despite our constant uncertainty and fear, out of inertia or necessity – or both – we continued going through the motions of our daily routine. Every day revealed to us yet another unpleasant aspect of our new reality. While my brother had managed, despite it all, to complete his medical studies at the University of Amsterdam, it was clear to me that my plans to study at the Hebrew University were now no more than a dream. It was at that time that I discovered that work – hard work – could serve as a kind of tranquillizer, as a means for shifting my thoughts away from the dark side of our lives. I divided my time between my duties in the leadership of the Zichron Jacob movement and my father's responsibilities in the firm, which had been entrusted to my care since his departure. To this day I am amazed how mobile we were despite all the travel restrictions imposed on us. For short trips I used my bicycle, the transportation of choice in Holland. As for my beloved car, which I had purchased at the flea market against my father's wishes, I had no choice but to part with it once Jews were banned from buying petrol. Through deception and a few calculated risks, I generally managed to obtain railway permits for my business trips.

Generally speaking, I was not deterred by danger. Was it courage, the reckless impetuosity of youth? I do not know for sure. I think my greatest motivation was a sense of responsibility towards the business tasks that I now filled in my father's absence. We had no contact whatsoever with Father, and there was no way I could seek his advice. Yet the fact that I had to make my own decisions undoubtedly had a very positive effect on me. I was inspired by Father in everything I did, and particularly by my constant desire to do what I knew he would have done had he been there with me. I often sought the answer to managerial problems by imagining how my father might have handled that particular situation. Clearly, the independence and self-confidence I had gained during my apprenticeship in Budapest now stood me in good stead.

BETWEEN GOD AND A GERMAN *REICHSKOMMISSAR*

A new name began cropping up in our conversations: Westerbork. This was a camp set up by the Dutch government in the province of Drente, with financial assistance from the Jewish community, to house Jewish refugees who came to Holland from Germany after 1933. In 1941 the Germans turned Westerbork into a transit camp where they processed transports to the death camps. Tens of thousands of Jews passed through this camp between 1942 and 1945. On 12 April 1945, when Westerbork was finally liberated by the Allied troops, they found only 876 Jewish survivors there.

I have gleaned most of what I know about this camp from existing historical records of its activities. In 1941, prior to its transfer to the Germans, the camp housed 1,100 inhabitants in 200 small wooden huts, and was run by a Dutch official from the Ministry of Justice. At the end of 1941, when the German administration decided to turn Westerbork into a transit camp, barbed-wire fences were erected, and twenty-four large barracks were added to the compound. These additions were funded by the proceeds from expropriated Jewish property to the tune of over ten million gulden. Westerbork had its own medical facilities and personnel: nurses, doctors, laboratories and a pharmacy. There was also a hospital that could treat up to 1,800 patients. The medical facilities in the camp were staffed by 120 doctors and over a thousand other medical personnel. As was the case in Theresienstadt in Czechoslovakia, the inmates of Westerbork pursued a rich cultural life with a bizarre, often feverish intensity, with the express approval and encouragement of the camp commander. Top performing artists incarcerated at the camp gave operas and cabaret shows. Confiscated Jewish money and property helped keep the camp amply stocked with food and everyday necessities, with the result that the inmates lacked virtually nothing in terms of their daily needs.

In the early part of 1942, 400 Jewish refugees from Germany were transferred to Westerbork. On 14 July transports of Jews from all over Holland began arriving at the camp. The very next day the first group of Jews who had arrived there were sent to the death camps, and from that time on deportations continued unabated from Westerbork directly to Auschwitz, Sobibor, Bergen-Belsen and Theresienstadt. Once or twice each week trains packed with Jews from the camp left and headed eastwards.

From February 1943 on, these trains left the camp regularly every Tuesday, and, judging by stories told to me by friends who were there, Monday nights turned into a nightmare. On the eve of a scheduled transport, the camp commander would hold a 'farewell party'. He and his colleagues would 'grace' these evenings with their presence. The performers sang, acted, and did their best to entertain those destined to leave the following morning for certain death, and in so doing they actually contributed to the fleeting illusion of wellbeing fostered by the camp commander. All told, 106,000 people went from Westerbork to their deaths.

At least initially, we in Amsterdam were not aware of the camp's true purpose. Westerbork's permanent residents, some two thousand strong, continued to lead seemingly normal lives side by side with the masses of people who were brought there in sporadic shipments, imprisoned for two or three weeks, and then sent to the east. Were the members of the Jewish Council also unaware of the camp's true nature? This question has troubled me for many years, because I knew, as everyone else did, that every decision relating to the fate of the Jewish community in Holland at that time was submitted to the Jewish Council for approval. The members of the council were responsible for the reorganization of the camp and the adaptation of the existing facilities to serve its new function. From the very first day of its operation as a transit camp there was brisk traffic entering and leaving the compound. Jewish merchants from Amsterdam delivered supplies to the camp, and left with articles such as shoes and textile goods crafted by the inmates in the workshop. I myself was asked from time to time to supply Westerbork with leather and other raw materials for the various cottage industries in the camp.

Whenever I think of Westerbork and of Jewish Amsterdam of that time I am immediately reminded of Theresienstadt. We in the city continued to live our lives as usual, and found that, paradoxically, we seemed to be living a fuller and more interesting life than before the Occupation. The forced separation from our non-Jewish neighbours was not, in itself, overly distressing. Having been forbidden to leave the Jewish quarter to go to performances or cultural events on the outside, we responded by creating our own cultural world, which included a local theatre company and an orchestra. The restrictive regulations of Jews' movements in town deprived the famed municipal symphony orchestra, the Concertgebouw, of the services of most of its Jewish musicians, and their absence there was sorely felt. Our own Jewish orchestra, by comparison, proved very successful with its selection of chamber arrangements. At the beginning of the Occupation, Willem Mengelberg, an authoritative and famous musician as well as a notorious anti-Semite, conducted the Concertgebouw Orchestra. When the curtain rose on his opening performance the astonished conductor found himself facing a virtually empty concert hall. In a unique act of protest against the honour that had been bestowed on the anti-Semitic conductor by the management of the orchestra, someone had purchased hundreds of tickets and on the night left all of those pre-purchased seats empty. Even if this story was slightly exaggerated, it still had a wonderful effect on our spirits.

With the help of our own comedians, singers and entertainers, Jewish cultural life in the city flourished. Since curfew regulations made it impossible for us to leave our homes at night, performances were held in private homes during the daytime hours. Despite the sudden burgeoning of cultural life in Jewish Amsterdam, there were artists who suffered greatly from the erosion of their hard-earned prestige. Willi Rosen, a famous songwriter whose songs had accompanied many German films of the twenties and thirties, the humorist Franz Engel, and other important artists had to take on extra work, such as door-to-door sales, to supplement their income.

The curfew also brought about other changes in our daily lives.

Meeting with friends became a permanent feature of our lives. Often these evenings with friends turned into entire nights spent together and, paradoxically, the restrictions imposed on us drew us much closer together. Who knows how many love affairs flourished and then waned, how many joys and broken hearts from those days can still be found in the collective memories of my generation.

'Life' acquired a totally new meaning, as though the usual, everyday stuff of life suddenly expanded and grew in intensity. Despite their ever-present fears and anxieties, people managed to take an avid interest in events taking place around them. Almost all of us knew someone who had disappeared never to return, and had non-Jewish friends who could be counted on to provide shelter in case of a sudden *aktion*. My brother and I had just such a safe haven in the home of one of my non-Jewish friends from elementary school. These arrangements were always accompanied by a nagging doubt: what if these friends could not be trusted really to stand by us in a time of need? Eventually we, like many others, were let down by our 'concealers': a short while after we gave him a handsome sum of money in exchange for providing us with a hiding place, my friend began hinting that we should look for some other place to hide. 'People have been sniffing around and they know that there is something going on in my house,' he said repeatedly. And we had no choice but to take our things and look for other benefactors.

At least on one occasion we were pleasantly surprised. One day I passed by an elderly neighbour of ours, a doctor who used to visit his patients around town by cart. He was also the director of Calvinist studies in the city, and a very devout man. Until then the sum total of our relationship had been the occasional polite 'hello' or 'good-day'. On that day, however, as I passed by him in the street, he whispered, 'The key to our garden is on the windowsill. You can hide in the pergola in the back whenever you want to.' He then continued on his way, leaving me deeply moved by his unexpected offer. In the event, we did not need to take advantage of his generosity, but to this day I am grateful to this wonderful man for his profound humanity. His fate was no less cruel for all that. One day he received a letter from Hitler's Reichskommissar, Dr Seyss Inquart, ordering him to include Nazi subjects in the curriculum of his religious school. The doctor-cum-educator refused. 'Education,' he said to the Gestapo officer, 'has been entrusted to me by God. For me, making a choice between Him and a Reichskommissar like yourself is a very simple matter.' Soon afterwards he was sent to a detention camp, and was never heard from again.

It was strange, but in most cases the *aktions* followed a predictable pattern. We always knew in advance when they were about to occur, and, in most cases, the rumours of impending selections for deportation turned out to be reliable. Any event that displeased the Germans sooner or later evoked an inevitable response: yet another transport to the east. On these occasions, neither my brother nor I, nor the rest of our small group of friends, ever waited in Amsterdam to find out if the rumours concerning the impending *aktion* were true. Instead, as soon as we could, we mounted our bikes and fled southward to our friends the tanners. At that time, Mother and Ya'akov had little cause to fear deportation, so we felt relatively confident about leaving them and fleeing the city. For some reason, our friends from the Dutch provinces seemed to us more reliable than the city folk. On several occasions during 1941–2 we took shelter with them.

THE NEW YEAR'S EVE PARTY, 31 DECEMBER 1941

New Year's Eve 1941 was one of the most unforgettable evenings of my life. To celebrate the coming of the new year, we gathered together, forty of us, all in our early twenties, at the house of my good friend B——. Both his parents were dead, and a few months earlier, at the age of twenty-four, he had married and set out to create a new family for himself. His father had been a successful industrialist, and had left him a great deal of money and a beautiful, spacious apartment. It was the perfect place for our grand party.

I took one of my girlfriends on my tyre-less bike, and another girlfriend promised to make her own way from Rotterdam to the party. I was enamoured of both these young ladies, and found it impossible to choose between them, since I simply couldn't bring myself to give up either one. The girl from Rotterdam spent the night at my friend's house, and the girl from Amsterdam eventually rode back with me on my bicycle. On that New Year's Day of 1942 she turned twenty-four. Nine months later I learned that it was the last birthday she would ever celebrate. The girl from Rotterdam was no more fortunate, and likewise ended her young life in the death camps.

But at that party, which went on throughout the curfew, from eight in the evening to four in the morning, we barely gave the future a thought. We danced, we sang and we laughed, and were carried away by our own blithe, youthful exuberance. I have relived that night hundreds of times in my mind, piecing together all its details again and again, sensation by sensation, memory by memory. The recurrent appearance of visions from the party both in my dreams at night and in reveries during long hours of wakefulness has become a permanent fixture of my long life.

What was it that made that night so significant for me? To this day, as images from the party keep me awake at night, I am possessed by an unresolved sense of guilt. My close friends' faces float before my eyes; for a moment I see their youthful figures dancing, laughing, happy; and then the screen goes blank, and the happy faces disappear. I might have so easily shared their terrible fate, but for some reason it was my destiny to survive. It is often difficult for me to deal with these feelings; yet, at the same time, I do not for a moment regret those enchanted, unforgettable hours we spent together. We loved each other so much! Perhaps after all that was the most beautiful way for us all to part for ever.

5

ESCAPE

Our never-ending efforts to sidestep the harsh realities of our lives at that time came to an abrupt end one day in March 1942. As part of my activities in the underground, I transmitted messages and helped create and deliver false documents. On that fateful day I received a bulky pamphlet from my friends in the underground. In a covering letter it said the following: 'Read this yourself, then make five copies and distribute all six copies to our other friends.' I read the pamphlet and felt the blood drain from my face. I had no idea what exactly it was, but I did realise that it was an authentic Nazi document which spelled out in great detail the methods that were to be used for the total annihilation of the Jews – men, women, old people, youngsters and children. Since my experience with the Nazis had taught me that they eventually carried out almost everything they planned to do, it was clear to me that the Germans would make every effort to fulfil the chilling intentions spelled out in this document. Many years later, I became convinced that the document I had been given was a report of the Wannsee Conference, the meeting that took place in January 1942, at which the heads of Nazi Germany made their decision on 'the final solution to the Jewish Problem'. It was not clear who had written the pamphlet or why, nor did I know if this was a draft copy or an original. Nevertheless, upon rereading the document, it slowly dawned on me that its contents were not at all a fanciful hypothesis.

It is hard to describe the profoundly disturbing impression this document had on my state of mind. The words in this mysterious manuscript shot through me like a voice from the underworld. As I copied it out over and over again, as I had been asked to do, its true meaning was brought home to me with far more clarity than if I had just read it through once. At that moment, as I saw it, there was only one possible conclusion: to separate myself instantly from those who still entertained some second – hopeful – thoughts about the Occupation, and take the path of unremitting pessimism. I realized that this would do nothing to make my life easier or more tolerable, but I was absolutely convinced, beyond a shadow of a doubt, that sitting idly by and doing nothing would be tantamount to sentencing ourselves to certain death. But what could we do? Even attempting to flee the country would not guarantee salvation. The most such a course of action could offer was a glimmer of hope as opposed to the deadly possibility of a transport. Despite the agonizing dilemma, I was no longer willing to sit by passively and await my death.

Why was it that only at the beginning of 1942 – two years after the beginning of the Nazi Occupation – did I finally make up my mind to escape? There is no simple answer to this question, and much of what I described above illuminates, to some extent, the excruciatingly complex choices facing Holland's Jews at the time. On the one hand, there were the terrifying conclusions of the document that had fallen into my hands, conclusions that we were slowly beginning to absorb in their full horror. But on the other hand, we were also well aware of other deadly risks: the trumped-up show trials of captured escapees and their executions; the seeming impossibility of making an escape by sea or by land along an extremely hazardous route that crossed three international borders. And, in any case, why risk certain death when the future, however bleak and threatening, somehow seemed to hold out a faint hope of safety – or so we preferred to believe. Over and over again we weighed the alternatives the one against the other, and as long as the danger of fleeing outweighed the danger of staying put, we opted for the latter. And indeed, of the few Jews who did take their fate into their own hands and attempted to flee the country, many were caught and either put to death immediately, or else imprisoned and later sent to the death camps. Only a handful managed to make their way to freedom, with the help of groups or individuals who specialized in border crossings, and helped them flee the country – usually for a fee.

Some escape attempts succeeded, although the word 'escape' is not an altogether appropriate definition for the disappearance, in 1942, of groups that included the members of half a dozen wealthy families. Some of them paid a very high ransom for their freedom, others reached safe havens for other unknown reasons. Perhaps, in keeping with their demonic psychological manipulation, it was the Germans' way of sig-nalling to us: 'You see? This isn't a siege or a trap. Don't be afraid! Nothing will happen to you. There are some people who are allowed to leave with our full permission.' Even though I knew it was a psychological trick, at the same time I still clung to the hope that perhaps we would be among the lucky ones allowed to leave. If we could manage to flee the country in any way, we had a clear goal in mind, however distant and difficult to reach. Argentina, the country into which my father had disappeared over two years earlier, and from where he could not contact us after the German invasion (10 May 1940) of the Netherlands. Thereafter we were forbidden to write letters to him and had no alternative means of com-munication. All we could do was hope that he was well, but at the same time we were not unduly worried about him. We simply yearned for the day when we could all be reunited. At that time Zigi and I believed that only the two of us were in any real danger. We had not yet reached the point where we would have to confront the agonizing moral and emotional dilemma encountered by all those who had tried to escape from Poland, or from any of the other occupied countries: do we go alone or attempt to escape with the entire family? Eventually, when the time came to face this issue squarely, we made up our minds without a moment's hesitation.

Despite the very real dangers involved in any attempt to flee the country, our resolve to go through with it was unshakable, particularly because we firmly believed that in the end we would be reunited with our father, and that once we managed to cross the border out of Holland, we would not be lost or homeless refugees. And so, a few weeks before I was given the 'Wannsee' document, I began looking into possible escape routes and dealing with various practical aspects of our flight out of Holland. I knew some people who had been issued exit permits, and learned from them that a well-known forwarding company, Brasch & Rottenstein, had dealt with the permits. I was also told that it had been a straightforward business deal, brokered by the Swiss Consul in Amsterdam, Dr Lanz, between the group seeking to leave Holland and the Gestapo. It was very clear to me that our departure from Holland would involve payment of a ransom for every member of my family: my mother, my brother Shimon, his young wife Leah, my younger brother Ya'akov and myself.

Dr Lanz was a highly respected lawyer, and his father was an equally well-known surgeon and professor at one of Holland's top universities. When I discussed my plans with him, he told me that his diplomatic status prevented him from extending us any kind of direct assistance. He sent us to another lawyer instead, one Dr Anton Wiederkehr from Zurich, who was known for his contacts with the SS in Berlin. At our request, Dr Lanz agreed to arrange a meeting for us with Wiederkehr at our home. When the Swiss lawyer arrived, he gave us the impression of being a very decent person. What he had to tell us was that the SS would be willing to provide us with exit permits in exchange for a total of 25,000 Swiss francs, the equivalent, in those days, of the average annual income of an upper-middle-class family, or a luxury apartment in Amsterdam. As part of the proposed arrangements, my father would have to provide a letter of credit for that sum, made out to the SS account at the Dresdner Bank, that could be cashed only after we had made it safely across to Spain. We realized that reaching Spain meant crossing the borders of Belgium, France, Vichy France and Spain itself, and had no idea of the risks we might have to take or the dangers we would have to face along the way. Nevertheless, with typical Gitter optimism, as we talked about our still hypothetical escape, we already imagined ourselves safely beyond the reach of any danger.

After we had authorized Dr Wiederkehr to try to find Father in Buenos Aires by placing a phone call to the Dutch Embassy in the Argentinian capital (which represented the Dutch government-in-exile), the lawyer returned to Switzerland. To Wiederkehr's surprise – and even more so to ours – he did not need to look very far. It turned out that my father had gone into partnership with the highly respected honorary Dutch Consul, Herman Van Waveren, a well-known inter-national businessman, and as a result, had an office in the same building as the Dutch Consulate. Father immediately deposited the required letter of credit at the Dresdner Bank, and following his prompt response to the request, Dr Wiederkehr informed us that the Commander of the Gestapo in Amsterdam wished to see all of us in his office. This was the end of February or the beginning of March 1942.

Gestapo headquarters were in a building that had in the past been a noted high school in one of the best parts of town, an area inhabited by many wealthy Jews. From the moment the administration of the

Nazi Occupation moved into that building, the Jews of Amsterdam had given that part of town a wide berth. And yet, on that day, we found ourselves walking straight into that very area, filled with apprehension and fear. Mother was pale, Zigi and Leah looked very grave, and little Ya'akov seemed to be wondering what all the fuss was about. As for myself, I could not escape the feeling that I was about to meet a client whom I knew for certain was going to swindle me.

We were in for a surprise: the Obersturmbannführer was extraordinarily polite to us. At least he's not really German, we reassured ourselves as we heard his unmistakable Austrian accent. And there was one other seemingly comforting sign: he was dressed in civilian clothes. The tall, handsome official shook my mother's hand, for all the world like a European gentleman of excellent breeding.

'Do you mean, sir, that I will be able to see my husband soon?' she asked, choked with excitement.

To which the German gentleman responded gallantly, 'Madam may consider this meeting as her first kiss with her husband.'

My mother was overcome with joy.

'When will we receive the permit, Herr Kommandant?' I asked, trying to be practical in the midst of all the tension.

'In about a week or so. And if you don't hear from me in a week's time, don't hesitate to come here again.'

This extraordinary invitation was no less of a surprise than the SS officer's excessive politeness towards us: Jews were not ordinarily invited to pay courtesy visits to Gestapo headquarters, oddly nicknamed 'the Temple'. I filed that highly irregular invitation in my mind to be used in a time of need.

As we descended the stairs we were all overcome by an overwhelming sense of relief. For days after that strange meeting, my moods shifted wildly from euphoria to fear, to a maelstrom of other emotions that I could not even identify. Two or three weeks passed without a word from the Gestapo office and the tension in the house grew unbearable. With deep apprehension, I decided to take up the Kommandant's offer, and to venture once again into the lion's den.

How different this second meeting was from the first! I waited outside the Kommandant's office on a bench for six hours, totally ignored by everyone, until at last I was ushered in to see the Obersturmbahnführer. His tall figure was now encased in a resplendent SS uniform, with highly polished knee-high boots. As I stared at this new image of the man, he seemed to me like a messenger from hell. I had taken no more than one step into his office when he began screaming at me at the top of his voice: 'What did you think, you dirty little Jew, that for a few measly pennies you'd be able to save your stinking skins! I don't want to talk to you! Only through your lawyer! Tell him he must contact me!'

I quickly left the office, utterly humiliated – but alive! As soon as I could, I called Dr Wiederkehr, and he reported that the Germans had indeed doubled, tripled and even quadrupled the sum of the ransom. My father notified him from Argentina that he was willing to pay whatever we had been asked to pay. Within two weeks the ransom price had shot up from 100,000 Swiss francs to 250,000. Two weeks later, after having been in Berlin and Zurich, Dr Wiederkehr came to see us. As soon as he entered the room I could tell that he was not the bearer of good tidings. 'Look,' he said, as he saw our anxious faces. 'It's not going to work. They're already talking about one million.'

Mother went deathly pale. The lawyer spoke quietly and earnestly. 'I don't know if your father can even issue a letter of credit for that amount. I don't know what Mr Gitter will do in Argentina. He has reiterated his willingness to pay, and will no doubt do so. But how? By robbing a bank? Stealing? Taking a loan? But that's not the issue. I am convinced that the Germans are simply toying with you. They'll keep raising the sum of the ransom payment, then take the money, and then, in the end, they won't issue you the exit permits. They now have you in their sights, and they can so easily get rid of you.'

'What do you suggest we do?' Zigi asked.

'In my opinion,' Wiederkehr replied, 'you have to get out of here. You either have to find refuge elsewhere in Holland, or, if you have the courage, you must make a move to escape. The decision is yours.'

We hesitated. In May Dr Wiederkehr came to see us once again, and this time he was even more determined than before. 'There's no point in waiting another moment. Forget about getting out of here legally. The Gestapo may very well surprise you and then you'll be lost. Hide, or try to escape over the Green Border that runs through the borders of Belgium, France, and Spain.'

As far as we knew, these borders were hermetically sealed, more so than ever before. We discussed the various alternatives. The lawyer sounded as though he knew exactly what he was talking about.

Months later, in a safe haven, we read about the Nazis' systematic methods of deception: many individuals and families were duped by the Germans' promises, and after handing over all their money and property to the Gestapo, they disappeared without a trace. We also read that the Americans had blacklisted Dr Wiederkehr as a collaborator. We were convinced that this was a mistake. He took great risks just to meet us; he gave us completely accurate reports on the situation, and gave us advice that eventually saved our lives. Later we learned from Father that he had also asked for a negligible fee for his work on our behalf. In time, Wiederkehr was cleared of the accusation of collaboration with the Nazis when he managed to prove that he had belonged to a Swiss salvation group known as the Group of 200 that saved the lives of many Jews.

'... AND DON'T FORGET YOUR TOILET THINGS, A TOOTHBRUSH AND A TOWEL'

Until such time as we could put together a detailed plan for our escape, Zigi and I went underground. We hid in a shelter that a friend allowed us to use for a fee. Looking back on these events, how futile and senseless were these attempts to hide from the Germans. Like many others, we too tried to ascribe aims, motives and explanations for the Nazis' actions. We thought we could understand the logic behind them, but in fact we were deluding ourselves. And our mistakes stemmed from the psychological mistakes the Germans themselves made. We thought, for example, that they only wanted young people, those who could be of some use to the German war effort. Consequently we hoped that working for the German Reich would buy our families' right to live. What a pitiful and grotesque misconception that was! Although we were not aware of it at the time, the decisions taken at the Wannsee

Conference concerning the so-called 'Final Solution' were already being implemented.

The members of our community in Amsterdam continued to turn a deaf ear to the ominous news reaching us via the underground organizations. As law-abiding citizens, who believed that their Jewish faith and fundamental equality were part of their birthright, they simply refused to draw the conclusions that would bring their view of the world crashing down about them. Every scrap of ostensibly bad news was considered an exaggeration, or as an attempt to sow panic or demoralization in the community. And those who, despite it all, did realize the truth of their predicament, were convinced that in any case there was nothing they could do about it.

Until my turn came to confront this stark reality, I too was among those who preferred to deny the facts we received through the underground networks. However, in that summer of 1942 there was little room left for illusion. While Zigi and I were still weighing the alternatives and wondering how to go about arranging our escape, danger appeared on our very doorstep. In July 1942, a short while after Dr Wiederkehr's last visit to our house, I received an order, signed by the Jewish Council by order of the Chief Gestapo Officer: 'You are to report to the central square near the railway station on 14 July to join your unit on its way to Camp Westerbork.' I was one of several hundred young bachelors who received these instructions that would eventually change the course of their lives. For the naïve and unsuspecting ones among us, the notices seemed perfectly routine. Instructions of this sort were regularly distributed to youngsters going to summer camp: you must bring with you so many pairs of shoes, so many pairs of pants and shirts, and don't forget your toiletries, a toothbrush and a towel. Once again, the well-oiled machinery of the Jewish Council obediently carried out the orders of its German masters. For well-behaved souls like us, the Jews of Holland, the message was clear: if you 'behave yourselves', if you obey your patrons' instructions, no harm will come to you. You will work hard, true, but you will go on living.

As I held the notice in my hands, I knew for certain that I would not be there on the appointed day at the railway station to meet my friends who had been given the first orders. Somehow, one way or another, I would leave Holland! I informed my family of my decision.

85

The next day, Zigi and Leah told me that they wanted to come with me. They were both convinced that unmarried young men would not be the only ones to suffer, and that soon, once the edict concerning bachelors had been absorbed into the system and forgotten, married couples would be added to the transport lists.

'But you're pregnant, Leah! This could be terribly dangerous for you and your baby,' I said, trying in vain to dampen their enthusiasm. Leah was in her seventh month, and I was extremely reluctant to take on this added responsibility.

'Don't worry! I'm strong!' my brave sister-in-law answered.

And what about Mother and Ya'akov? My head swam with all these problems, but we did have to think of ourselves. The deeply ingrained Jewish injunction of *pikuach nefesh* – saving lives – stood above all else, and at that point we, the twenty-year-olds, were the ones directly threatened. Apart from that, we did not believe that my mother, who was forty-eight at the time, and my brother, who was not quite ten, would be up to the gruelling demands of so hazardous a journey. Mother felt the same way.

We notified Frans Bernards, a non-Jewish friend of ours, and one of the directors of our company. We did not agonize too much about letting him in on our secret: he was a good friend and very loyal to the family. We needed to have someone we could trust who would be able to deliver messages from us to our family without fear of discovery. We also desperately needed the objective opinion of someone who was not directly affected by the problem. 'Either you all escape, or else find some place where you can hide until the end of the war,' Bernards stated categorically. He was genuinely surprised that we hadn't come to the same conclusion ourselves. 'What do you think?' he asked, almost rhetorically. 'That the Gestapo will let your mother and brother live once they learn that you have escaped right under their noses? And what if something happens to them after you make it to safety, what will your escape be worth then? Will you ever be able to forgive yourselves? And if you are caught along the way, the Germans will seek out and punish any other members of the family left behind. That's why none of you can stay here.'

We all accepted his advice unconditionally. Now that the decision had been made, we had to see to numerous and no less weighty problems: how would we conceal our departure, which, as we planned it, was going to take place over a number of days? What route would we take? Where would we get help? We knew that we had to reach the Belgian border, but who would take us across and where? In the past we had had some contacts in Brabant, in the south of Holland, but approaching the wrong person could prove disastrous. We recalled one of our acquaintances there, who had been employed at the tannery and had later continued to supply us with black-market foodstuffs. From time to time we had asked him half-jokingly if he also smuggled people. 'That's not me, that's my brother,' he used to reply. And it was through him that we eventually contacted his brother, Mr Gieles.

Mr Gieles turned out to be a true hero, as the heroic manner of his death proved to us later beyond a doubt. To our amazement, he treated the mission in a most professional manner, but behind the dry, detailed pragmatism of his approach was the soul of a true idealist. He offered us two escape routes, one for 100 gulden and the other for 150 gulden – a ridiculous price considering the challenge at hand. The difference in price reflected the different modes of transport, and, consequently, different routes, he was offering: either on foot, or on bicycles which Mrs Gieles would provide for us. We chose a bicycle for Mother, while we, being younger and stronger, chose to travel on foot.

'LEAD US NOT INTO THE POWER OF SIN'

Before going on with the story of our escape, I will digress here briefly to illustrate how the predicament of Dutch Jews strained goodwill on all sides. I had two good and faithful friends, A—, and B—. B— was well-to-do: his parents had died and left him with a great deal of property. A— came from a poor family. His father was a devoutly religious man who was forced to provide for his family by working as a bus driver. This caused him profound anguish, since his job forced him, on occasion, to desecrate the Sabbath. On those occasions, if he finished his work before sundown on Saturday, he would walk home, sometimes for over two hours, so as not to continue to violate Jewish laws prohibiting any form of travel on the Sabbath. All three of us received orders to report for the transport to Westerbork. It was clear to me that I would never show up at the central railway station to join the rest of the young people who had been summoned. Out of a sense of true friendship, and after swearing them to secrecy, I told both A— and B— of my plan to escape, and suggested that they come with us. B— said that he and his family had already found a hiding place. A— remained silent. We went on to discuss the relative merits of escape or going underground. As I spoke to them about all this I was not the least suspicious – after all, we were friends!

A few days later, B— came to see me, visibly upset and very angry. He was holding a letter, written in flowery Dutch handwriting, which looked to us like imitation German script. It was, without any doubt, a blackmail letter. The anonymous author wrote that if B— did not agree to part with a considerable sum of money, which he was to transfer to a certain address, he would feel free to inform the authorities of B—'s plan to go into hiding. The anonymous author of the letter made it very clear that he knew the time and the place of B—'s proposed move into the underground.

B— had not spoken to anyone else about his plan to go into hiding. Who, apart from our 'good friend' A— could have passed on this vital information to a third party? We then understood that the letter had been written by none other than our friend A— himself. Our suspicions tormented us, and we were determined to find out if they were indeed true. We went to a Dutch police officer we knew, one of the precious few who proved to be a true friend of the Jewish community. Immediately after hearing our story, he arrested A— and put him in jail for one night. During that night in the cell, A— confessed to writing the letter. We knew that the police officer would not hand A— over to the Germans, even though he found A—'s actions totally repugnant. And, indeed, after confessing to the attempted blackmail, A— was released and sent home.

Another such story involved A—'s father. After the beginning of the German Occupation of Holland, Jewish bank accounts were frozen. At the same time, Jews were also not allowed to keep substantial amounts of money in their homes. Anyone who dared to keep large sums at home did so at great risk. A—'s father was known to all as a deeply religious man, and as such enjoyed a fine reputation in the community. One of my acquaintances asked A—'s father to keep a sum of 10,000 gulden for him for a time of need. Given the man's good name, my acquaintance was convinced that his 'deposit' was safe and that it would be returned to him in full whenever he needed it. A short while later, he did indeed require the money (or in any case something happened that caused him to ask for his money back urgently). He came to the man he had entrusted with this significant sum of money, and asked for the entire deposit. When A——'s father heard what my friend had to say, he went bright red. He went into the bedroom and emerged with three notes of one hundred gulden each. 'This is all that's left,' he sighed, placing the notes on the table.

'This is all that's left of 10,000 gulden?!' my acquaintance gasped, shocked to the core.

'No, this is the 300 that is left of the 1,000 that I took – I had to.'

My acquaintance calmed down somewhat and said nothing. In the end, he received his money – less 700 gulden.

These stories are not meant to blacken the names of my friend or his father, but rather, as I said, to show how the Occupation affected basically good, honest people. A—— was a wonderful friend, a good and intelligent person, as was his father, who, apart from his devotion to religious principles, was also highly respected for his honesty, and his highly ethical behaviour. A——'s father did not want to desecrate the Sabbath, or to take money that had been given him for safe-keeping; his son did not want to blackmail anyone. However, the extreme privations of the situation we lived in, and the fear of what might happen at any time, made them both forget the famous words from the Jewish morning prayer, *shachrit*: 'O lead us not into the power of sin, or of transgression or iniquity, or of temptation, or of scorn.'

I never saw A—— or his father again after these events. And of the tragic fate that befell B—— I heard from friends of mine after the war. In the middle of 1942 he and his family went into hiding together with twenty other people. B—— found it difficult to adjust to the stuffiness of the tiny, overcrowded basement, and every so often had to go out to get some air. On one of these occasions, as he emerged from the hiding place, he was caught by the Dutch police and handed over to the Gestapo. He was subjected to unspeakable torture by the Gestapo, and in the end gave away the location of the hiding place, causing the death of all the people who had taken refuge there.

THE JEWISH COUNCIL COMPLAINS ABOUT DISLOYALTY

Our escape from Nazi-occupied Holland began early on the morning of 7 July 1942, a week before I was supposed to report for the transport to Westerbork. We did not take suitcases or any large bags. We took nothing from the house except some valuables and money, all of which we hid in the soles of our shoes. My mother was nervous but very calm. Now that the decision had been made, I no longer worried about her – I knew she would be equal to the ordeal that awaited us. Zigi and Leah left a day earlier, together with our friends Felix and Irma Levenbach. We hoped with all our hearts that our smuggler had succeeded in getting them across the border safely, but at that moment we were wrapped up in our own private tensions. A few days after we set out, my younger brother, Ya'akov, turned ten. We had not discussed our plans with him so as to prevent him from inadvertently revealing them. Nevertheless, he had guessed what was about to happen, and throughout the entire journey behaved like an adult. My mother had an identity card belonging to the mother of Tineke, our beautiful and intelligent friend who was engaged to my brother's good friend Abraham Pais. Abraham himself had considered joining us, but at the last moment decided against it. For a while he hid in Holland, and later managed to reach Denmark, where he became a close friend and assistant to Nobel Laureate Professor Niels Bohr. Immediately after the war Professor Bohr and his assistant went to Princeton. Professor Pais became Albert Einstein's assistant and collaborator, and eventually wrote the authoritative biography of the great physicist. He never married Tineke, who is today a well-known psychiatrist in her own right in the United States. Her husband, also a well-known American psychiatrist, passed away a short while ago.

On the actual day of our escape I had no reason to fear any surprise inspections by the police as the Jewish Council had provided me with an official travel permit for that day. Putting on Gentile-style expressions of self-confidence and *ennui*, but with hearts pounding in fearful anticipation of the least mishap that might put an end to our dreams of freedom, we boarded the first train to Rozendaal, a town near the

Dutch-Belgian border. An hour and a half later we disembarked at our destination. At the railway station we mailed our papers back to Tineke and the Jewish Council. Years later I learned that some members of the council never forgave me for what they regarded as a terrible breach of faith. They believed that I should have returned that same day and, like an obedient Dutchman, joined the group being sent to Westerbork. They also accused me of deserting my leadership post in the youth movement.

We made our way to the town of Putten, near Rozendaal. It was there that Gieles and his wife operated out of the fenced-in compound of the Jewish cemetery, which was situated on the border between Holland and Belgium. A dearth of burial sites in Belgium forced the Belgian authorities to move the dead from their individual burial sites in the cemeteries into mass graves every five years, an act strictly forbidden by the Jewish faith. It was for that reason that wealthy, religious Belgian Jews preferred to be buried in the Putten cemetery, which was located on Dutch soil, close to the border between the two countries. Part of the borderline itself traversed a small valley that was partially concealed from sight. After leaving the deserted graveyard, we went down into the valley, and after a short while we met Mrs Gieles. The couple gave us some heartening news, that they had encountered no problems in getting my brother and his group across the border the day before. And, so far, luck had been on our side too. Mrs Gieles provided my mother with a bicycle, as planned. Guided by our smugglers, we crossed the 700 metres or so to the border along a barely visible path, partly under earth, our pulses racing with tension and fear. The slightest unexpected sound froze the blood in our veins. Once we had crossed the border into Belgium, we parted from our guides, and continued on our way in Belgian territory for about twelve kilometres until we reached the outskirts of Antwerp.

Looking back at all this now, I am amazed by the mixture of courage and daring involved in our decision to escape. At moments like these one does not tend to stop to praise oneself, and I also have no intention of doing so now in retrospect. However, when I once again analyze the details of our escape, I believe that luck played a major role in our success. Belgium was also under Nazi occupation; as refugees we were highly conspicuous, and could have been arrested at any moment: in the crowded tram in Antwerp, or on the fast train from Antwerp to Brussels, which we boarded after a nail-biting wait in the bustling station, with nowhere to hide from the staring gaze of other travellers.

Despite the fact that Brussels was under the martial law of the Occupation, it was still relatively peaceful. In contrast to the tough methods used by the Gestapo and the local police to control Amsterdam, the Wehrmacht governed Brussels in a slightly more 'humane' manner. The authorities often turned a blind eye when Jews removed their yellow badges and left their homes at night in violation of the official curfew. Our friends there, the Mo'ed family, suggested that we spend the night with them. We had not seen them for two and a half years – since the outbreak of the war – but when we knocked on their door they greeted us with such warmth it seemed as though they had been expecting us. Their younger son, Jackie, was our Ya'akov's friend. Jackie had just returned the day before from a visit to his grandparents in Amsterdam. It was only then that we made the connection and discovered that the warm welcome was in fact Ya'akov's doing. My little brother, who was not supposed to have known anything about our plans, had known all about them for quite some time, and had even brought his friend, Jackie, in on the secret.

The Mo'eds were much more optimistic than we were. 'Stay here in Brussels!' they implored us. 'Why should you go on wandering for ever?' Our hosts' rosy view of the situation made little impression on us, and we, instead, tried to persuade them to join us. 'For you, escaping from Belgium means you have one less border to cross,' we exhorted them, but they remained adamant. Eventually, they too paid the price of their complacency, and disappeared into one of the camps, or went to their deaths in some other terrible way during the war.

BLESSÈD SLEEP

In the end, after trying in vain to turn down their hospitality, we spent our first night in Brussels with the Mo'ed family. However, we were determined not to stay in Belgium any longer than was absolutely necessary. We had no explanation for the panic that now gripped us. My brother and his wife and their friends stayed with Jules Goffard, who had been our agent in Brussels before the war. He and his wife were our main contacts in the Belgian capital. We heaved a sigh of relief when we all met again, and quickly exchanged important bits of information. Through Shumer, the father of a friend who had also fled from Holland, we learned of another contact, a Mr Gottlieb, and Zigi arranged to meet him on the following morning at nine. Gottlieb was supposed to put us in touch with a guide who would take us across the border into France.

Tired and highly agitated after the experiences of our first day on the run, we all overslept. Highly embarrassed about being so late, we decided to call Gottlieb to apologize and to ask him to postpone our meeting for an hour or two. At the other end of the line, a voice with a heavy German accent answered. This person did not seem to know anything about our planned meeting with Gottlieb, but suggested, 'Why don't you come anyway, just as you planned?' We were instantly on our guard. With great trepidation we called Mr Shumer to find out what all this meant, and he explained immediately: 'Gottlieb was arrested last night by the Nazis. Everyone who showed up at his house was thrown into jail.' Once again, fortune was on our side.

We quickly revised our plans. We now had to find alternative escape routes and to avoid using the same guides; it was clear to us that we had to split up now and continue separately. We reasoned that if anything happened to any of us Zigi could come and help us, and vice versa. At the very worst we would at least not all be caught together. We abided by these hastily proposed guidelines most of the time. We stayed with the Mo'ed family until we put together all the details of the new plan. On 14 July, Bastille Day, we joined the Goffards and a few of their French friends for a celebration. We raised a glass to France and ate a festive meal, totally forgetting for a while that there was a war going on, and that the shadow of death was lurking just outside the door.

A few days later, my mother, my brother Ya'akov and I set out from Brussels for France with our new guide, a Jew known in the underground only as 'Otto'. He put us in a crowded coach where there were no empty seats. My mother, who always impressed people with her gentle manner and pleasant appearance, was soon offered a seat by a Belgian gentleman. At the next station, when some of the passengers disembarked, we grabbed seats for ourselves as well. Otto brought out a paper bag, and offered the people sitting opposite us some fragrant Belgian peaches. 'Offer one to the man who gave my mother his seat,' I begged him in a whisper, but he refused.

'There's no point in wasting any attention on him if he's so nice anyway,' he replied *sotto voce*.

Clearly, he preferred to invest only in those who might pose a threat to our safety. As it turned out, he also had something to hide: under the ripe, sweet-smelling peaches he had concealed a few dozen contraband gold watches, which were the real reason for his making this trip. He would divulge this secret to us only after we reached our destination safely.

We got off the train at a small Belgian village called Menin, not far from Tourcoing in the north of France. Menin was a Protestant enclave in a predominantly Catholic country. The village was so small that it did not even have a church. As soon as Otto settled us down for the night we fell asleep, and the following morning at dawn, dressed like the local farmers, we set out once again. We were accompanied by a few of the villagers who were well aware of their role in this part of our escape. Our guides were from the Maquis, and these farmers were their allies, and helped them on many of their missions. Belgian and French customs officials and bored German policemen barely glanced at us as we arrived at the border, not even bothering to inspect our bags. As far as they were concerned, we were obviously a small group of local people, routinely crossing the border checkpoint.

We were all completely worn out. Our guide at this point, a Jewish woman, took us to a hotel to rest. We had to be at the railway station at four in the afternoon to board a train for Paris. The sight of German soldiers in shiny uniforms going up and down the hotel stairs sent shivers down our spines. We feared a trap, but in fact our guides had cleverly assumed that no one would suspect anything that was right under their noses: the so-called 'hotel' was actually a brothel, and was therefore a very safe place of refuge for us.

We changed out of our dirty peasant clothes and boarded the train for Paris. Two hours later we arrived at the Gare du Nord. From there, our brave guide put us on a bus heading for the Gare de Lyon, in the south-east part of the city. There was no time to take in any of the wonderful sights of the City of Lights. Before nightfall we were once again aboard a train, this time the Paris–Lyon–Marseille line, on our way south to Dijon, the last city before the demarcation line between Vichy France and the Nazi-occupied countries.

From Dijon, our journey took a particularly bizarre and adventurous turn. After spending the night in a place chosen for us by the Maquis, we were taken to a workshop that specialized in the manufacture of wooden crates, dog kennels, and other such objects. My mother and a Parisian woman we did not know were squeezed into a half-finished dog kennel. Ya'akov and I, together with the son of the woman from Paris, were crammed into another one. I curled up, drew in my legs, and stuck my head between my knees, so as to make room for the other two boys. Once we were settled, after a fashion, inside, a roof was hammered into place over our heads, leaving only a small opening, big enough for a small or, at most, a medium-sized dog. We were told to remain still and wait patiently until we received further instructions.

Voices filtered in from outside our wooden box. We felt our kennel being lifted on to a horse-drawn cart, buffeted by other kennels and crates that were piled up next to ours. The horse trotted along the road leading to the railway station. We heard whistles, voices, loudspeaker announcements, and a cacophony of other sounds – until at last we were thrown into a boxcar. Once again we heard voices speaking in French and German. The inspection of the boxcar passed without a hitch.

After a while I could feel something hot and wet on my skin: my two travelling companions had wet themselves, and, in those totally cramped circumstances, there was no way I could avoid the spreading urine. What could they do, squeezed tightly like that into a doghouse with no way of relieving themselves? Apart from that incident, I hardly remember anything about those thirty long hours in the doghouse on the train – except my concern for my mother. Throughout the entire time I couldn't stop wondering how she was weathering this torturous trip.

Suddenly we heard new sounds: an axe splintering the roof of the doghouse, and a deep male voice saying: '*Sortez, mesdames et messieurs, vous venez d'arriver en France libre.*' Sweet words! We crawled out of the doghouse and stretched our aching bodies, and then found ourselves facing a French railway conductor dressed in a highly theatrical uniform. To this day I have a very clear memory of the man: a broad smile below a large moustache that curled down along his jaw, a shiny fob watch proudly adorning his waistcoat. After providing us with railway tickets to Lyon, he accompanied us to one of the passenger cars. Some time later in our odyssey to freedom we heard that he had been captured by the Germans during an underground rescue operation, and had died a hero's death.

The trip from the frontier to Lyon took two hours. About half an hour after we left the station, a police inspector entered our compartment. We showed him our false papers, and I told him that we had fled the Nazis with the help of these forged documents. He took them and left without a word.

Our real passports were safely hidden in the soles of our shoes. We hoped the inspector would believe us and not demand that we take off our shoes and cut open the soles. After all, they were the only shoes we had, and our journey was far from over. But the inspector told me there was nothing to worry about, that he would take us to a reception centre and everything would be all right.

We soon found out that the 'reception centre' was the police station at Lyon-Perache. No one had asked to see our passports yet, and we sat idly in the large hall, waiting to see what they would do with us. They are probably looking for some decent place for us to stay, I thought to myself, and assured the official who was dealing with our papers: 'There is no need to worry about us; we have the means to pay.' The man gave no sign that he had heard what I had said, but informed us that we would be sent by train to Macon, a city on the border of Vichy France. The only thing I knew about that city was that it boasted some very fine wines. 'We are totally exhausted. Will we have a good hotel there?' I asked. The look on his face set off some alarm bells in my mind, but I still hoped that it was a false alarm and that everything would be all right in the end. 'You'll be put up at the finest hotel in town, the Hotel Joubert,' the official said, his thumb stuck into his belt dramatically, Napoleon-style. For some reason I believed him.

Time and again I have asked myself how I allowed myself to fall into the trap. I believe that the answer is actually very simple, which, of course, does nothing to alleviate the enormity of my failure. After two and a half years under German occupation, and with the words 'You have reached Free France!' ringing in my ears, I simply couldn't imagine we would encounter any more obstacles, acts of betrayal, or disastrous errors of judgement of any kind. Distraught and agitated by our ordeals, I didn't take into account all the possible ramifications of the fact that we had arrived in a region controlled by the despised Nazi collaborators of the Vichy régime.

Over the years, I have stopped blaming myself for the mishap, because I know now that our chances of evading the Vichy police were minimal to begin with. The Belgian identity cards that we were carrying were so rare, particularly in that region, that they would no doubt have given us away instantly or at least made the authorities very suspicious. Later I also learned that the Vichy régime was one of the darkest and most despicable that ever existed, wholly dedicated to the execution of the Nazis' sinister intentions. In terms of their attitude towards the Jews, the local civilian population in that area of France were much worse than their Dutch counterparts. The only people we met who truly deserved praise for their heroism and humanity were the members of the Communist railway workers union, and, of course, the members of the Maquis underground.

Not fully aware of the true nature of our situation, we were put into a closely guarded passenger car on a train going back in the direction we had come from. Surrounded by policemen, we were taken to Caserne Joubert, a filthy hostel now turned prison, where for many years derelicts and political refugees from Spain, Algiers and the Arab countries had found shelter. The officer disappeared, and we were left waiting behind bars inside the dilapidated building. From my conversations with some of the people there I learned about the scores of refugees who had been handed over to the Germans every night, a few kilometres from the border.

By now the state of our affairs was very clear: our grand plans for escaping the Nazis had come to a dismal end. The following day I was called in to the commander of the jail, and underwent a lengthy interrogation in his office. At the end of the session he informed me that we would be handed over to the Germans either that same night or on the following day. I spent the night racking my brains trying to think of some way out of our predicament, but the situation seemed beyond hope. I decided to risk everything and offer him a bribe; under the circumstances, and after a long and sleepless night, it seemed to be the most plausible scenario I could come up with. 'Money is not an issue. Name a sum and we'll pay it,' I said to him when we met again. The barest flicker of interest crossed his face, and I knew instantly that I was on the right track. Not a single franc without some cast-iron guarantee, I warned myself silently, bolstered by the thought that both sides were interested in the deal, and that in itself was a step in the right direction. Despite our profound mutual distrust, I forced myself to stay calm. I had learned an important lesson about ransoms at the Gestapo headquarters in Amsterdam. 'My father lives in Argentina, and we have enough money to pay,' I told the commander.

'How will the money get here?' he responded, his question about the technicalities softening somewhat his seemingly tough exterior.

'No problem,' I said, with a show of confidence that I didn't really feel. 'I'll speak to friends of ours in Lyon, and they will call mutual friends in Switzerland, to convince them that we are indeed here and alive. Our friends from Lyon know who we are. The money from Switzerland will be sent to them.'

'All right,' the commander said. 'Go and make your phone call, but your mother and brother stay here.'

That was all we needed now – to be separated and leave him with hostages! 'Absolutely not!' I insisted. 'Unfortunately, that is out of the question. We all have to go to Lyon. Only if our friends from Switzerland hear each one of our voices will they be ready to believe that it is not a trick of some kind.'

This was a critical moment, and there was a pause as the commander considered his options. Finally he said, 'All right, so be it. But I will escort you personally to Lyon, and we'll settle the account right there.'

Our friends in Lyon were the owners of Tanneries Lyonnaises, and our mutual friends in Switzerland were their agents, just as we had been in Amsterdam. Before we set out on our escape route, I had carefully memorized the names of the two directors of the company. I had never met Messrs Vourloud and Coifon, and I fervently hoped that they would not let me down. I asked the commander of the jail to bring an official document signed by an official representative or person of authority in Macon, in case Vourloud and Coifon would ask to have some proof of their payment of the ransom money, and he agreed. As part of the deal, he issued us a temporary residency permit for Tournus, and we parted from the bizarre inmates of the fetid old building. Under the conditions of our house arrest, we had to report to the police station in Tournus five times a day, but under the circumstances, totally preoccupied as we were with the daily hazards we were facing, no one had the strength to think of tomorrow.

We travelled to Lyon, and from there called our friends in Zurich. We received their answer only on the following day, concerning the transfer of the money from our friend Fritz Mannes. The actual sum we paid in ransom seems ludicrously small today, but at that time that was what was required to save human lives. To his credit, the commander of the jail was as good as his word, and even sold me a veritable treasure: a block of officially stamped and approved travel permits – *laissez-passer.* Armed with these permits, I could travel anywhere in Vichy France without fear of arrest. What is more, eventually these permits also allowed me to help save refugees who had come to a dead end in Lyon and in Marseille.

The hotel at Tournus, our *résidence forcée*, was one of the worst imaginable. The food was completely inedible, and we had no choice but to live on the peaches and apricots that we bought in the local market. But we were alive, and, to all intents and purposes, free. Nothing else mattered! Still, reporting to the police very day, in the basement of a singularly ugly building, forced us to bear in mind where we had come from and where we could not yet go. The endless interrogations and the hostility of the officials we had to report to turned every visit there into torture. But, as luck would have it, even in that depressing basement office, we found a French officer who seemed desperately in need of financial help to improve his standard of living. We had no illusions on this count whatsoever: it was crystal clear to us that whoever agreed to help us would do so solely for financial gain.

FROM THE HOUSE OF TORTURE TO THE TOURIST RESORT

Forty-five years later I returned to Tournus. I was on a trip to France with my two grandchildren, Yif'at and Sharon, and about to introduce them to the glories of the Loire Valley. After spending a night in Dijon, I suddenly decided to pay a visit to Tournus, eighty kilometres away. The closer we came to the town, the more nervous I became. It was August – the same month I had been there with my family so many years before under very different circumstances. I had absolutely no recollection of the beautiful scenery, the vibrant yellow of the tall sunflowers, and the rippling seas of ripe wheat that now assailed our senses. The rolling hills of grain stretched out into the distance, framed by the beauty of the hills beyond, and the radiant yellow of the sun-flowers followed us all the way into the town. I was surprised to see the signs indicating the city's attractions. On one sign, just outside the entrance to the city, Tournus was described as a beautiful medieval city boasting numerous tourist attractions, among them the old City Hall with its intricately decorated balustrades. All these things, which had completely escaped me the first time I was there, induced in me a strange sense of alienation.

New sights battled inside me with those sights that I did remember: like the 'hotel' we had lived in, for example. I found it quite quickly, a few hundred metres from the entrance to the city. I turned into the street, and suddenly came face to face with the building. It had been recently renovated and was amazingly clean and richly furnished. I could hardly believe my eyes. Where were the stairs that led from the dismal, so-called 'dining-room' to the rooms upstairs? When I asked the owner about this, he told me he had made extensive renovations and had had those stairs removed. Continuing this difficult journey back in time, I looked for the City Hall and the police station that used to be housed inside it. How strange! The building looked completely different! The last time I had been here, I never noticed the 'wonderful medieval architecture' praised so highly by the new tourist brochures. I could not erase the stubborn memories I had had of the building for so many years, and found it impossible to accept the building's new look. I took the stairs down to the dingy basement where we had been forced to report every day. Time had dulled the nightmare, but as I stood there, all my memories of the place were reawakened. I looked for some telltale sign of those terrible times, something – anything - that would give mute testimony to the tortures administered there to so many people. But the freshly painted walls kept silent, and there was nothing at all left of my traumatic memories.

Ever since we had left Brussels we had had no contact with my brother Shimon and his wife. Now that we were out of any immediate danger and could take time to think of things other than what was about to happen in the next few minutes, we began wondering what had happened to them on their escape route. We hoped that they had not encountered the same kind of dangers we had met during those crazy days on the road. Our contacts at Tanneries Lyonnaises managed to find out that Shimon and Leah had been delayed for a few days in Brussels before setting out, and that they had been forced to change their plans and take a different route. Despite numerous phone calls to our friends in Lyon, we learned nothing more, and our uncertainty about their fate grew. The tension, the worrying and the diet of peaches and apricots wreaked havoc with our health. Mother suffered most of all, but as soon as she heard my brother's voice on the other end of the phone line, our troubles instantly vanished into thin air.

Shimon and Leah arrived in Lyon after a much less tortuous trip than ours, in a boxcar containing cloth for uniforms destined for Vichy France to be turned into uniforms for the German army. And as soon as we had spoken to them I set about planning our reunion. For the first time in a great while I could use travel tickets issued in our own names, but first I had to bribe the commander of the police, this time in order to be allowed to stay in Lyon more than the usual three days before going back to our house-arrest arrangement.

Nervous and overjoyed, we made our plans for the trip to Lyon. There was an express train from Tournus to Lyon once a day, which covered the distance in two and a half hours. The local trains that stopped at all the stations on the way took five hours or more. Our hotel was only a few minutes' walk away from the railway station, and it was with all this information in mind that I planned our departure. But the two extra minutes that were required for the sandwiches that my mother insisted on making at the very last minute were critical, and as we arrived huffing and puffing at the railway station, we saw the express train pulling out without us. And so, after so many trials and tribulations – three meticulously orchestrated illegal border-crossings, numerous life-threatening moments, and imprisonment by the Vichy police – this time our plans fell through because of sandwiches, and voices were raised in frustration and anger. In the event, those sandwiches turned out to be a boon in disguise, for we certainly needed them on the five-hour journey by the local train. Once they recovered from the initial excitement of the reunion, even Shimon and Leah enjoyed those that we left especially for them. And my mother, beaming with happiness, couldn't restrain herself from saying: '*Nu*, I was right after all, wasn't I!'

We stayed during those days in Lyon at the Hôtel D'Angleterre. During my nostalgic trip back to that region, I discovered that it no longer exists.

OSCAR WENT OUT FOR A WALK AND WON'T BE COMING BACK

While we were struggling to stay alive and more or less managing to do so, the Jews of Poland had no chance at all. Two and a half years had passed since our last contact with my Aunt Toncia, my mother's elder sister. At the end of August 1942 we suddenly received a postcard she sent to some Swiss friends who knew where to find us. 'The weather is fine now,' my aunt wrote in German, as the Jews of Poland were forced to do whenever they were given the rare privilege of writing a letter. 'Oscar went on a long trip. He enjoyed himself so much that he probably won't be coming back.' The next postcard was the same: 'Izzy went on the same long trip and joined Oscar there.' The first one to die, then, was Oscar, Toncia's son, and then Izzy, her brother and my uncle. One by one, the postcards related to us the deaths of all the members of the family. They all died, and were buried in the eleven holes that had been prepared as mass graves in Stanislawow.

PASSPORTS TO CURAÇAO

In Lyon we faced a new situation: some two thousand refugees from Holland and Belgium had taken up temporary residence in the city, with many more pouring in each day. They all lived in small hotels within a one-kilometre radius of the Lyon-Perache railway station. We were acquainted with some of them, and there were those among them who amazed us with their courage. We were profoundly moved by every one of our encounters; it was as though our friends from the past had just been reborn before our very eyes. Rumours came thick and fast in the small community, together with endless tales of narrow escapes and harrowing journeys, of people who had been caught in Belgium or France and put to death, and of others who had disappeared without trace.

The affairs of the Dutch refugees in Vichy France were handled by several different offices. In Lyon the Dutch representatives were known as 'Office Neerlandais', while in Marseille it was the 'Chief Commissioner for the Affairs of the Dutch Refugees'. Fortunately, in Lyon, a Frenchman named Jacquet was in charge of the Dutch refugees. Before the war he had been appointed Honorary Dutch Consul in Lyon, and retained his title and position throughout the war as well. Previously he had been the French representative of a well-known Dutch insurance company in Utrecht, and was known for his great love of Holland and the Dutch people. His deputy, Sally Noach, took charge of matters on the ground. Noach was a Dutch Jew who had little formal education but was nevertheless one of the most fascinating conversationalists I have ever met. Having spent many years in Belgium, he was more fluent in French than in Dutch. Hundreds, perhaps thousands, of Jewish refugees owe their lives to Sally Noach. He arranged for them to leave Vichy France as rapidly as possible, and until such time as he could arrange for their escape, he passed information to them about informers and potential troublemakers, and helped them find a place to stay and a means of subsistence. Food ration cards were hard to come by for most people, but not for Noach. He was thoroughly honest and well versed in the complex realities of wartime. In the course of the war he rose to prominence in the Dutch resistance movement. He was later transferred to England where, as a private in the army of

Her Majesty Queen Wilhelmina, he became one of the most prominent figures in the Princess Irene Dutch Brigade. A story about him that made the rounds told how the Queen of Holland picked him out of the troops during a military parade, and cried out to him, 'Mr Noach, you have no idea how happy I am to see you here!' Sally responded gaily from the ranks, 'And I likewise, Your Majesty, am very happy to see you!' My friendship with Sally will for ever remain one of my life's most cherished experiences.

I have a vivid recollection of some of Sally's heroic exploits. One day he got wind of an agreement that had apparently been signed between the Office Belgique (that dealt with Belgian refugees in France) and a South American country that was interested in Catholic agricultural workers. This snippet of information fired Sally's imagination; he saw it as a fortuitous opportunity to arrange for the escape of some of 'his' Dutch refugees. What difference did it make if they were Jewish and not Catholic, and city-dwellers rather than agricultural workers? As far as Sally was concerned, these were insignificant details. Jacquet was brought in on the plan, but notwithstanding his agreement to go along with it, no visas could be issued without the official approval of the High Commissioner for Dutch Refugees in Marseille. So Sally was sent to Marseille to see if he could find a solution to the problem, and he suggested that I come along with him. We spent a great deal of time together in those days and became very close friends.

'Do you imagine for one moment that I would risk my good name and undermine my own authority by allowing a Mr Lifschitz from Amsterdam to go to South America in the guise of a Catholic farm labourer?' the High Commissioner asked us when we submitted a few passports for his signature.

Sally was not one to give up easily, and he replied, 'Well, in that case, could you perhaps issue a few entry permits to Curaçao?'

To which the Commissioner replied indifferently, 'No, that's not such a good idea either. The governor of Curaçao informed me that the island is packed with people, and we should not issue any more visas.'

What could we do? The entire venture appeared to be on the brink of abject failure – but not in Sally's eyes. 'Allow us to give the matter some more thought and we will get back to you,' he promised, signalling me to move towards the door.

We made our way to a café near the beach, and sat there feeling thoroughly dispirited. 'I have an idea,' Sally said over his second cup of coffee. 'I have fifteen passports. We are going to add a visa to each one of them. Yes. Yes. We'll insert: "Valid for visit to Curaçao." In the meantime, call up the Swedish Consulate, and ask for the person in charge of Dutch affairs. Tell them that you are speaking from the Dutch Refugee Office, and that we're sending them fifteen passports for their signature. Give them the phone number of the office, and ask them to phone for confirmation. I'll keep the boss busy until you give me a signal that it's all been arranged.'

I did as he requested, and everything worked out perfectly. Fifteen passports with temporary visas to Curaçao were duly signed and approved. One additional passport – mine – visa included, completed the collection. I didn't need it, but I wanted a souvenir from this successful 'operation' in which I had played a part. The fake passport bearing Sally's handwriting is one of my most cherished mementos of this heroic man whose path crossed mine during an unforgettable period in my life.

That was not the last of Sally's heroic rescue operations. After weeks of deceptive calm, the Gestapo and the French police surprised us with an *aktion* reminiscent of the darkest days in Amsterdam. The police rounded up over 1,500 refugees, most of them from the small hotel area near the railway station, all of them without papers, citizenship or a place they could call home.

We were more or less safe since Father had sent us the revalidated Argentinian papers as soon as we arrived in Lyon. The Argentinian Consul in Amsterdam had signed the original documents in April 1940, but owing to the Occupation we had been unable to have our passports stamped with Argentinian visas. Even if we had held *bona fide* Argentinian documents, we would not have been able to use them in Holland because of the closure imposed on the Jewish community. It was only with the help of our friends in Switzerland that we received new copies of our papers in Lyon, this time stamped with the required visas. Nevertheless, we knew that we couldn't rely on the decency of the fickle officials. Anything could happen – if not to us, then to the people we had become so closely attached to during those weeks in Lyon. As a result of our common fate, we felt a strong sense of brotherhood and responsibility for many others, some of whom we did not even know.

It was at this point that Jacquet brought the full force of his authority to bear on the issue. He immediately dispatched Sally to the government offices at Vichy, to the terrifying place popularly known as 'Le Deuxième Bureau', which was in fact the office of the Intelligence Service. Sally managed to get an appointment with Laval, the Vichy Prime Minister, and took with him a large file crammed with documents and official papers. Laval signed them all without comment. Why he did so is a question that may never be answered, because Pierre Laval, the greatest French traitor of the war years, was brought to trial and executed shortly after the war.

The trip back from Vichy to Lyon with the documents took eight hours. Despite his fatigue, Sally went directly to the building where the refugees were being held. Sally walked in, waving the papers in the air, exclaiming, 'Here are the documents! All these people are free to go. Look, here is the Prime Minister's signature!'

The officer in charge at the detention house was not impressed, scrutinized the documents with deep suspicion, and then said, 'Come back tomorrow morning.'

Sally bristled. 'You are addressing the Dutch Consul in France!' he said, raising his voice and glaring at the man. The prison commander was unfazed by this display of authority, and looked Sally over without responding. 'And my being a diplomat means nothing to you?' By now Sally was roaring, banging his fist on the table.

The officer stared at Sally with bemusement. The 'diplomat' was, without a doubt, incredibly insolent, but his fearless behaviour earned him the grudging respect of the French officer. 'All right, all right,' he said, finally acquiescing. 'Take them to wherever you want.'

By now, Vichy France had revealed its true, ugly face. From August 1942 on, the situation deteriorated. The changes were subtle and gradual, and only those people sensitive enough to notice them in their initial stages could detect them. Had we arrived in Lyon at that time, it is highly unlikely that the bribes, which eventually saved our lives, would have had the same effect. By September 1942 the Germans had strengthened their hold on Vichy, just as they had done earlier in Belgium and Holland. French government officials and police officers fell over each other trying to display their loyalty to the German conquerors. The local police joined forces with the Gestapo in sadistic attacks on both the refugees and opponents of the régime.

The refugees' predicament was worse than ever. Marseille, Lyon and Vichy, which up to then had tried to maintain at least a façade of local rule, soon lost any pretence of independence. Local politicians feared for their lives, and as a result 'troublemakers' (i.e. anyone traceably Jewish) could no longer count on municipal officials for protection, and requests for emigration permits were swiftly denied.

Where could we run to now? Switzerland, which had proclaimed its 'neutrality' at the outbreak of the war, had sealed its borders, and only a few hundred Jews somehow managed to get into that country and save themselves. Border inspections were redoubled, and Jews who had entered Switzerland on foot along the treacherous mountain passes were resolutely and cruelly sent back across the border.

It was at this time that we managed to contact my father once again through our friends in Switzerland. We already had emigration papers, and now all we needed were *laissez-passez* documents to get us through Spain. We applied to the Spanish Consulate in Lyon for the required papers, and were treated with exemplary kindness. If it hadn't been for the wonderful Spanish officials at the Consulate, everything we had endured to ensure our escape would have been in vain. Without a doubt we would have joined the thousands of other refugees who were trapped in southern France and sent to their deaths in one of the concentration camps. As I ponder these events over and over again, I cannot escape the feeling that my life was given to me as a gift, through some ineffable act of grace, of which I was no more worthy than anyone else.

6

FREEDOM

The Spanish Consul in southern France displayed exemplary generosity of spirit when, in order to speed us on our way, he sidestepped the usual – and cumbersome – bureaucratic procedures relating to transit papers. 'Monsieur Gitter,' he said, 'if you wish to save your lives, take advantage of your visas immediately! Don't stay in France even one hour more than is absolutely necessary! Remember what I have said!' he added, and completed his act of charity by waiving the need to wait for the approval of our papers by Madrid. And indeed, only hours after my meeting with him, we seized the very first opportunity that came our way, and crossed the border into Spain. We left Lyon for Spain at a moment's notice, without any idea of what awaited us there, or if the Spaniards would be on our side or not. Our fears soon evaporated when we set foot in Barcelona. We were overwhelmed with displays of friendship, sympathy and goodwill from all directions. And how different was the Spaniards' sense of the burning issues of the day! As opposed to the repeated calls for us to 'sit tight until it blows over' that we had heard in Lyon even from our very best friends, the Spaniards advised us to leave Europe and Spain as quickly as we possibly could, for our own good.

It was abundantly clear to us that we had to move quickly, but the prospect of setting out once more on yet another escape route was almost intolerable. My sister-in-law Leah was in the late months of her pregnancy, and it would have been better for her to remain in Lyon – or in any other city with good medical facilities – until after she gave birth. At the same time, after hearing what the Spanish Consul had to say, we were primed with a dire sense of urgency. My brother, who was a practising physician, stocked up in Lyon with whatever medical supplies and instruments he thought he might need for a delivery under emergency conditions. Three days after we arrived in Barcelona, on Rosh Hashannah (the Jewish New Year), 14 September 1942, we set out again on another leg of our odyssey to freedom. My mother was appalled that we had decided to travel on Rosh Hashannah of all days, fearing God's wrath for desecrating His holy day. But we were fleeing for our lives, and according to the sages the Biblical injunction of *pikuach nefesh* – saving a soul – takes precedence over any religious observance, including the holiest day of the Jewish year: Yom Kippur. Our next destination was Bilbao, and all along the way we were in a state of high nervous tension. Travelling on the important Jewish holiday, the anticipation of the birth of Leah and Zigi's firstborn, our sense of imminent freedom, the resumption of our hazardous journey and the rapidly approaching reunion with Father – all these contributed to our heightened agitation.

Little details, like openly buying a ticket for a sleeper compartment on the night train in cash at the ticket counter, gave me inordinate pleasure. From the time of the Occupation of Amsterdam every trip we made using false papers had been fraught with danger. And now we felt a tremendous sense of relief, and a resurgence of our self-respect, as we entered the *wagon-lit* as ordinary citizens, just like anyone else. A new life seemed just around the corner.

A few hours after the train left Barcelona, my brother woke me up. 'Benno, get up, Leah is having her baby!' He was clearly very excited, but also very much in control. The train officials had already been notified, and the chief conductor had sent for boiling water from the engine.

'What's our next stop?' I asked, somewhat confused.

'Zaragoza, in another forty-five minutes,' my brother replied. 'The conductor has already sent word ahead of our imminent arrival. An ambulance will be waiting for us at the station to take Leah to the hospital immediately.'

We were already quite adept at making quick family decisions: Mother, Ya'akov and I would continue on to Bilbao to make all the preparations for the boat trip as planned. We would then wait there until Zigi and Leah and their newborn child could join us. I remember how excited we were when, upon our arrival in the Spanish port city, we received a telegram from Zigi: 'We have a daughter. Everything's all right. Her name is Adina.'

My brother's stories of the events surrounding Adina's birth were suffused with deep gratitude for the wonderful way they had been received by the medical team at the magnificent private clinic in Zaragoza – La Clinica Opertoria del Doctor Horno. Dr Ricardo Horno Alcorta and his son, the owners of the clinic, put themselves entirely at the service of the young mother and her baby daughter. My brother, more out of his deep desire to be with his wife at this wonderful moment than out of a yearning to practise his profession, was allowed to witness the birth. Dressed in a white coat, he felt like a respected professional colleague. For him this was the realization of a dream he had hardly dared to envisage: welcoming his newborn daughter into the world and being at his wife's side during the delivery.

After this momentous event everything appeared to be brimming with hope. Even the name of the ship we were to sail on – *Cabo de Bueno Esperanza*, the Cape of Good Hope – seemed to bode well for this last leg of our journey. Within two weeks, the doctors had said, Leah and Adina would be able to undertake the trip to South America.

During our stay in Bilbao I was able, for the first time in many long months, to place a phone call to my father. I decided to share all the good news with him at once. I don't recall the order in which I blurted out all the information, but I told him that we were in Bilbao, that we were all well and closer to him than at any time during the two and a half years of his absence. I probably began by telling him the good news of the birth, and that must have provided some consolation for him after many months of loneliness, separation and fear: 'A few days ago you became a grandfather!' I cried. His excitement, joy and thankfulness seemed to leap across time and space.

I also told my father that the letter of credit that had been handed over to the Germans in return for our safe passage had not been cashed, since the date on the note had expired and apparently no action had been taken on it. Even though the news about the money was not the most important thing, nevertheless I was pleased to be able to tell him that in the end the Germans had not been able to lay their hands on his money. My father had not been aware of the expiry date of the letter of credit, and did not want to cancel it until he was certain we had arrived safely at our final destination. Much later, my father would make a gift of an identical sum for a purpose that was close to his heart: the building of a Jewish elementary school, a magnificent synagogue, and a library, on Moldes Street in our neighbourhood in Buenos Aires. He sought to commemorate in this way the greatest event of his life: the miraculous salvation of his entire family from Nazi persecution. A memorial plaque stating this purpose was fixed on the wall next to the Ark of the Torah Scrolls in 'his' synagogue.

As the fear for our own lives lessened, we could finally take some time to think about the fate of our friends in Holland and in Lyon. For us Bilbao was an undiscovered country. We knew no one there and had no way of finding out anything about the people we had left behind. The days passed uneventfully. We had already had our fill of excitement and tension, but Leah and Zigi's arrival with their baby Adina was cause for a fresh round of rejoicing.

Zigi told us a few stories about his experiences, some of which helped restore our failing belief in mankind. Ten days after the birth, my brother consulted Dr Horno Alcorta about the trip to Bilbao. 'It's still a bit dangerous for a ten-day-old child to travel by train,' the doctor advised. 'But my son is gong to San Sebastian, and he'll be happy to drive through Bilbao on the way. It won't be too much of a detour.' My brother eagerly accepted the offer, which, in the event, turned out to be much more generous than he could have imagined. The trip from Zaragoza to San Sebastian via Bilbao, which the young Alcorta offered to make for us, in fact required a detour of some three hundred kilometres – all this at a time when petrol was strictly rationed. Nevertheless, the doctor absolutely refused to accept payment for the extra petrol or any of the expenses of the trip. And that was not the end of the doctor's generosity. When my brother requested the hospital bills, Dr Alcorta told Zigi, somewhat evasively, that he would give them to him when he left. When he was ready to leave, my brother looked for the doctor. He had simply disappeared, but had left an envelope addressed to my brother on his desk. Zigi opened the envelope, and inside he found the bill with a large, round zero next to every item. Beneath the total, the noble-hearted doctor had added in handwriting: 'We are not Fascists.'

Forty years after these events I had an opportunity to express my profound gratitude for our Spanish benefactors' wonderful warmth and humanity. It was in 1986, the year that diplomatic relations were established between Israel and Spain, and official contacts between Spain and the Jewish people were renewed after a rift lasting 500 years, from the time of the expulsion of the Jews from Spain in 1492. A few weeks after the official ceremonies marking the inauguration of diplomatic ties between the two countries, I received an invitation from the Israeli Foreign Ministry to participate in a symposium that was to take place at the Round Table Club in Barcelona. After a brief investigation, I discovered that this prestigious club, which had been active in Franco's time as well (on condition that it stayed out of politics), dealt with economic issues, and among its members were statesmen, scholars, businessmen, industrialists and bankers. Following the resumption of diplomatic relations, the Spaniards requested that an Israeli businessman address the club. They requested a speaker who was involved in Israeli industry, preferably a banker, but in any case not a government official, and, if possible, Spanish speaking. 'Would you agree to take up this challenge?' I was asked by officials from the Foreign Ministry, who also informed me of the topic of the lecture: 'Economic Ties Between Israel and the United States of America; could this closed circle be widened to include Spain as well?'

Naturally, I immediately accepted, not least because I did not want to disappoint my good friend Shmuel Hadass, Israel's first ambassador to Spain. Normally I give speeches and lectures easily and without notes, but on this occasion I realized that I would have to prepare a written address in order to treat this impressive forum with the gravity it deserved. An advance copy of the speech by the French Minister of France that was to precede mine made it crystal clear to me that if I was to serve myself and my mission well, I would have to deal with the issue at hand on the highest possible level. Never before had I invested such concentrated energy into fashioning a speech as I did then. In the month I had to prepare for the event, I recruited economics experts from Tel Aviv University to advise me, and hired the best Spanish translator I could find to go over the speech and check my use of the Spanish language. I added statistical data, slides, diagrams and transparencies – until finally I was satisfied with the results of my hard labour. On the eve of my trip, I asked my brother for the 'receipt' that Dr Ricardo Horno Alcorta had given him.

When it was my turn to speak, I began by saying that I had prepared a lecture on the subject I had been requested to address. 'Here are the papers, the transparencies and all the numbers. But, before I begin,' I added, 'I must first pay a debt of honour and gratitude to the citizens of Spain, residents of Barcelona, or their children and relatives who may be sitting in the audience, who helped me and my family during the war.' You could have heard a pin drop in the hall as I recounted the story of our escape. I stressed the differences between the attitude and behaviour of the people of southern France and the people of northern Spain in relation to our predicament. I related the story of my niece's birth in the middle of our journey, and showed the audience Zigi's 'receipt' with its large round zeroes, an expression of infinite human compassion. I believe I felt a stir of excitement in the audience as I told this story. I then continued with my planned lecture: forty minutes of learned, academic discourse. Questions were asked, and comments were made, and then we were invited, my wife and myself, to a pleasant dinner with the chairman of the club.

The following day the phone in our hotel room didn't stop ringing for a minute. People called to tell me how moved they were by my story, and to give me the names of their relatives who might have played a part in the success of our escape. Neither Dr Ricardo Horno Alcorta nor his son called, despite the fact that the newspapers and television stations carried extensive coverage of the story throughout Spain.

THERE IS NO REPLY FROM THE HOUSE OF ORANGE

The final destination of the boat we were about to board was Buenos Aires. Our sailing date approached rapidly. Due to the special circumstances of the war and the various naval blockades, we estimated that the voyage would take at least fifty days. This would include ten days of questioning by the Allied intelligence officers in Trinidad and the other ports of call: Curaçao, La Guayra, Rio de Janeiro, Santos and Montevideo.

One day after leaving Bilbao we anchored in Lisbon. To our great surprise and happiness, I picked out the familiar figure of our friend

Sally Noach on the pier. 'What are you doing here?' I asked after we embraced warmly.

'Things are too hot in Lyon, much more so than when you were there,' he said. 'The people in our office advised me to go to some neutral country. We have an embassy here in Lisbon that will take care of me. I can live in Portugal in a quiet place by the sea and forget about the war. In fact, what I really want to do is to get to England, and join the Princess Irene Brigade.'

I asked him what he was doing in the meanwhile.

'Nothing,' he replied with a shrug. I knew that doing nothing – even against his will – was not my energetic friend's style, and he soon told me the real reason why he had rushed to Lisbon after us, and how we would be spending the next twenty-four hours in the harbour. 'We have to make some plans to rescue the people in Lyon,' he said, looking at me gravely.

'What can we do?' I asked. After considering and rejecting a number of possibilities, we finally decided to try our luck and present ourselves at the Dutch Embassy. Sally had already informed the people there of our escape from Holland and our arrival in Lisbon harbour. We made an appointment to meet a Mr Luns, the second or third secretary in the embassy, a promising and dependable young diplomat, who served as liaison officer between the embassy and Queen Wilhelmina in London. We described our anxieties concerning the fate of the Dutch Jewish refugees being held captive in France. At that time, the Dutch government-in-exile still had one KLM plane, a DC3 that flew from Lisbon to London every Friday. 'I know what you should do,' the young man said to my brother and me. 'Write a letter to the Queen, tell her everything you know about all this, make some suggestions, put forward some proposals. I promise to deliver the letter to her personally on Friday.'

Tragically, the conquest of southern France was completed much more swiftly than we had imagined, and our appeal ultimately failed to reach its destination in time, or perhaps there was simply no one there to deal with it. Her Majesty's reply reached us a few months later: 'The Dutch authorities did everything in their power,' the Queen's secretary wrote, offering as proof the fact that our family had been saved. Lip service, I thought, as I read the letter. With all my respect and fondness for the House of Orange and its representatives, I knew very well that they had contributed absolutely nothing to the success of our escape.

It was in Lisbon that I heard about the heroic death of Mr Gieles and the French train commander who had helped us cross the border at great personal risk. The news broke our hearts. How could anyone possibly compare the actions of these heroic individuals with the indifference of the Dutch authorities in France? There were a few exceptions, among them Sally Noach, who had the added incentive of being Jewish. I am not a believer in acts of revenge, but before we left Europe I felt I had to do something. I bought a postcard and addressed it to the Austrian Obersturmbahnführer, c/o the head offices of the Gestapo in Amsterdam. 'Dear Gestapo Commander!' I wrote. 'Thank you for your very useful advice. Thanks to your help we have reached a safe haven. We are also grateful to you for seeing to it that our money did not reach the SS.' We signed our names and posted the card. If, as a result of our card, our Austrian friend was sent to die a hero's death on the Eastern front – as was customary in the case of lapsed SS officers – then he most certainly received his just desserts.

Luns, the kindly First Secretary of the Dutch Embassy in Lisbon, eventually rose high in the ranks of Dutch politics. He served as Dutch Foreign Minister for twenty years, and was then elected to the post of Secretary-General of NATO. Twenty-five years were to pass before we met again. The Dutch ambassador to Israel presented me to him at a reception in Jerusalem. 'My dear friend,' Luns said, with typical humour. 'I must tell you that since our last meeting you haven't lost one gram of weight.'

TRAVELLING COMPANIONS AND GEFILTE FISH

By the standards of those days, our sea voyage to South America aboard the *Cabo de Bueno Esperanza* was a pleasure cruise, even though it was insufferably long. In the spirit of the times, there was a large portrait of Generalissimo Franco on the wall of the dining-room. Out of sheer boredom, we younger people took to mimicking the older passengers by throwing the cutlery – and sometimes even the glasses – overboard. Actually, the boredom only set in later, despite the excellent band, the dances, the entertainment, and the flamenco dancing. At first we savoured an exhilarating sense of freedom. We were well aware of the fact that only our ship, its sister ship – appropriately named *Cabo de Hornos* (Cape Horn) – and a few other flimsy vessels even older than ours regularly plied the route to South America and back, carrying people from Europe to the free world.

Initially, we were also overwhelmed by the sheer quantities of food we were served. We boarded the ship healthy, but quite thin. During the voyage we stuffed ourselves in a feeding frenzy that was a form of compensation for the lean years of food rationing. The food was wonderful, and seemed to be limitless. During the fifty-two days that we were at sea, I ballooned twenty kilos above my regular weight! Zigi spent a great deal of his time looking after passengers suffering from seasickness or other ailments. All of us, including Leah and the baby, Mother and my younger brother Ya'akov, were bursting with good health.

Apart from partaking of the ship's many attractions, we also began taking an interest in the other passengers on board. We soon identified a small group of undercover police agents. Strangely enough, of all the people on the boat, it was with them that we managed to make a few good deals in foreign currency, despite the many signs posted all over the ship cautioning against such activities. There were also some monks and clerics among the passengers. One of them looked at Adina in her egg-basket crib, and remarked that it was a shame that she would not gain entrance 'into heaven', referring to the Catholic concept of eternal life promised to all those baptized in the Christian faith. Adina has paid little heed to these prognostications, and continues to enjoy her life with her family and her success as a scientist.

While waiting to board the ship we met the Kroch family. Hans Kroch, his son Ernst, and his three daughters were among the very few people officially allowed by the Gestapo in Amsterdam to leave Holland. Kroch was an important banker from Leipzig who had fled to Amsterdam with his family. His wife, who took a separate escape route, was caught by the Germans and sent to a concentration camp. For a number of years Kroch made valiant efforts to secure her release, until word finally reached him that she had died in the camps. I knew some members of their family in Amsterdam. The son, a talented and wonderfully well-mannered boy, belonged to the group I led in the youth movement. He eventually went to Palestine, and became a member of Kibbutz Mefalsim. Later, he was killed in battle during Israel's War of Independence. A few years after the establishment of the state, the elder Kroch also came to Israel, and built the Holyland Hotel in Jerusalem, where he also created the superb model of Biblical Jerusalem and the Temple, to this day one of the capital's distinctive tourist attractions.

Many of the passengers were at pains to hide the fact that they were Jewish, so much so that at first we thought that the Krochs and ourselves were the only Jews on board. From time to time we spoke Hebrew to each other. On one such occasion one of the passengers, a woman, came up to us and asked if we were Jewish. When we said yes, she told us, to our amazement, that she was from Palestine, and then proceeded to reveal to us yet another story illustrating the tortuous path of Jewish destiny. After studying in Belgium before the war, she married a Jew from Yugoslavia who had served in Michaelovitch's army. The rivalry between Michaelovitch and Tito soon turned into civil war, and she decided to leave the war-torn country. Somewhere along her escape route, before she disembarked from the ship that was carrying her to safety, she received word that her husband had been killed by Tito's soldiers.

There were quite a number of people on board who spoke German with traces of a Yiddish accent, and who we were certain were Jewish. Despite the imposing crosses they wore on their chests, we were able to discern their true identity. I particularly recall one of them who boasted frequently about his large donations to the Church, and made a point of telling us he had hardly ever met any Jews before boarding the ship. We were itching to reveal his true identity. One evening we invited him to join us for a fish meal, but he refused, explaining that ever since a bone had got stuck in his throat, he only ate 'gefilte fish'. Beneath his pedantic pronunciation of the German language, his Lithuanian-Yiddish origins were unmistakable. He used the Yiddish 'fis' instead of 'fish', and, besides, how did he know anything about 'gefilte fish' in the first place? Today I am much less judgemental, and tend to be more tolerant of the ways in which fears and traumas undermine the soul.

There was also a group of Dutch people on board, all of whom had fled Occupied Holland. Some of them intended joining the Dutch army in exile in Curaçao. Among them were a few Jews who did their best to conceal their Jewish identity. As for us, we did the exact opposite. After years of persecution, the ship's decks were the first place where we no longer needed to fear for our lives, and we proudly paraded our Jewishness for all to see. We made no secret of our desire to live in Palestine eventually, spoke Hebrew whenever we felt like it, and, of course, maintained a traditional Jewish lifestyle. I think the Dutch group regarded our display of Jewish life and customs as a nuisance.

Now that they were on their way to a new life, there were some passengers who made every effort to shed their dark past. One of these was a pleasant-looking 'diplomat' – a Paraguayan Consul from some obscure town. The more he boasted about the many Jews he had saved and the many Paraguayan visas he had issued, the less we believed him. Even assuming that he was not lying about the visas, he most certainly did not do it for the love of God, and probably pocketed a tidy sum in the process. We were not at all sorry when he was taken off the ship at one of our ports of call, never to return. Nor was he the only one to suffer this fate. In Trinidad, for example, a number of passengers were interrogated and then taken off the ship. Rumour had it that they were spies.

There were also people on board such as Mr Malbran, the Brazilian ambassador to Rome, and his wife. On one occasion, when British Spitfire aeroplanes flew over our ship, this charming couple applauded enthusiastically. To mark the occasion, they treated all the other passengers to champagne. Later, Mrs Malbran recalled that her hands stung from clapping so loudly and so long.

Lasting friendships were also forged on that voyage on the *Cabo de Bueno Esperanza*, particularly with Nessim Seroussi and his family, a friendship that has spanned continents and decades, and has not waned to this day. In his personality, manners and appearance, Nessim Seroussi was the perfect gentleman: always consummately turned out, fluent in French, Italian and Spanish, a Grand Signor unfettered by personal ties but with a string of rumoured previous marriages, one of them to a Russian princess (we heard these spicy details from others, never from him). Nessim originally came from Sudan, lived in Egypt for a while, and then moved to Italy. From Milan, where he made his home, he moved to the Côte d'Azur in France. He later fled from Nice when Vichy France turned into a Nazi-occupied country like all the others. When we met him he was on his way to Montevideo, the capital of Uruguay, to visit his brother, the head of the local Jewish community there. Montevideo, he confided to me, was too small and provincial a city for his taste, and his brother – a wonderful man – was too religious. He warmly invited me to come and visit his brother's family. Should he not be there when I came to Uruguay, he added, I would probably find him in Rio de Janeiro, at the Copacabana Hotel, where he intended to live until the war ended.

And, indeed, soon after my arrival in Buenos Aires, I happened to be in Montevideo. Nessim Seroussi was no longer there and had gone to Rio as planned, but I was glad to get to meet his brother and his brother's wonderful wife. Elias Seroussi was a marvellous combination of patriarch and saint. Unlike his brother Nessim, Elias was not a very successful businessman, but thanks to his good reputation he managed to provide amply for his large family. The Seroussis gave their six children – five boys and one girl – an excellent Jewish education and humanitarian upbringing.

In 1944 we received an urgent telegram from Hinde, my father's sister, who had found refuge in Switzerland with her family. The tone of her telegram was clearly panic-stricken. Rumours had spread like wildfire in the refugee camp where she had been staying that the Swiss intended to return all the refugees to the Germans on the other side of the border. Despite the fact that it was the Sabbath, I called Elias Seroussi. If the rumours were true, I told him, only those who already had a valid visa to some destination outside Switzerland would not be turned over to the Germans, and my aunt and her family did not fall into this category. 'Don't worry,' he promised. 'I am meeting the President of Uruguay today. Come and see me tomorrow, and you'll have the visas.'

The following day I went to Montevideo. Six weeks later, my aunt and her family arrived in Uruguay, where they lived for a number of years. To be fair to the Swiss, the rumours – even though they were not entirely unfounded – never materialized.

There is a Zionist chapter in the Seroussi story as well. When the state of Israel was established, their son Rafael joined the MAHAL (an acronym for Mitnadvei Hutz La-aretz – Volunteers from Abroad), and then remained in the army when it became the Israel Defence Forces. Eventually, all the young Seroussis except the youngest brother – who became a famous computer expert in the US – emigrated to Israel. The Seroussis played a prominent role in almost every aspect of Israeli life: in the army, the universities, in business, industry and commerce. Later, their parents joined the children and their families, and took the greatest pleasure in being so close to their expanded family. On the occasion of the Seroussis' sixtieth wedding anniversary, more than seventy of their offspring gathered together to congratulate them and a forest was planted in their name by the Jewish National Fund.

IN TRINIDAD

By this time we were impatient to complete the journey. Occasionally, out of sheer fear and tension, some of us imagined we saw German warships or submarines coming after us in pursuit, but these were all false alarms. I had absolute confidence in our crew, and during the trip my natural optimism had gradually been restored. Nevertheless, I was relieved when we dropped anchor in Trinidad. We were received at the harbour by British intelligence officers. There was something about these tall figures, dressed in the uniforms of His Majesty's government, which inspired us with confidence. They questioned each of us, asking us to tell our life stories, from which they tried to extract vital information about the German enemy. In my case, they questioned me at length about the topography of southern Holland. I had no idea why the needed all this information, but with the help of my penchant for details and my excellent memory, I answered all their questions patiently. There were particularly interested in the years 1941–2.

As I mentioned earlier, during those years the Germans had forbidden us to drive our cars, making it extremely difficult for us to maintain our business contacts around the country. However, in order not to lose these important clients and suppliers, I made a habit of stealing into trains or pedalling my bicycle as much as thirty kilometres each way to meet them. Some of these trips took me through Gilze-Ryen, a small town in the south of Holland, which split up into twin towns on either side of a main highway. We had many business contacts in this region, which, over the years, had become a national centre for the production and supply of leather. In each of the many villages that closely dotted the countryside, there were hide suppliers or leather workers. I would make my way from one village to the next on bicycle trails, visiting many of the small workshops in the area. The trail to Gilze-Ryen, the divided town, wound past an old military airfield, and every time I went that way I had to look for a way around the large complex the Germans had built there. I could not help but notice the buildings they had erected which they camouflaged as farm buildings. Scattered around them in plain view were artillery pieces and other military equipment. I described all these things to the British officer who questioned me, and he wrote it all down meticulously, asking a few questions to clear up anything he wasn't certain about. Three days later the intelligence officer called me in again, and showed me a highly detailed map of the area I had described. What he wanted to know was how closely the map resembled the actual terrain as I recalled it. I looked over the map, made a few corrections based on what I remembered, and then forgot all about it.

A few months later, in our haven in Buenos Aires, I read in the newspaper a report on the partial destruction of Gilze-Ryen in a British bombing raid. Breathless with excitement, I read the item out loudly to my family, feeling for a moment as though I had actually played a role in the heroic aerial attack that had been carried out by the RAF.

In moments of nostalgia and contemplation I often go back to those ten days in Trinidad. If someone were to tell me that I would have to endure the fifty-two-day voyage ten times over, to cross the Atlantic in our flimsy vessel, and relive all the dangers we had encountered on our journey in order to help the Allies, I would do it all gladly, if only to experience once again the elation I felt when I realized that I had played a tiny part in one of the Allied successes.

ANTI-SEMITISM IN CURAÇAO

The ship lowered its anchor in Curaçao, in the middle of the Caribbean Ocean. One of the last vestiges of the crumbling Dutch Empire spread out before our eyes. The sight was astonishing: little houses with pointed, red-tiled roofs, delicate curtains in the windows, meticulously landscaped gardens – Dutch scenery at its best. Everything looked as though it had been lifted straight out of our childhood memories. With the motherland – Holland – languishing under German occupation, and the colonies of East Asia under Japanese occupation, Willemstad, the island's capital, was the only free Dutch city in the world. That may have been the reason why the government officials treated us with such pompous officiousness, not altogether free of traces of latent anti-Semitism, as I was soon to find out. Standing in the local police station, I accidentally overheard a conversation between the commander of the police force, Van der Kroeft, and his superior, the governor of the island. 'We know there are a number of Jews among the Dutch group on board, but they deny it,' the officer said. 'I am certain we can extract a confession from them to that effect. What do you think?'

'See to it that they all confess to their identity,' the governor replied. 'We already have enough Jews here, we don't need any more.'

I was furious when I heard this, and felt acutely uncomfortable, as though I had suddenly been forced to breath poisonous fumes once again instead of fresh air. How far does one have to go to get away from anti-Semitism? I asked myself. The Dutch people they were discussing were, indeed, Jewish: idealists who had come to the island to join the Dutch army. They had not been able to hide their Jewishness from us, and the local Dutch people had little trouble detecting it. I asked myself why do people choose to take on an alien identity? What could be their reason for denying their birthright? I could never understand that. We had never tried to hide our Jewish identity, even when we had to escape in order to stay alive. For this strong sense of belonging I am greatly indebted to our parents, who instilled in us profound self-confidence and Jewish values.

In the years following our brief stay in Curaçao, Governor Kasteel did not change his views in the slightest. Years later I heard that this same Kasteel was about to be appointed Dutch ambassador to Israel. I wrote letters to the Foreign Ministers of Israel and Holland, explaining my opposition to the appointment. I never received any response to these letters, but the Dutch government decided to send someone else, instead of Mr Kasteel, to be its ambassador to Israel.

My unhappiness over these events was totally offset by the warm welcome we received from the local Jewish community. We were welcomed in the homes of Rabbi Jeshurun Cardozo, and other members of the community with whom I soon established a deep friendship. To this day I am happy to meet these people whenever my travels abroad take me to that part of the world. Old-timers as well as new residents of the island welcomed us. Max Tak, formerly first violin for the Amsterdam Concertgebouw, took us on trips the length and breadth of the island, revealing its secrets to us one by one. We were deeply impressed by the Sephardi synagogue, which was a perfect replica, on a smaller scale, of the famous Esnoga of Amsterdam. I was convinced that this was the last time I would ever see a reconstruction of the synagogue, and just looking at it kindled a profound yearning for the long-gone days of my childhood. I had no way of knowing that the Germans had not harmed the Esnoga – not out of any feelings of compassion of decency, but in an attempt, for their own reasons, to retain some of the authentic atmosphere of the city.

At the port of La Guayara near Caracas, the 'Catholic' passengers, still sporting their large crosses, bade us farewell. Many years after we parted company, I chanced to meet some of the women of that group at a charity for the United Jewish Appeal, or perhaps for Tel Aviv University. Time had taken its inevitable toll. I looked at them carefully: instead of the large crosses that had dangled on their necks back then, they now wore large, diamond-studded Magen Davids.

BRIBERY IN RIO DE JANIERO

Our ship was slowly approaching its final destination. After Curaçao we docked at Rio de Janeiro. Some of my father's good friends and competitors (in my entire life I have never met anyone like my father, with his uncanny knack of turning even professional rivals into close friends), boarded the ship at his request to escort us to Santos, the port of São Paulo. We were thrilled, and felt as though meeting them was a prelude to our long-awaited reunion with Father. It did not occur to me at the time that behind their cordial welcome they were also intent on laying a small trap for me. After all, I was only twenty-three, and was considered an excellent *shidduch* (match) for one of their daughters. Like myself, the potential bride – whoever she may have been – was probably totally unaware of their plans. We spent a pleasant time together on the deck, and then went on a tour of the beautiful city, which included my first swim at the enchanted Copacabana beach. We dined in the elegant Copacabana Hotel, and by nightfall I was back on the deck of the ship, dancing a *paso doble* to an authentic Spanish melody. And that was the end of our romance.

Unbeknownst to us, there was a drama unfolding behind the scenes. Another one of my father's acquaintances, also a competitor in the leather business, did not like the close ties that seemed to have sprung up between my father and his colleagues in the trade, and was eager to disrupt them in some way. At the same time he desperately wanted to be regarded as our champion and score points with my father. In order to try to achieve both of his goals, he concocted a convoluted plot. He told a police officer that the Gitter family intended leaving the ship illegally, and in exchange for a sizable fee asked the policemen to detain us on board while the other passengers went on a tour of the town. I refused to have anyone restrict my movements. After everything we had been through, I was not prepared to endure any form of house arrest – even in the relative luxury of our ship's excellent accommodation. I offered the police officer a tip higher than the original bribe, and went ashore, a free man. This event remained engraved in my memory as a first lesson in the ways of South America: there is virtually nothing on that continent that doesn't have a price tag.

BEGINNING TO PICK UP THE PIECES

On 14 November 1942, almost five months after we left Holland, and two and a half years since we had parted from Father, our ship docked at Montevideo. The first thing we noticed was the hulk of the famous German battleship the *Graf von Spee*. A year earlier, the world had been rocked by the news that the ship had been mortally damaged by British shells after a relentless chase by the British navy.

'There's Father!' I heard Zigi cry out. Father? How was that possible? Our hearts skipped a beat. Mother almost fainted. My eyes swept the dock frantically, until finally I saw him. There he was, on the pier, hat in hand, exquisitely dressed in an expensive suit and fine hat, tall and handsome as I remembered him. His face was slightly blurred, possibly because of the distance to the pier – or could it have been because of the tears in my eyes? It was very evident from the way he was craning forward that he was desperately anxious to see us at long last. He had spent the previous night crossing the Rio de la Plata, which separates Argentina from Uruguay, in order to be at the pier when the boat docked. We embraced and wept, and gazed at each other, finding it hard to believe that this was really happening. All our heroic travails suddenly shrank into insignificance. We hardly knew where to begin telling our story. I was exhausted and excited and terrified by the thought of the distance that had separated us all these years.

With gestures both simple and grand, Father led us gently into the self-confidence of his new status and wealth. He almost certainly did so out of some embarrassment, or perhaps he wanted to make us happy by sharing his – and our – successes. We also felt suddenly shy. How difficult it was going to be to bridge the long period of separation! All at once I looked at our little group as though from a distance, like a stranger. We were poorly dressed in our threadbare clothes and wooden-soled cloth shoes, the ones we had bought in France after our original Dutch shoes, stuffed with money and diamonds when we left home, had worn through beyond repair.

Within minutes this initial awkwardness fell away. It was a wonderful, moving reunion. We sat on the deck of the boat the whole night, huddling close together in the crisp air as it made its way to Buenos Aires. The long hours we spent together that night were still too brief for us to fill in all the gaps of time and events that had separated us. We had so much to make up for! One tiny voice inside me asked if Father would ever truly be able to understand the meaning of per-secution and flight, life-threatening risks, and the wiliness that we had acquired by force of circumstance. Another voice inside me told me to relax, put an end to this kind of speculation, and just enjoy the miracle of our successful escape.

We sat there until sunrise, unable to part for a moment. But were we truly sensitive to our parents' feelings and needs? Just like any other young people, our fifty-three-year-old father, and forty-eight-year-old mother seemed ancient to us, and we displayed what can only be described as youthful egocentricity. We wanted them both to ourselves all the time. In our minds they were 'parents', not man and wife, and it took a considerable time before we finally gave them time to be alone with each other.

The following day, when we docked at Buenos Aires, we were greeted by the family of Ernst Calvary, who had left Holland and travelled to Argentina before the war. Our excitement knew no bounds as we waved to them over and over again, calling out our greetings, and then fell into each other's arms and couldn't stop hugging and kissing them!

Always the practical man, Father had begun preparing for our arrival the moment he received word of our reaching Spain safely. We stood gazing in wonder at the new house he had bought and furnished from top to bottom in anticipation of our arrival. How strange! Throughout the trials and tribulations of our ordeal, I had never once stopped to think about what kind of life we would have when it was all over. My fantasies had taken me as far as our reunion with Father and no further. I gave no thought to the house we would live in, our daily routine, or the resumption of our life as a family. Now I had to say something. Father looked at us, waiting for signs of wonder and gratitude. The house was large and spacious, shining and fresh, beautifully set in landscaped gardens, in a fine suburb of the city. The furnishings were tasteful and expensive. Naturally, each of us had a separate room. Even our house in Amsterdam was no match for this new residence, which had been designed – in accordance with Father's hopes – to house all of us under one roof. Father wanted to keep us together, and have us live as one large happy family in the family mansion. However, a few months after we arrived, Zigi and Leah and their daughter Adina moved into a separate flat not far from our house.

There was another little surprise that Father had prepared: a brand-new small car, a belated birthday present for me. Clearly, he had softened somewhat over the years. I still had a vivid memory of his stiff opposition to the first car I bought when I was eighteen. I bought it against his wishes in the Flea Market with my own money – eighty gulden. Now I had to get used not only to driving on the left side of the road, but also to the ease of having material possessions that I had managed to lose during our long separation.

PART II

ARGENTINA

7

SETTLING IN

Our ordeal was over and we were safely lodged in a beautiful, sparkling white house; depression soon replaced the initial euphoria. I remember clearly how frightening this despondency was: the knowledge that nothing could assuage the sorrow, neither the car, the lovely house, nor even the feeling of togetherness and the joy of our final deliverance from danger. Suddenly, after all the tension, our lives seemed to have emptied of all significance. The inbred energies which are so much a part of my very being, and which had kept me going throughout the harrowing journey to safety, suddenly disappeared like air escaping from a punctured balloon. Day and night I was flooded with memories of the endless days of the escape, the sea voyage, Amsterdam under the Occupation, the close friends whose fate had no doubt been sealed and who I would never see again. During the days, these thoughts crowded into my mind, tormenting my waking hours and dragging me into the depths of despair, while at night my sleep was racked by endless dreams.

In Amsterdam my father had been addicted to cigars. Once a year he would buy a few thousand Hajenius cigars, among the most prestigious and famous brands not only in Holland but also throughout the world. One of the recurrent dreams I had at that time involved these cigars. In the dream I have a craving for the cigars. I know I have no choice: I simply have to go back to Amsterdam. I enter our house, everything is in place. I open the door – nothing has been touched. The furniture, the *objets d'art*, the books, the paintings, everything is exactly the way it was when we left. I go to the cupboard, open the door, and pull open the drawer. The cigars are all there, as usual. Hundreds of them, in neatly stacked boxes. I touch them, sense their special aroma, and savour the anticipated pleasure. But, despite my profound longing, I don't have time to smoke even one cigar. My mouth waters. I can imagine the taste, and the wonderful, heady aroma. But no – Mother is waiting for me. Everyone is waiting for me. I quickly stuff the pockets of my suit and raincoat, and even put some cigars inside my shirt, then close the drawer. I can't take all of them with me. It's a shame, but it doesn't matter, these will do for now.

But wait! I must destroy the rest of the cigars so they don't fall into German hands. That's it. Now I can leave. I am not the least bit worried about finding my way back. After all I know every road and border crossing here! Mother said: you'll find your way back in the same way you found your way there. I leave the room, go to the entrance and open the door. Two men are standing in the doorway in dark hats and long raincoats. I recognize them instantly: they are Gestapo, in plain clothes. A cynical smile plays on their lips as they ask me: 'Benno Gitter? Is that you? We knew that some day you'd be back to pick up the cigars. Come here, you're under arrest!' And at that moment I would wake up, sweat pouring down my face. What a relief! It was only a dream, a dream that haunted my sleep for months on end.

Initially it seemed as though I would never be able to bridge the chasm between the life I had left behind and my new life in Buenos Aires. Whenever I tried to share my feelings with other people – Jews, of course – I was bitterly disappointed. They simply refused to understand what I was talking about. On one occasion, a friend of my father's, an orthodox Jew from São Paolo, asked me not to bother him with my stories – he was busy making up kosher food parcels for the Jews at Bergen-Belsen, Mauthausen and Auschwitz. Whenever I tried to talk to people about what was happening in Europe, I was greeted with open disbelief. They preferred not to talk about it; and more often than not asked me not to trouble them with my apocalyptic fantasies. What they seemed to be telling me was: 'Is this why you made this entire journey: just to make our lives miserable?' Safe in their remote haven, which they believed to be the hub of the world for the simple reason that they lived there, they could afford to chide me for my stories about the horrors of the war in Europe. Buenos Aires was so beautiful, the world there was at peace, and life couldn't be better: why put a damper on things? The things I tried to describe to them – and to which they refused to listen – were indelibly seared into my soul, and throughout my life have had a profound effect on my actions and my conscience. Fortunately for me, at that time I was young and healthy, and daily life had its own headlong dynamic, which ultimately proved to be stronger than any sorrow. Slowly but surely, I returned to my former self. Our tightly knit family fortified me against the gnawing despair, and ultimately helped me regain my equilibrium and get back into a routine of hard work. The new business challenges which my father, in his infinite wisdom, now charged me with playing a major part in my cure.

Once the crisis had passed, I began getting used to our new life, and soon became a passionate admirer of Argentina and Buenos Aires. I gradually began to grasp the sheer size of my new country, and found it amusing to compare it to my little homeland in Europe, which had been forced to 'steal' land from the sea in order to increase its habitable areas. The vast open spaces thrilled me, filling me with a sense of unlimited possibilities. There was an ingrained atmosphere of tolerance in the country, the result either of its immense size, or the endless variety of its scenery. It may also have stemmed from the fact that Argentina was a developing country with a large immigrant population. In this melting pot there were people from Spain, Italy (some sixty per cent), a few Indians and other nationalities. Unlike Brazil, which had taken in thousands of African slaves, Argentina was ethnically a much more homogenous country. The Argentine people, whom I was now beginning to admire, were pleasant, courteous, had a great love for music, theatre and art, and were open and unabashedly joyful in moments of celebration or happiness. They were industrious, creative and work-oriented, despite the rampant inflation that bit deeply into their meagre salaries. Many of the residents were immigrants from overseas who worked on contracts and sent most of their money to their relatives back in their home countries. Those among them who grew fond of this beautiful, spacious new country and decided to make it their home sent their relatives money to enable them to make the long trip over to Argentina. I recall one employee in my father's firm who, after working with us for several years, finally managed to save enough money so that his eight children could join him in Argentina. When he left them they had all been children and young adults between the ages of ten and twenty-five. When he was finally reunited with them in Argentina, he had to get used to the fact that they were all grown men and women in the prime of their lives.

I sometimes wonder if my parents, who lived in Argentina for over twenty-five years, ever compared the two countries that they called home. Holland had a long history of stable and efficient government, while régimes in Argentina rose and fell in rapid succession, and tended more often than not towards dictatorship; Holland was imbued by a strong tradition of proper official conduct, while none of the many different leaders of Argentina were averse to corrupt practices and nepotism; the economic affairs and institutions in Holland were highly organized, while in Argentina inflation was a regular feature of the economy; the Dutch monarchs fervently upheld the principles of equality and the need to make every effort to close the socio-economic gaps that existed among their subjects, while in Argentina class discrimination was accepted as the natural order of things. And yet, notwithstanding all of this, Argentina, like Holland, was an extremely pleasant place to live.

BULL (OR LEATHER) FIGHTER

By the time we arrived in Argentina, Father had already established himself in the local leather industry. When he left Holland, he had been on his way to buy leather on the Argentine markets. Within a very short time he completed what he had originally set out to achieve: he bought a sufficient quantity of leather, paid the suppliers, and made all the arrangements to have the material shipped to Holland in good time. By making these purchases in South America, far from the war that would ravage half the world, Father managed to bypass the difficulties of production, supply and transportation facing his competitors in Europe. South America, which was so far away from the theatres of war in Europe, the Balkans and the Middle East, was a place where many products that had disappeared from European markets – including, for example, animal hides – could be easily purchased. I have no idea if, prior to his departure, Father had had any premonitions concerning Holland's security in the face of German Nazism. If he had, it was not evident in the manner of his parting or in the tone of his first letters from Argentina. Father first heard about the German invasion of Holland from a radio broadcast on 10 May 1940. At that very moment all his carefully laid plans collapsed. There was no way for him either to return home or to bring us over to join him, and no way of finding out what had happened to us. He was totally cut off.

Despite this calamitous turn of events, my father refused to succumb to despair. With the help of some of his friends, he made a first, critically important, move: he applied for, and was granted, permanent resident status. In time he repaid his adopted country many times over for its hospitality. What my father did for the Argentine leather industry was no less than a 'one-man revolution'. This country, the largest cattle-rearing country in the world, had an enormous potential for trade in animal hides, but bureaucratic obstacles and bad management had prevented it from achieving the international prominence in this field that it deserved. First of all, there simply weren't enough knowledgeable professionals in the field. Second, the traditional ways of raising cattle on the *pampas* often resulted in irreversible damage to the hides, which lowered their value considerably. Throughout the year vast herds of cattle grazed outdoors with little or no supervision. As a result their hides were badly marred by insect and mosquito bites, or by rubbing against barbed-wire fences. Another problem was the extensive damage caused by the large brands used by the cattlemen to ward off potential cattle rustlers. My father explained to the ranchers that they could change all this without incurring any losses, and that, on the contrary, if they cooperated with him and instituted a few changes their profits would soar, since trade in top-grade Argentine animal hides would undoubtedly grow by leaps and bounds. They were easily convinced.

There was no doubt about it: Natan Gitter was the right man at the right time for the Argentine leather trade. The new immigrant from Holland proved himself superbly. Within a short space of time he found solutions for most of the industry's fundamental problems, and then proceeded to bring it out of the primitive state it had languished in for centuries into a world of new potential. Single-handedly, my father turned the previously lethargic trade in Argentine leather into one of the most advanced in the world. Apart from his professional acumen, and his technological innovations, my father was blessed with another unique quality. Although he lacked any formal schooling in economics, he was extraordinarily adept at calculating – with amazing accuracy and efficiency – expenses against profits and market prices in the light of supply and demand. With his razor-sharp intuition, he sensed when and where markets were opening up for industrial products, and where they could be purchased at the best possible prices.

It was into this fascinating world of business and commerce that my father now introduced me. The experience I had gained on my visits to England, France, Belgium and Hungary, and the period when fate forced me to take my father's place at the company in Holland – all these, it transpired, were a priceless boon. Initially, however, my position in the firm was not at all clear. Was I an independent businessman on my own merits, or was I Natan Gitter's son? This question troubled me every now and again, but paled into insignificance in the heady excitement of the day-to-day work. It was clear to everyone that my father considered me an equal partner in the business. To his credit I must say that he constantly urged me to take on new and more demanding challenges. Unlike the case in many other father/employer relationships that I knew about, he was never judgemental or critical in any way that might have indicated any fear on his part of being 'deposed', nor were there any traces of a hidden father–son rivalry. In fact, at times I thought he gave me more credit than I deserved. He always praised me lavishly for any business deals I concluded, as though he himself could not have done better.

However, not everything was as idyllic as this description may lead one to believe. We had arguments, just like any other father and son. And, strangely enough, in these arguments it was as though we switched roles: my father had somehow managed to retain a measure of naïveté and belief in his fellow man far in excess of my own, and I often had to take steps to protect him from his own ingenuousness. One of the reasons for this was, no doubt, the vastly different life experience each of us had undergone since he left Holland. The grim period of the Occupation, our confrontation with the brutal reality of Nazism, and our great escape – all these were etched into the very fabric of my soul, while he had experienced nothing even remotely similar. After the initial excitement of our arrival in Buenos Aires, he could immerse himself in the continued development of a successful business, while I had to make a very rapid and profound adjustment, and become accustomed once again to normal routines of life, as though the many narrow escapes from certain death that I had been through only months before never happened. He had no experience of the kind of depression that overcame me soon after arriving in Argentina. He was almost always brimming with enthusiasm and happiness, and could not conceive of anything untoward happening to himself or any of his loved ones. Looking back now, there was something odd about this, since he had heard from us and from many of his acquaintances about the terrible fate we had managed to elude in Europe. In this context, his boundless optimism seemed totally misplaced. These differences in our personalities could not but cause occasional friction between us, but deep in our hearts we held each other in the highest esteem. As is often the case with sons' relationships with their fathers, I am not certain I truly knew how to appreciate my good fortune, and – like many other young men – I, too, tried to do things my own way, and move away from his protective shadow. Nevertheless, to this very day I am profoundly grateful to him. He gave me free rein, and gave his blessing to everything I did.

A wonderful aspect of our relationship was a kind of telepathy that we developed in our work together. Occasionally, I would call him to report on sales I had made abroad, or remind him that we must replenish our stocks, and he would interrupt me with, 'Benno, don't worry! We have enough raw material. I already bought some.' Such things occurred with amazing regularity, but neither of us gave them a second thought. When I think about this unspoken understanding between us, I find it hard to fathom. How did it come about? Was it our common business interests, our spiritual or biological relationship, or a combination of all of these?

Thanks to my father's support and trust, I entered the world of business with enormous enthusiasm. In business matters I am rather like a bullfighter: I seek success not out of a desire for blood, but more out of a deep love for the challenge of the game. Business for me is like a sport, where in order to win you must be one step ahead of your opponents, understand their tactics, and make the winning moves.

VAN WAVEREN-GITTER

The revolution in the leather industry was not the only business enterprise my father was engaged in. When the Germans invaded Holland and all trade routes in and out of the country were cut off, he was no longer able to retrieve the leather he had purchased and already sent to Holland by sea. By a bizarre coincidence it was the Dutch government-in-exile in London that saved this first shipment of Argentine leather. The Netherlands' Royal Company for Shipping and Trading, which was set up immediately after the German Occupation in May 1940 with the blessing of Queen Wilhelmina and the financial assistance of the government-in-exile, seized the goods that were on their way to Occupied Holland, claiming that these were the property of Free Holland, and that the Germans were likely to appropriate them. All non-perishable goods, including my father's precious cargo, were kept in storage by the government-in-exile. Some of these goods were appropriated by that government for the duration of the war, who eventually paid their rightful owners in full for the seized shipments. As the war dragged on, other goods, which were found unsuitable for long-term storage, were sold, and all the proceeds were handed over to their owners.

Since passage to large parts of Europe was impossible as long as the war still raged in Europe, my father realized that he had to stake his claim in Argentina. He proposed to some of his business acquaintances, owners of the leading firm in the Dutch leather trade who had also emigrated to Argentina, that they set up a partnership. Since his financial resources were limited, Father offered them his highly valued talents and boundless energy, in return for less than the accepted percentage of profit, until such time as he was able to make his way on his own. He promised them that, with his help, their firm would create new standards of quality leather goods that would be sold on the few open markets left in the world: the USA, Canada, a few countries in Europe, and South Africa. The traders he approached were wary of setting up such a large company. They had not yet fully recovered from the trauma of losing their business empire in Holland, but had managed to bring out enough money to try and set themselves up again without partners.

Undaunted, my father decided on a different strategy. He knew that the leather he had sent to Holland had been seized by the Dutch Shipping & Trading Company of the government-in-exile, and therefore decided to go to the Dutch Embassy in Argentina and make an official request to retrieve his merchandise or its cash equivalent. The Honorary Consul-General of Holland in Argentina at that time was a man named Herman Van Waveren, an industrialist and entrepreneur with impeccable credentials, who had been appointed by the Dutch government-in-exile. The name Van Waveren was not new to my father. He had headed a family business that was involved in international trade in grain and seeds. During the hundreds of years of its existence, it had gained a worldwide reputation as the largest tulip-bulb exporter in Holland, and maintained its headquarters in Haarlem, the centre for the growing and exporting of flowers and bulbs. Over the years, the company had expanded and set up offices in the Dutch colonies in Indonesia and in Argentina, and in time these branches surpassed the mother company in Holland in their volume of business.

From their very first meeting, my father and Van Waveren found that they had a great deal in common and soon developed a profound mutual respect for each other. My father was fascinated by his host's personality and honesty, and gave him a detailed account of his financial situation and business plans. 'You may rest assured that I will help you in any way I can to get government approval for the release of your merchandise,' the Consul said. 'But why are you asking your competitors to enter into a partnership with you for so small a percentage of the profits, when it is very clear that it will be you who will be investing most of the know-how and doing most of the work? I suggest, instead, that you and I set up a new company together, that will be called Waveren-Gitter. You put up only ten per cent of the initial costs, and as soon as we succeed in obtaining payment for your goods from the Dutch authorities in exile, we'll go fifty-fifty.'

This was an offer my father could not refuse. Overwhelmed by the honour, he politely refused to have his name appear on the company letterhead, but Van Waveren insisted, and eventually a compromise was found: the logo for the joint company was designed as a crown over the letters WG – Waveren-Gitter. The crown, the traditional Van Waveren crest, had been bestowed on the company by the Dutch monarchy many generations earlier. Shortly after the new partnership was launched, Van Waveren & Partners became the largest leather exporter in the world. Over twenty years later, when my father passed away in Tel Aviv, an obituary appeared in one of the Argentine newspapers, extolling his accomplishments in developing the leather trade in that country, and helping Argentina become one of the world's principal exporters of leather.

Their beginnings were modest. My father discovered warehouses and production facilities where large quantities of hides were being stored, often without the manufacturers being aware of their true – and much higher – value on the international markets. My father redirected these stocks of raw material to the right markets, at prices that matched world demand at the time. Van Waveren looked on wonderingly at my father's decisive and agile business moves, his ability to set prices perfectly in tune with market conditions without missing a beat, and the lucrative long-term agreements he managed to sign with suppliers. Just as he had done in Holland, my father worked only with suppliers who had proven their professional expertise, stability and loyalty. Those he chose to work with were favoured in all their dealings with him, while at the same time he taught them the secrets of the trade and his methods for running a profitable business.

He devoted two and a half years to this industrial project, working day and night to make it succeed. He was driven by unbounded enthusiasm and dedication, and the natural ambition of an industrious man seeking perfection and success. At time this drive was also fuelled by despair and frustration. His total devotion to his work filled up his days, and gave him some comfort in his years of loneliness. During the empty night hours, when tension and anxiety could otherwise have preyed on his mind, my father sank into his bed in his lonely apartment, too tired to think.

SHOES – DURING THE WAR AND AFTER

As my father was wearing himself out in his new life in Argentina, something happened in Holland that was to affect us all. While Holland itself languished under the heavy burden of German Occupation, the Dutch government-in-exile displayed extraordinary pragmatism, almost to the point of prophesy, and began giving some thought to what the Dutch people would need to eat, dress, and put on their feet once the war was over. This was one of the reasons for their seizure and purchase of non-perishable goods. The Dutch government-in-exile displayed its unshakable confidence in an Allied victory in many other ways as well. I remember listening with some of my friends to the underground Orange Radio which operated out of Queen Wilhelmina's residence in London, and hearing her calling on her countrymen in a voice charged with emotion not to lose hope: 'Peace will come, in the not too distant future.' These words sounded like a vision of the Hereafter, particularly when she added that at the end of the war, when life returned to normal, there would be food for everyone, and every one of Holland's seven million inhabitants would have at least two good pairs of shoes.

As I listened to this broadcast on Radio Orange, I never imagined that my father would soon become part of the Dutch government's plans to provide shoes for its citizens. By the same token, I had no idea that I, too, would play a part in this project from my safe haven in Argentina. One way or another, these plans did finally get under way, and despite minor adjustments that had to be made to their projected time frame, the Dutch government-in-exile gave an excellent example of practical foresight.

In 1941, after the Dutch government-in-exile authorized Van Waveren & Co. to buy finished leather on its behalf, the government of Norway followed suit, albeit on a smaller scale, for its population of five million inhabitants. The famous Swiss shoe company Bally, and others as well, soon followed with similar demands. The leather earmarked for the citizens of Norway, Holland and Switzerland after the war was stored in Argentina. The funding for these transactions was transferred between banks through notes of credit without any problems.

These massive purchases gave my father control over the entire market, including its long-range planning and pricing. Van Waveren & Co. regulated the rate and timing of production, and instead of resting on their laurels as exporters of untanned hides, the company developed its industrial capabilities in tanning and curing as well. This new workplace required hundreds of new workers, and thus the entire trade, which had been in the doldrums for many years, suddenly took off into a dynamic and promising new future.

After I arrived in Argentina, my father told me a story that I remember to this day. In the course of his business dealings with the Dutch government-in-exile, the Dutch Minister of the Economy, Mr Steenberghe, arrived in Buenos Aires. He was a well-known businessman, and had been president of the Catholic C&A Company in Holland prior to the war, and a brilliant member of the Catholic Party in Holland. He was joined on this trip by a businessman named Kees Van Stolk, who was living in New York at the time, and managed the Dutch Shipping & Trading Company from there. They came to Argentina to oversee the development of their business interests and to expand them together with my father's company with the help of a new deal they had in mind. The contract for this deal had already been hammered out into a near-final draft. It lacked only a few details and the relevant signatures. Since travel was dangerous, and every trip to and from Europe required meticulous planning, the minister and his entourage were in a hurry to make their way back to their home ports. Van Waveren duly informed my father that the signing of the contract had to be pushed forward to Saturday – the Jewish Sabbath. 'In that case,' my father replied, politely but firmly, 'I will not be able to be there.'

'Are you seriously considering refusing to sign a multi-million-dollar contract because of the Sabbath?' he was asked.

My father looked up from his desk, and saw the minister in person standing in the doorway of his office. 'Your Excellency,' my father replied, attempting to give the minister a succinct explanation of the articles of his faith. 'If you were to tell me that my presence there was of vital importance to my country, Holland, and to the war effort, I would set out on foot and walk the fourteen kilometres from my house to the office; if you told me that my absence would cause grave damage to vital national interests, I would not hesitate for a moment. But I cannot see the urgency in signing a bill of sale for goods that will in any case arrive at their destination only after the war. I cannot participate in this part of the deal.'

The minister held out his hand to my father, and said, 'Don't worry!

We will close the deal at the beginning of the week. You enjoy your day of rest, and I will enjoy mine.'

In December 1945, during my first visit to Holland after the war, my father asked me to contact his friend Steenberghe, who had resumed his post as president of C&A. 'Are you Natan Gitter's son?' the former minister asked me excitedly over the phone, and immediately invited me over to have lunch with him. When he saw me, he held out his arms and embraced me warmly. 'May I call you Benno? I have prepared a meal for you that even your father would find acceptable,' he added.

'I do not keep kosher like my father,' I said, somewhat embarrassed.

But Steenberghe led me to the table and said, 'I cannot imagine that Natan Gitter's son would disregard the rules of kosher food.' He too was a very religious man, and this was one of the reasons why he held my father in such high regard. So, I sat down and ate the impeccably kosher meal that had been prepared especially for me.

Leather shoes are a consumer item that the world cannot do without at any time. During those long years of armed conflict, the Allied armies required vast quantities of shoes of all varieties. After Van Waveren & Co. established itself as a major supplier of animal hides, the company was approached by officials from Washington, as well as from a number of other countries in the Western Hemisphere and South Africa, all of which had, until then, been buying fine leather from leading European tanners.

My father now immersed himself in this new aspect of his business. Apart from running the business and overseeing the marketing of their merchandise for military and civilian use, my father placed great emphasis on maintaining contacts with his suppliers, and often instructed them on how to produce high-class leather goods for refined tastes. The local industry had begun to supply domestic demand as international orders from countries such as South Africa, Venezuela and a few others kept larger firms busy. Even Brazil, a major supplier for the British army, bought leather for its shoe industry from Van Waveren. Another important contact that was renewed was with the Bally family, owners of the famous Swiss shoe company. Before the war they were among my father's regular clients. Because the company required large amounts of leather to keep up its production, they were extremely concerned about the possibility of a shortage of raw material after the war. They had contacts with tanneries in Argentina and Brazil, but contacted Waveren as well, to ensure their supply. They also required extensive storage space, and my father offered to keep their stock for them in his warehouses, suggesting that they apply to the International Control Company in Geneva, or top officials from Holland Bank, Citibank, and the Bank of Boston, for supervision. 'Store in your storage facilities; Gitter's supervision is sufficient.' This was the wording of a telegram signed by Ernst Bally, the chairman of the company. We placed this telegram in a fine frame and hung it up in the room my father and I shared in the company offices.

Our good reputation spread far and wide. Our company was the only one awarded a very special privilege by the United States government: to be allowed to appoint comptrollers from among its own staff to stamp and number all its products for control purposes. All the other companies were monitored by US government-appointed officials, a procedure that was considerably more cumbersome. We monitored our own stocks and thus gained an added advantage in our pricing policies.

At work I made use of everything I had learned about the leather trade: I knew how to make the best possible use of damaged hides, I instructed owners of leather goods firms, and knew how to talk to everyone, from the porter to the bank manager. I was very ambitious and full of energy. I was young and in the thrall of the comfortable, good life in Buenos Aires, even though somewhere deep inside me I was still torn between my tendency to enjoy life and my feelings of guilt at having been spared, and my longings for the friends who had been left behind. Business, and the dynamic forces that keep it moving, were just what the doctor ordered to enable me to deal with this agonizing internal conflict.

I fitted in very easily with the friendly and harmonious relations between my father and his partners. Since my status and authority in the company remained vague and undefined, I understood that I would have to carve out a place for myself. Consequently, I looked for an available niche that would suit my energy and abilities, and found it in the contacts with other South American countries, such as Brazil and Uruguay among others. Their own leather industry was growing rapidly, but they had not yet reached the level of their Argentine counterparts, nor did they enjoy as abundant a supply of raw material.

A large part of our business was with the government of the United States. Major American leather manufacturers came to Buenos Aires as official representatives of various US government departments. I negotiated with them on behalf of the company, and over the years became very friendly with a few of them. Among these was Emory Holderness from Chicago, the director of a large leather manufacturing company which had stopped production during the war, and Ed Melzer, one of the top executives in the Florsheim shoe company of Chicago. I became their principal supplier, and their consultant on buying sole leather from my competitors. I sensed that these personal contacts, which grew out of our business dealings, were more important by far than any immediate, visible profits.

One day I was in my office dealing with routine matters when the phone rang. At the other end of the line was the general manager of the Bank of Holland in Argentina. 'I would like to refer to you a potential client for sole leather. He has a credit note to the tune of a million and a half dollars.' That was in 1944. The war was still raging in Europe, and trading was very difficult. The letter of credit was from South Africa, a detail that could have complicated the transaction, because we had to acquire a *laissez-passer* for the goods – known as NAVYCERT – from the Allies before we could make any practical moves on the deal.

'Excellent,' I said to the bank manager. 'Send him along, and accept my thanks even before we close a deal.'

'But I think you should know – he is a bit strange,' the manager added. 'He is a count, and the cousin of King Zog from Albania. His name is Count Toptani.'

It was all very intriguing. No more than fifteen minutes later, my secretary notified me that the count had arrived. I rose to greet him. He was a very tall, handsome figure, and entered my office wearing jodhpurs.

We began talking business immediately. I told him that with the sum he had at his disposal, he could purchase one million kilograms of hides.

'Is that your last price?' the count asked.

'Of course,' I replied. 'And it's a good price at that.'

'All right, I'll take it. I'll give you my letter of credit for one and a half million dollars.'

Obtaining official approval for the deal was complicated, and there were times when I thought the whole transaction would fall apart. The South African ambassador called me in the presence of the count in order to clarify a few things, but finally, Count Toptani and I shook hands and the purchase went through. It was only years later that I found out that the goods were destined for Jordan, and that, through a convoluted set of circumstances, part of the consignment actually reached the black market in Palestine.

I was fond of the count and had great respect for him. He was a generous man, who after the war purchased various goods with his own money and shipped them to Albania at his own expense. He despised his cousin, the King, and was not unduly sorry when the Albanian monarch was forced into exile.

As time went on, our friendship deepened. I met his wife, the beautiful actress Tilda Tamar, one of the most famous actresses in Argentina at that time. At our wedding he appeared dressed in elegant tails with royal medals of honour on his lapels. Later he separated from his actress wife, and we gradually lost contact with each other.

One day I received a letter from him, bearing the royal crest. 'Dear Benno,' he wrote. 'I always enjoyed doing business with the Jewish people, and you have been their faithful representative. Unfortunately, other people have brought me to financial ruin and despair. This is a letter of farewell, because I intend to take leave of my life. Your friend, Count Toptani.' The following day all the newspapers carried the story of his suicide: he had shot himself in the head and died immediately.

FOR EXPERTS ONLY

By now I had begun to regard myself as a native Argentinian. Soon after arriving in the country I took private Spanish lessons, and within a year I became fairly fluent in the language, and began to feel a part of my new country's culture and way of life. As an immigrant in a country that absorbed newcomers from all over the world, I did not feel at all like an outsider. Slowly I became acquainted with the political life of the country, including its shady and less attractive aspects, which – despite vehement denials by all concerned – were actually common knowledge. Everyone talked about the widespread corruption in government circles, which worsened after right-wing nationalist parties began taking control of the country. Soon after we arrived in Buenos Aires, General Rawson came to power. The very next day there was a military *coup d'état*, and a General Ramirez seized control. At that time we were not fully aware of the impact these frequent revolutions had on the country.

The nationalist governments, some of which rose and fell in rapid succession, tried to gain complete control over the economy as well, and it was this that brought about the collapse of the grain business owned by our friend and partner, Consul Van Waveren. Government officials appropriated his huge grain silos at the mouth of the River Plate, arbitrarily set prices for the grains, and then shamelessly siphoned off a large percentage of the profits into their own pockets.

Fortunately for us, we were not involved in this aspect of Van Waveren's business empire. My father preferred to deal only in those areas where he could bring his expertise to bear, and continually turned down offers to expand the range of his business partnerships. There were two exceptions, neither one of which turned out particularly well. There was a ceramics-manufacturing firm, which only barely covered its costs, let alone showing a profit. A few years after our emigration to Israel I sold the firm off to some good friends, who released us from its heavy burden, and, to my great satisfaction, eventually managed to turn it into a profitable enterprise. My father was right: every area has its experts, he used to say. These friends of ours were very experienced in the design, manufacture and marketing of household goods, an area in which we had no knowledge whatsoever.

The other business venture we entered into, at Van Waveren's insistence, were the *estancias* – cattle ranches. My father finally agreed to invest in them for nostalgic reasons: he himself had grown up in a small farming village in Poland where his father had been a farmer. When we were children my father used to take us for walks in the fields and talk to us about various methods of cultivation and teach us how to identify different animals and species of grains. However, even after he purchased the Christina *estancia*, I don't recall him visiting that remote ranch very often. Generally speaking, my father had no interest in real estate. Even in Holland we rented the house we lived in, an accepted practice in those days. As for land holdings in Argentina, despite our great love for the country, my father was certain that we, his sons, would not spend the rest of our lives there. As a result, he did not invest any of his money in commercial real estate, except for the minor and almost forgotten incident of the *estancia*.

LEAH: FROM PALESTINE TO ISRAEL VIA ARGENTINA

When we first arrived in Argentina, my brother was not allowed to practise medicine until he passed all his medical exams once again. This was a regulation that had become law in Argentina in 1939. Up until then he had been very lucky in his studies, and was one of the last Jews to be awarded a doctor's diploma in Holland before Jews were no longer allowed to study medicine.

At the time, in Buenos Aires, we felt that these regulations governing the employment of immigrant physicians reeked of anti-Semitism that had somehow managed to cross the ocean from the Old World to the New. To this day I am not altogether certain we were right about this or just overly sensitive. Nevertheless, the fact that Argentina (like Uruguay, Brazil and other South American countries) had given immigrant visas to numerous German immigrants, many of them open supporters of the Nazi Party, was very suspicious. These people found their way into all walks of Argentine life and soon occupied highly influential positions. Could it have been they who made life difficult for immigrant physicians, most of whom were Jewish? We only had questions and hypothetical theories about these things, but no hard and fast answers.

My brother refused to give up hope. He turned to Professor Bernard Houssay, an internationally famous physiologist and pharmacologist, and asked him for a research position in his laboratory. They had a brief, businesslike conversation, which centred primarily on the professor's expectations from his researchers and my brother's qualifications. Before they parted, the professor apologized and said that he could not offer my brother a position at the university because of the infuriating law relating to the hiring of immigrant physicians. The professor was a well-known opponent of the government ruling on this issue, but as an employee of a state-run university, he was not free to follow the dictates of his conscience, and had to toe the government line. He apologized once again and asked Shimon to leave him his telephone number. My brother was not sure if this boded well for the future or was merely a gesture of courtesy.

A few months later, this affair took a surprising turn. Professor Houssay invited Shimon to join a research institute for experimental medicine and biological research. Houssay had been relieved of his position at the university in Buenos Aires on orders from the rightist government, and had been invited to join a private research facility organized by Professor Braun Menendez, the son of a farming and industrial tycoon. A few years later this research institute received the highest possible international recognition when Professor Houssay was awarded the Nobel Prize for Medicine. Because of the scientist's vociferous opposition to government policies, news of his prize was buried in a small item on page seven of Argentina's largest daily newspaper, *La Nación*, after the news of the day, and the soccer, road racing, and betting results.

Being accepted into the research team was a turning-point in my brother's life. His entire lifestyle changed, and his chances of achieving his professional goals improved considerably. After the war, he returned to Amsterdam to complete his studies in his chosen field and write his PhD dissertation, and then continued his specialization in physiology and pharmacology at Oxford University in England. In 1949 one of Israel's top scientists, Professor Ernst David Bergman, came to Argentina, and was warmly received by the Jewish community of Buenos Aires. Professor Bergman had come to the country with the express purpose of persuading young and promising Jewish scientists to come to Israel and contribute to its development through their knowledge and expertise. At a reception in Bergman's honour held at our home, my brother became attracted to the idea, and within three days he and his wife reached a decision to emigrate to Israel. My parents had no objections. They knew that Zigi had dreamed of *aliya* (emigration) to Israel ever since he was very young, and it was only the tragic events of the early forties that had postponed the fulfilment of this dream.

Zigi and his family were the vanguard of the Gitters in Israel, and within a very short time he was recognized as one of the top physicians in his field. After serving in the Science Corps of the Israel Defence Forces, he became the deputy director of the Rogoff Research Institute at one of Israel's major hospitals, Beilinson in Petach Tikva (recently renamed after the late Prime Minister, Yitzhak Rabin). In 1964 my brother and his old friend from Holland Professor André de Vries were among the founders of the Faculty of Medicine at Tel Aviv University. Professor de Vries was elected to serve as the first Dean of the faculty, succeeded by Zigi who became the second Dean.

Leah, my brother's wife, was his helpmeet in every possible way. She had always felt that Argentina was not an appropriate place for the development of a scientific career. But that in itself was not the main reason for her willingness to go on *aliya* to Israel. For Leah, *aliya* meant the closing of a deeply significant circle in her life. As a young woman, Leah had been active in the Zionist movement, and in 1937, true to her Zionist ideals, she went to live in Palestine. For a short while she worked as a teacher, and then in 1940 returned for a brief visit to Holland. The German occupation of Holland made it impossible for her to go back to Palestine, and so it was that she ended up in Argentina with Zigi and her baby. As far as she was concerned, Argentina was only a station on her way back to Israel. When they arrived in Israel, she began doing graduate work in mathematics – her own chosen field.

Our younger brother, Ya'akov, was ten years old when we came to Argentina, and his childhood years were totally different from ours. He learned Spanish very quickly, and integrated smoothly into Argentine life. When he grew up he married a woman from Uruguay – Lilliana – and worked with my father until he ultimately decided to return to Holland.

8

ALICE

In 1944 I was an old-young man of twenty-five, without friends, male or female, of my own age. During the first two years of my life in Argentina I plunged headlong into the business world, and my social circle included very few of my contemporaries. I socialized either with businessmen who were, for the most part, older than me, or with people from Zionist circles, most of whom were also older. The many business interests and responsibilities, which I took upon myself with my father's encouragement, kept me away from the lively social life of the city. It is also quite possible that at that stage I had not yet totally completed the process of internalizing and dealing with my feelings of guilt at having remained alive. Dance music of any kind still reminded me of that last party in Holland on New Year's Eve of 1942.

And so I lived a solitary and rather desolate life, whose true nature I was hardly aware of until my first encounter with Alice. We met for the first time at her sister Eva's eighteenth birthday party; Alice was twenty years old. Her uncle, her mother's brother, Hans Kaufmann, and her Aunt Alice had come to Buenos Aires shortly before the war, and had rebuilt the family hide empire that had been founded in Germany at the beginning of the century by Alice's grandfather, Carl Kaufmann. The Kaufmanns had developed sharp instincts that warned them of the danger threatening the Jews in Europe, even though they themselves had distanced themselves from the observance of most Jewish traditions. And so it was that Uncle George sailed to the United States in 1939, while the other branches of the family moved to Argentina in 1940. Among them was a sister, Mali, who had earlier divorced her husband, Walter Rosenberg, and her two daughters, Alice and Eva.

Hans, Alice's uncle, was a few years older than I was, and we developed a close business relationship. After listening with amazement to the story of our odyssey to Argentina, his wife suggested, 'Tomorrow we are celebrating our niece Eva's birthday. Our two nieces, Eva and

Alice, are very nice. We would be very happy if you would come.' And with sound feminine intuition she added, 'It would be good for you to meet a few people your own age, don't you think?'

I went to the party, and the evening was a total bore. The young people danced or chatted, but I had little or nothing to add to their conversations. The things they talked about didn't interest me in the least, and what did interest me was totally alien to them. I had not yet acquired the knack for light and non-committal small talk. I have since acquired the habit, and grown to understand its importance at social events.

I stood there by the wall, feeling lonely and out of place, until a very beautiful young woman with black hair and a lithe figure came down the stairs and spoke to me. She introduced herself as Alice, the Kaufmanns' niece. Our conversation flowed effortlessly in English and Dutch, in both of which Alice was fluent. From that moment on, everything changed. Alice became the centre of the party for me, and, although I was only dimly aware of it at the time, the party itself turned into a highly significant event in my life.

Almost from the very beginning we talked like old friends. I had no reservations about telling her my difficulties in integrating into Argentine society, and she told me about her life at an English boarding school. Many of the people I knew at that time had gone through traumatic experiences, and Alice, too, had undergone a number of major changes in her life, albeit for private family reasons. She was born in Berlin, and a few years after her birth the family moved to Rotterdam, the city where her grandfather Carl had his family hide business. His grandmother, the ambitious Mrs Amalia Kaufmann, came from Muhlheim in the Ruhr district. It was she who had set up the first Kaufmann hide business in the backyard of their house at the end of the nineteenth century. After moving to Rotterdam, Carl decided to turn that city into his company's home base. When Alice was fourteen, her mother, Mali Kaufmann, decided to leave her husband, Walter – a very unusual step in those days. The ex-husband moved to The Hague, while Mali Kaufmann and the two girls remained in the family home in Rotterdam. When Grandfather Carl Kaufmann died in 1938, the first gusts of the ill winds that were about to spread like a malignant storm throughout Europe were clearly felt. Mali Kaufmann, restless as always, was just waiting for the first opportunity to leave the city where her marriage had ended so badly. Thus her personal predicament and the general situation in Europe now combined to give her a one-time opportunity to make a break. She quickly dismantled the household, stored the furniture and began looking for somewhere else to live, somewhere more peaceful and calm, which had more to offer herself and her daughters.

First they moved to London where Alice was accepted at an exclusive boarding school. The emphasis at the school was more on horsemanship than on modern history or sciences. Nevertheless, the time she spent there were not wasted. It was there that she began cultivating one of the abiding interests of her life: English literature.

When the war broke out, Mali took her two daughters and moved to the United States. At the same time, most of her family dispersed throughout the Free World. Mother and daughters remained in the United States on tourist visas until they received word that Argentina was willing to issue them immigrant visas. Argentina's hesitant internal affairs policies were believed by many to be a deliberate bureaucratic delaying tactic. Mali Kaufmann decided to go there after her brother Hans who had already set out for Buenos Aires. Aware of the difficulties of obtaining a visa, Mali preferred to make her way first to the Dutch colony of Curaçao. A short while after Hans arrived in the Argentine capital, Mali Kaufmann received entry visas to the country for herself and her two daughters. They lived in a two-storey house on 11th of September Street, and it was there that we met.

I watched Alice and listened to her voice, and did not want our conversation to end. She had a gentle, pleasing manner when she talked. In her company I experienced none of my usual clumsiness or sense of advanced age. Since my arrival in Buenos Aires, I had not been attracted to a young woman as I was to her at that party. But what was I supposed to do next? I was terribly shy and plagued by inhibitions. My conscience tormented me over any of life's pleasures, or any attempt I made to return to a semblance of a normal life. How easy it was to discuss business or problems pertaining to the Jewish community, and how difficult it was to talk about matters of the heart!

I had no idea if Alice felt the same way about me. In those far-off days – 1944 – it was up to the man to take the lead in a relationship.

Gauche as I was, I missed the right moment to arrange a time for us to meet again. I was also too shy to ask for Alice's exact address, and instead took to driving along her street a number of times each day. She had to come out at some time during the day, I reasoned, and then, as I imagined it, when I saw her coming out, I would say something like, 'What a wonderful coincidence! I was just on my way to the office!'

But this hoped-for coincidence never took place, and I can only blame my faulty memory for the long time that passed before we met again. Alice's street – 11th of September Street in the Belgrano district – was named after an illustrious military victory led by General Belgrano, an important figure in Argentine history. In the same neighbourhood there is another street, 3rd of February Street, named after another illustrious battle, and I had confused the two. So, every day for six months I walked the length of 3rd of February Street looking in vain for some sign of Alice. I peered into the houses, but they all looked alike to me. I looked longingly at the tall fences, wondering which one hid the object of all my thoughts. But Alice was nowhere to be seen. Of course, I could have chosen much simpler ways to seek her out, but my shyness and embarrassment got the better of me.

But God, or fate or perhaps luck, works in many mysterious ways. In the Argentine summer of 1945, a full six months after our first encounter, we met again, this time on the Mar del Plata beach, a resort some four hundred kilometres from Buenos Aires. Somehow, among the thousands of people basking on the broad expanse of sand, we were drawn to each other. I regarded it as a kind of miracle or omen, and after the ridiculous mistake of the wrong street name, I was determined not to leave our fate up to chance again. From that day on we hardly left each other's side.

Alice's parents had a stormy relationship that was marked by constant fights. Her father, Walter Rosenberg, a strikingly handsome man, treated everyone – except his own family – very politely, particularly when it came to members of the opposite sex. He once read me a letter from his father-in-law, Alice's grandfather, which he received in hospital, where he was being treated for appendicitis: 'Dear Son-in-Law, I wish you the best of health. No one here misses you in the least. Take as much time as you like to get better – even without you business is bad.' It was only when he put the dog-eared letter back in his pocket that I understood why he had read it to me. Clearly he was trying to frighten me, to warn me about the family I was about to enter.

As I grew to know Alice better, I felt that, like me, she was mature beyond her years. This could have been the result of the complexity of her family life, but was also, possibly, the result of her long battle with asthma, an illness that had stalked her like a dark shadow from the age of fourteen. It was then, soon after her parents' divorce, that she had suffered the first of many terrible attacks. Alice loved her mother deeply, and life after the divorce was not easy for either of them. Her mother remarried, but this marriage too ended disastrously. Alice, who was vulnerable and sensitive, suffered greatly from these upheavals in her family. Her vulnerability to the disease was probably the result of unhealthy genes that had remained dormant in her body from birth, but it was the difficult emotional circumstances of her life that seemed to have brought about the actual outbreak of the illness when she was a young teenager. To this day asthma is regarded, to a great extent, as a psychosomatic disease that is latent in the body from birth, and can appear suddenly in times of severe emotional or physical duress. In most cases the disease is dormant, and it is fatal only in very rare and extreme cases. Despite rapid advances in medical science, and improvements in medication that can alleviate its symptoms to some extent, asthma remains a disease that severely affects the quality of life of its victims.

Alice never concealed her illness from me. In fact, she told me about it at our very first meeting. Was it to prevent any future mis-understandings that she was so frank about these problems, or was it an indication of the seriousness of her intentions towards me? From the time she was a young woman she was never given to superficial conversation and non-committal remarks. Even if I had known more about her illness at the time, the optimism of youth is boundless, and which one of us at that time of our lives wants to tear away the rosy veils of the future? Which one of us, in our youth, does not believe in his or her power to overcome every obstacle or dictate of fate in the name of love? What I was incapable of understanding at that time was that from the outset our relationship was to be a *ménage à trois*: Alice, myself, and her illness, which would be with us at all times, throughout our life together.

Alice had chosen to become a nurse. Being intimately aware of suffering herself, and highly sensitive, what she wanted more than anything else was to be able to alleviate the pain and suffering of hospital patients. She had studied nursing at the British hospital of Buenos Aires. I often waited for her in my car for hours until she finished her rounds. Unfortunately, she was never able to fulfil her dream: the physical demands of nursing were beyond her strength, and the nursing diploma remained unused in a forgotten drawer.

Our relationship grew stronger and closer. Her involvement in my life added colour and meaning to everything I did. She was very attracted to my Zionist activities, a fact that I found pleasantly surprising, since her own family had removed itself from any involvement in Jewish or Zionist affairs. Her interest in my business came much more naturally to her. After all she was the scion of a wealthy industrialist's family. Conversation at our dinner table centred primarily on business. A few months after we renewed our acquaintance, Alice and I already considered ourselves a couple and spent most of our time together. We were filled with optimism and love, and our lives seemed like an enchanted trip into a future where all the elements of our life together would blend into one: work, family, social life, ideals and, of course, free time and vacations.

As usual, my social and business contacts intermingled. Alice and I spent many a pleasant hour in the company of our dear friends, the Americans Emory Holderness and Ed Melzer. One of the most amusing adventures of this period almost cost the two properly behaved innocents, Alice and Benno, their good names. At the time, we were anything but amused. It was during one of those hot Argentine summer months. Our American friends and a few other people invited us to join them at Bariloche, a wonderful and well-known resort, 2,000 kilometres from Buenos Aires. Alice had just finished her nursing diploma exams, and was in dire need of a vacation, and as for myself, I was not about to forego the opportunity to enjoy myself in the company of my good friends. Since the train was the most convenient mode of transport for Alice, we set off in good time, hoping that our friends, who had left Buenos Aires forty-eight hours earlier by car, would arrive there at about the same time as our train. After forty hours on the train, we arrived at our destination looking like chimney sweeps. The heat along the way had been so oppressive that we had been forced to open the windows of our compartment, and the smoke and soot from the locomotive covered us with a thick black crust.

When we arrived at the Corentoso Hotel at Bariloche, no one there knew anything at all about our friends' imminent arrival. We wondered what had happened to them. And as if that concern were not enough, we unexpectedly ran into friends of my future mother-in-law who had come to the same hotel. They were quite appalled to see us there on our own – how dare an unmarried young man and woman stay together at a hotel! Alice and I had booked separate rooms, but at that particular moment it was too embarrassing to try to explain. In a desperate attempt to prevent malicious rumour-mongers from working overtime on this titbit, we explained that we were waiting for friends who were due to arrive at the hotel any moment. That explanation seemed to lay the issue to rest – but barely.

A day passed, and our friends were nowhere to be seen. 'Where are these friends of yours?' the guardians of public morality enquired suspiciously, and we did not know what to say to them. The following day we were asked again, 'What happened to your friends?' We were very nervous and worried. After three days, they no longer bothered to ask us any questions. As far as they were concerned, we had overstepped all bounds of decency. We knew that this meant only one thing: when we returned to Buenos Aires we would have to deal with a veritable campaign of whispers and slander.

However, our main concern – for the fate of our friends – grew from day to day. They finally arrived at the hotel almost a week late. Unluckily for them, their car broke down just before the *pampas*, and they had to abandon it and hitchhike the rest of the way to Bariloche.

Typically impatient, we youngsters soon grew tired of Bariloche. We were drawn to the Sierra Lopez, the highest mountain in the area. Climbing the mountain on horseback was a popular pastime. We hired a guide, and he brought all the necessary equipment, including shoes and mountain-climbing clothes. Eventually, we returned to Bariloche so as to leave by the evening train, and booked rooms at a hotel in the centre of town, not far from the railway station, where we intended to rest before our trip back. Our mountain-climbing guide came to my room to pick up all the equipment and his fee, and seemed to be in a hurry to be on his way. I opened the door a crack, handed him his money and the equipment, including the mountain trousers we had used, said goodbye. It was only then, alone in my room, that I discovered, to my utter disbelief, that the suitcase with all my clothes, which was supposed to have been sent along from the Llaollao Hotel, twenty-five kilometres away, had not arrived, and I was left with only my underwear. It was an excruciatingly embarrassing moment. I called the hotel and they promised to send the suitcase by taxi immediately. I paced the room impatiently, highly agitated, until finally, unable to wait any longer, I decided to take a taxi myself to retrieve the missing suitcase. What happened next could only have been planned by the devil himself: as I rushed out into the corridor – dressed in my drawers – I once again encountered one of my future mother-in-law's acquaintances. He had already met Alice and me once before in the Corentoso Hotel, and had probably labelled me right then and there an archenemy of chastity and proper behaviour. And now here I was facing him in another hotel in my underwear! The man walked past me, taking in every juicy detail. I could hear him muttering, 'Scandalous, simply scandalous!' Naturally, when we returned home I had to go to some lengths to explain my supposedly disreputable behaviour to several people, including my future mother-in-law. Fortunately, the unpleasantness surrounding this entire incident soon evaporated.

A MOVABLE WEDDING

By the first half of 1945 the war in Europe was about to end.

It was a time for celebration and we could now begin to think of a wedding, but Alice was still suffering from asthma, and another attack, more serious than usual, forced us to postpone the ceremony. Alice's doctor recommended an innovative treatment and suggested that we put off the wedding for a while and delay any thoughts of starting a family. Alice accepted the news with her characteristic stoicism.

We set the wedding for 1 May 1946. May has been a month of landmarks in my life: my birthday, the day of the German invasion of Holland, the day I received my Certificate of Immigration to Palestine, and now my wedding. What is more, 8 May was V-E Day, the official date of the Allied victory in Europe over Nazi Germany. After we had finally set the day, we had to change our plans once again for an unexpected reason. Giving the people of Argentina less than a week's notice, President Juan Peron declared 1 May a national holiday. When the manager of the elegant Alvear Hotel, where we had planned to hold our wedding reception, explained that he could not possibly hold our wedding party on that day, we decided to hold it on the following day. But that created an added difficulty: the hall was already booked by friends of ours, the Mirelmans, for a wedding in their family. The management of the Alvear then came up with another solution: they offered to send out telegrams, at their expense, inviting all our guests to the Plaza Hotel, which was considered even more elegant and luxurious than the Alvear – and that was what they did. Finally, after all the delays, our guests, about a thousand people – business and social acquaintances from both families – gathered to celebrate our marriage with us at the Plaza Hotel.

The religious ceremony, the *huppa* (bridal canopy, and symbol of a Jewish wedding), was held at my father's synagogue on Moldes Street. My father was, of course, deeply attached to that synagogue which he had built with the ransom money he had promised for our release that the Germans had not cashed. According to Jewish tradition, the bride and groom are supposed to be kept apart until the actual ceremony begins, when the groom comes to the bride and covers her face with the wedding veil. Alice and I were duly placed in separate rooms. But as the minutes ticked by and nothing happened, I grew increasingly impatient, and finally began banging on the door and yelling, 'Where is my family? If they don't come out immediately I'm leaving.' I simply couldn't control myself, and Carla Kaufmann, Alice's fourteen-year-old cousin, was so terrified by my bellowing that she fainted. To this day she bears a small scar on her forehead as a memento of our wedding.

As far as I could gather through the haze of excitement that enveloped me, our wedding was an impressive society event. All the social codes were strictly adhered to: the women wore long evening gowns, the men were dressed in tuxedos and sported top hats. I still cherish the photographs that appeared in the social columns the next day, in the *Nación* and the English-language *Buenos Aires Herald*.

We spent our honeymoon in the United States – my first visit to that great country. I will never forget the warmth with which relatives from both sides of the family welcomed us.

Contrary to the liberal image it tried to project, the United States of 1946 was a far cry from the equal rights paradise it purported to be. In many aspects of daily life Jews and blacks were discriminated against by their white Christian fellow citizens. One day, Alice and I met for coffee with Emory Holderness and his wife at a café at the country club on the beach at Edgewater, Michigan. Emory, a non-Jew, leaned back comfortably in his chair and remarked: 'Benno, Alice, you know this is the most beautiful country club in the entire area, but we can't become members because we're Gentiles.'

'And what about your club?' I asked pointedly. 'Do you accept Jewish members?'

Emory was hard put to come up with a satisfactory answer, but since neither of us wanted to undermine our friendship, we did not pursue the issue any further. I must admit, compared with the kind of anti-Semitism I had witnessed and experienced first-hand in Europe, the discrimination against Jews in American country clubs did not seem to me to be that critical an issue. Perhaps out of a desire to regard it in as positive a light as possible, I thought of it as more of a mutually accepted form of social distinction than as an expression of anti-Semitic feelings. I may have treated the issue too lightly or else, perhaps, I was simply sick and tired of having to deal with it.

Apart from these few awkward moments, I have nothing but praise for my relationship with Emory Holderness, who remained my closest friend until the day he died. Neither he nor I ever felt that our backgrounds were of any importance whatsoever. I had many other non-Jewish friends in the USA, most of them considerably older than I was, and no longer with us.

9

AFTER THE WAR

Soon after the war was over in Europe and the Far East, the Argentine leather industry underwent extensive changes. My father and I were forced to make tremendous efforts to adjust to the new reality. As I have already mentioned, prior to the war, Argentina had exported only low-grade, untanned and partially tanned hides, and also, as a result of my father's reorganization of the industry, the local leather industry had since grown by leaps and bounds. Among his innovations was the recruiting of export tanners, most of them Jewish refugees from Czechoslovakia, Hungary, Holland and Poland, who, under his tutelage, taught the Argentine leather workers all the secrets of the trade. Among other things, they introduced far-reaching technological innovations that revolutionized the standard of Argentine leather.

With the war over, we felt as though we were being shunted aside, despite our important contributions to the industry. It was abundantly clear to us that despite the enormous strides taken by the local leather trade, for which we were largely responsible, the Europeans would now be re-entering the market, and the Argentine leather industry was heading for a crisis. Even though major improvements had been made in the quality of the merchandise, and in the means of shipping them from the New World to the Old, there was no way we could ensure the quick, safe and continuous export of finished leather goods from Argentina to Europe. I knew that our contributions as traders and industrialists during the war would soon be forgotten. It was only a matter of time, we feared, until thousands of workers in the Argentine leather industry would be laid off.

As long as leather firms in other countries continued to suffer from a shortage of trained professionals, Argentina maintained its position as a leading producer of leather, but my father and I were convinced that this was only temporary. After the post-war years the leather industry was once again about to become totally dependent on the whims of the fickle world of fashion. In order to create fashionable shoes and clothing European and American manufacturers would prefer buying leather from suppliers closer to home. The times when manufacturers ordered and maintained large stocks of leather were over. In an era when trends and fleeting fashions dominated the market, holding on to large, standardized stocks could spell ruin for these companies.

The future did not look too rosy, but we never lost hope. Undaunted by the problems, and as persevering as ever, my father carefully reviewed the new situation, and soon came up with a typically imaginative solution: he suggested that the tanneries in Argentina concentrate on producing semi-tanned hides. These cheaper hides would be snapped up by American and European firms who could then finish the tanning process at their convenience, adapting the raw material to suit the local fashion trade. In this way, he suggested, prices could be kept high, and the leather trade in Argentina would be able to survive and retain the many thousands of workers who depended on it for their livelihood.

To the Argentine government's credit it must be said that it immediately understood the financial potential of such an arrangement. The decision to set a lower rate of currency exchange for raw material, and another rate for tanned or semi-tanned hides (a difference of up to twenty per cent), was a positive incentive for our clients from abroad. In this way we could still compete with lower-priced suppliers from Greece, Italy, Turkey and the North African countries which had recently entered the international leather trade.

In Argentina my father's ideas were received enthusiastically, but in Europe some of the biggest suppliers were furious over what they felt was unfair trading. They feared that the wholesale purchase of semi-tanned hides would gradually close down their own businesses. And that is in fact exactly what happened: the weaker companies in Europe closed down, and the centres of enterprise and production moved to South America, North Africa, Korea and, eventually, to China and Thailand as well. My job was to persuade European governments and some of the larger suppliers to adopt our proposal for everyone's benefit. In many cases, my efforts bore fruit.

The entire field of leather production remained my principal business concern until I emigrated to Israel, when I gradually changed direction and moved into banking. Our competitors in the Argentine leather trade followed our lead and were very successful, becoming world leaders in the business. One of these, Walter Lebach, originally came to Argentina as an investment consultant, and soon became a highly successful leather manufacturer. He pleaded with me to go into partnership with him, but I told him that I was preparing for my imminent move to Israel. He said that where I chose to live was of no consequence, and that we could maintain a partnership even at a distance. Turning down his offer was one of the few truly wrong-headed decisions I made in my life. We eventually did do business, after a fashion, when, following my father's death, Walter purchased a large share of our firm's business. Walter Lebach has remained one of my dearest friends to this day. On a number of occasions Walter and his wife joined Alice and me on joint family vacations, and he was always ready to assist me in all my public endeavours in Israel. I was deeply saddened when, a few weeks before the completion of this English version, Walter, my best friend of sixty years, passed away at the age of ninety-three.

EVITA AND JUAN PERON

Argentina is a fascinating, multi-faceted country, with a rich and diverse ethnology and history and a long tradition of volatile politics. As I mentioned, in the very first days after our arrival, we found ourselves in the midst of a short-lived revolution. In a swift *coup d'état*, General Rawson took control of the country, and in an equally rapid counter-coup by a General Ramirez, he was deposed. (From a purely personal point of view, Rawson's brief flirt with power was not a total loss: according to the Argentine constitution, his few days as head of state entitled him to a full pension for the rest of his life.) The man who replaced him, General Ramirez, was a weak and lacklustre politician, who, by his very weakness, paved the way for a takeover by a strong totalitarian régime. As far back as 1943, the high-flying political ambitions of a young army colonel by the name of Juan Peron, an avid disciple of Mussolini's Fascist military thinking, caught the eye of savvy political analysts. In the meantime, the country was being run by General Farrell, yet another in a long line of power-hungry military men, and the scion of a family known for its revolutionary inclinations.

Peron was appointed – or appointed himself – Minister of Labour in Farrell's government, a seemingly minor government position, but one that in fact contained tremendous potential for personal advancement in a country where the gap between rich and poor was so enormous.

At that time, labour relations in Argentina were at a low ebb. In fact, blue-collar and low-level white-collar workers suffered from harshly discriminatory working conditions: the kind that feed the flames of revolution and produce grassroots leaders. Employees were fired without notice, and basic social benefits such as severance pay, pensions and social security were all no more than vague rumours from distant countries. These problems provided all the ingredients for a social and political time bomb, and the wily and ambitious Juan Peron bided his time waiting for just the right moment to make his move.

And the opportunity soon presented itself. A severe earthquake rocked the city of San Juan, and Peron swung into action, raising money and recruiting volunteers to rebuild the ravaged city. An impressive obelisk, that rose higher and higher as contributions poured in to the devastated region, honoured the donors for all to see. One hundred and fifty million pesos found their way into the coffers of the ambitious Minister of Labour, who, rather than transferring the funds to reconstruction projects, kept them salted away for a time of need. He revelled in the universal recognition and acclaim he garnered for his swift and decisive action in the disaster, and then waited for an opportune moment to reap the rewards of his dedication to the people, and seize control of the country.

As Minister of Labour, Peron brought a breath of fresh air into the creaking Argentine system of labour relations, introducing social changes that were gratefully received by the lower classes, and universally opposed by reactionaries from among the hard-line Catholics and the wealthy. These deeply conservative elements in Argentine society treated Peron's one time mistress and later wife, Eva, with hostility, taking every opportunity to drag her name through the mud. A collision was inevitable, and the ruling classes played into Peron's hands by giving him his martyrdom: like his role model, Napoleon, he was ordered into exile on a prison island. This was Eva's finest hour. Popularly known as Evita, she organized a mass rally in support of her lover. Hundreds of thousands of *descamisados* ('shirtless') cried 'Peron!

Peron!' in support of their exiled hero. The message carried by the masses into the streets rang out loud and clear, and that very night the country's rulers rescinded the exile order, and Juan and Evita Peron appeared together to receive the multitudes at Casa Rosada, the Argentine seat of power. In a dramatic gesture, the usually impeccably dressed Peron appeared in simple worker's garb to demonstrate his solidarity with his 'shirtless' supporters, who now surrounded him in absolute adoration. From that moment on, there was no stopping Peron's inexorable march to power.

The true force behind the leader was his beautiful Evita, a strong-willed woman who fought her way out of the slums to the very pinnacle of power. Lacking any formal education, she was self-taught and extraordinarily intelligent. Rumour had it that she had been born in the alleys, and it was perhaps this strong sense of inferiority that fuelled her insatiable passion for power. She was a woman driven by many contradictory forces. She was, by all accounts, a true benefactor of the poor and the dispossessed, but at the same time she maintained an extravagantly luxurious lifestyle that many of the most decadent Roman empresses might have envied – and gained herself many enemies in the process. Her dubious 'marriage' to Juan Peron, which was deeply disturbing to the Catholic clergy and the morally self-righteous, in no way contradicted her vaunted devotion to the Catholic faith, rites and icons. These contradictory aspects of her nature were mirrored by the conflicting feelings she aroused in her countrymen: from loathing and abomination to blind adoration and total obedience. Evita's authority, influence and prestige were in no way inferior to that of her husband, and indeed, at times, she overshadowed him. Ironically, the high point of her story was not her life, but rather her death from cancer at the age of thirty-two. Her tragic early death turned her into a national heroine, transforming her from villain to saint, a symbol of all that was good and sublime in the world.

Argentina had a long history of dictatorial régimes and corruption in high places, and the Perons very quickly – and uniquely – formed their lives as rulers in the self-same mould. In this respect, at least, they were no different from many of their predecessors. When Peron, an open admirer of Fascism, assumed power in 1945, fear spread throughout the Jewish community. While previous Argentine governments had hedged their support for any of the sides in the global conflict – Axis or Allies – it was well known that Peron was fascinated by Mussolini and possibly also by Hitler, though in the latter case – if indeed it was true – he was clever enough to conceal his sympathies.

However Argentina – regarded at the beginning of the twentieth century as the 'El Dorado of the Southern Hemisphere' – was ultimately dragged down to financial ruin not by politics but by the collapse of its economy. At the turn of the century many immigrants from the Old World were drawn to the country. As was the case in Switzerland, Argentina's liberal monetary regulations encouraged trade and foreign currency deposits, and local and international businesses prospered. In time, serious mistakes in monetary policies and rampant inflation brought the country's economy crashing down. In a desperate effort to halt the collapse, all imports of foreign capital were banned, as were investments from abroad. Precious time was lost until the perpetrators of these bizarre economic concepts finally began to grasp the disastrous consequences of their mistakes. The government's hasty nationalization of any moderately successful business caused further irreversible damage to an already weakened economy. Up until then, the railway and telephone systems and other public utilities were owned by American, British and French firms. Britain regarded the development of the railway system as a colonial goal of the first order. Under the auspices of the British crown, or the French Republic, these companies were both active and efficient. For a relatively small margin of profit they invested huge sums of money to maintain and develop these services so as to meet the needs of their clients: the Argentine people. But the Argentine rulers regarded these companies as foreigners who were drawing their life's blood. For those of us watching from the sidelines it came as no surprise when General Peron, like the proverbial farmer who killed the goose that laid the golden eggs, decided to nationalize these companies in the hope of filling his coffers with their profits.

It soon became clear that nationalization – in most cases – was a disastrous mistake. Purchasing the utilities companies involved an enormous outlay of much-needed capital; maintenance or replacement of obsolete or outdated equipment proved immeasurably more expensive than expected; and somehow, whenever money was urgently needed for these purposes, there were always more pressing needs elsewhere, such as upgrading the country's primitive road system. The rapid decline in the level of public services produced a growing bitterness among Peron's constituents, and made deep inroads into his support among the lower classes. The masses who had brought him back from exile and swept him triumphantly to power were soon going to bring him down.

At first, the Jewish community remained untouched by the actions of this volatile régime, whose most consistent characteristic was its steady decline. My father and I were businessmen, and we were used to working under adverse conditions. The distinction between a 'normal' and an 'abnormal' business atmosphere was largely irrelevant for us, and our continuous efforts to maintain profit levels despite the difficult circumstances became a kind of ongoing challenge.

All the manifestations of corruption, nepotism, and anti-democratic activities of the Peron administration centred around the personality of his wife, Evita. Today, at a remove of many years, the lives of Juan and Evita Peron remind me of the convoluted – not to say farcical – plot of a burlesque operetta. My own meetings with Evita and Juan Peron now seem to me like an almost hallucinatory episode among the many accumulated experiences and memories of my life. I do not wish to pass judgement on the Perons as to whether they were 'good' or 'bad' for Argentina. Many books, stories, and even a famous musical have been woven out of their biographies. At the time when I was an occasional visitor to their palace, I never stopped to try and decipher their enigmatic characters. There was only one criterion of success or failure as far as I was concerned: the extent to which our meetings helped advance the Zionist cause or the interests of the state of Israel among the powers-that-be in Argentina. My thinking on these matters was totally pragmatic and goal-oriented, as in the age-old question that has always been on the minds of a persecuted people: 'Are these people good for the Jews or bad for the Jews?'

To their credit, and despite our initial fears, the Perons were in fact good for the Jews: for the local Jewish community, for the state of Israel and even for Jewish individuals in Argentina. There were some four hundred thousand Jews in Argentina at that time, with a vast majority – 350,000 – living in the capital, Buenos Aires. Peron regarded them as an important electoral and economic constituency, even though very few Jews held positions of any importance either in government or the army.

10

LINKS WITH ISRAEL

Apart from the family business, to which I devoted most of my energies, a new focal point began emerging in my life in Argentina: Zionism. I was, of course, no stranger to Zionist activities: I had been deeply involved in the Zichron Jacob Zionist youth movement in Holland, and had applied to study at the Hebrew University in Jerusalem as part of my irrevocable determination to go on *aliya* to Palestine. However, fate and history intervened to prevent me from realizing these dreams in my youth, and at the same time brought me round full circle, and allowed me to realize them in my manhood. As is often the case in such things, my initiation into Zionist activities in Argentina was totally unplanned. It has been my good fortune, at various important junctures of my life, to meet a number of people who opened my heart to Zionist aspirations, thus giving my life content, meaning and a clear direction. In this case, it was my acquaintance with Dr Yoseph (José) Mirelman, and his brother Simon, among the most unique and impressive figures in the Jewish community of Buenos Aires, indeed in the whole of the Latin American continent. It was they who drew me in to the Zionist activities that I soon embraced with great fervour.

Dr Yoseph Mirelman was a partner and one of the managing directors in the Mirelman family textile business, Manuseda. However, books and literature were his true and abiding passion. Almost single-handedly he massively enriched Jewish cultural life in Argentina by translating into Spanish and publishing books on Jewish subjects in the fields of philosophy, science, and Jewish law – much like the Schocken publishing house in Berlin before the war.

A few weeks after my arrival in Argentina, Yoseph Mirelman invited me to join him at a *brit mila* (ritual circumcision) at the home of one of his friends. He thought this would be a good opportunity for me to meet a broad cross-section of people from the Jewish community and to begin to familiarize myself with their social milieu. In Buenos Aires circumcisions like these were generally held on Sundays so that the *mohel* (circumciser), who made his living elsewhere, would be free to come and perform the ceremony. This use of Sundays as '*Brit* Day' was also convenient for the guests who greatly enjoyed their pleasant social gatherings on their day of rest.

The event in question was the *brit* of Daniel Barenboim, the newborn son of two well-known musicians. In time, this infant would become a world-renowned child prodigy, who is today famous the world over as a pianist, conductor, and artistic director of important orchestras and opera houses. In keeping with age-old Jewish tradition, eight days after he was born, Daniel Barenboim was initiated into the Jewish faith. On that same occasion I was initiated into the Zionist life of my adopted city. Three hundred people attended the event, and I, of course, had no way of knowing just how important all these people were to be in my life. My first social contacts in South America were made at that celebration.

I have often been asked how it came about that a staunch Zionist such as myself remained in Argentina for over thirteen years. My standard response has been to refer my interlocutors to the bountiful fleshpots of Argentina. I usually speak of this jokingly, but there is a kernel of truth in every joke, and Argentina did indeed exert on all of us a kind of gravitational pull that was difficult to resist. The years just before our emigration to Israel were wonderful. I married Alice and we brought our two lovely daughters, Beatrix and Judy, into the world. Alice, better versed than me in the country's lifestyle, took to the social circles there like a fish to water. I gradually overcame the difficulties I encountered during my first few years there, and soon blended into the society. I loved Argentina, the Argentine people, and the Jewish community there. Through my involvement in Zionist activities I found my true place in the community and defined my life's goal.

My active involvement in Zionist affairs began in earnest in 1946. Together with Yoseph Mirelman and my brother Shimon, I did whatever I could for the Jewish Yishuv in Palestine in the last few years of the British Mandate. We contacted the Jewish Agency, which at that time was preparing the financial infrastructure for the 'state in the making'. Two years later, following the declaration of Israel's independence, we became deeply involved in providing aid to the young country in the difficult first years of its existence. We hoped and believed that we would be able to contribute to the fledgling state in our areas of expertise – business and finance.

In 1948 the entire Jewish population in Israel numbered only 600,000. But between 1949 and 1951, a great 'ingathering of the exiles' was carried out in massive airlift operations – Operation Magic Carpet from Yemen, On the Wings of Eagles from North Africa, Ezra and Nehemia from Iraq – all of which doubled and even tripled the Jewish population in Israel. Immigrant absorption was the call of the hour, and what this meant was the immediate creation of an industrial infrastructure that would create as many jobs as possible for the many thousands of new immigrants.

In 1946, then, Yoseph Mirelman initiated and headed the creation of a pioneer group of investors from Latin America: ARPALSA (Argentina – Palestine Sociedad Anonima). During that year, Mirelman travelled to Palestine, and, totally ignoring the bureaucratic machinery of the British Mandate, began looking for suitable investment opportunities to help support and develop local trade and industry. During his visit he was deeply impressed by what he learned about the activities of a group of American investors who had organized themselves under the title of the Palestine Economic Corporation (PEC). The group was headed by important leaders of the Jewish community in America, such as the Secretary of the Treasury, Henry Morgenthau, Supreme Court Justice Louis Brandeis, Robert Szold (Henrietta Szold's nephew), a member of the Zionist Executive, Jerome Swope, the founder and C.E.O. of General Electric, Julius Simon, and others. Among others, the PEC established the Union Bank and several industries, and purchased land in many different parts of the country. Dr Mirelman worked out an agreement between ARPALSA and PEC, according to which the two groups would cooperate fully in all their enterprises.

And indeed, ARPALSA's investments in Israel grew rapidly. As a third holding group, together with PEC and Discount Bank, we purchased land in Rishon le-Ziyyon and Holon in the Tel Aviv area, and further north in the Haifa Bay area. This latter acquisition was based on Zionist needs rather than hard-nosed business considerations. The Jewish Agency, which was regarded as 'the government in making' of the state to come, asked us to purchase the land in order to enable its Settlement Department to develop, under Jewish ownership, the open spaces between the sea and the Carmel Mountains overlooking Haifa Bay. Intensive building in these areas, it was reasoned, would ensure Jewish territorial contiguity in the Haifa area, and undermine the British plan to concentrate the Jewish population of Haifa halfway up the Carmel Mountains, in an area known as Hadar Ha-Carmel, leaving the area of the port and its surroundings to the Arabs. We went ahead and built rows of apartments and single homes in these suburbs north of Haifa. This would eventually prove to be a distinctly unprofitable investment, since the Tenant Protection Law enacted by the Knesset shortly after the establishment of the state was exceedingly favourable to the tenants, leaving the landlords with little or no profit. Nevertheless we never regretted our involvement in this project. We found consolation, as the Bible enjoins us, in the rebuilding of the country.

At the end of 1948, just after the establishment of the state of Israel, ARPALSA decided to look into further investment possibilities in the new country. We organized a mission, headed by Yoseph Mirelman and myself, and including over a dozen leading Jewish businessmen from Argentina. The difficulties of travelling to Israel in those times were daunting. As a result of the War of Independence, all commercial air connections to and from the country had been severed, and had not yet been restored. Only one airline, a Czech company, remained loyal to the isolated country, and sent a twin-engined passenger plane once a week from Rome to Israel with a stopover in Athens.

In December 1948 I travelled to Israel one week ahead of the group to arrange our itinerary. On my way I stopped in Europe to tend to some business which, as I found out unexpectedly, required an urgent and unplanned trip to France and Holland. This, in turn, forced me to cancel my reservations for the flight to Israel on the Czech airline from Rome that week. With the help of a Dutch friend who worked for KLM in Rome, I managed to secure a place on the next flight out, a week later. The aeroplane, a DC3, shuddered and creaked most suspiciously during the flight. The stewardess serving us was pale and frightened and could hardly hold back her tears. I couldn't help but ask her why she was crying. 'I shouldn't be telling you this,' she answered, her voice choked with tears, 'but last week's plane crashed, and the pilot, my fiancé, was killed.' I tried to comfort her, but at the same time I could not help thinking: Here I am, only twenty-nine years old, and once again I've been miraculously saved from death.

There were a few adventures in store for me on the way back to Argentina as well. Shortly before I was due to leave Israel, I read an article in the local English-language daily *The Palestine Post* (precursor of the present-day *Jerusalem Post*), about the first four-engined plane that would be making a direct flight from Israel to Rome without any stopovers. I contacted the newspaper and they put me in touch with an unknown airline company, where I was told that it was a charter flight operated by an airline called Trans Caribbean. I asked to be put on the flight scheduled for Wednesday of that same week. I was delighted to learn that there was a seat available on the plane, and hoped for a faster, safer and more comfortable flight than the one I had endured on the way to Israel, without the loss of time involved in the overnight stop at Athens. However, from the moment I stepped aboard the plane, I realized that someone had not told me the whole truth about this flight. First of all, it was most definitely *not* a civilian airliner. We were all crowded into two rows facing each other, just like the customary seating arrangement on military aircraft. Finally one of the passengers managed to discover the secret: this was one of the planes used to transport Jewish immigrants from Yemen in Operation Magic Carpet, and in order to make a profit on the return trip the company sold seats to innocent, unsuspecting passengers like myself. Never mind, I reasoned, the main thing is to avoid the annoying stopover in Athens and get to Rome in one piece. Not fifty minutes later the aircraft began shaking and spluttering, and a plume of smoke rose ominously from under one of the wings. A few minutes later we made a truly miraculous belly landing.

Frantically we checked ourselves for bruises and injuries, and tried to control our panic. We all wanted to escape from the grounded monster as soon as possible. Where had we landed? A sharp voice with an unmistakable British accent blared at us from the doorway: 'Do not get off this plane! This plane has made an emergency landing in Nicosia, Cyprus.' It was the commander of the airfield, who had boarded the aircraft wearing a British army uniform with RAF wings on his shirt front.

I was furious. 'Why shouldn't we leave?' I asked him angrily.

'Because you have just come from nowhere,' he replied archly.

'Israel is nowhere?' I asked this insufferably condescending British officer.

'Yes. We've never heard of it,' he replied and stalked out of the plane.

The aircraft needed repairs. One wheel had to be replaced and there was damage to other parts of the plane as well, all of which would take a day, a week, or even two. It was obvious that we would have to spend the night in Nicosia, a city even more dismal than Athens. I did not want to miss my connecting flight to Argentina. One of the other passengers on the plane was from Holland, and together we demanded to see the Dutch Consul in Cyprus, who eventually managed to release us from our forced detention the following day.

Despite the truly bizarre and sometimes frightening aspects of that incident, in the event I had no regrets about my forced landing in Cyprus in the least. This strange series of accidents was to provide me with a very special experience: a unique and memorable – the first of its kind – visit to the DP camps in Famagusta, where the British were holding Jews who had attempted to enter Palestine illegally. They had been intercepted by the British naval blockade that was attempting to seal off the country, and taken to Cyprus aboard unbearably crowded prison ships. I splashed through the mud around the tents, and spoke to the would-be immigrants, many of whom were quite young. Not long before this they had been refugees, 'Displaced Persons' in the official post-war terminology of the time. Now they were doing their best to maintain some semblance of orderly life in the camp. Babies were born, infants took their first steps, food was cooked, laundry was hung out to dry on makeshift clothes-lines, tailors mended clothes, and ironmongers turned sheets of metal into pots and pans. No one knew how long they would be forced to remain on the island (it was only after the camps were dismantled that I learned that some of them had stayed there for over a year), and despite the harsh winter, these people accepted their fate stoically. There was something very heroic and moving in their fortitude. I identified with them in the most profound – perhaps even tribal – way. Many of my long-held feelings of admiration for Churchill's country, Great Britain, faded after that visit, to be replaced by a burning rage over its callous treatment of refugees who had survived the death camps of Europe.

It is always the small, unusual and accidental events that remained etched in our memories. Among the tens of thousands of refugees at the camps I struck up a conversation with a young man from Romania. As we talked, it turned out that I knew his brother, who had emigrated to Argentina years earlier, and had worked in Yoseph Mirelman's firm. I knew that in Romania this young man had been regarded as a first-rate neuro-surgeon. I promised to give his brother his regards, and to notify his relatives in Israel of his expected arrival. A few months later I was pleased to learn that he had been accepted with open arms at the Beilinson Hospital in Petach Tikva. A short time afterwards, the father of my friend Mordechai Shneerson, the minister at the Israeli Embassy in Argentina, was diagnosed as suffering from a rare type of brain tumour. He was rushed to Israel, where he prepared himself for the worst. The operation was indeed very complicated, but Professor Ashkenazi, my acquaintance from the camp in Cyprus, performed the surgery with great skill, and my friend Shneerson's father survived the ordeal and lived to a ripe old age.

Our first visits to the country were most successful, and boded well for the additional trips we were planning. The rapid development of modern long-distance air travel brought Buenos Aires and Tel Aviv so much closer together that brief trips between the two countries became a matter of course. At that time there was little to see in the small country that was still licking its wounds after the War of Independence, but the air was full of hope. We were deeply gratified that we had the means and opportunity to make some of these hopes into a reality.

PIGLETS FOR ISRAEL

At the beginning of 1949 the first delegation of Israeli diplomats was sent to Latin America to set up an Israeli Embassy which would represent the state of Israel in all the countries of the region. Since Argentina had not yet officially recognized Israel, it was decided to set up the first embassy in Montevideo, the capital of Uruguay, a country that had supported and recognized the Jewish state from the very beginning. The diplomats included the ambassador, Ya'akov Tsur, the

minister and counsellor, Mordechai Shneerson, and the second secretary, Yitzhak Navon (later to become Israel's fifth President). It was
they who performed the ritual ceremony of attaching the *mezzuzah*
(lintel amulet) to the doorway of the new Israeli Embassy.

I have absolutely no doubt that this first meeting between the Israeli
diplomats and the Jewish community of South America has remained
indelibly engraved in their memories. The reception was held at the
beautiful resort town of Punta del Este, quite a distance from Montevideo. Mauricio Litman, a good friend of mine who was very active
in Jewish affairs in Argentina, suggested holding the function, and even
offered to host it at his country estate at Punta del Este. Mauricio was
the first president of the Israel-Latin America Chamber of Commerce
that I had set up, while I served as his vice-president. When he built
his magnificent home at Punta del Este in 1943, he invited me to come
for a visit and went on at some length about how he wanted to use it
for social and cultural events of a humanitarian nature. I was overwhelmed by the magnificent mansion, and was often invited there for
golf or tennis tournaments, or for foreign film festivals that Litman
hosted at the estate.

I couldn't have imagined a more spectacular setting for special events
of this kind. And indeed, that night, everything seemed perfect: top
chefs had been specially flown in from Buenos Aires to prepare the
meal; the atmosphere was wonderfully congenial; the guests were
resplendent in their evening clothes; and our beaming hosts couldn't
have been happier. And then the lights dimmed, the pianist struck up
an Israeli melody that touched our hearts to the core, and the waiters
strode in. Long lines of splendidly uniformed men in tails and white
gloves, carrying gold-plated platters with the specially prepared main
course of the evening: roast piglets, each delicately illuminated by
candles and gaily bedecked with blue and white Israeli flags...

A few months later, after Argentina officially recognized the state of
Israel, the Israeli legation moved to Buenos Aires, and officially opened
its doors to the public on 11 May 1949. At about the same time the
Argentine government invited an official trade mission from Israel to
come on a visit to Argentina. The mission included Ambassador Tsur,
the Plenipotentiary for Uruguay, Yitzhak Navon, and Yehudit Bergman,
an Israeli diplomat who proved to us yet again what a small world we

live in: her former name was Yehudit Fingerhut and we had met her aboard the ship en route to Argentina. She was the woman who had fled from Yugoslavia, and, while still at sea, had received word of her husband's death.

'YOU'LL BE COMING BACK TO ASK ME FOR MONEY'

The leaders of the young and impoverished country were inexperienced, but they made up in courage and humour for everything they lacked in experience. Israel's dire financial straits placed economic issues high on the list of national priorities. Prior to the establishment of the Bank of Israel, Bank Leumi, one of the oldest banking institutions in the country, was entrusted with all the important national monetary activities including printing bank-notes. The managing director of the bank was a pleasant and cultured religious Jew by the name of Dr Aharon Bart, who wrote books on philosophy in his spare time. One of these books, *Our Generation and Questions of Eternity*, was a very popular Bar Mitzvah present among religious Jews in Israel in the fifties. At a reception marking the issue of the first Israeli bank-notes, someone remarked to Dr Bart: 'There's nothing here to eat or drink, so why are you wearing a *kippah* [skullcap]? To bless the bank-notes?'

Unfazed, Dr Bart instantly replied, 'I'm wearing a *kippa* because right now my head is the only thing I'm certain that I can cover.'

During one of our visits to Israel, I requested a meeting with the country's first Minister of Finances, Eliezer Kaplan, and the Director-General of his office, David Horowitz (who later established the Bank of Israel and became its first governor). My mentor from the Zionist movement in Holland, Peretz Bernstein, who had recently been appointed Minister of Commerce and Industry in the first government of Israel, helped arrange the meeting. I held Dr Bernstein in the highest esteem. He had come to Holland from Germany and settled in Rotterdam, where he tried his hand at the tobacco business. However, his total devotion to Zionist affairs kept him away from his office so often that his business suffered. Whenever he was not actively involved in community affairs, he wrote articles for the Jewish press in Holland. When he came to Israel he used his years of journalistic experience in

Holland to found a daily newspaper called *Ha-Boker*, which was affiliated to the Liberal Party. His book, *Anti-Semitism as a Social Phenomenon*, is a classic, and, in my opinion, one of the best books ever written on the subject – a must for anyone attempting to understand the issues involved. I am particularly proud of the part I played in publishing the Hebrew edition of the book in Israel.

Bernstein was not well when I called him, but he ignored his illness and did whatever was necessary to arrange an immediate meeting for me with the Minister of Finance. In order to whet Eliezer Kaplan's curiosity, Bernstein told the minister that we were looking into the possibility of setting up several businesses in our area of expertise. When we met with the minister and his Director-General, we described our plans to them in detail: setting up industrial plants that would help alleviate unemployment in the country; earmarking most of their products for export; importing the raw materials for producing rayon – which is the basis for nylon, orlon and other materials – from abroad, for example from Argentina. We promised them that the DuPont Company, with which Dr Simon Mirelman had strong business connections, would supply the raw materials, while all other expenses would be covered by the anticipated profits.

My own personal proposal was very similar: I offered to set up a tanning business that would import its raw hides from Argentina. The finished products would be similar to those we were producing in Argentina, and they too would be earmarked primarily for export.

The minister listened impassively. 'The answer, I'm sorry to say, is no,' he said at the end of my brief presentation. 'What you are proposing is unrealistic,' the minister said. 'Israel will never become an industrial country because we have no raw materials or cheap labour.'

'But you will undoubtedly need industrial products, so what will you do – import everything you need?' I retorted.

'And when your businesses get into trouble,' said the minister with a somewhat accusatory edge to his voice, 'you'll come to me for help in purchasing foreign currency, and I don't have any! What can I do? I simply don't have any money!' Eliezer Kaplan raised his voice slightly on this last sentence. He was apparently convinced that, despite all our promises, some day we would come to him cap in hand begging him to bail us out. How was I to persuade him that this was simply not the case?

I was deeply disappointed, and made no effort to conceal my feelings. 'So we have come all this way just to have our proposals turned down?' I asked sharply. 'And our idea of creating jobs for new immigrants simply goes down the drain? That's it – nothing at all is going to come of our dream?'

Kaplan looked at us, his expression betraying his sympathy. He certainly appreciated our good intentions. I respected him, too, for his honesty and humanity. It was easy to see why he was among the best liked of Israel's political leaders, right across the party lines. It was difficult to be angry with him, even though at that moment we were at loggerheads. As for myself – as usual, I was certain that I was right.

'Look,' he said at last. 'Setting up industries here is a problem because we have no basic raw materials. But we do have three kinds of raw material that have hardly been exploited at all so far.' Here he paused for a moment and looked at us. 'If you can find some way to make use of them, I'll be more than willing to help.'

'What materials?' we asked in unison.

'Very simple: the triple S – Sand, Sea and Sun. These are Israel's real raw materials. If you are willing to help us develop tourism to Israel by building a hotel, I promise to provide you with whatever help you need. I am certain that Jewish tourists from all over the world will come in droves to visit the Jewish state. Industry has no future in Israel: tourism does.'

After thinking it over for a few minutes, we agreed. I shall return later on to the story of my unfortunate venture into the Israeli tourist trade.

THE STORY OF A DONATION

Our first step was to set up a company in Israel that would work directly with our company, ARPALSA. This was the ISAR (Israel-Argentina) company that I headed after my arrival in Israel. Although it was in every way a thoroughly commercial business, much of the work I did there was voluntary.

Doing voluntary work for good causes had become a way of life for me in Argentina. I was active in fundraising for the United Jewish

Appeal (UJA) and Israel Bonds. In many ways the UJA was set up along the existing lines of the Jewish National Fund and the bonds were an extension of Keren Hayesod. Both the state of Israel and those who purchased the bonds made a good deal: Israel received vitally needed foreign currency for its daily needs, and within a few years the bonds yielded their owners a fair interest on their investment.

I remember the celebration held at Simon Mirelman's elegant home on 1 May 1951, when the bonds' fundraising appeal was launched in Buenos Aires. Simon, the elder brother of the Mirelman tribe, and the uncrowned leader of the Jewish community, graciously agreed to sponsor the event and head the bonds sales; this following five years of devoted service as head of the UJA, and only after his fifth brother, Leon, (better known as Bubby) agreed to replace him in that organization. In honour of the occasion, Dr Joseph Burg, the Minister of Posts in Ben Gurion's government, was sent over to represent Israel. In his own unique fashion, he spoke with a great deal of wit and humour, opening both hearts and wallets. Simon Mirelman spoke in praise of the bonds, which, he said, were not merely a donation. The purchasers' capital and interest were insured by the Treasury, while in the meantime the funds were put to use in developing the young state of Israel. He then turned to the audience and addressed the invited guests directly: 'Who will be the first to buy Israel Bonds?' Meir Mirelman, the grandfather of the Mirelman tribe, rose at the back of the hall, and said in a loud and clear voice: 'I will!' He quoted a very generous sum, which provided the fundraising event with an impressive opening bid.

A collective gasp rose from the direction of the Mirelman brothers. 'Father,' the eldest of the sons, said, 'do you have any idea when these bonds mature?'

'Yes, my son,' the old man replied, 'in fifteen years. *Nu*,' he added with a sigh, 'that leaves me with plenty of time.'

Old man Mirelman was then already nearly eighty years old. Fifteen years later I was present when he personally received the proceeds from the bonds he purchased on that evening – a very old man but still in full possession of his faculties.

One of the tasks I was asked to take upon myself by the head of the Jewish community in Buenos Aires was to find people who would be willing to donate money in support of the state of Israel. I could fill volumes with the stories of all the fascinating meetings I have had with Jewish philanthropists and donors over the years. At that time, in the late forties, I primarily targeted Jewish refugees from Central and Western Europe. I understood the mentality of these people, spoke their languages and knew how to approach them. It was for that reason that I vividly recall how disappointed I was when a very wealthy man of Dutch origin turned me down. He was one of the biggest cotton traders in the world, and in Argentina had bought up most of the stock of a well-known banking institution. The most he was willing to contribute to Israel was 500 pesos (the equivalent of about $125). Given his extremely prosperous financial situation, I felt that this was an insult rather than a donation, and I made no secret of my feelings. 'You have no right to determine the size of my contribution,' the man hissed between clenched teeth.

I maintained my composure even though inside I was boiling. I told him as calmly as I could that I had been taught never to refuse a donation, however small. But then I added: 'The day will come when you too will learn how important Israel is for you and for Jews all over the world, and then you'll regret what you did today.'

Twenty years later I came to Buenos Aires with the Israeli Minister of finance, Pinhas Sapir. We had left Israel at a particularly tense moment in the country's history: it was 4 June 1967, at the height of the events that eventually led up to the Six-Day War, and just two days before the war actually began.

'Someone has called for you twice, and is looking for you desperately. He wants you to call him back the moment you get in.' That was how the Israeli ambassador to Argentina greeted me as we arrived. I asked for the man's name and telephone number, and it turned out to be the same wealthy gentleman who had refused to donate anything significant to Israel so many years before. I was mildly surprised, and quickly calculated that he must be well over eighty.

At the elderly gentleman's request I invited him to the embassy. As soon as he sat down, he turned to me and said, 'Do you remember telling me twenty years ago how the day would come when I would regret giving you such a meagre contribution? You were right! Now that the state of Israel is in real danger, I understand that if, God forbid, something happens to that country, it'll be the end of us all.' He produced a cheque book and a gold-plated pen. 'I don't want to keep you long,' he said. 'I am writing a cheque for one hundred and twenty-five thousand dollars made out to the state of Israel. When you get to Europe in a month's time, there will be an identical cheque waiting for you at my office.' Two hundred and fifty thousand dollars! That was a vast sum! In my heart of hearts I savoured my moral victory as well. Nevertheless, I could not help but admire the man, who was willing to admit his mistake and make an impressive attempt to correct it. This was not the last contribution this man made to Israel. He helped establish a number of important institutions in the country and con-tributed generously to many worthy causes up to the time of his death. Happily, his children have followed in his footsteps in this respect.

Had I but time enough and space, I could add many other stories of unusual donations and donors. I suppose if my life had been more conventional I would never have become acquainted with the many faces of the people who made up the Jewish community in Argentina. I got to know them intimately through my Zionist work, and found them fascinating. Many of these Jews appeared to have simply imported their previous lifestyles from Warsaw, Lodz or Plonsk, to Argentina. They continued speaking Yiddish just as they had done in Europe, and remained loyal to their non-Zionist, 'Bundist' orientation (so-called after the anti-Zionist Socialist Party, the Bund, first established in 1897 and very active in Poland up to the Second World War). In 1944, at the best of the three Yiddish-speaking theatres in Buenos Aires, the actors sang: '*Yossel, ti es noch a mol.*' ('Yossel, do it again.') Yossel was the Jewish nickname for Joseph Stalin; and while I too was very happy about the Red Army's victories over the Nazis, I felt that the audiences' enthusiasm was somewhat excessive. Judging by their excitement, Stalin – the 'Sun of the Nations' – was their hero, and it was only by sheer accident that they weren't wearing his uniform and fighting on the battlefield under his banner.

At the beginning of the fifties I was given another opportunity to discover how deeply Communism still held many of Argentina's Jews in thrall. I met a Jew from Poland who was the leading importer of false teeth from Israel to Argentina. His purchases through ARPALSA ran into many thousands of dollars and were regarded as quite substantial. In the course of our mutual business contacts we became rather close, and when he told me that he intended taking his family and returning to Poland, I was dumbstruck. Since I truly liked him, I tried to dissuade him, but to no avail: the man was convinced that he belonged in his native country. 'And what will you do with all your money?' I asked him. In my estimation, he had amassed a small fortune in Argentina, and was a wealthy man, certainly by the standards of any Communist country.

'I'll take the money with me,' he replied. 'My country needs the money, and perhaps I will need some of it too.'

I tried to tell him that in a Communist country his money would be of no use to him. To this day I don't know how or why he allowed me to persuade him to leave a large part of his assets to the state of Israel. 'If life in Poland turns out to be unsuitable, in five years' time you can get back everything you have given to the state plus interest,' I promised him.

Simon Mirelman, head of the UJA in Buenos Aires, added: 'If we don't hear from you by the end of five years, then and only then will we regard that sum as a contribution to the state of Israel.' After all the details were worked out to everyone's satisfaction, we set it all down in writing.

Somewhat naïvely, all three of us believed that this story would have a happy ending. In fact, once my friend disappeared behind the Iron Curtain, he was never heard from again. Nowadays, when the crimes committed by the Socialist 'Utopia' are common knowledge, it is obvious that by deciding to go back to Poland he signed his own death warrant. Perhaps the money he took with him to Poland marked him as an 'international imperialist agent' and as such an enemy of the régime. From time to time I think about him with great sadness.

GAUCHO BOOTS INSTEAD OF A LAWYER'S ROBE

In addition to the die-hard Communists and the Bundists, both of whom revered 'the Sun of the Nations', Joseph Stalin, I also became acquainted with the descendants of the first Jewish settlers in Argentina.

These were the most impressive and most intriguing of all the groups that comprised the Jewish community. Their forefathers were brought out to Argentina by Baron Moses de Hirsch at the end of the nineteenth century, at the same time as the first Zionist pioneers, the Bilu-im (an acronym of *beit yisrael le-chu ve-nelcha* – 'the House of Israel, go forth and we shall follow'), and the pioneers of the First *Aliya* set out for Palestine. Most of these people had been very poor in their native countries, and from a distance Argentina seemed to them like a land of plenty. Upon their arrival they were taken to remote settlements, thousands of kilometres from Buenos Aires, in God-forsaken agricultural areas. The baron's people tried to turn these peddlars and *luftmenschen* ('people who live on air', inhabitants of Jewish villages in Eastern Europe who lived off charity or makeshift employment) into professional farmers. But lacking any true motivation or adequate training, and without the slightest inclination on the part of these émigrés towards tilling the land, this romantic notion of the new Jewish farmer soon dissipated. All that was left was the harsh daily reality, the Sisyphean toiling in the sun, which blistered their hands, bent their backs, and yielded pitifully poor crops.

These frustrated first-generation farmers had one overriding goal in life: to protect their children from a similar fate. And indeed, the sons and daughters of these first settlers soon found their way to the universities, many of them making names for themselves in their chosen professions – medicine, law and the like. I was amazed to discover that, unlike their parents, some of these young people yearned for a life closer to nature after having been cut off from it by their parents at an early age. They fulfilled their love of the land by buying estates in rural areas. It was strange to find these cultured Jewish gentlemen exchanging their lawyers' robes for *gaucho* boots and broad-brimmed hats, and their shiny limousines for dusty Jeeps. Some of them imported stud bulls from Scotland and top-grade black and white milk cows from Holland. So devoted were they to their work that they garnered many international prizes for the quality of their cattle.

By a strange twist of fate, these descendants of the first settlers made Baron de Hirsch's dream of Jewish agricultural a reality. However, despite my admiration for these people, it was a dream that never particularly fired my imagination. In the contest between the two great

Jewish philanthropists of the nineteenth century, Baron de Hirsch and the Baron de Rothschild, I always favoured the latter, who became known in Palestine as Ha-Nadiv Ha-Yadua – the Famous Philanthropist.

The generation of founding fathers of the Argentine Jewish colony was strongly connected to the Jewish heritage that had been so central to their upbringing in Europe. Some of them were true *talmidei hachamim* – Talmudic scholars – who were well versed in Jewish thought and enjoyed studying the Talmud whenever they had the time. Their sons, forty- to sixty-year-olds in the 1940s, had not been exposed to Jewish tradition in the same way. In Buenos Aires, the educational centre of Argentina, these second-generation settlers underwent a transformation that distanced them from Judaism and caused many of them to assimilate into the non-Jewish culture of the country. They lost virtually all contact with the fundamental values of their forefathers, such as traditional Judaism and the Hebrew language. Nevertheless, I was convinced that if I looked hard enough I would rediscover in each of them a Jewish heart, and I set about looking for ways to contact them and interest them in contributing to Israel. We scanned the registers for names and addresses, and approached them all, one by one, suggesting that they join in the wonderful adventure of helping to create the Jewish state – and they did indeed contribute. The sums of money we raised were somewhat smaller than those raised among the Jews of America, for example, but in this context it is important to note that in Argentina such contributions were not tax-deductible.

'THE CLERICS' AND OVERWEENING GREED

Those early days of the state-in-the-making opened up for me yet another area of activity on Israel's behalf. Herman Hollander, a close friend of mine, was a senior official in the Jewish Agency. His father, Julius Hollander, had emigrated from Hamburg, in Germany, to Sweden, and was one of my father's biggest competitors, which of course never deterred him from staying with us and enjoying my mother's kosher cooking every time he visited his company's offices in Amsterdam. His brother, Fritz Hollander, who also lived in Sweden, was a good friend of mine as well. When the Nazis came to power in Germany, Herman Hollander emigrated to America, where he became one of the leaders of the religious Mizrahi movement. He might have spent the rest of his days there, realizing his Zionist aspirations from afar, had it not been for the fact that in 1948 the newly appointed Israeli Minister of Commerce and Industry, Peretz Bernstein, asked him to come to Israel and take up the post of Director-General of his ministry. Hollander could not turn down this request, so he packed his bags and emigrated once again – this time to Israel, at a time when emigration from the United States to Israel was virtually non-existent. Being a wealthy man, Hollander accepted the position at a token salary. It was no wonder, then, that everyone treated him with such great respect. I was among those who held him in the highest esteem, and after I emigrated to Israel, he was a role model that I tried to emulate. Since Peretz Bernstein preferred to spend time on other matters, such as literature and politics, Hollander soon became the supreme authority in the Ministry of Commerce and Industry.

Prior to his emigration to Israel, we used to meet, Hollander and I, at least three times a year, when he came on his frequent trips to Buenos Aires to purchase hides and leather. As a result he became very familiar with the social fabric of Argentine Jewry. He knew me well as a friend, a rival in the trade, and a tough – but fair – opponent. He also knew that of all the people he had met in the Jewish community of Buenos Aires, I was the one who could 'deliver the goods'. On his last visit before emigrating to Israel, he came looking for different products: this time what he was seeking was a supply of meat for the citizens of Israel. Meat exports to the new country had been drastically reduced after Israel's traditional suppliers, Imperial Packers and Cold Storage of South Africa, joined the embargo imposed by the British Empire on what they regarded as an upstart little country. The embargo and naval blockade imposed by the British navy made it impossible for ships to dock at Haifa or Akko (Acre). Even after the end of the Mandate, the British Empire continued to obstruct the development of the struggling young country, and shortages and economic problems did indeed threaten its very existence.

Argentina came through in this crisis with flying colours. As I see it, the Argentine government's readiness to supply Israel with meat in those early days of its existence deserves the highest praise. During the transfer of power from the British Mandate to the provisional government of Israel, Argentina simply ignored the British embargo and sent a ship packed with meat products to Israel's shores. The first captain who ran the blockade aboard the *Rio Gallegos* undoubtedly earned himself a place of honour in Israel's history.

But beyond these pioneering efforts a regular supply route had to be established between Argentina and Israel. Herman Hollander brought to my attention the potential of the Argentine merchant marine fleet. 'If you can persuade them to run the blockade, we can build solid economic relations based on the supply of kosher meat, supervised by the Chief Rabbinate of Argentina. Once that precedent is set, we can go on and purchase other goods from Argentina,' he said, adding a tempting morsel of bait to make sure I would bite.

Our work was now cut out for us. The first order of business was to win over the people running Argentina's shipping companies. One of ARPALSA's board members was on friendly terms with a high-ranking admiral in the Argentine navy. We persuaded him to run the blockade once again, and a large shipment of meat soon arrived safely in Israel, deep in the bowels of the sister ship *Rio Gualegaychu*.

Following the success of this venture, I asked Herman Hollander, as the representative of the Ministry of Commerce and Industry, to provide us with a document that would attest to the fact that ARPALSA had been officially recognized by the government of Israel as a shipping agent for goods to Israel. There had already been quite a few expenses that we had covered with our own money, and this letter would help us in our negotiations with the authorities. The reply we received, under the official letterhead of the Ministry of Commerce and Industry, was addressed to José (Yoseph) Mirelman, and was worded very politely but also very vaguely. I understood from the tone of the letter that the Israeli government was not willing to commit itself totally to our company simply because we pioneered the contacts. Nevertheless, for the time being, this letter was sufficient; it was, at the very least, an official document that we could certainly present to the Argentine authorities. And yet, as I was to learn from personal experience in Israel over and over again, a gentleman's agreement is never enough, even among friends.

The heady euphoria that we all experienced at the birth of the state soon dissipated, and as the representative of ARPALSA (and not as a private businessman looking for a profit), I was left with the responsibility for the meat trade between the two countries. It was not all smooth sailing. I look back on the ten years that I dealt with this issue with neither nostalgia nor particular satisfaction. As a matter of fact I was left, rather, with memories of frustration and anxiety. Most of all, I underwent a complete change of heart concerning Israel's 'clerical' bureaucracy: the rabbis, *shochtim* (men responsible for ritual slaughter), and supervisors of various kinds, with songs of praise for God and *kashrut* ('kosherness') on their tongues, and nothing but greed in their hearts.

The rabbis in Argentina were not much better. Predictably, cooperation with them was arduous, and nothing came as easily as we had expected. The ever-spiralling wage demands, from one shipment to the next, were outrageous and exasperating. And yet, somehow we managed to overcome all the obstacles. Everything we did was on a non-profit basis, and the company covered its expenses with help from the community. On orders from Peron himself, some of the Argentine export regulations were overlooked – to our benefit. The Peronist authorities were very appreciative of the fact that we took nothing either for the company or for ourselves in these transactions, and the community thus enjoyed a substantial saving in foreign currency expenses.

One of my most unforgettable meetings with Peron took place in connection with our financial agreements. Leaning back comfortably in his chair, he said, 'You know, the only reason the Arabs are fighting against you is because they're hungry. What do you say to the idea of your buying wheat, meat, and other foodstuffs from us, and shipping it all to them by sea?'

'But, *Senor Presidente*, where will we find the money to buy food for millions of Arabs?' I asked, barely able to conceal my astonishment.

He laughed, dismissing my response with a wave of his hand: 'Don't try to play the innocent with me! The newspapers all say that you people control world industry, and that the Jews control Wall Street.'

I was quite taken aback. What could I say? That it wasn't true? That this theory had already been expounded at length in the infamous

'Protocols of the Elders of Zion'? The President was drawing upon the same old preconceptions that fuelled the anti-Semitism of dictators and peasants alike all over the world. Luckily, Peron did not hate the Jews. On the contrary, he rather admired them. Strangely enough, he believed quite ingenuously that the Jews wielded the power and influence of a superpower, albeit a secret one. 'Hitler was a fool! If only he had used the Jews on his side, he would have controlled the world today,' he said. None of my explanations – about Nazism's inherent anti-Semitism, or the fact that Hitler waged a satanic war against the Jews simply because they were Jewish – made the slightest dent in his theory. Peron was simply incapable of seeing things any differently.

11

OFFICIAL BUSINESS BETWEEN ARGENTINA AND ISRAEL

In 1949 the Economic Planning Department of Israel's Foreign Ministry appointed me a member of the committee set up to promote economic ties between Israel and Argentina. The ambassador-designate to Argentina, Ya'akov Tsur, the Economic Attaché, Dr Mordechai Shneerson, and the Director-General of the Ministry of Commerce and Industry, Herman Hollander, came to Buenos Aires to look into the possibility of setting up formal economic ties between our two countries. Clearly, my Zionist activities and extensive business contacts with Israel had a great deal to do with my appointment. My knowledge of English, Spanish and Hebrew gave me a considerable advantage as well, and in effect made me a central figure on the committee. A translator can be a very important mediator in certain circumstances, as we shall see.

Both countries were equally eager for the talks to succeed. It was only natural for the newly established state of Israel to be interested in setting up a firm and stable economic infrastructure, and this required strong foreign trade. The country was desperately in need of imported goods, specifically meat products, which were in plentiful supply in Argentina. What was Argentina's interest in all this? It's difficult for me to say. Perhaps it was Peron's superstitious belief in this insidious and all-embracing influence of the Jews on world affairs. Or perhaps it was his feeling that Israel could become a lucrative trading partner in the near future. One way or another, Argentina, which had voted in favour of the UN Partition Plan, and had thus helped in the creation of the state of Israel, treated the young country as a parent might treat a toddler who must be taught how to walk. Initially, the atmosphere at the negotiating table was friendly, with a great deal of goodwill on both sides, and I enjoyed being a part of it all. It was an opportunity for me to expand my horizons and bring some benefit to both countries: Argentina, which had given me a warm home; and Israel, my home of the future.

Leading government ministers represented Argentina at the talks: the Minister of Finance, Ramon Cereigo, and the Minister of Commerce, Roberto Ares. Senior officials from both sides examined the technical aspects of the contracts. Whenever we reached an impasse, President Peron was brought into the picture. We had several crucial meetings with him, and when the time came to reach conclusions and make binding decisions, we turned to Evita. Even though she was not a member of the cabinet, she had a powerful influence on the outcome of all negotiations.

We were not talking about a large volume of trade and, looking back, the disparity between Israel's needs and its ability at that time to pay for them, either in cash or in export products, seems to me somewhat absurd. What could the fledgling Israeli economy offer a country like Argentina? Burners for Primus stoves, false teeth and some citrus fruit. The latter was the most attractive because it meant that Argentina would have a supply of citrus fruit during its summer season – the height of winter, and of the citrus season, in Israel. Israel, on the other hand, needed a constant and growing supply of beef. There were also technical problems we had to overcome in order to ensure a steady supply. The refrigerated ships used for citrus exports were not always suited for shipping meat. However, the real importance of the talks lay not only in their practical outcome, but also in their potential for developing mutual trade in the future. Israel was the poor relation, which had to be treated with a measure of kindness and a great deal of patience. The question was, how long would this be the case? In July 1995 I spoke to the Argentine Foreign Minister, Dr Di Tella, at Tel Aviv University while he was on a visit to Israel. It was nearly fifty years after those difficult early years, and here we were discussing once again the importance of expanding trade between the two countries, but at issue now were computers, high-tech products, and industrial know-how. We had certainly come a long way from Primus stoves and false teeth . . .

Any negotiation process between people, companies or countries is, in the final analysis – once we go beyond official protocol and the careful choice of words – a relationship between individuals. History is replete with stories of personal animosity between leaders, which produced disastrous results for their respective countries. On the other hand, important mutual projects between nations have on occasion been greatly enhanced by 'good chemistry' between national leaders. The issues we were dealing with in the trade negotiations between Israel and Argentina were not of major national importance for either country. Nevertheless, they too stalled at times simply because of a lack of 'chemistry' between the negotiators. The Argentine Minister of Finance, a thoroughly unpleasant man, and our own Herman Hollander, a stubborn man in his own right who did not give ground easily, faced off against each other like butting goats. In these situations, it was always Evita who eventually managed to soothe frayed nerves and flaring tempers. I remember that on one occasion we asked to come and see her when it was close to midnight. When we arrived we found her surrounded by the kind of people whose company she particularly enjoyed: authors and poets, actors, artists and several admirers from government circles. She was dressed in an elegant gown, with a profusion of expensive jewellery adorning her arms, fingers, throat and earlobes.

Despite all her efforts to minimize the conflict, Evita was very much aware of the continuing animosity between Hollander and Cereijo. 'You don't really like my minister, do you?' Evita asked Hollander at some point with a small smile. I was afraid that an explosion of some kind was imminent, and tried to ease the tension by phrasing the question less bluntly in my translation into Hebrew. But some things need no translation, and Hollander, impulsive and easily angered, understood Evita Peron's question very clearly. The sour look on his face did not go unnoticed by the Argentine minister, and from that day on he was never again seen at the talks. As for Hollander, some time before the conclusion of negotiations he returned home to Israel for some undisclosed reason, and it was only Evita's charismatic intervention that eventually brought the talks to a successful conclusion. The first trade pact between the two countries was signed at an official ceremony attended by the Israeli ambassador, Ya'akov Tsur, the Economic Attaché, Mordechai Shneerson, my friend the general manager of the Holland Bank in Buenos Aires, Dr Baruch, and myself.

The events of that evening have remained imprinted on my memory like scenes from a film. President Peron and his ministers waited for Evita to arrive, and she eventually appeared in a simple but superbly regal outfit. I could not help but notice how pale she was, a fact that even her make-up could not disguise. The Argentine ruler and our ambassador signed the documents, and shook hands. *Maté* – a non-alcoholic Argentine herb tea – was served in silver cups, and Peron praised the medicinal properties of the local drink, bragging that whiskey or gin, drinks distinctly reminiscent of the hated Americans, would never be served at Casa Rosada, the presidential palace.

The deathly pallor of Evita's cheeks was indeed a clear indication of the terminal state of her illness. In 1952, three years later, Evita Peron died after a lengthy and agonizing battle with cancer. I still have a vivid recollection of her funeral, which was shown over and over again in the cinema newsreels. Through the transparent cover of the coffin in which she was borne to her final resting-place, we could see the full beauty of her angelic and delicate features. Masses of people thronged the pavements and streets, casting flowers at the receding hearse.

The story of Evita's death also had its Jewish angle. Immediately following her death, when Juan Peron was inundated with condolences and expressions of sympathy, the Chief Rabbi of Buenos Aires, Rabbi Amram Blum, found a unique way to the grieving President's heart. Together with Peron he recited *Kaddish*, the traditional Jewish prayer for the dead, for the everlasting life of his beloved's spirit. The Jewish words of acquiescence to God's will, translated and explained, brought tears to the President's eyes. Rabbi Blum soon became a close advisor to the ruler. The Gitter family found the rabbi's new status rather amusing. For us he had always been the religious *shaliach*, the emissary from Israel, the man who ate at my parents' table for many years for lack of proper kosher restaurants in the bustling metropolis. We had always found him to be a great busybody, this rabbi of ours, as he tried to preach to us about returning to strict religious observance. When Peron fled the country, the Chief Rabbi followed in his wake, never to return. I was told that he died a few years ago after serving as a rabbi in Hollywood.

'DON'T TALK NONSENSE!'

I recall a number of stories that demonstrate Juan Peron's support for the state of Israel. One day in 1952 our embassy received word that the government of Argentina had donated 1,000 tons of wheat to Syria through the Evita Peron Foundation. In fact, as we later found out, it was not strictly speaking a gift, but rather a consignment of wheat sold to Syria at a considerably reduced price. Ambassador Tsur and I requested a meeting with the President to discuss the matter. We told Peron that in all fairness, Israel should be given the same kind of 'gift'. 'Of course you should,' the President agreed with a bright smile. 'I am a friend of both countries.'

As we were sitting there, I suddenly had an idea, which, of course, I had not had time to discuss with Tsur. With wheat shipments from the United States and Canada covering all the shortfalls of local production, Israel had no shortage of grains. I therefore asked the President if he would be willing to consider providing Israel with finished products from other Argentine industries, such as timber, wool and leather, among others. This way, I said enthusiastically, quite carried away by my moment of inspiration, Israel would get to know Argentina not only as an agricultural country but as an industrial giant as well, and the rapidly expanding Israeli population would eventually become a good client for Argentine industrial products.

It seemed to me that Peron was quite impressed by my proposal, but Ya'akov Tsur was profoundly embarrassed. He was convinced that I had just ruined any possibility of obtaining the wheat grant and had stirred up a diplomatic scandal into the bargain. What was more – and worst of all – I had made it possible for the Syrians to receive a great deal more from Argentina than Israel, and perhaps – who knows? – even opened the door for the Syrians right into Peron's heart. 'Give me a little credit,' I whispered to Tsur. The ultimate value of the deal that eventually went through was significantly higher than Peron's original offer. Not only that, but the consignment of 1,000 tons of wheat was still given to us at a greatly reduced price. In short, Israel profited from every aspect of the transaction.

I can still recall the tension that surrounded another round of talks we held at that time. In those days, Argentina was the principal supplier of meat to many countries around the world, among them Belgium, Switzerland, Holland and Germany. Argentina's largest client for meat products was the United Kingdom, which imported a total of 300,000 tons of meat annually. All meat exports from Argentina were handled by a company called IAPI, which charged a seven to ten per cent handling charge for all exports they handled for the Argentine government. Naturally, local producers did not like this form of taxation, because it forced them either to absorb the extra costs or to raise prices at the consumer end. At that time, Israel made purchases of up to 2,000–3,000 tons of frozen meat from Argentina, according to the terms of a standing contract that was renewed every few months. Up until then, the largest quantity of meat Israel had ever purchased from Argentina at any one time was 5,000 tons, and it was regarded as such an unusually large one-time purchase that it required the approval of the Finance Committee of Israel's parliament, the Knesset.

Trade relations between Argentina and Britain had deteriorated steadily by that time, and a confrontation appeared to be inevitable. Using its leverage as the largest buyer of Argentine beef, the UK demanded to be allowed to set the prices, while the Argentines, true to their fiery Latin temperament, were quite willing to throw the entire deal back in the Britons' face. The Minister of the Economy, Miranda, put it very clearly: 'I prefer selling to ten other countries at our prices than giving in to the prices the British want to dictate to us!' I knew nothing about this affair until I returned home late one evening and Alice told me that the Director of IAPI was looking for me urgently and wanted me to call him immediately. We were good friends, and when he asked to see me without delay, I took a brief nap to refresh myself and then set out in the middle of the night to see him. He told me that at eleven a.m. the following morning a British delegation was supposed to come to see him to put the finishing touches to their gigantic annual beef purchase. To avoid caving in to their pressure on price, would I be willing, he asked me, to undertake the purchase of one-tenth of the total consignment – 30,000 tons of beef – at $100 million on behalf of the state of Israel? He went on to say that Argentina would be most grateful if Israel would help Argentina in this way.

'That's not so easy,' I replied quickly. 'I cannot possibly undertake such a commitment without the approval of the ambassador. And he too will not be able to make a move without the approval of the Israeli Minister of Agriculture and the Knesset Finance Committee. And the chances that the Minister of Agriculture, Pinhas Lavon, the Minister of Finance, Levi Eshkol, and the Minister of Commerce and Industry, Pinhas Sapir, will all agree to such an enormous outlay of foreign currency seem very slim indeed.'

The minister went over to his desk, opened a drawer, took out a letter and handed it to me. I read the letter carefully. 'And after reading that, do you still think there is no chance?' It was an official letter from the government of Argentina, promising us the freedom to cancel the entire deal or parts of it, at any time, without any explanation. 'Yes, this does indeed change the entire picture,' I said. 'But give me a couple of hours to think it over.' It was now two a.m. and I promised to get back to the minister before five o'clock in the morning. I walked over to the embassy building. The counsellor was not there, and the ambassador, after I managed to wake him up, was somewhat confused. Finally he said to me, 'Do what you think is best. But if you do sign the deal, you had better be prepared to back up your decision before the Knesset Finance Committee.'

I knew that I had gone too far, that this entire proposition was a bit crazy, but I had always been attracted to high-risk adventures of this sort. I crossed the street and went into the IAPI offices once again to sign the contract. The minister smiled and handed me the signed letter of annulment as though he were providing me with an insurance policy. I once again returned to the embassy. Mordechai Shneerson and I drafted a cable to the Minister of Agriculture, detailing the deal. Within hours we received Pinhas Lavon's irate answer, severely reprimanding me and demanding that I come to Israel at once to explain my actions.

The following day I took off on a forty-hour flight to Tel Aviv via Rio de Janeiro, Lisbon, Amsterdam and Rome. My first stop was at the offices of the Inspector of Food, Dr Picker. I had met him once before when he was one of former Minister Dov Joseph's advisors. In that capacity, he was one of the officials charged with implementing the Austerity Plan designed by Dov Joseph to shore up the country's shaky economy in the state's first few years. Everyone who knew Picker, myself included, liked him and admired his mild-mannered ways. We both spoke the language of commerce, and our business connections brought us closer. Without offering his own opinion about the uproar I had created, he told me that the minister was furious, and was expecting us both in his office immediately.

Minister Lavon did not seem overly keen to meet me. First he let me cool my heels in his secretary's office, and then I was called in and forced to listen to a veritable torrent of reprimands. According to Lavon I had virtually committed a crime. He promised that he would turn heaven and earth to cancel the catastrophic agreement I had signed. At that point I pulled out my 'alibi': the letter of annulment. 'The Argentine government will call off the deal at any time we ask them to do so,' I said in my defence. 'After all, they only wanted to use this sale to us and to nine other countries as a ploy against the British, so that Britain wouldn't believe Argentina was in their back pocket. And if you endorse this contract,' I went on, 'we will only have to abide by the terms of the agreement as long as we can actually afford it. It's an unbelievably low price,' I insisted. 'Only thirty cents per kilo – that's next to nothing! It isn't as though we've signed away our lives here, and we should take advantage of the opportunity.'

'Don't talk nonsense!' the minister retorted, raising his voice. 'Have you lost your mind, or what? This letter is a joke. If we call off the deal, Argentina will sever diplomatic relations with us!' I refused to be drawn into his overheated rhetoric. Lavon was a labour leader and a seasoned politician, but in matters relating to international trade and business he was a rank amateur. Herman Hollander, who was a member of the Finance Committee, tried to give me some hope when, in a private conversation, he said to me: 'What a shame I never got wind of a deal like that when I was in business for myself.' After this initial onslaught by the minister, I was more than a little concerned about my meeting with the rest of the members of the Finance committee.

The committee met in due course, and, before hearing a word about the letter of annulment, voted against the deal. I chose my moment carefully and then, like a conjurer, produced the letter. In the light of this crucial piece of information, the atmosphere in the committee changed, and suddenly the deal did not seem like such a bad idea after all. Even Lavon showed some signs of having second thoughts, and asked me rather hesitantly, 'And what if Argentina suddenly decides to raise its prices?' I told him that I knew Argentina at least as well as he knew Israel, and that it had its own strong code of ethics, so that no matter what happens, even if governments rise and fall, any Argentine government will always honour the commitments of its predecessors. Eventually the deal was approved, albeit with great reservations, and those 30,000 tons of beef eventually made their way to Israel over a period of three years. The deal eventually turned out to be even better than we had dared to imagine: towards the end of this three-year period, prices of Argentine beef on the world markets rose considerably, but, just as I had promised, the Argentine government honoured its side of the bargain, and every consignment that was still part of the original agreement was shipped to Israel at the original contract price.

PURE AS THE DRIVEN SNOW

Thinking back now to the 'Beef Affair', and to other, similar incidents, I cannot help but wonder where I had acquired the relentless – Israeli-style – confidence that everything would turn out all right in the end. I don't really have a good answer to that question. But my memories of politicians and businessmen, and my 'victories' over them, pale before the recollections I have of my confrontations with the Chief Rabbinate. Unlike some of my clashes with politicians, I never managed to win a single round against the rabbis. In fact, I wandered into the combat zone of religious bureaucracy unwittingly and ill-advisedly. At issue, in the case of the beef sales, were the slaughtering procedures approved by the Chief Rabbinate of Argentina, which were not considered kosher enough by the Chief Rabbinate in Israel. Perplexed, I asked my father, who reminded me that the long and complex history of the Jewish people has been rife with similar acrimonious conflicts on religious issues. For example, he told me, at one time the local rabbinate of Hamburg in Germany banned all the kosher meat prepared by *shechita* (ritual slaughter) in the neighbouring Jewish community of Altona across the River Elbe, and the local rabbinate of Altona responded in kind. What was behind these clashes over *kashrut* – ostensibly waged in God's name – were powerful economic and political interests.

A large refrigerated meat ship was about to set sail from Argentina to Israel with 3,000 tons of frozen beef in its holds. An irate *mashgiach* (*kashrut* inspector) was standing on the dock, adamant in his refusal to give the shipment the kosher stamp of approval. No wonder, then, that Dr Picker cabled me once again in a panic – 'Come quickly, we have a problem!' – and once again I set out, this time for a most unusual meeting at the Jerusalem home of the Chief Rabbi of Israel, Yitzhak Halevi Herzog.

Rabbi Herzog was a truly great man. Before coming to Israel he had been the Chief Rabbi of Ireland, and was endowed with that unique combination of *Toreh ve-derekh eretz* – religious scholarship and courtesy – that I had learned to respect from childhood. Surrounded by some of his aides and accompanied by his son, Ya'akov, who served as his secretary at that time, the rabbi seemed rather angry when he asked me why I was defending the *shechita* in Argentina. I explained to him that bringing over *shochtim* or *kashrut* inspectors from Israel to Argentina would cost money, and either the government or the consumers in Israel would have to foot the bill. The rabbi responded cuttingly but with typical British courtesy: 'If you are so worried about the state of Israel's financial situation, why don't you cut your percentage of the profits?'

The blood rushed to my head, and if I hadn't reminded myself – just in time – whom I was speaking to, I would have exploded. I checked my rage and began to speak in a low voice, 'Like many others, the Honourable Rabbi is perhaps not aware of the way things are done in the Jewish community of Argentina. I am connected to the UJA and do all my work voluntarily. As a result, it is a little difficult for me to give up my profits – because there are none. The UJA receives a small, symbolic sum for its services, and that, too, serves only to enable us to continue to give the trade relations between Israel and Argentina the benefit of our experience and professional expertise.'

Still furious and deeply upset, I left the room. Just beyond the door, the rabbi's son caught up with me. 'Please be so kind as to come back. My father must certainly have been misled. Please, let us continue the conversation.'

When I respond in anger I don't always choose my words carefully, and this time was no exception. 'I'm very sorry,' I replied sharply. 'It's already one o'clock in the afternoon, and for the first time in my life I'm really dying for a non-kosher meal.'

Ultimately a compromise was found, which was actually a great political victory for the religious parties in Israel: rabbis and *shochtim* were sent to Argentina in order to set up a mechanism for *shechita* according to the dictates of the Chief Rabbinate of Israel. The state had to bear the expenses of course, and the 'clerics' were the big winners. Some of them liked what they saw in Argentina and decided to stay there after their work there was completed. Some eventually returned to Israel, much richer than before, and equipped with every new electrical appliance on the market as well as brand-new cars. I did not begrudge them their new-found wealth, but I did eventually become sick and tired of this *shtetl*-like bickering (*shtetl* – a small Jewish village in nineteenth-century Eastern Europe). I decided that I had done my share, and that from now on I would let the two sides fight it out among themselves. I would no longer have anything to do with it.

The chronicles of political life in Israel are filled with stories of religious crises, real or artificial, political or economic, which always ended in surrender to the religious parties. For my own part, I regarded the concessions made in the case of the 'Argentine Beef Affair' as an ill omen of things to come.

Despite the bitter pills I had to swallow at the time, the beef deal had its brighter side as well: it brought me into contact with two people who had an enormous influence on my life.

The first was Ya'akov Herzog, the Chief Rabbi's son. He was a man of prodigious talents. An ordained rabbi, he was offered the position of Chief Rabbi of Britain, but turned it down. I have never met anyone who was so universally admired and respected by so many different people. His wisdom and erudition, his cordial manner and extra-ordinary character endeared him to everyone. Oddly enough, as a result of the incident at his father's house in Jerusalem, we became very close friends and enjoyed a wonderful friendship that was sadly cut short by his premature death.

The second relationship that developed out of the 'Beef Affair' was with Pinhas Sapir, then Minister of Commerce and Industry. We met briefly just before I left for that ill-fated meeting at Rabbi Herzog's home, but nothing in that brief encounter in any way presaged the profound, and sometimes stormy relationship we were to share over the next twenty-five years, from the time I emigrated to Israel until the time of Sapir's death.

I returned to Argentina with little to boast about, but I was happy to have made the decision to relinquish all my voluntary involvement in the meat business. Yoseph Mirelman agreed with me, and together we decided to merge ARPALSA with one of our competitors, CAIPI, while in Israel ISAR continued to monitor the transaction. It was an important decision for both of us. In so doing we made it clear that we were no longer going to serve the state of Israel on a voluntary basis in matters of imports and exports. Apart from saving myself the expense of buying my own aeroplane tickets, I also spared myself any further heartache. I was sick and tired of the meat business and of arguing with rabbis and *shochtim.*

LETTERS TO GOD, BLESSED BE HE

Despite my decision to step back from my voluntary involvement in the meat business, my other contacts with Israel were not damaged in any way. Once a year, and occasionally two or three times a year, I would come on a visit, ostensibly as a tourist, but in fact as a foreign investor, a representative of an Argentine-Israeli firm, and chairman (at first active and later honorary) of the Argentine-Israel Chamber of Commerce. In Argentina I looked for ways of doing things for Israel in any area, both as a private individual and as a member of the Jewish community in Argentina. A large part of my time was also devoted to hosting the Israeli dignitaries who came to Buenos Aires. During those early years of statehood in the fifties, Israel went through a period of claustrophobia. The opportunities to travel outside the country were few and far between, and every trip abroad was a cause for celebration.

Argentina was one of the preferred destinations for those few who could afford to travel, and particularly for Israeli government officials. In my various official and private capacities, I met with all of the top echelons of the Israeli bureaucracy. I have a particularly vivid recollection of the visit by the Foreign Minister, Moshe Sharett, who later became Israel's second Prime Minister. He had been invited to Argentina by the UJA and the Argentine government as the guest of the Argentine Foreign Minister. The ambassador, Ya'akov Tsur, was very nervous and excited about the visit. There was a great deal of work involved in arranging the schedule of meetings with the heads of state – including Juan and Evita Peron – interviews in all the media and meetings with representatives of the Jewish community. We knew that Sharett was a stickler for language and grammar and that we would instantly be taken to task for even the smallest mistake in Hebrew.

Since Sharett did not know Spanish, I was asked to serve as his interpreter. He refused to have me translate simultaneously, sentence by sentence, requesting instead that I listen each time to a short segment of what he was saying, make certain that I fully understood it and then translate it. Once, as I was translating a fairly lengthy passage, he suddenly exclaimed, 'That's not what I said!' It transpired that although he was not fluent in Spanish, he understood quite well what was being said.

To our enormous relief, the visit went off without a hitch, save for one embarrassing incident. When Sharett's wife, Tsipporah, paid an official visit to Evita Peron she arrived wearing a hat, as was the custom at the time. There was only one problem: to her chagrin, she discovered that Evita Peron was waiting for her in the identical hat.

Perhaps it was because of my 'failure' as an interpreter, or for other reasons of which I am not aware, but right from the start Sharett and I did not hit it off. Later, we met again after he had become Prime Minister, when I came to introduce him to the members of the Israel-Argentina Chamber of Commerce, and to tell him of our activities and plans for the future.

Yoseph Sprinzak, the first Speaker of the Knesset, also came to Argentina on a visit. On the eve of his arrival, Ya'akov Tsur called me in some consternation. 'Do you by any chance have any cigars? Sprinzak smokes cigars.'

'Don't worry,' I promised him, and the following day showed up in his office with a fancy wooden box filled with my favourite brand of Brazilian cigars.

Sprinzak selected one of them from the box, lit it and inhaled once, then flung the cigar on the table in disgust. 'Phew! Haven't you got any real cigars? I can't smoke this,' he complained. Before becoming Speaker of the Knesset he was a fully fledged member of a kibbutz and an outstanding leader of the labour movement.

There was one other amusing story connected with Sprinzak's visit.

I was standing next to him at the reception in his honour given by the embassy, when my friend Mordechai Shneerson introduced him to a tall, mysterious-looking gentleman. 'Mr Speaker,' Shneerson said formally, 'allow me to introduce you to *un alto, chefe' de la policía* (a high-ranking police officer).

Sprinzak, visibly excited, smiled broadly with the kind of smile usually reserved for old friends, slapped the man on the shoulder, Israeli-fashion, and said to the surprised gentleman, '*Fein, fein!* adding that he was overjoyed to meet him.

Shneerson sensed the onset of a comedy of errors, so he repeated the introduction, stressing that the man held a high rank in the police force.

Sprinzak responded with yet another clap on the shoulder, and said, 'I'm always glad to meet an *alter haver* [Yiddish for 'old friend'] from Poalei Zion [Labour Party].'

After Sprinzak, the Minister of Posts, Joseph Burg, visited us. Burg's speeches were always a splendid combination of wisdom, down-to-earth philosophy, practical suggestions, witticisms and humorous anecdotes. Everyone loved to hear his stories, and looked forward eagerly to each punch line. One of his anecdotes went as follows: 'A letter arrived at the Post Office, addressed to 'The Holy One Blessed Be He'. The writer asked God for ten Israeli pounds to enable him to buy food for the holidays. Just to make him feel good, we sent him a reply with a five-pound note in it,' Burg told us, to peals of laughter. 'The man sent a reply, thanking the Holy One Blessed Be He, and added that the next time He sent him anything He should not send it through the Israeli postal system, because those thieves at the Post Office stole half the money.' Five hundred people roared with laughter when he related the following anecdote at a dinner given in his honour: 'This morning I received two letters: one from Ben Gurion and one from my young son, Avraham. The letters were identical: both of them asked me when was I coming back, and what was I bringing them.' When I congratulated him on his speech, as I always did whenever I listened to this wise and erudite man, he smiled and said. '*Nu*, next week you'll have to say the same thing to the Minister of Health who's coming here as a guest of the UJA. It won't be difficult for you to tell the difference.'

The Minister of Health's visit passed without incident and was soon forgotten, but a year later, in 1953, there came the unforgettable visit of Levi Eshkol, the Minister of Finance. Eshkol was a man after my own heart: pragmatic, down-to-earth, and equipped with a healthy sense of humour. I was invited to meet him together with Simon Mirelman. We were both well known to him as businessmen who were active in the Argentina-Israel Chamber of Commerce, in the Bonds and the UJA, not to mention our independent investments in Israeli enterprises. He confided in us the real reason for his brief visit to Argentina. At that time a conflict had arisen between Henry Montor, the chairman of the Bonds, and Joseph Schwartz, the head of the UJA. Both men, each widely acclaimed in his own field, claimed pride of place at the head of the Jewish organizations in America. The Jewish fundraising effort in the United States was the largest of its kind in the Jewish world, and the contributions raised there were staggering. Any controversy or scandal within the ranks could endanger this great enterprise and cause grave damage to Israel. It was no wonder that Eshkol was worried.

'Those two bodies should have a joint leadership. That's the way it should be everywhere,' Eshkol told us.

'Here too?' I asked.

'Here too,' he replied.

I realized that Eshkol had done his homework and had been well briefed on our internal politics. Power struggles were quite a well-known phenomenon in our circles too, although they were not nearly as intense as those in the USA.

'You must get all the leaders and activists in your local UJA and the Bonds to agree to unite,' he demanded. 'And if you need help, bring them to me for a meeting.'

For the next two days I hardly slept a wink. I lobbied intensively, meeting with every one of the people involved individually, and eventually managed to win an overwhelming majority for the leadership unification plan.

Eshkol was still not satisfied. 'That's not enough. I need something in writing, signed and sealed,' he ordered.

There were only twenty-four hours left before his departure. Nevertheless I made the rounds again, and managed to bring him the signed document at the airport.

He thanked me warmly. 'When they see this document in America, they will have no choice but to follow your lead,' he said with undisguised satisfaction. And then, without warning, and looking at me as though he were seeing me for the first time, he suddenly asked: 'And when are you coming on *aliya* to Israel, *jungerman* [Yiddish for 'young man']?'

I did indeed have every intention of emigrating to Israel, but up until then had simply not had the time to take the necessary steps to make the move. 'Next year,' I replied, and immediately realized that I had just made a momentous decision. 'But I do have some problems,' I added, backpedalling somewhat as I realized the magnitude of the commitment I had just made.

'What problems? There are no problems that can't be solved.'

When he was being practical or humorous, Eshkol tended to be somewhat patronizing, but I carried on: 'I live in a country where there are no restrictions on transactions in foreign currency. How will I be able to keep up my businesses abroad if I am living in Israel?' I asked him.

'Just come, and we'll work it out,' Eshkol said, waving away my concerns with a shrug of his shoulders.

We still had a few minutes left in the airport lounge, and Eshkol asked me: 'And what will you do in Israel?'

'I still don't know,' I replied.

'Come and work for us in the Ministry of Finance,' he offered. 'We need people like you.' His habitual smile deepened.

'This is the first time I've heard that you intend to resign,' I quipped, answering him in kind.

Following my emigration to Israel, I met with Eshkol at his office on numerous occasions, and we maintained a cordial friendship. He often sought my opinion, even though he dealt with issues that were not in my area of expertise. Eshkol was true to his word about my businesses abroad, and facilitated my settling in Israel. These personal concessions concerning foreign currency later turned into official government regulations that applied to everyone, and made it easier for businessmen from abroad to come and live and do business inside Israel and abroad.

IN THE FAMILY CIRCLE

All these diverse public activities were, naturally, only one part of my life. During those years my family grew, as my two daughters, Beatriz and Judith, were born within two years of each other. Argentina was going through a paroxysm of nationalist frenzy, and, among many other draconian regulations, children born in Argentina at that time could only be given Spanish or Biblical names. We therefore named our eldest daughter Beatriz-Juana (Beatriz after the Crown Princess of the Throne of Orange, and Hanna, after my maternal grandmother). In time she became known by her nickname Bixie. Our second daughter we named Judith-Amalia (Amalia, after my mother-in-law Mali, who had died a year earlier), and was soon known in the family only as Judy.

Bixie and Judy grew up as lovely girls who brought happiness to all of us and to everyone around them. We raised them as well as we knew how in those days. That is why I cannot help but wonder why I am so often troubled by gnawing doubts about the way we raised our girls. When Bixie was born, my mother-in-law, Mali, was very ill. In order to be near her as much as possible, Alice arranged for her delivery at the same hospital where her mother was being treated, rather than at a regular maternity hospital. Nine months after Bixie was born Mali died, having suffered greatly before her death. Throughout this entire time we spent many hours at her bedside, with Bixie in her cradle in the same room as her dying grandmother.

The girls' early years passed pleasantly. Alice and I made every effort to raise our small family in a special atmosphere, combining Jewish tradition, strong devotion to the state of Israel, close ties with the Jewish community, together, of course, with the Argentine aspect of our lives. We were loyal citizens, and were not conscious of any contradiction between the various different elements of our lives. For this I owe a deep debt of gratitude to Alice, who always strove to create a life filled with harmony and a profoundly aesthetic and unique spiritual, cultural and emotional ambience. She agreed to my request to observe Jewish traditions in our home, even though the Jewish education she had received in her family was very rudimentary. Observing Jewish customs in our home was important for me not only as a gesture of respect to my parents, nor for purely religious reasons. I felt – and convinced

Alice – that observing Jewish tradition was the only way for Jews living abroad to bring up their children.

As long as we lived in Argentina, we maintained an observant life-style. We were not fanatical about it, but we were strict: our kitchen was kosher, we did not speak on the phone or drive on the Sabbath; and we observed all the Jewish holidays. The Sabbath day of rest brought a special sense of peace and relaxation into my life. On that one day of the week I had to cut myself off from the hectic world of business, ease my involvement in public affairs, and devote myself entirely to my family. I have particularly fond memories of quiet, leisurely and deeply satisfying family weekends. I believe we gave our daughters a liberal Jewish upbringing. We explained to them that as soon as we moved to Israel we would ease some of the religious restrictions that we observed in Argentina. I remember how amazed my daughters were on our first Sabbath in Israel when we got into our car and headed for the beach. I tried to explain my reasoning to them as best I could and in a way they could understand. I felt since in Israel virtually everyone was Jewish, we had no need to strengthen our sense of identity through religious observance. I tried to explain to them that unlike Argentina, with its two-day weekend, Saturday was the only day for rest and recreation in Israel, and it was therefore the only day we had for family outings. The girls wanted to go to the beach, of course, but something inside resisted these unexpected changes. Apparently we had not explained ourselves very well.

Our home in Buenos Aires was large and elegant, surrounded by a broad expanse of garden, with its own swimming pool in the garden – one of the few private swimming pools in town at that time. On Saturdays and Sundays our house was usually filled with guests. The ambassadors, Ya'akov Tsur and Aryeh (Leon) Kubobi who succeeded him, were frequent house guests, and senior embassy staff were regularly invited to parties or festive dinners we hosted. Whenever we left town, we deposited our keys at the embassy.

Alice and I often took vacations in the Cordoba Mountains, the Tucuman Gardens, or the beaches at Mar del Plata. I loved the Argentine resorts, which are among the most beautiful in the world, and the national park of Nahuel Huapi at San Carlos de Bariloche. After our first tragi-comic visit to Bariloche, we made a habit of going there every summer. Married now, with children of our own, we laughed when we recalled our adventures there a few years earlier. We also took some wonderful vacations at Mar del Plata, the place where Alice and I had met for the second time, never again to part. We often took these vacations with friends. From time to time we went to the Christina *estancia* in the Cordoba region, with its 8,000 head of cattle, which we owned jointly with Van Waveren.

WARNING SIGNS

Business went on as usual, and we wanted for nothing, but some ominous warning signs began to make themselves felt. In fact, the situation in Argentina began deteriorating rapidly only a short time before we emigrated to Israel. In 1954, two years after Evita's death, and without her guiding hand, Peron's hold on the reins of government began to slip, and within a short time he was forced to flee Argentina and sought refuge in Spain. He remained there for fifteen years, stoking the flames of his Napoleonic dreams in his own mind and in the minds of his supporters, until 1969 when the Peronist party won the elections in Argentina. In a dramatic move, so typical of South American republics, the old general was called back to become President once again. By that time he was a feeble and pathetic shadow of his old self. Accompanied by his new wife, a dancer named Isabella – a poor imitation of Evita – he returned to power having learned nothing or forgotten anything during his years in exile. And it soon transpired that the Argentine parliament was no better: it took him a very short time to persuade them to appoint his wife Vice-President of Argentina.

The wave of Argentine nationalism that swept the country in the fifties destroyed almost every positive aspect of daily life in the country. Some of its excesses bordered on the absurd, particularly the new holidays, invented to inculcate a sense of national pride in the populace. For example, Peron canonized San Martin, the legendary freedom fighter who had wrested Argentina's independence from Spain. All the former rulers of Argentina who preceded Peron (excluding, of course, the 'Holy' Evita) were excised from the country's official history – a history that had, in any case, not been very extensive to begin with. Daily life was regulated in nonsensical ways, such as the daily radio announcement at precisely eight twenty-five, when the sonorous voice of an announcer would remind the Argentine people: 'It is eight twenty-five, the exact hour when Evita left us and went on to life everlasting.' As has always been the case under totalitarian régimes, cultural events were tightly controlled: books, poems, and even music required official approval before they were made available to the public. The only kind of music that did not require official permission was indigenous Argentine music. Rock music or anything that remotely resembled anything American was strictly banned.

If the actions taken by the régime had been restricted to stupidities or to a short-lived dictatorship, they might have been bearable or even ignored up to a point. Unfortunately, however, the Peronist régime, which was disastrously inefficient to begin with, put into motion long-range consequences that destroyed the very fabric of the country. Peron's death in 1974 before the end of his second term of office two decades after his exile in 1954, and his last wife's inability to run the country after she succeeded him as President, marked the beginning of a lengthy period of extreme political instability. It did not take too long for a few army colonels to depose the ineffectual Isabella, and Argentina soon became a police state, generously rewarding the junta's yes-men and mercilessly persecuting its opponents, often to death. And yet, despite it all, there were many people both inside the country and beyond (including people in Israel) who still regarded Argentina as an enlightened country, when in fact it had descended – with terrible consequences – into an era of darkness. Human rights were trampled, tens of thousands of people died or disappeared without a trace (among them a large percentage of Jews, in excess of their proportion of the overall population of the country), the economy collapsed, and whatever was left of the country's good name simply evaporated. And this beautiful country, blessed with so many resources, slipped into an unimaginable abyss, until it dared to declare war on Great Britain in order to conquer the Falkland Islands, marking the beginning of the fall of the disastrous regime of the colonels.

All these dreadful things happened after my emigration to Israel. During the early fifties, before we left, the great majority of the Argentine people kept silent, hoping for a miracle that would save them, and turning a blind eye to the social ills, the travesties of justice, and the dangerous rise of xenophobia. My experiences in Holland during the war had taught me something about self-preservation, and I could see very clearly where things were heading. I clearly foresaw Peron's imminent downfall, and understood with equal clarity that whatever would fill the vacuum he would leave behind after his death could only be worse. Alice, who always saw reality in the clearest light, agreed with me completely, particularly after her relatives decided to leave Argentina and settle in the United States. All this led us, inevitably, to one conclusion: we decided to leave Argentina. Luckily for us we were young enough not to have to worry about the prospect of leaving behind everything we had achieved, including family and friends, and starting over again. My parents, on the other hand, like so many others of their generation, simply could not muster the physical and emotional strength to do the same, and chose to remain behind.

But where were we to go? We had three options: the United States, Holland or Israel. From a purely practical point of view, Holland and the US were preferable. During the years preceding our departure I had travelled extensively throughout Europe on business, keeping away from Germany as far as possible. Even though I was still deeply attached to my native country, I could not see myself going back to live in Holland. Fully ninety per cent of the Jews of Holland – among them many of my friends and acquaintances – had disappeared off the face of the earth. When I returned to Amsterdam soon after the war, to the city that was so much a part of my very being, I felt very clearly that I could not set up house and bring up my daughters there. In Israel, on the other hand, a number of possibilities began emerging that suited my active disposition. I decided to try to combine the last two options: to make a home both in Europe and in Israel, and to spend at least half of my time abroad. Our family business still maintained offices in Holland, and from there it would be easier to be in contact with Argentina.

After moving to Israel, I spent less and less time in Buenos Aires. Apart from the occasional visit, I handled my part of the business there from a distance. My cooperation with my father in all this was extraordinarily productive.

Those were good years for our business. Father dealt with the management and financial planning, while I saw to marketing and sales. I developed extensive business contacts throughout South America, as well as in other parts of the world, including South Africa. In Europe and the United States I expanded our previous contacts and opened up new markets for our products. Trying to develop our business in Israel was frustrating at times, but after a while I let it go: the market for leather and hides in Israel was so small that often it wasn't worth the effort. I did, however, do some good business in Israel at the end of the period of austerity, during the first difficult years of statehood. At that time the government was interested in flooding the market with products in order to bring down prices. My friend Herman Hollander, the Director-General of the Ministry of Commerce and Industry, knew that only Argentina – in other words, our company – could deliver the relatively large supply of hides that the country needed. This was one of the swiftest and easiest deals I have ever made.

Looking back now, it was during the years between 1942 and 1948 that I became fully integrated into Argentine life, while the years 1948 to 1954 were spent in Buenos Aires preparing for my *aliya* to Israel, and taking care of everything that was required by such a transition, without, at the same time, neglecting our business in Argentina and the rest of the world.

PART III

ISRAEL

12

A NEW LIFE

Moving from Argentina to Israel was an intense time of uprooting, leave-taking and settling in again, all in the space of a few months. In the middle of 1954, the hotel I had invested in, the Accadia Hotel in Herzliya, was officially opened. I flew to Israel to attend the opening, and spent a week in the country, during which time I came to the conclusion that I could contribute best to the success of the hotel if I lived nearby and not halfway across the globe. Alice and the girls had already left Argentina, but were staying in Holland for the meanwhile. After the gala opening, I flew to Holland, and for a few months we lived in a rented apartment in Scheveningen. In September of 1954, at the beginning of the school year, we came to settle in Israel. Alice and I thought that the best solution for us during this initial period would be to stay at the Accadia. The hotel was still empty most of the time, so we had a choice of rooms to pick from, a beach just outside the dining-room door, and all the amenities and services that a hotel could offer. We chose a couple of rooms for ourselves and settled in, and the girls started attending the Brandeis School in nearby Herzliya.

For a while we were certain that the girls, like us, were enjoying the comfort and luxury of hotel life, but we were sadly mistaken. One day, when we were visiting some friends, our daughters asked the host if it was all right to shout in their house. 'Of course,' he replied, and to our utter amazement, the two girls proceeded to yell at the top of their voices. I sometimes think that if it hadn't been for those shouts, we probably would never have found out that Bixie and Judy were in fact suffering in the unnatural living accommodation we had chosen for ourselves, even if it was only temporary. Living in a hotel meant that they were not allowed to shout or go wild and just behave naturally like other children of their age. Today I believe that we were indeed not sensitive enough to the deeper levels of our girls' souls. We failed to grasp that even a 'deluxe' move from one country to another, such as we had experienced, leaves an indelible imprint on young children. Perhaps we were thinking of ourselves and how we had grappled with difficult situations in our own past experiences, but we had been older and stronger, and the time and circumstances were different as well.

At the beginning of 1955 we moved to Tel Aviv, and rented a small house at number 17 Maharal Street. The street was unpaved and dirty, and there was sand piled up all the way to our doorstep. I wrote a sharp letter of complaint to the municipality about the state of the street, asking them if I needed to buy a camel in order to cross the desert wastes in my neighbourhood, or had the city perhaps decided to preserve the street in its present state as a historic monument. My letter seemed to do the trick, because it was soon transformed into a properly paved street with pavements and trees. Once we made the final move to a house in Tel Aviv, Bixie and Judy began going to the Le-Dugma School.

These frequent changes of schools and social frameworks underline just how much our two daughters suffered from the many adjustments we imposed on them. They moved from country to country, from one language to another, from one school to the next, and each time there was a difficult period of reorientation. For the first few months after our arrival in Israel they needed private lessons in Hebrew. When they began studying at Le-Dugma School in Tel Aviv, one of Bixie's teachers gave Judy private lessons, while one of Judy's teachers taught Bixie after school. There was one other aspect of our family life that must have made things even more difficult for them: up to 1959 I regularly spent several months of every year abroad, while the family remained in Tel Aviv.

At the beginning of the summer of 1957, one day before we were all due to leave for a visit to Argentina, I learned that a three-storey house at 18 Maharal Street, directly opposite our own, was up for sale. I went in to talk to the owner, and within half an hour came out with a signed agreement in principle to buy the house. The timing couldn't have been better: Alice was pregnant with our third child and we would be needing a larger home. The house was indeed spacious and beautiful, and was literally across the street. I was particularly pleased because this meant that we would not be moving to yet another new neighbourhood

Benno Gitter (circled) at his high-school class in Amsterdam (1933). The school, called 'Maimonides', is still open today.

Thanks to the wide-ranging work of Benno's father, Natan Gitter, Argentina became one of the world's leading exporters of leather.

Benno Gitter accompanies Emory Holderness, the chief buyer from the US government, through the tannery in Buenos Aires in 1943.

Rio Gallegos – the first ship to run the naval blockade after the War of Independence, 1948. Middle row, 4th from left: Benno Gitter; next to him, Mordechai Shneerson, Economic Minister at the Israeli Embassy in Argentina, the Captain and ship's officers.

Benno Gitter inaugurates the Israeli Chamber of Commerce in Argentina, 1950.
From left: Jacob Zur, first Israeli Ambassador to Argentina, Simon Mirelman, a
distinguished member of the Jewish community, Benno Gitter and Jacob Murmis.

Prime Minister Moshe Sharet signing the guest book at the inauguration of the
Accadia Hotel on Herzliah Beach (1954). At the right of the picture is Avraham
Schuster, one of the partners from Buenos Aires and the grandfather of the musical
virtuoso Daniel Barenboim.

Alice and Benno Gitter in 1947 with their eldest
daughter, Bixie.

Jenny (née Fishler) and Natan
Gitter, Benno's parents celebrating
Natan's 70th birthday at the home
of Benno and Alice in Tel Aviv.

The three brothers pictured in 1964. In the centre, Benno; to his left, his
elder brother Zigi (Shimon) and to his right, Jacob, his younger brother.

As personal adviser of the Minister of Finance, Benno Gitter tries to convince Pinchas Sapir of his point.

Benno Gitter introduces the Prime Minister, David Ben-Gurion, to the participants of the first General Assembly of CLAL (1963).

The start of relations with Ahron Dovrat in Buenos Aires. Subsequently Dovrat replaced Benno Gitter as Director-General of CLAL.

A trip to Japan for the launch of a tanker carrying the name of Mathilda Recanati. From right: Mathilda Recanati, Alice Gitter, Dani Recanati, Benno Gitter. A cheerful quartet who used to travel and work together.

Alice Gitter has the honour of launching El Yam's tanker *Har Addir* in 1967.

Ariela, the youngest daughter of Alice and Benno, greets the guests at her sister Bixie's wedding in 1966.

Benno with two colleagues. Centre: Augusto Levi, Professor at the Hebrew University and the first Director-General of Discount Investment Co. Right: Major-General (res.) Dan Tolkovsky, the second commander of the Air Force and later Director-General of Discount Investment Co.

A conference in Mexico with the Minister of Foreign Affairs, Abba Eban (sitting, circled), and Israel's ambassadors to all the Latin American countries. Gitter (standing, circled) – serving as a roving ambassador in these countries – acted forcefully to encourage economic investment and immigration to Israel.

Ambassador Eduardo Ham decorates Benno at a ceremony in the Argentine embassy in Tel Aviv in 1989.

Benno Gitter delivers his address to the Board of Governors of the Shaarei Zedek hospital in the Chagall Hall at the Knesset. From right: Samuel Lewis, US Ambassador to Israel, Professor Y. Meyer, first Director of the new Shaarei Zedek hospital, Professor Efraim Katzir, President of Israel.

With daughters Judith and Bixie, revealing the plaque at the Surgical A Ward in memory of Alice Gitter, at the Souraski Medical Center in Tel Aviv, 1989.

With the late prime minister, Yitzhak Rabin, on the occasion of Gitter's 70th birthday.

A special lecture at Tel Aviv University in honour of Benno Gitter's 75th birthday.
From left: Professor Yoram Dinstein (President), Professor Dan Amir (Rector), Sir
Leslie Porter (Chancellor), Prime Minister Yitzhak Rabin and Moshe Porat (chairman
of the executive council).

Family and friends gather in Beit Ariela for a gala concert in honour of Gitter's
75th birthday.

Benno Gitter at his 75th birthday raises the wine goblet he received at his Bar Mitzvah in Amsterdam in 1932.

From left to right: Professor Dotan, Benno Gitter, President Weizman, and the donors of the synagogue at Tel Aviv University, Mr and Mrs Norbert Cymbalista, 1997.

and the girls could remain at Le-Dugma School. We sent a message to Argentina asking my parents to send us all the furniture, paintings and *objets d'art* that we had left behind, as well as anything else that might enhance our sense of stability and permanence in our new home. We moved in to the house at 18 Maharal Street just before Rosh Ha-Shanah of that year, and spent thirty happy years there.

THE HIGH PRICE OF LEARNING A LESSON

Until 1959 I had relatively few business interests in Israel: some scattered investments, the ISAR company, in which I was heavily involved, and the Accadia Hotel. Our investment in the Accadia was a venture that ran aground because of a very fundamental mistake. We dived into the world of hotels and tourism without any prior experience, without taking the time to learn the business first, and without any real knowledge of the business climate in Israel. I had always been much more impulsive than my father, always eager to invest in any local business, as long as it bore the aura of a Zionist endeavour. The result was that I paid *rebbe gelt* (Yiddish for 'tuition fees', literally 'money for the rabbi'), and learned an important lesson: in business, as in love, it is extremely important that both sides be happy. In the case of the Accadia Hotel, I believe that, ultimately, the government of Israel had many more reasons to be satisfied than the investors.

At the beginning of the fifties Israel had very few hotels, fewer still in the luxury range. In Tel Aviv there were only two that could be included in the category of 'luxury hotels': the Kaete Dan, a family-run establishment which was later razed and replaced by the five-star Dan Hotel, and Gat Rimon, a two-storey building with no elevator. Neither hotel had more than fifteen to twenty rooms. With the help of some influential friends, I managed to get a room at the Gat Rimon on one of my visits to the country. When I arrived there, the bellboy at the door looked on indifferently as I dragged my heavy suitcase inside. This introduction to the hotel's standard of service made me realize that no one was going to help me take my things up to my room, so I asked the reception clerk if there was an elevator – using the English word 'lift', that was commonly used among Hebrew-speakers in Israel at that time. 'Open the window, and you'll have plenty of *lift*,' he replied, certain that I had used the Yiddish word for 'breeze'.

These incidents reinforced my conviction that there was a crying need for a good, five-star hotel – equal to the best available abroad – somewhere along Israel's coastline. I put together a group of investors who were all certain, as I was, that this was an investment that couldn't go wrong, and that a hotel of this kind would be an instant success. Together with my brother Shimon and the Mirelmans, we found several people who were willing to invest in a 150-room hotel to be built on the beach at Herzliya, just north of Tel Aviv. My brother agreed to represent the group's interests on a voluntary basis until I arrived in the country. Raising the money, pushing the plans through the endless red tape of planning commissions and building permits, and then actually building the hotel, took three years. We invested a great deal of love, too, in this project, as well as considerable sums of money. We supervised the entire project, down to the minutest details of the interior design and the choice of furniture. Young and promising Israeli artists such as Kastel and Jean David, who were just starting out then, were given a boost by our purchase of their works for the hotel, where they still hang today, forty-five years later. Despite the excruciating agony and heartache I suffered as a result of my disastrous venture into the hotel business, there was a positive side to the story as well: my investments in the hotel business introduced me to a whole new world of art appreciation. Strongly encouraged and influenced in this by Alice, I soon became an art collector myself. Years later, and no doubt as a direct result, I became involved in the building of the Tel Aviv Museum.

The hotel was named Accadia after the ancient Accadians who are mentioned in the Bible. According to Moshe Sharett, whose suggestion it was, these people were coast-dwellers, thus making the name particularly appropriate for a hotel on the shoreline. Sharett was inordinately proud of the Hebrew ring of the word Accadia, but as a stickler for language he stipulated that the word be pronounced with the stress on the last syllable, as in the correct Hebrew pronunciation of other names such as Herzliya, Haifa and Netanya (in Hebrew: Herts-e-li-*yah*, Hay-*fa*, Ne-tan-*ya*). The gala opening ceremony, which took place in the middle of 1954, was attended by the Prime Minister Moshe Sharett, the Minister of Posts, Joseph Burg, the Minister of Commerce and

Industry, Peretz Bernstein, and many other prominent public figures and businessmen, among them a large contingent from South America. The broad smiles that were flashed at the cameras and immortalized in my album of the event were a measure of the high hopes we all nurtured that the hotel would attract many tourists and be a great success. But this was not to be. As it turned out, we couldn't have chosen a worse time to open a luxury hotel in Israel. Palestinian terrorists, known at that time as *fedayeen*, had mounted several murderous attacks inside Israel. Even though these had taken place in the south of the country, far away from Herzliya, they deterred many tourists from spending their vacations in Israel. If we needed any further proof of our colossal mistake, on 6 December 1954 we held a party at the hotel in honour of Alice's birthday with twenty invited guests. A full complement of 120 members of staff attended us – and we were the only guests at the hotel. The orchestra played for us and us alone. The outbreak of the Sinai Campaign, in the autumn of 1956, naturally did little to improve the state of tourism in Israel.

At the height of this drought in tourism, I asked my friend Felix Shinar, Israel's ambassador to Germany, who was heading the negotiations over German reparations to Holocaust victims, if he could bring the high-ranking German government officials he was dealing with to the hotel. He rejected my request out of hand, saying, 'I refuse to bring official guests from Germany and put them up in luxury hotels in Israel.'

My investment in the hotel was not only financial. I also had a deep emotional attachment to the project, and that is perhaps why I was so profoundly frustrated by its failure. At about that time I met the young American ambassador to Israel, Ogden Reid, and I spoke to him very frankly about my troubles. Reid was an enthusiastic friend of Israel who had studied Hebrew before taking up his post here, and, as befitted the son of major newspaper publishers in New York, had an excellent sense of timing. 'Thanksgiving Day is not too far off,' he said. 'I'll call the Pentagon, and ask them to send you some American servicemen from our bases in Europe. They'll be happy to spend their vacation in the Holy Land.'

It sounded too good to be true, but a few weeks later the ambassador informed me personally that two days before Thanksgiving, two Constellation passenger planes filled with American soldiers from Europe would be landing in Israel. The hotel staff went into high gear, preparing all the rooms and entertainment areas. I gave orders to polish up the best silver, get hold of as many turkeys as we could lay our hands on and prepare them for the festival meal. Two days later the hotel was spick and span, delectable aromas arose from the kitchen area, and the entire staff was poised and ready to serve the guests. The atmosphere in the hotel was crackling with nervous excitement in anticipation of their arrival. And then, on the day before Thanksgiving, the ambassador called and informed me that there had been some unexpected problems, and the soldiers had been ordered to remain on their bases. With a heavy heart I slowly made my way towards the kitchen to inform the staff of the cancellation, and then sat down next to the chef – and we both burst into tears.

Right then and there I decided to sell the hotel. I flew to Istanbul to meet with Conrad Hilton, one of the owners of the Hilton hotel chain, but we were unable to strike a deal. I could not meet his financial expectations, and he was not prepared to make any concessions. Then we'll sell the hotel to some organization, I muttered to myself over and over again, recalling how the Kastel Hotel in north Tel Aviv had been sold to the Mizrahi party. What became clear to me was that our salvation could only come from inside Israel.

Until such time as we could find the right buyer, the hotel remained open, and we still had to run it as usual. Israel at that time had no schools teaching hoteliering skills such as reception, haute cuisine or other tourist services. The average Jewish mother was never too keen for her sons or daughters to enter any kind of service profession, and as a result it was almost impossible to find good professional staff for the day-to-day running of the hotel. Since there was little chance of finding an experienced hotel manager in Israel, we had to import one: Commendatore Ridelli from Italy, who was referred to us with excellent letters of introduction. Apparently he had helped to open and had managed several luxury hotels in large cities and resort areas in Italy. We hired him on his merits and on the basis of his references, but failed to take into account one major problem: the differences in mentality between Israel and Italy. For instance, Ridelli had no idea of the enormous power and influence of the Histadrut, Israel's monolithic

General Federation of Labour. Whenever a member of the staff talked back to him, Ridelli would call in the wayward employee, pull himself up to his impressive full height, and shout in Italian, 'A casa! – Go home!' The employee – who, had he been in Italy, might have taken his things and crept out of the back door with his tail between his legs – generally stood there facing the fuming Commendatore totally unfazed, just waiting for the Italian to allow him to leave, and then went directly to his union representative to lodge a complaint against Ridelli and the hotel. The Histadrut would then enter the fray with all its authority, turning heaven and earth until the employee was awarded full severance pay. I knew many hotel employees who made the rounds in this manner between all three top hotels in the country in turn: the King David in Jerusalem, the Dan in Tel Aviv, and the Accadia in Herzliya. Occasionally, having worked briefly at all three, they would start the rounds all over again. Some would move from land to sea, and take jobs on one or more of the Zim passenger ships. On one or two occasions, I even met some of my former employees from the Accadia who had jumped ship at one of the South American ports, and made a fortune in business ventures there, some of them even becoming industrial tycoons. With so few trained hotel workers to choose from, hotel managers in Israel often had to turn a blind eye to the absence of any sense of loyalty on the part of their employees towards their place of employment.

We wanted to close the Accadia, but the government – quite rightly – refused to allow us to turn it into anything but a hotel. They were not willing, for example, to give us the loans we needed to turn the lovely building in the centre of the country into a medical centre, or an office building. The government even turned down the idea of selling the building to an important embassy. The hotel never showed a profit, and, in the days when Ridelli was manager, it was difficult even to get accurate details of the number of guests staying there. 'How many of the 150 rooms are booked?' I would ask Ridelli on the in-house phone every morning at nine. 'I haven't had a chance to find out yet,' he would reply, adding nonchalantly, 'but in the Dan Hotel only sixteen rooms are occupied.' We were well aware of our situation, and we knew that our losses were the result of the tough labour laws that gave such extensive protection to the employees. Unlike in other countries, we could not hire a hotel worker just for the tourist season. This problem was particularly acute in a hotel of the size and standard of the Accadia, which required a staff of 150 in season but a much smaller number during the off-season.

While all this was going on, we learned that one of our regular guests had not paid his bill. I asked to see him, and discovered that it was Leon Uris, the famous American novelist. He had earned a great deal of money from, among others, his wartime bestseller *Battle Cry*, but chose to waste his royalties on pleasurable pursuits – such as luxury hotel suites – and had now run out of money. Surprisingly, he offered to pay off his bill by working as a night guard at the hotel for a while, and I agreed. He seemed like a trustworthy man, and in any case, there did not appear to be any better solution to the problem. A few days later, the Sinai Campaign began, and Uris was hired by Reuters to be their chief war correspondent in Israel. After the war, when Reuters no longer needed a full-time military correspondent in the region, Uris returned to the United States. Before leaving, he settled his bill, and as a token of his gratitude, gave everyone – except me – a present for having allowed him to remain at the hotel and for making his stay such a pleasant one. When he returned home, he wrote his great bestselling novel *Exodus*, one of the most successful novels of all time. Apart from its historical, Zionist and literary value, the novel proved to be a great boon for tourism to Israel. Twenty years later, Alice visited him in his home town of Aspen, Colorado. Uris remembered her fondly, and was very kind to her during her stay there.

Following the financial failure of the hotel the other investors wanted to pull out, so as to salvage at least part of their investment. In order to avoid any unpleasantness, Yoseph Mirelman and I bought them out, and within a short time we were the sole owners of the Accadia Hotel. We were very anxious to close it, but the Minister of Commerce and Industry, Pinhas Sapir, refused to allow us to do so, possibly in order to avoid setting a dangerous precedent. It was only at the end of 1956, after the Sinai Campaign, and in the wake of the general uncertainty in the country at that time, that we managed to close the hotel for an indefinite period. At long last we could heave a sigh of relief: finally we were able to staunch this devastating drain on our finances resulting from the endless losses the hotel had incurred. Sapir offered us a large loan to reopen, but despite our deep admiration for Sapir we stood our ground and refused. The lesson we had learned, from bitter personal experience, was simple but painful: you can sell flowers, vegetables, books or fashion items at half price, or give them away to the needy, and enjoy the mere fact of giving charity, but a hotel room that is not occupied at yesterday's price is a net loss. At last, after carefully surveying the market, we came up with an idea of how to get rid of the hotel and gain Sapir's blessing at the same time: 'Give Yekutiel Federman a loan at the same rates you offered us, and help him expand his chain of Dan hotels,' we suggested. Sapir liked the idea, and the Accadia was duly sold to Federman. We had absolutely no regrets about the sale.

The money we received – ostensibly from Federman, but in fact from the government – was deposited with the Treasury until such time as we could find a suitable investment in Israel that would receive the ministry's blessing. Three years later we found exactly the investment we were looking for.

ARIELA COMES INTO OUR LIVES

After purchasing the house at 18 Maharal Street in Tel Aviv in the spring of 1957, we also rented a home in Kilchberg, in a suburb of Zurich near the lake, in May of that same year. We had a wonderful time there; those were good, quiet and restful days, marred only by occasional rain. Alice was nearing the end of her pregnancy. We were not too impressed by the local children's hospital, and hoped that the maternity clinic would be better. Shortly before we arrived, I read an article about a new method of painless childbirth that was used by a famous professor in Lausanne. I was very anxious to provide Alice with all available comforts for the birth: air-conditioning, a modern delivery-room, and a single room with a phone, but most of all I wanted to ensure her an easy, painless delivery. So I went to Lausanne to see the professor's clinic at first hand. I sat in the waiting-room, and a nurse came in and took down all my personal details: who I was, the name of my company, etc. After that, I was left in the waiting-room and no one paid the slightest attention to me. I could see the director of the institution in her office, talking into the phone and not even glancing in my direction. Suddenly an elderly gentleman came in. The director jumped up and rushed out to greet him. 'Hello, M'sieu Shaplan! How are you, M'sieu Shaplan? Would you like to drink something, M'sieu Shaplan?' It was none other than the famous actor Charlie Chaplin (whom she referred to, with her French accent, as 'Shaplan'), who had come to visit his wife Oona after the birth of one of their children. As I watched the director of the clinic fussing over 'M'sieu Shaplan' it suddenly struck me that unless I was someone of the stature of the great actor Charlie Chaplin, Alice would probably not receive the treatment I thought she deserved.

That being the case, Alice registered for her delivery at the local canton hospital, which was headed by a famous gynaecologist, the favourite of all the Jewish women in the region. We felt very reassured and waited patiently for the day. One afternoon, our Swiss neighbour invited us to tea. The invitation was unusual, as the Swiss are not particularly well known for their hospitality to strangers. The conversation, too, took an unexpected turn. 'At which hospital has your wife registered for her delivery?' the neighbour asked me.

'The canton hospital,' I replied.

The neighbour was deeply shocked. 'You're endangering your wife! If she goes into labour in the middle of the day, by the time you get through the traffic and cover the distance to the hospital, she'll have her baby in the taxi. The best thing you can do is to register her at Sanitas. The doctors there are all devout Catholics with many children of their own, and they know a thing or two about delivering babies. They're the best in town. And besides, the nurses are all nuns, and their devotion and patience are truly angelic.'

What could we do in the face of such passionate advice? We felt that a native of the area like him was bound to be better informed than visitors like us, and therefore cancelled our registration at the canton hospital, and, following our neighbour's advice, registered Alice at the Sanitas.

At noon on 21 August 1957 I received word in the middle of a meeting that Alice had been taken to the hospital. I raced to the Sanitas, breaking half a dozen traffic regulations on the way. The doctor – a devout Catholic with ten children, just as my neighbour had promised – examined Alice and then left her in the care of a nurse. When he saw me, he hurried over to me, buttoning up his coat as if he were preparing to leave. 'How is my wife?' I asked.

'Oh. She's perfectly fine. There is plenty of time yet until the delivery; six or eight hours at least,' he replied.

'Are you leaving?' I asked him with some concern in my voice.

'Yes, but I will be back in time, don't worry. You're in good hands.' He patted me reassuringly on the shoulder, waved lightly and disappeared out of the door.

The chief nurse now appeared, carrying a white gown. 'Why do I need that?' I asked her, aghast.

'To wear in the delivery-room,' she replied.

This was too much. 'I did not attend the birth of either one of my daughters, and I think I prefer to wait outside this time as well,' I said firmly.

'That sounds like a bad joke,' the grim-faced nurse retorted.

At that very moment, my brother Shimon appeared. He had arrived in Zurich with his wife just a few days earlier. My parents had also come to Switzerland to be with us for the exciting arrival of another Gitter into the world. 'The doctor was here earlier but he left,' I told Shimon, my voice betraying my anxiety. Shimon went over to the nurse, introduced himself as a physician, and asked to be allowed into Alice's room. A few seconds later I heard him shouting from the room: 'Nurse! A gown! Instruments! A midwife!' All at once there was a flurry of activity. I could clearly hear my polite, soft-spoken brother cursing like a trooper. The midwife, in nun's habit, made no comment. And that was the way my daughter Ariela came into the world – delivered by my brother.

THE RECANATIS COME INTO MY LIFE

During the ten years between 1945 and 1955 Argentina was part of the bi-lateral trade agreements between many countries around the world, among them Brazil, Uruguay, the Scandinavian countries, France, Holland, Belgium and Germany. Much of the trade with these countries went through the port of Rotterdam, the city where both my family firms, Kaufmann and now Van Waveren had offices and large warehouses. Our companies had business dealings with many of the firms that traded with Argentina in hides, wool and other goods. It was a highly volatile business, characterized by wild swings of prices in both directions. Problems with the weather, natural disasters, supply and demand, the tactics of the competition: all these were but some of the reasons for the price swings that make the import/export commodity business almost as wild a ride as the stock market – if not more so.

In the decade immediately following the Second World War the market was particularly unstable. The economic situation in countries with bilateral trade agreements shifted rapidly from capital surpluses to severe financial shortfalls, depending on the volume of trade and the actual pace of the buying or the selling. While the prices of finished products were fairly steady, the prices of raw materials remained highly unstable, and this was one of the reasons for the fluctuating fortunes of the market and the all too frequent risk of incurring losses. To offset their losses, countries with mutual trade agreements tended to sell the unsold parts of these bilateral currency-contracts to commercial companies, which bought them at reduced prices (a practice known in the business as 'switch'). In this way exporters and importers could make a profit, and balance any losses they may have incurred in pricing their products. People who bought out contracts through this 'clearing' system could often earn a very tidy profit, but at the same time risked taking heavy losses whenever too many of these deals came on the market at the same time, and prices dropped accordingly. This form underwent many adjustments and eventually became known as 'arbitrage' or 'switch'.

I did some arbitrage trading for our company, and over the years, as I developed a knack for it, many other people asked me to trade for them as well – among them some of our clients, and even some of our competitors. This added an interesting sideline to my daily work: I was no longer just a trader in leather, but a financier dealing in large-scale transactions – virtually a banker – a profession that rated very highly in my own private list of prestigious callings.

As our business grew, I found that my need for communication services and professional banking advice increased too. It occurred to me that these services – telex machines and telephones, as well as advice on prices and exchange rates – were more readily available in a bank than anywhere else. Moreover, access to these services would be easier for me, in exchange for my business, at a medium-sized bank than at a large banking institution. In Paris I discovered just the bank I was looking for, Bank Danon, which gave me very satisfactory services. Later I heard about a small family bank in Geneva, and I looked into that alternative too. There was a special attraction for me in this small Swiss bank, since I soon found that it was in fact a part of the Israeli Discount Bank, owned by the Recanati family. Harry Recanati, the eldest brother and acknowledged head of the family, ran the branch in Geneva, while the second brother, Dani, ran the head office in Israel. A third brother, Raphael, operated out of New York, where he ran the family's shipping business.

On a summer's day in 1958 I arranged a meeting with Harry Recanati at his office in Geneva. The offices, housed in a lovely building with a finely carved marble façade, were in fact quite modest. The man who met me there was in his late thirties, a very polite, easygoing man who already stood at the head of a burgeoning business empire. I am a great believer in 'chemistry' between people, and am convinced that its importance in business and politics is incalculable. The relationship between Harry and myself was a classic case of instant 'good chemistry', which has sustained a close friendship for over forty years, despite a few – and occasionally extreme – crises and disruptions that engulfed us both. I found in him not only a business partner, but also a true friend. I was deeply impressed by his intelligence and his superb financial skills. Very soon after our first meeting, we embarked on joint business ventures and investments. Our group soon applied most of the excellent commercial advice that he gave me, and we enjoyed making use of his wonderful contacts. Whenever I walked into the bank in Geneva I felt instantly at home. I used his bank's services, consulted with him, and thoroughly enjoyed the hospitality he extended to me. This relationship has endured to this very day.

After a while, my conversations with Harry became more personal. 'What are you doing in Israel?' he asked me. 'How is it possible to live in one country and work in another?'

I told him that no one had offered me anything really interesting in Israel, that I was happy with my work abroad, and that I didn't even have the time to think about dividing my time any differently. As he continued to question me, I explained that it was very important for me to raise and educate my daughters in Israel. 'Living in Israel is a very special privilege. Actually experiencing Israeli life at first hand,' I told him, 'makes me feel as though I too am part of the miracle of the creation of the state.'

I was not sure if my words had moved him in any way, because he immediately asked me, 'And why don't you come to Geneva and go into partnership with me here at the bank?' He led me to an adjoining room with a large window overlooking the spectacular vista of the lake, and said, 'This could be your office.'

I was flattered, but once again I reminded him – and myself – of my commitment to my family. 'And besides, if I did decide to live in some other country in Europe, I would settle in Holland. I am part owner of a family business there, which has been going for over a hundred years.'

'Do you know my brother Dani?' Harry now asked me, doggedly pursuing his train of thought.

'No, I've never met him,' I replied.

'Good, well when you get back to Israel I'll arrange for you to meet him. It's unheard of that you should be living in a new country that is just beginning to grow and develop and not have a piece of the action,' he declared bluntly.

I had already had more than enough 'pieces of the action' in Israel with my ill-fated involvement in the Accadia Hotel, and now all I wanted was to engage in more secure areas of business. However, I didn't say anything to Harry and preferred to wait and see how the chips would fall.

Soon after I arrived back in Israel, a meeting was arranged between Dani Recanati and myself. Dani, too, made a deep impression on me. Why does he look so familiar? I thought. Have we met somewhere in the past? A few nights later the answer to my question struck me: he reminded me of a Portuguese Jew, one of the descendants of the Spanish Jewish nobility who fled to Holland after the Inquisition, and inspired some of Rembrandt's paintings. In my childhood I had seen faces like that at the Esnoga Portuguese synagogue in Amsterdam. We spent two hours together at that first meeting. He was extremely charming, I was friendly, and there was a great deal of goodwill on both sides, despite which we were unable to reach an agreement on a business partnership that would be mutually satisfactory. I found the ideas he proposed unacceptable, while he felt that my proposals were unrealistic and impractical. For a while it looked as though our budding friendship would remain limited strictly to social events. His intelligence, keen mind, and instant grasp of any issue we discussed impressed me. He was also blessed with a rare quality: he excelled not only at voicing his own opinions but also in listening to others expound theirs.

The Recanati family is descended from a line of Spanish Jews forced out by the Inquisition who maintained their Jewish heritage and traditions over the generations. After the expulsion of the Jews from Spain, the family made its way via Italy to Saloniki in Greece. The head of the family, Leon (Yehuda) Recanati, was an educator at the Jewish high school in Saloniki and one of the leaders of the Jewish community there. He was universally admired for his high ethical standards and his stature as an educator, but equally for his extraordinary business acumen, a quality he discovered only when he went into the tobacco business after retiring from his teaching career. Around 1933 he travelled to Germany on business to attend a tobacco fair. He was so deeply disturbed by the atmosphere in Germany and the rise to power of the National Socialists that he hurried back to Greece, and, without giving it a second thought, picked up his entire family and moved to Palestine.

The arrival of Leon Recanati and his family in Palestine caused quite a stir in the small Yishuv in Palestine, as well as in the Jewish community in Egypt where he was equally well known. People from the Sephardi community approached him, offering to deposit their money with him so that he could set up a new and unique banking institution. The founders wanted to prove that, even without any prior experience in banking, it was possible to set up a reliable bank that could be geared to meet the needs of a particular social sector. The bank was officially opened in 1935 and became an instant success story. Ten years later, in 1945, Leon Recanati passed away, in the prime of his life.

The death of the head of the family brought the second generation of Recanatis to the forefront. The eldest son, Harry, embarked on an ambitious programme to expand the bank's operations, which included opening many new branches in Israel and abroad. The name Discount Bank began appearing on bank buildings in Zurich, Geneva, Amsterdam, New York and several South American countries. Dani was demobilized from the British army at the end of the war, and soon joined the family business in Palestine. The aristocratic, even-handed and extremely cordial banker, and his impeccable character, impressed everyone who came into contact with him and his gentle demeanour became part of the bank's image in the public eye. Raphael Recanati ran the bank's business in New York, and the fourth brother, Ya'akov, settled in Haifa and went into the shipping business. Within a few years, Discount Bank became the second largest bank in Israel, after Bank Leumi.

Two days after my meeting with Dani I received a phone call from Harry. He suggested that we meet at the bank at three o'clock that afternoon, and try to iron out our differences and find some way to reach a decision on a business relationship between us.

'But how will you be able to get to Israel so quickly?' I asked.

'I'm already here,' he replied. 'When Dani told me that things were not working out, I decided to come right away. I arrived last night and I have to go back tomorrow morning.' After a brief pause he corrected himself: 'No, come to think of it, let's make it two o'clock, and arrange to stay here with us at least until nine. There's a lot of work to be done.'

'What work?' I asked, somewhat bewildered.

'We're going to set up a new bank together.'

13

AND A NEW CAREER IN
BANKING

At precisely two p.m. I arrived with my friend and partner, Yoseph
Mirelman, at the main offices of Discount Bank on Yehuda Halevi
Street in Tel Aviv. Harry and Dani Recanati received us warmly, and
we were joined by the bank's legal advisor, Dr Kurt Getzlinger, and
Henry Bourla, one of the bank's directors, a very gentle and pleasant
man. Our discussions were long and complex, but we managed to iron
out all the outstanding problems, and finally put our signatures to a
draft agreement setting up the partnership. In this memorandum we
agreed that we would establish a bank for development and mortgages,
that I would be its president, and that I would be able to retain my
other business interests abroad, albeit on a reduced scale. It was Harry's
proposal to set up a bank that would deal with both development and
mortgages under the same roof that clinched the deal for me, since I
had no interest whatsoever in running either a regular commercial bank
or only a mortgage bank.

We concluded the marathon meeting with an enormous sense of
relief and satisfaction on all sides. The idea of becoming involved in
the development of industrial firms and projects in Israel was a very
exciting one for me. After all, my background was in the world of
industry and commerce, and these were still my main areas of interest.
I knew that financial dealings as such could not sustain my interest
over a long period of time. We agreed that money for those industrial
projects that we chose to support would be borrowed from Discount
Bank's present and future capital. There would be twelve directors, six
from Discount Bank and six from ARGEL, the company in which Dr
Mirelman and I were partners, along with a number of shareholders
from Argentina. We were given the authority to represent ARGEL in
all decisions and appointments arising from this partnership. We
decided on a total of 750 founders' shares, of one Israel pound each
nominal value, equally divided between the Discount Group and our-

selves. The agreement went on to stipulate that our groups would retain seventy-five per cent of the voting rights on issues relating to increasing capital, dividends and the like. When the bank opened, it had an initial capital of one million Israeli pounds. Half of this sum was deposited in the new bank by Discount Bank, and half by ARGEL, the corporation that constituted my group. Most of the money we invested came from the money we had deposited for safe-keeping in the Ministry of Finance after the sale of the Accadia Hotel.

Once the agreement was signed, we deepened our contacts with the Recanatis through daily discussions. Even after we received official government approval to open the new bank, we did not rush into throwing its doors open to the public. We spent time looking for the right building, which we eventually found in a small street in the heart of Tel Aviv. At first we occupied only the ground floor, and later, as our business expanded, we took over the floors above us as well. We eventually renovated the entire building, and moved Discount Bank's investment company, and the Nechassim u-le-Binyan real estate and construction company and most of their branches, into the upper floors. From my offices on the second floor of the building I could oversee the many and varied activities that were concentrated under our one roof.

We invested much time and energy in preparing and painstakingly organizing everything we thought would be necessary for the success of the new banking institution. And then at last, on my fortieth birthday, 8 May 1959, the Development and Mortgage Bank was officially opened at a ceremony attended by the Minister of Finance, Levi Eshkol, the Minister of Commerce and Industry, Pinhas Sapir, and partners from Buenos Aires.

Within a relatively short time I learned that, because of its limited resources and low profit margin, a mortgage bank was not at all like a regular commercial bank. Our bank's principal function was to arrange Ministry of Housing loans for people buying apartments. Just like the other two large mortgage banks, controlled by Bank Leumi and Bank Hapoalim, our bank was not much more than a conduit for channelling government funds into the public's hands. The problem was that these loans were granted sparingly, and thus did not enable us to generate significant profits. I told myself that the only way to avoid losing money – and perhaps even to make some – was to run a tight ship with a small but highly efficient staff, and to invest the state funds that we handled carefully, without taking any unnecessary risks. In order to ensure the efficient running of the bank, I asked a top accountant – and a childhood friend of mine – Avraham Vredenburg, to become the bank's chief administrator, and brought in Karl Reich and Yossi Shemesh to take up other senior positions. Ten years later, Vredenburg brought in Meir Eldar. When we opened the bank, our entire staff totalled only ten people.

With such a superb team running the day-to-day business of the bank, I could afford to look ahead at more general developments and future trends both at Discount Bank Investments and at the Development and Mortgage Bank, with a special emphasis on development. As the issue of development gained momentum, my enthusiasm grew as well, and my involvement in this aspect of the bank's business became one of my abiding passions. I immersed myself in it with all my heart, exhorting people in Israel and abroad to invest in local companies, and persuading my friends from South America to buy shares in newly expanding Israeli industries. Simon Mirelman, the much-admired leader of the Jewish community in Buenos Aires, and my close friend, was one of the people I recruited for this purpose, and he graciously accepted my offer to become the chairman of the Board of Directors of the bank. In Argentina he was a leading industrial entrepreneur, and he invested significant sums of money in companies supported by our bank. When one of our foreign partners put his holdings in the El-Yam shipping company up for sale, I purchased them, and in that way became a director and shareholder in all the firms affiliated with the Discount Bank group.

Soon, Dani co-opted me on to the Board of Directors of Discount Bank. While I was not involved in any of the daily affairs of the bank, my voice was definitely heard on important general policy issues, such as, for example, setting up additional branches abroad. I firmly believed in the need for branches of Jewish banks in Latin America. According to my estimates, there were 250,000–300,000 Jewish families in these countries, and I was convinced that most of them would prefer doing business with an Israeli bank that had connections to other countries in the world, particularly the United States and Israel. I had no doubt that Jews would prefer to deposit their money, their contributions to Israel, and their investments in Israel, in an Israeli bank. Language was another important asset: Jews like to feel 'at home' when they're doing business, and what could be more like home than conducting their banking business in Yiddish, Ladino, or even Hebrew.

With my first-hand knowledge of the countries of Latin America and Western Europe, I drew up a proposal for the location of several new branches and representation offices of the Israel Discount Bank. I also recommended people who I thought would be suitable for responsible positions in these new branches. I was convinced of the enormous potential of the bank's overseas expansion, and time was to prove me right.

Recruiting capital investments by brokering shares did not give me the satisfaction I was looking for. Also, it simply did not generate the kind of revenues we needed for the goals we had in mind. Looking for another source of income, we decided to issue bank bonds – with government approval of course – and to sell them through government channels. Most of these bonds were earmarked for covering the government's budgets and helping to meet its day-to-day budgetary requirements. Nevertheless, on occasion, whenever we came across 'unattached' sums of money – funds that the state did not need right away – we made use of them by transferring them to our mortgage funds, which were not too well endowed to begin with. That was the only way we could compete with the older and better-established banks. And the fact that we managed to bring in foreign capital and help establish new industries soon gave us a good reputation for reliability. Within a short time we managed to close the gap between our young bank and the competition.

I mentioned our goals. But what were these goals of ours? If I were to say 'the greater good of the state of Israel', I might be accused of gratuitous self-righteousness. But at the same time, we must remember that at that time, in the very early and difficult years of the state's existence, it was exceedingly difficult to distinguish between the good of the country and the good of commercial institutions like our own. After all, we were involved in setting up industries and businesses that were destined to pave the way for a new economic reality in the country, and would change the face of the industrial and business community in Israel. Their development and commercial success were inseparably linked to the prosperity of the country as a whole. One of the examples of these joint successes was our idea of offering our bonds to the public through foreign banks abroad. I well remember the dire warnings and prophecies of doom that came our way from all the experts who strongly opposed what they believed could only end in disaster. On a certain level, one could even understand them, because this was an unprecedented move in the Israeli banking community. I ignored the criticism, and insisted on pushing ahead with the idea, and ultimately my determination yielded a very handsome profit indeed. We sold a few million of these bonds, for which we were paid in dollars. The Ministry of Finance had no objection to our using these funds to serve the bank's own purposes, some of which were totally devoted to the development of Israeli industry.

CLAL

My involvement in the numerous companies controlled by Discount Bank considerably expanded my business horizons. Forging ahead with the intensity I so relished, I became involved in the running of numerous firms, companies and projects. A few small vignettes that come to mind from my day-to-day activities in those years still warm my heart. For example, filling up with petrol at a Delek garage, and secretly checking out the service from the point of view of a shareholder; or leafing through the morning paper and, as I read the headlines, recalling the last meeting of the board at the Hadera Paper Mills; visiting one of our affiliated companies and sitting in on its board meeting; attending meetings of the Board of Directors of Discount Bank. As a representative of the leadership of Discount Bank I also met regularly with the heads of the various economic ministries in the government. Those were years of great personal and public growth for me. And throughout it all, there was one relationship in particular – with the Minister of

Commerce and Industry, Pinhas Sapir – that grew into a deep trust and close personal friendship, and was to have a profound influence on my life.

During the sixties several momentous events took place that were to shape the future of the country, and which were also significant and fascinating for me personally. I believe it was Sapir who first recognized my ability to promote the country's business and investment contacts in South America. From the time I joined the Discount Group he had his eye on me. He believed that, whenever the interests of South American Jewry were involved, I was the man with the magic touch, and consequently he drew me closer to him, both out of personal affection and the confidence that I would be able to serve him well. Sapir was a powerful man, not power-hungry, and never tainted by cynicism, but a consummate master of manipulation. He was driven by an enormous – indeed almost personal – sense of responsibility for the people of Israel and the country he served. He was absolutely convinced that I was motivated by similar feelings, and knew how to inspire me with his enthusiasm and drive.

In the early part of 1962 Sapir suggested that I set up a new company with investors from Latin America. These investors, he suggested, would control eighty per cent of the company's shares. Some of these potential investors already owned companies in Israel, but were finding it difficult to run them efficiently from a distance. Others were interested in investing in the country in order to transfer some of their money out of the unstable South American region. All of them were well known for their strong affiliation with Zionism. According to the proposal, the remaining twenty per cent of the shares would be held by the ten largest firms in Israel, which would give the company its local base. These were to be Bank Leumi, Discount Bank, Bank Hapoalim, the Development and Mortgage Bank, the Bank for Industrial Development, the Foreign Trade Bank, the Agriculture Bank, the Central Trade Company, Koor Industries, and the Solel Boneh contracting company.

Aharon Dovrat, then head of the Industrial Section at the Ministry of Commerce and Industry, and son-in-law of my friend Ya'akov Tsur, Israel's first ambassador to Argentina, agreed to come in on the new venture. Together we drew up a list of one hundred wealthy people whom we would invite personally, on Sapir's behalf, to the founding meeting of this new company. Everything went as smoothly as a well-oiled machine, and on 2 May 1962 one hundred people gathered in Miami, Florida, to launch the new company. Dani Recanati, whom I had managed to persuade to attend the meeting, was the one who came up with a name for the new company: Clal ('General' in Hebrew). After making the trip to Miami, he felt very much a part of the new enterprise and was pleased to have joined the project – as were all the other participants in the meeting who expressed their desire to join the new venture. Nobody could foresee, of course, that in time Clal would become the largest company in Israel's private sector, and would be controlled by the Recanati family. I am not certain if this latter development, which occurred only in recent years, is something for which I can take credit or be blamed.

I believe that all the participants – a veritable *Who's Who* of Israeli economic life – were moved by the event. To my deep regret, I am the only one who can testify to the electrifying atmosphere of that evening: of all the Israelis who were present at that founding meeting, only Abraham Friedman and I are still alive. And I was as moved as everyone else. I was given the great honour of opening the historic ceremony at which the founding of the new company was announced. I explained to the prestigious gathering the concept behind the creation of Clal, and then gave the floor to Pinhas Sapir. The Minister of Commerce and Industry gave the keynote address, and then I continued to chair the meeting. That evening we set a goal of $25 million to be raised for the new company – a very large sum at that time. We also established another company, Ma'aleh, on that same occasion, to be jointly owned by the government and the Israeli shareholders, aimed at helping investors from abroad sell their Clal shares once they came on *aliya* to Israel. There was a general feeling that the new company had a brilliant future ahead of it, and the Israeli economy was on the brink of a new and very exciting era in its brief history.

Once the initial euphoria died down, it became clear that enthusiasm alone would not get the job done. The Ministries of Finance and of Commerce and Industry sent a few senior representatives for a round of talks with potential investors, but nothing concrete ever came out of them. Six months passed, and still nothing happened. The problem seemed to be the make-up of the Board of Directors. Each one of the directors was an eminently capable and praiseworthy person in his own right, but they had trouble communicating with one another. Clearly, what we needed was a strong managing director who would take control of the companies and the directors, and provide them with an adequate ideological and practical framework. But no one volunteered for the job. Everyone knew just how difficult it was to realize even supposedly cast-iron investment promises.

The investors' impatience with the slow pace of the company's move towards achieving its capital investment goal was expressed succinctly by Dr George S. Wise, the chairman of the Board of Directors. In a terse statement to Sapir, Wise said: 'You had better either appoint a managing director for the company – or forget the entire thing.' This blunt approach worked, and Sapir and Wise quickly came to an agreement on a suitable candidate – and offered me the job. The offer created a major dilemma for me. On the one hand, my career at the bank was flourishing, and I found a great deal of interest and satisfaction in supervising our investments in industrial firms. I also asked myself how Dani Recanati might react if I suddenly got up and dissolved our partnership. As it turned out, Sapir was one step ahead of me. Before approaching me with the offer, he had discussed the issue with Dani Recanati, and secured his approval to release me from my duties at the bank for a year. As managing director of Clal it would be my duty to run the company and bring in the promised investments. How could I refuse now that Sapir had paved the way for me? I agreed, but waived payment for my work. I did not want to make any money from the change in my position and status, since I intended to return to my position at the bank at the end of the designated period. And, in any case, I had a substantial income from our leather business abroad, and did not need another salary.

As managing director of Clal I did indeed bring in the investment pledges, but it took me two and a half years to complete the task. Once my main assignment as managing director was completed, Dani Recanati reminded Sapir that the time had come for me to return to IDB and Discount Bank. Sapir reluctantly agreed, but on condition that I be appointed chairman of Clal's Executive Committee. I remained in that capacity from 1965 to 1988. When I retired from the position of managing director in 1965, I recommended that Aharon Dovrat replace me, which he did, and very successfully too.

The Executive Committee of Clal established a model of business administration that was unknown in Israel up to that time. Over the years, after this model proved itself in Clal, a number of other companies successfully adopted the concept. The Executive Committee functioned on the basis of authority delegated to it by the Board of Directors. This was necessary because of the sheer size of the board: some fifty directors representing the various shareholders in Israel and abroad. Naturally, reaching mutually acceptable decisions in so cumbersome a body was exceedingly difficult. Moreover, the shareholders' representatives came to Israel only once or twice a year, making it difficult to ensure the proper day-to-day functioning of the company. To overcome this problem, a fifteen-man Executive Committee was set up to serve as a liaison between the Board of Directors and the managing director.

With a balance sheet in the black from its very first year of operation, Clal became an integral and significant part of the Israeli economy. Clearly, the fortuitous timing of its establishment enhanced its financial success. And yet, in the mid-sixties, when Israel plunged into a serious recession, many of the investors expressed concern over the fate of their investments. Clal suffered just like all the other companies whose shares were traded on the Tel Aviv Stock Exchange, and its shares began to decline, even though the company was invested in profitable ventures. The foreign investors seized the opportunity of the recession to pull out of Clal by selling off their shares on the stock market. Other investors sold some of their shares just to test the waters, and see if their investments in Israel could indeed be realized. Clal's management, principally Dovrat and myself, followed these developments with some concern, and soon decided to set up a subsidiary company to buy up these shares as an interim measure. After examining the problem from every possible angle, we reached the conclusion that the banks were the only financial institutions that could possibly absorb all the Clal shares that had been put on the market. This meant going against one of the basic guiding principles of the company, namely that Israeli firms would hold no more than twenty per cent of the concern's total shares; but under the circumstances, we had no choice.

After lengthy discussions, we finally offered the large banks the opportunity to buy up Clal investors' shares. We took these steps very carefully and deliberately, and in constant consultation with all the relevant economic and financial bodies. When the management of Bank Leumi hesitated before giving us an answer, we sold most of the shares to Bank Hapoalim and Discount Bank, while Bank Leumi eventually purchased a smaller number of shares and got rid of them shortly afterwards. After all these complex transactions, only 400 of the original 1,800 Jewish foreign investors remained on board.

The Six-Day War pulled Israel out of the grave recession of 1966, and gave Clal, among others, a much-needed boost into the bargain. But, as was often the case with large companies, Clal's greatest days came in the era of large-scale mergers that followed much later. The first of the mergers was with Gus-Rasco, a company owned by Sir Isaac Wolfson and Sir Charles Clore, and run in Israel by Haim Herzog. Afterwards there were additional mergers that enabled Clal to expand its business interests considerably. The biggest and perhaps most important merger in Israel's economy was that of Clal with the Central Trade Company, one of the largest industrial and commercial firms in the country. Headed by Gershon Gurevitch and Abraham Friedman, the Central Trade Company was just as keen as the Clal people on going ahead with the deal. In fact, the Central Company was one of the ten Israeli companies that had founded Clal in the first place. Avraham Friedman was appointed deputy managing director of the company. In the wake of these business successes, Clal took additional companies under its wing, such as the Nesher Cement Company, the Nazareth Vehicle Company, Electra, Ordan and many others.

I devoted much time and energy to these developments. I was deeply involved in all of them, appointing directors and supervising the company's manifold activities in all its firms, branches and affiliates. Undoubtedly, efficient management played a major role in the company's success. In its first year it was run by a small, tightly knit and highly efficient team that worked out of offices at the Bank for Industrial Development. Soon the company needed more office space, and moved to the El Al Building on Ben Yehuda Street in Tel Aviv. As Clal flourished, the time came for the company to move into its own building – the Clal Building on Druyanov Street in the centre of Tel Aviv. To this day, long after my departure from Clal, I still have offices in this building. It's almost as though I cannot tear myself away from the place where I spent so many productive and happy years.

At the end of the eighties I resigned from the Board of Directors and from the Executive Committee of the company. Like any other dynamic company, Clal too had changed over the years. By the time I left, it no longer had its original South American flavour, and only my occasional conversations in Spanish with Dovrat reminded me of those far-off Latin American days. The company went public, and the intimate contact with the original investors was lost. Nevertheless, I look back on my years there with deep satisfaction: within less than thirty years Clal became the largest private industrial and commercial company in the country. Aharon Dovrat, its former managing director, deserves much praise for his excellent leadership. My own contributions to the company, particularly the strong ties that I cultivated between the shareholders and the directorate, played a major role in Clal's success over the years.

FAREWELL TO FATHER

My father's life came to an end in the middle of November 1961. His greatest wish – to come and live out his last years in Israel – never materialized. His sudden death came as a shock to all of us, but we consoled ourselves with the thought that at least he had died in Israel, surrounded by his family, and had passed away relatively painlessly. The fact that my father never came on *aliya* to Israel did not prevent him from regarding himself to his last day as a true Zionist. He and my mother contributed generously to Israeli institutions, and came regularly, at least once a year, on visits. They generally stayed at the Dan Hotel in Tel Aviv, or at the old Sheraton. My father took great pleasure in the atmosphere he found at the Ihud Shivat Zion synagogue, led by Rabbi Yehuda Ansbacher, and he never missed any of the services or the Talmud lessons in the old building at the corner of Ben Yehuda and Frischman Street in Tel Aviv.

My father was only seventy-two years old when he died, but he had been growing steadily weaker over a number of years. His health had begun deteriorating for no apparent reason. He lost weight, frequently complained of fatigue, and had difficulty walking. Gradually he sold off his business interests, and the idea of coming to live in Israel began taking precedence over everything else. Zigi and I had no difficulty in persuading him to retire, to leave his beloved Argentina and begin planning a life of ease and comfort in Israel, close to his two sons and five granddaughters.

Always the practical man, my father took advantage of his annual visit for the High Holidays to look for a house. We eventually found the perfect place, just down the road from Zigi's house. In a buoyant mood, my father told me about it as we went on our regular Saturday morning walk near the hotel. 'Go to the owner and give him his asking price. Don't haggle,' he ordered, eager not to miss this golden opportunity. His eyes shone as he described the house to me: comfortable, beautiful, not too expensive, and, best of all, right next door to his son the doctor. 'Zigi can come in whenever he likes to check my blood pressure – it's just a few metres away from his house!' he said, beaming.

We continued on our walk. It was still summer in Israel, but the heat of the day had abated, and a welcome cool breeze blew in from the sea. 'How is business here?' he asked. He had never been involved in any of my business affairs, even though I had always taken an active interest in his.

'Father,' I said, 'you know that I am not interested in making any profits from my business interests in Israel. I've told you this before; that's the way it's been ever since I came on *aliya*.'

My father knew this, of course, but he had never been too happy about these self-imposed rules of mine. He couldn't comprehend the logic behind them. He had always loved making money, so how was it possible that his son chose to disregard the very meaning of the word 'commerce'? In an effort to understand, he asked, 'So what are you going to do in the future? Are you just going to go on like this?'

I stuck to my guns: 'Father, you know I am not a poor man. I have our business abroad, so in Israel I almost always work voluntarily. I feel bad about working for a profit here.'

'That's impossible!' my father remonstrated, more adamant than ever. 'A merchant, or an industrialist, or a craftsman – whatever – has to earn something from his work. What you do with your money afterwards is nobody's business, but you have to know, for yourself, what your work is worth. You should also look out for your own interests, so that you don't feel exploited. In a country where everyone gets paid for their work, it's unheard of that you should be the only exception.'

He was right, of course. But it took me many years to understand the wisdom of his advice. He was implying that people who are different are generally looked down upon by their society, regardless of how beneficial their 'difference' may be to everyone around them. He knew that volunteering was regarded by many as an invitation to exploitation or even contempt.

That evening, I prevailed upon my parents to come with us to the cinema. My father had difficulty walking, but enjoyed the double pleasure of seeing a film and doing so in the company of his family. When it was over, we made our way through the audience that thronged the exit. I glanced at my father as we moved with the crowd, and was shocked to see how pale and fatigued he looked. All night my conscience troubled me: why did I have to take him with me into that crowded cinema? In his state of health it was too much of a strain. The following morning he called Zigi and told him he was not feeling well. Zigi immediately took him by ambulance to Beilinson Hospital. At that time, ambulances were not as well equipped as they are today, and emergency medical treatment was also less sophisticated. A few years later, my doctors told me that the heart attack I suffered was much more severe than the one that caused my father's death. Unfortunately, he never lived to benefit from the advances in cardiac medicine. When my father died I was a grown man, with a proven track record of accomplishments in everything I had touched, and yet upon his death I suffered a crushing sense of loss.

Immediately after the funeral I tried to honour his memory by doing things I felt would have made him happy. I began by regularly attending services at the Ihud Shivat Zion synagogue that he had loved. I usually went to the later morning services, but on occasion I rose early and went to the first *minyan* at six fifteen in the morning. Rabbi Ansbacher noticed my regular visits, and asked if I wanted to lead the prayer service as was customary for the bereaved.

'I don't think I'm suited for it,' I replied. 'I am not as observant as my father was. If the people who worship here see me driving on the Sabbath, they will be very angry with their *sh'liach tsibur* [prayer leader] who does not observe the Sabbath properly.'

'Well then,' Rabbi Ansbacher suggested, 'I have an idea: don't drive on Shabbat!' He was not joking.

'I can't,' I replied, no less seriously. 'It's a matter of principle.'

'All right,' he relented. 'I'll ask the regulars. Come to the early *minyan* tomorrow so that I can ask the people who come to the second *minyan*.'

To my amazement, the majority of the men in the *minyan* decided that I was suited to lead the morning prayers, even though I continued to drive on the Sabbath. The prayer services in the synagogue and the *Kaddish* that I recited there for my father were a source of great comfort to me, giving me the strength to come to terms with my father's death. My conversations with the ever-patient and sympathetic rabbi were interesting and deeply moving, and also helped me in my grief. I understood then why my father had admired him so much: he was one of the only rabbis I have ever met who truly knew the meaning of tolerance and the love of Israel. If only we had a few more rabbis like him, this country would be a very different place...

Some ten years later I mourned over the loss of my youngest daughter, Ariela. At about the same time, the Ihud Shivat Zion community moved into a beautiful new building on the other side of Ben Yehuda Street. I was pleased to be able to help Rabbi Ansbacher by contributing the community centre of the new building, which is known to this day as the Nathan Ben Shimon (Gitter) Community Centre.

SAPIR AND THE MISSING SUMS

I have only a fragmentary memory of my first meeting with Pinhas Sapir. I believe that it was at a business meeting or social gathering during one of my visits to Israel with a group of South American investors. We exchanged a few pleasantries, nothing more. I had already heard much about him, and had admired him from afar. I was told that before the country achieved its independence he had been Israel's major arms purchaser. His knowledge in the fields of arms procurement was phenomenal, and many years later he could still quote at will the price of a Messerschmidt aeroplane that he had purchased in Prague in 1948, or the differences (in price, not technology) between the more modern French Mirage and Mystère jet fighters that Israel purchased in the sixties. He was the first Director-General of Israel's new Ministry of Defence, until someone decided, quite rightly, that he could bring much greater benefit to the state by moving to the area of economics.

Later I met Sapir at the farewell party for the managing director of the Hadera Paper Mills. This company, a pioneer of modern industrial technology in Israel, became one of the leading firms in Clal Industries and Israel Discount Industries. I remember regarding him on that occasion with some derision: it was such a small country, and here was this man making so much noise! My initial reaction was totally misconceived. I subsequently learned that one of Sapir's abiding virtues was his sure instinct about the exact moment when it was prudent to pull back from any further attempt to change his interlocutor's mind. When I came to know him better, I discovered some of his other sterling qualities: his brilliant mind, and innate, unaffected modesty. He was constantly surrounded by wealthy people, and was very well aware of the value of money and of ways of earning it, but in his own personal and family life, he was frugal to a fault.

In this context I remember the following story. On our way back from one of Sapir's visits to South America, our flight was delayed at the airport in Caracas. It was late and we were both rather hungry. We sat at a counter at the airport restaurant, and I ordered and paid for a couple of sandwiches for both of us. After we finally boarded the plane and took our seats, Sapir produced his wallet, and carefully counted out eight dollars. 'What's that?' I asked in amazement.

'You paid the waiter sixteen dollars, so I owe you eight,' he said, proffering the bills.

With all his modesty and apparent disregard for material things in his own life, Sapir understood, better than most people I know, the true nature of a profit-oriented economy. Knowing that only substantial profits can ensure repeat investments, he sought every means possible to attract local and foreign investors and help them succeed in their business ventures in Israel. Their satisfaction was very important to him. In his vision of the Zionist dream, Israel was to be not only the emotional and spiritual heart of the Jewish people, but an international centre of finance and commerce as well. Sapir's version of Zionism was anything but airy idealism that was out of touch with reality.

As part of my duties as managing director of the Development and Mortgage Bank, Dani Recanati appointed me, informally, as the 'Foreign Minister' of Discount Bank and their holding company IDB – their liaison with the government authorities on bank business. This task brought me into frequent contact with Sapir, and we soon developed a rare mutual understanding. We began meeting outside his offices, generally on Saturday mornings at his home in Kfar Saba just north of Tel Aviv. I remember these meetings with crystal clarity. Since both of us were early risers and hated wasting time, I used to show up on his doorstep at seven a.m. on a Saturday morning. I would sit in the deeply cushioned armchair while he sprawled on the couch across the room, his pen poised over his ubiquitous black notebook, ready to jot down any idea that might occur to him that required further thought or development. At eight in the morning his small grandchildren – his daughter Rina's children – would come tearing in from their house next door like a small whirlwind, and proceed to dance on their grandfather's ample belly. Sapir allowed them do their worst, glowing with pleasure – and without missing a beat in our conversation. Often his special advisor, Yossi Sarid, would come in at nine to receive instructions. On other occasions, members of the Knesset, businessmen or foreign investors would show up, and I would stay or go depending on the circumstances.

At times we would have these meetings on weekdays as well. Sapir would call me and ask in his deep bass voice, 'Gitter [that's what he called me, and I returned the compliment by calling him simply Sapir], can you make it tomorrow morning? Let's meet as usual.' 'As usual' meant at six in the morning at the Ra'anana barbershop where he got a shave every morning. Sometimes we drove from there to Jerusalem, either in his official car or in mine. It was during these meetings with Sapir that I came to understand his views on economics. His ideas in no way resembled learned theories one might acquire at university. Instead, they were all the direct result of common sense, experience, daring and intuition. He was also possessed of an extraordinary memory, and never forgot any new turn of phrase, technical term or definition that popped up in the professional jargon of economists, and always knew how and when they applied. If necessary, he could handle any situation in Yiddish or in English as well. These were the ingredients that went into the making of Sapir, the 'mythological' Minister of Finance of the state of Israel.

Despite the fact that he could outclass any economics expert on his home turf, Sapir always felt that a formal education would have enhanced his abilities and increased his self-confidence. But this was one of the few ambitions that Sapir was unable to realize. Every time he was about to take some time off to study (like a course he enrolled to take in London), he was called back to take up another, more senior position in the government hierarchy. In 1955 David Ben Gurion nominated Sapir as Minister of Commerce and Industry. In June 1963, when Levi Eshkol was elected Prime Minister, Sapir was appointed Minister of Finance, but also retained the portfolio of Minister of Commerce and Industry. After Eshkol's unexpected death, in 1969, and then again after Prime Minister Golda Meir's resignation in April 1974, conditions seemed ripe for Sapir to move into the Prime Minister's seat. I believe to this day that he had all the qualities necessary for the position, but for some reason he never made a move to secure it. Some of his closest associates claimed that he did not feel up to the demands of the top position in the state of Israel. His fears may have stemmed from a sense of inadequacy owing to what he felt was his lack of academic training and background. His last real opportunity to study slipped away towards the end of 1964 when he agreed to serve a second term as Minister of Finance.

Sapir was a man of action who paid attention to the most minute details. Whenever anyone approached him about setting up an industrial company, Sapir would always ask: How far is it from Tel Aviv? If the potential investor had done his homework he knew that the further his projected plant was from Tel Aviv, the greater his chances were for getting help from the Treasury. Then Sapir would go on and ask some more questions: How many employees will your company need? What is your projected volume of production? Will the firm cover its costs (or in Sapir's picturesque Hebrew: 'Will it be a live body that carries its own weight?'). And then, whenever necessary, he would do a complete about-face and ask contrary questions: How many employees can you do without? What percentage of imports will your plant replace? How can your export quotient be increased?

Sapir was a great believer in the dispersion of the population – a major socio-economic concept in Israel's early years. But in time the enthusiastic momentum of this seemingly positive slogan produced some enormous social mistakes. New immigrants were brought to undeveloped areas of the country where there was little likelihood of making a decent living. In an attempt to overcome that problem, non-priority industrial enterprises were set up around the so-called development towns. One of the most glaring examples was the Kitan textile factory, which was set up in the town of Dimona. To Sapir's credit it must be said that for years Kitan Dimona provided jobs for 3,000 employees in the Negev development town, and saved many families from unemployment and hunger. For the new immigrants who were brought to the region, Kitan played the same role as did the Israel Defence Forces: a melting pot where newcomers could make the transition from their previous social and cultural milieu into the new and unfamiliar Israeli society. Through their employment at the plant many new immigrants learned Hebrew, underwent professional training, and integrated into society and into the country.

The name Kitan Dimona came up during one of my first important meetings with Sapir. I came to him for help with our first public offering of Development and Mortgage Bank bonds. The idea of issuing the bonds had received only lukewarm support both inside and outside the bank, and the preparations were taking longer than I had anticipated. Also, it was not at all clear whether the offering was going to yield any profits. From time to time, instead of sending the proceeds from public offerings directly to the Treasury, the bank was allowed to use some of the funds it received from the sale. As guardian of the bank's interests, it was up to me to persuade the Ministry of Finance to allow us to do so as often as possible. In that meeting with Sapir, I repeatedly tried to shift our conversation to the topic I had come to discuss.

'Let's talk about Dimona,' Sapir said, seemingly ignoring the drift of my conversation.

'Dimona?' I asked, somewhat bewildered.

'They are building a factory there that will employ 3,000 workers who will learn Hebrew and a trade there,' Sapir said pointedly. 'If we don't build factories we'll never have a city there, and then what will all the people living there do? Build more unnecessary roads?'

'But that doesn't solve my problem,' I blurted. 'I can't invest in a factory that's bigger than any of the factories we already own, just in return for your help!'

Sapir immediately changed tack. 'And apart from the business of the bonds,' he said smoothly, 'where else are you hurting?'

'I need help in securing a loan to buy equipment for our cable manufacturing company in Haifa. If that works out, I'll try to think of something,' I replied, relenting somewhat.

There was no obvious connection between the first issue, Kitan Dimona, and the other two, the bonds and the cable factory, but in Sapir's little black notebook all these apparently disparate pieces fitted neatly together.

Sapir was a never-ending source of new ideas for building infra-structures to bolster the Israeli economy. The Centre for Investments and the Alleviation of Institutional Taxation, which was a boon for investors and industrialists, was a case in point. The idea of tax-free donations to the country was another, and was one of Sapir's greatest contributions to the country's economy. Sapir followed the excellent example set by the United States in the area of corporate contributions. The US Treasury strongly encourages voluntary donations, and makes them tax-deductible. I brought to Sapir's attention the fact that in America donors can claim tax deductions not only for contributions made inside the US but also for contributions to Israel. I felt, however, that this was not sufficient for our purposes, and suggested that in order to encourage people to help cultural, educational and health institutions, potential donors should be given some added incentive, apart from the tax exemptions. The incentive should take the form of financial assistance – matching funds – from government sources, particularly in cases where the government in any case intended to invest its budgetary resources.

My relationship with Sapir very quickly developed far beyond mere formalities. Sapir and his wife Shoshana, and Dani and Matti Recanati, were among the friends we invited to a festive family dinner we gave in honour of my daughter Bixie's marriage. Sapir spoke warmly on the occasion, stressing the strong ties of friendship that bound us together. He was at my side in times of happiness and of sorrow. To my profound distress, years later shifts of time and fortunes eventually eroded our friendship. Nevertheless I could never find it in my heart to be really angry with him. Our relationship went through a dark period of misunderstanding and alienation, but in the end we arrived at a reconciliation.

Sapir truly enjoyed it when his advice was sought after and respected. He could not bear condescension of any kind. We were lucky enough to benefit from his support and respect for our work, possibly because we involved him from the very early stages of its development. We frequently sought his advice on important matters, some of them even of a private nature. As for my relations with the Recanati brothers, he followed my contacts with them fairly closely, and tended to favour Dani somewhat over Raphael.

Occasionally, Sapir would invite me to accompany him on his trips to South America to assist him in his contacts with the leaders of the community there. My contacts and my knowledge of Spanish were a great help to him. One trip we took together, at the beginning of the seventies, brings a smile to my lips whenever I think of it. Our first stop was in São Paulo, Brazil. The representative of the Mossad there had warned us of a possible attempt on Sapir's life, and as a precaution the embassy had booked an entire floor for him at his hotel. Sapir stayed in one room, I in another, and there was a living-room area connecting the two. An Israeli security officer was posted outside our door twenty-four hours a day. On the last night of our stay we attended a gala fundraising dinner for the UJA, and Sapir's presence spurred the wealthy guests to open their wallets and give generously. Sapir returned to the hotel quite excited and could not fall asleep.

'Let's go over the pledges again,' he requested.

It was already very late. 'Can't we do it tomorrow morning?' I pleaded with him.

It was just four hours before we would be leaving the hotel, and I desperately needed a few hours' sleep. But Sapir insisted. Reluctantly, I took a pen and paper, once again calculated the pledges we had been given, and handed him the piece of paper. I woke up at four in the morning, shaved and stepped into the bath. As I was relaxing in the warm water, I suddenly heard stealthy footsteps outside the bathroom. The door to the bathroom opened. I was convinced that the guard outside had fallen asleep on the job. I closed my eyes, and warm drops slid down my cheeks – water or sweat, I was not sure. Once again there was a muffled sound. My heart was beating wildly. In my imagination I could already see the assassin the Mossad had warned us about aiming his revolver at me. My eyes snapped open – and there was Sapir, sitting on the closed toilet seat. He pointed an accusing finger at me and said, 'There's a mistake in your figures!'

14

POLITICS AND DIPLOMACY

Today I find it rather amusing when I think of the chain of events hinted at in the title of this chapter, which almost propelled me into a minister's seat in the cabinet. At the time, I was filled with the bitter sense of a missed opportunity. At a remove of all those years, what is left in my memory is the endless manipulation, the manoeuvring, the insults and the bruised feelings, the anger and the frustration. But, over the years, I have become increasingly aware of some of the more comic elements that were also an integral part of the story.

It all began with the sudden death of Levi Eshkol in February 1969. Golda Meir succeeded him as Prime Minister, and Pinhas Sapir, who was Minister of Finance, was given the Commerce and Industry portfolio as well. Golda was very apprehensive about giving one man in the government so much power, not because she didn't trust Sapir, but because she didn't believe that anyone – no matter how gifted – could responsibly discharge so many important duties at once.

One evening, I received a phone call from Sapir at my home. He was on one of his rare vacations in the northern city of Zefat (Safed). 'Come to Zefat! Today!' he ordered. 'I have something important to tell you.' I tried to put off the trip until the following day, but to no avail. I arrived at his hotel in Zefat after ten at night, and found him dozing in an armchair. When he saw me he awoke instantly. 'Golda does not want me to be in charge of both ministries. But she is willing to let me choose my successor for the office of Minister of Trade and Industry. She doesn't care who it is as long as I find someone quickly.'

My initial astonishment quickly turned to anger. This was why he had demanded that I leave my home at the end of a long day's work, and make the four-hour drive to Zefat and back, up and down treacherous mountain roads at night?

'She said it was totally up to me. She does not intervene in economic affairs,' Sapir repeated, rephrasing his words slightly and looking me squarely in the eye. I think he was smiling.

And then it hit me. 'Does this have anything to do with me? Do you mean to say that you talked to her about me?' I stammered.

'*Mazel Tov*! My, aren't we quick-witted tonight,' he chided.

'And what did she say?' I asked, very nervous now.

'She's not overjoyed, but I already told you: she's leaving the decision entirely up to me. But what do you think?'

My thoughts were in turmoil. At first I was flushed with a pleasantly warm sensation. Coming from Sapir and – for all her reservations – from Golda as well, this was a tremendous compliment. It was also a huge compliment for a new immigrant like myself, who had never been one of 'the boys' in the Hagannah or the Palmach, or even on a kibbutz, for that matter. Nevertheless, I had to keep my wits about me. Deep inside I knew that, compliments aside, I was not cut out to be a government minister. Finally, I said to Sapir; 'I have to think about it. I must consult with Alice. I don't think she's exactly dying to be the wife of a government minister in Israel.'

'Let *me* talk to Alice,' Sapir rejoined. 'Don't decide anything yet. We've been invited to dinner at Golda's tomorrow at six thirty. Come with me, and let's see what happens.'

Up to the very moment I knocked on the front door of the Prime Minister's residence in Jerusalem, I wrestled with myself as never before. On the one hand, I was deeply touched by this display of confidence in me. On the other, I wondered how I could abandon my many business interests. What would happen to all the factories, projects and people I was responsible for? And if I did not cut myself off from all of them, how could I avoid conflicts of interest or, worse still, favouritism? And what would my partners say? And the most difficult question of all: was this really my kettle of fish? Would I be able to handle political pressures, partisan and non-partisan, without the solid backing of a political party? How long would Sapir be able to protect me, and when would our friendship turn into a handicap?

As I expected, Alice vehemently opposed the idea, and, in what was a highly unusual step for her, she shared her feelings with one of my good friends from Brazil who happened to be in the country at the time. 'Get that crazy idea out of his head,' she begged him. Her unequivocal opposition reinforced my own doubts about the wisdom of the move.

Until then, I had known Golda Meir only superficially, and much of what I knew came from the stories and myths spawned by her unique personality. In my mind's eye I had imagined her famous 'kitchen' – where she often held important meetings with members of her cabinet – as a mysterious place where fateful decisions were made, kings were crowned and political heads rolled. As it turned out, the reality of Golda's kitchen was a far cry from all these mystical fantasies. First of all, when I arrived I couldn't see anything vaguely resembling preparations for dinner. We sat in the living room and sipped cold drinks. From where I was sitting I could see the kitchen table out of the corner of my eye, and it had neither a tablecloth nor any trace of silverware on it. I was nervous and impatient, and kept thinking that at any moment we would get to the point of the meeting. Apart from Sapir and myself, the Minister of Justice, Ya'akov Shimshon Shapira – a frequent visitor at Golda's home – was also present. I had no idea why he was there or where he stood on the issue of my appointment: was he in favour or against it?

'Here we talk only after the meal,' Golda interrupted me as I tried to bring the conversation round to the question that was on my mind, but I still couldn't see the slightest hint of any kind of meal in the making. Then Golda made a tiny gesture and the two ministers flew out of their chairs, hurried into the kitchen and began fussing about with the plates and silver. I watched with utter amazement as Sapir, who in his own home never lifted a finger to pick up the tiniest spoon, not to mention a plate, skilfully set the table like a true professional.

The food was quite good, and the two ministers lavished praise on Golda's cooking. She received their praise coolly. I was rebuked once again when I tried very gingerly to bring the small talk around to the only subject that I cared about at that moment. 'If we can't have a moment's rest even while we're eating, how are we ever going to get any work done?' Golda asked sourly. I bit my tongue to hold back an imprudent reply.

Once the meal was over, Sapir and Shapira, for all the world like two overgrown children, put on aprons and cleared the dishes from the table. Now that we had eaten, I assumed it was safe at last to broach the issue. 'First I want to smoke a cigarette in peace and quite,' Golda said archly, and sat there for a long time enjoying her Kent cigarette. Finally, at long last, she sat up in her chair and said, 'Now we can talk.'

But it was still not my turn to ask questions or to say what was on my mind, because Golda took the floor instead, and launched into a lengthy peroration on her doubts about the appointment. She talked about the difficulties the position entailed, and her opposition to having one man hold so much power in the government. She mentioned her supposed non-involvement in the whole issue, and then summed it all up with a blunt question: 'Sapir thinks you can do the job. I have my doubts. What is your answer?'

Until that moment I had not known what my answer would be, but now, instantly, I knew what to say. I smiled and said decisively, 'Thank you, but no!'

Shapira and Sapir were stunned. Golda was annoyed, but immediately regained her composure. 'I told you,' she snapped at the two ministers in her most patronizing tone of voice. 'I told you he's a snob!'

Now it was my turn to be angry. 'Excuse me, Golda,' I said to her. 'Allow me to give you my reasons. After all, you invited me here to discuss something, and so far you have not given me a chance to get a word in edgewise.'

'There's actually no need,' Golda muttered angrily. 'But if you insist...'

'Look, Golda,' I said, 'I was not born on a kibbutz. We do not come from the same background. I am a member of the Labour Party, but I have never been a blue-collar worker. On the contrary, I employ blue-collar workers. If I take the job I'll have to deal with all of that and learning about it will require a great deal of time and effort. How much time is there, anyway, until the elections?'

'Ten months,' Sapir answered.

'And will I stay on in this job after the elections?'

'Do I know if we'll win the elections?' Golda asked, in her inimitable manner. 'Even Sapir and Shapira have no guarantee that they'll be ministers in the next government.'

'But supposing they are, will I be a minister too?' I persisted.

'Absolutely not!' came the rapid-fire response.

'In that case, it's hardly worth my while to make such radical changes in my life for only ten months,' I said. 'But I must tell you one more thing.' I looked squarely at the tough lady across from me and said, 'Now that this conversation is over, I have only one more question: which one of us is the snob?'

And that is how I did not become a minister in the Israeli government. Golda, who was well known for her vindictiveness, ignored me for the rest of the evening. In time our relationship improved, and years later, when she was no longer in office, she even asked for my help on a personal matter. I gladly offered to do whatever I could, and we developed a fine friendship that erased any rancour that may have lingered from the past. I once asked her why she had treated me so harshly that evening. She thought it over for a minute, then said, 'Because at that time I really didn't know you very well.' I will always cherish this sincere compliment from the great lady of Israeli history.

A ROVING AMBASSADOR

The abortive meeting in Golda's kitchen receded into the past, leaving no ill feelings. I tried not to waste energy on regretting a missed opportunity. Above all, I was pleased by Alice's evident relief. I did not want to cause her any pain. Because of her continuing illness, our lives had begun moving in separate directions. Alice noticed this even before I did, and it was she who encouraged me to keep up the intense pace of my life, even though she could not always be part of it. Therefore, while I busied myself with trips and my many business interests, she made a life for herself. Apart from raising our daughters and educating them, she also created an intellectual and spiritual world of her own. Studying and reading filled her life and soul. She developed a fine taste for art, and acquired a beautiful collection. I joined her in her purchases, amazed by her profound understanding and love of the arts, and by the time she devoted to cultural affairs.

A short time after that meeting at Golda's, I was invited to an informal meeting with Sapir. I had the feeling that my friend had yet another surprise in store for me. Indeed he did, and it was a particularly appealing offer. In those days, the status of Latin American Jewry was on the decline, not so much because of anti-Semitism, but for historico-political reasons. Some of the South American governments of the time were extremely unstable. Chile was ruled by the Marxist Salvador Allende; Brazil, Argentina and Uruguay were governed by dictators whose totalitarian régimes posed a potential threat to the Jewish minorities. The collapse of democratic rule and the rise of the military junta in Argentina resulted in a further deterioration in the economic situation of the Jews there. The early seventies bore the telltale signs of a reign of terror: people were kidnapped off the streets and disappeared simply because of their suspected opposition to the régime. Many young Jews were involved in protests against the government, and were forced to flee the country, either because of their own involvement in the protests, or the involvement of relatives. In their hasty departure they left behind all their property and personal belongings. This situation created a double bind: those who remained ran the risk of losing their civil rights, while those who fled were in danger of losing everything they owned. The situation prompted many people to give more serious thought than ever before to the idea of going on *aliya* to Israel, but most of them were beset by doubts that rendered them almost incapable of making a decision one way or the other. What would they do in Israel? What would they live on? Many of the potential immigrants feared that the unfavourable rate of exchange between the peso and the Israeli pound would make it impossible for them to buy an apartment with the money they would be allowed to take out of the country with them. The glut of apartments and houses on the market in Argentina brought prices plummeting down, while in Israel, on the other hand, demand for housing was enormous, and prices – by Argentine standards – were sky-high.

Sapir was well aware of all these developments, and it was for this reason that he wanted to see me. What he had in mind was to send me to South America as a 'roving ambassador' to facilitate the *aliya* of those wanting to come to Israel. When I came to see him, he compared the situation of the Jews in South America to the plight of the Jews in Germany in the thirties. He told me about a similar *aliya* operation carried out successfully by the Jewish Agency in Germany after Hitler's rise to power. A few years before the outbreak of the Second World War, Jews who emigrated to Palestine, or wanted to do so, were reimbursed for the property they left behind through an exchange agreement with the German government. As a result, while the rest of the Western world boycotted German products, Palestine was flooded with Mercedes cars and German electrical appliances. I refused to accept the analogy. 'How can you compare what happened in Nazi Germany to what's happening now in Argentina?!' I argued. In my opinion, the Jews in my former country were not in any kind of mortal danger, though they were facing severe financial difficulties. Despite my protests about the analogy with Germany, I was aware of the terrible damage these financial restrictions might inflict, and agreed with Sapir about the importance of extending a helping hand to the Jews of Argentina. I accepted his offer, and soon began preparing for a new mission to South America, this time as a *bona fide* Israeli diplomat.

At that time, similar efforts were being made to salvage the property of the Jews of Morocco. The problem arose following a forgotten but unpleasant incident in relations between Morocco and its Jewish minority. An attempt had been made on the life of the King of Morocco, and, in a bizarre twist of logic, because of the prominent position held by a number of Jews in the King's court, Jews became prime suspects in the abortive assassination attempt. Fear of riots against the community or pogroms in the Jewish quarter prompted many Jews to consider *aliya* to Israel. Although here too questions arose concerning the fate of the property of those who decided to leave, it transpired later that this was never really an issue: the rich Moroccan Jews emigrated to France, Spain, Canada and the United States, while the poor came to Israel.

Since my proposed appointment as ambassador came from outside Foreign Ministry circles, government approval was required. Golda pushed the issue through at a cabinet meeting that I was invited to attend. She treated me rather condescendingly, and made no mention at all of our previous meeting. Golda demanded that I report to her directly after every trip I made in my new capacity as roving ambassador to South America. Once my appointment was approved, I began attending meetings of the ministerial committee on *aliya* whenever the agenda included issues touching upon my work in South America. I worked out all the necessary legal aspects of my mission with the Minister of Justice, Ya'akov Shimshon Shapira, formulating with him which of my business interests I would have to relinquish, and which I could retain. The Attorney General Aharon Barak (presently the President of the Supreme Court) also examined the legal issues raised by my appointment, and naturally, as a civil servant, my work was to be monitored by the State Comptroller. I was to retain my position at Clal, which in any case had many dealings with South American Jewry. Looking back now on that entire process, I believe there was no justification for such a minutely detailed examination of all my achievements and failures, since, after all, I had agreed to accept the job on a purely voluntary basis. As usual, I also took it upon myself to cover most of the expenses involved out of my own pocket.

I began my activities as roving ambassador through the Fimaro Company, which I set up to deal with the property of South American Jews who wanted to come on *aliya*. The company eventually did very well, particularly in Argentina. We had offices in Buenos Aires that were run by my assistant, Asher Michaeli, a man with a great deal of experience and know-how in all things relating to the Jews of Latin America. The managing director of the company, Yoram Ravin, came from the top echelons of the Israeli civil service, and had served earlier as the Accountant-General of the Ministry of Finance. There was also a Board of Directors that was appointed, as was customary in Israel, along party lines. My position as ambassador prevented me from sitting on the board. The chairman of the company, chosen at my recommendation, was Ya'akov Tsur, formerly Israel's first ambassador to Argentina. I have no idea what Golda had against him, but her hostility towards him became apparently clear upon my return from one of my official trips. Before coming to report to her as she had requested, and in order to save myself the trouble of presenting my report twice, once to her and once to Tsur, I asked her permission to bring Tsur along to our meeting. 'Then perhaps it would be better if you didn't come at all,' was her reaction. That was Golda: a woman of strong likes and equally vehement dislikes.

Fimaro bought up all the apartments that new immigrants had difficulty selling, and the disparity between their value on the depressed Argentine housing market and their true value was made up by the government or the Jewish Agency. Over a period of time we managed to sell all the apartments we held – at times even for a nice profit, but in any case never at a loss. In the final analysis, the state of Israel profited from Fimaro's financial dealings in Argentina. But financial profit was only a by-product. After all, the company's main purpose was to extend aid to emigrants wanting to come and live in Israel, and help them purchase decent housing for themselves in their new country.

In Chile things were different. During the Allende régime many Jews wanted to come on *aliya*, but government regulations required that they leave all their property behind. I found this situation intolerable, and requested a meeting with President Allende in the hope of persuading him to see our side of the story. I must admit I was somewhat surprised by Allende's pleasant manner during our meeting. He reminded me of the kindly country doctor that he actually was. He listened carefully and with apparent sympathy to my request. When I asked him what he thought of Jews who wanted to return to their historic homeland in Israel, he replied, 'What a question! Anyone who wants to leave can do so immediately, and no one will stop them.'

'But just a moment, Mr President,' I countered, taking full advantage of the opportunity. 'What about their possessions? Are they indeed going to have to leave them here without any compensation for their property, as the Chilean law stipulates? How will they manage in Israel without any means of livelihood? Is that fair – to send them to a new country like beggars?'

If I had any illusions about touching the leftist President's heart with my plea, I was totally mistaken. His face hardened, and he shrugged his shoulders angrily. He had never promised to solve all the problems of the Jews in his country, he said, and went on: 'I'm not sending anyone away or holding anyone back. But what you are asking me to do now is to discriminate against my own countrymen. If I allow money to be taken out of the country, I will be encouraging people to leave. I can't make exceptions for the Jews, because I can't give special privileges to people who choose to leave the country.'

Unlike our profitable efforts in Argentina, in Chile we had no choice but to take on heavy expenses. The disparity between the price of the flats and their real value was enormous, and we could not provide any help in selling them as we had done in Argentina. Those Chilean Jews who made the choice to come on *aliya* received grants from us, and that, to some extent, eased their absorption in their new country. In North Africa, things were done differently, but the time has not yet come to divulge those fascinating stories.

For two or three years I made a number of tours of Argentina, Chile and North Africa. I deliberately set my sights quite low, so as not to be overly disappointed, but as it turned out – to my surprise – I actually managed to do some good. The position intrigued me, and I planned to devote two years to this important mission. I must admit I enjoyed the aura surrounding diplomatic service, the contacts that it brought my way, the broad horizons of the work, and the opportunity I was given to meet people from all walks of life. Once again I found myself at an important intersection of people and events where I could do some good, and I regarded every success in the field as a personal achievement. I loved being at the hub of the action where I could excel and give free rein to my abilities, offer satisfaction and receive some in return, and bask in the glow of my achievements. I enjoyed reporting to the cabinet, as well as delivering the keynote address at a meeting of all the Israeli ambassadors to Central and South America, which took place in Mexico City, in the presence of Foreign Minister Abba Eban.

And then, at the height of all this activity, a sword's blow from fate split my life asunder.

OUR LAST PESACH WITH ARIELA

Brief, all too brief was the life of my youngest daughter Ariela. Her sudden death, at the age of fourteen and a half, has remained with me every moment of my life since then. If it hadn't been for Alice's precarious health, we might have brought more children into the world. In fact, having Ariela was a calculated risk that we had decided to take despite the odds. Nothing in Alice's pregnancy or Ariela's birth gave us any warning whatsoever that we were courting disaster. But before she reached the age of one year, our baby daughter already suffered her first asthma attack. That was how we learned that this disease, with which Alice had been contending since the age of fourteen, was hereditary.

We did everything we could to make sure that Ariela lived a healthy, normal and happy life, just like any other child of her age. I think we did manage to free her of the constant dread of her illness, just as we made a conscious effort to downplay the fact that her father was a man of means. When the principal of her school asked me to help them build a gymnasium for the school, I agreed but only on the condition that Ariela would never hear a word about my contribution. We tried to protect her as best we could, and at the same time to raise her as a normal, ordinary child.

As she grew older, Ariela's attacks of asthma came more frequently, and things became more and more difficult. The doctors prescribed ever-increasing doses of cortisone, and I was not fully aware at that time of the dreadful side effects of such heavy medication. Cortisone can indeed save the lives of asthmatics, but heavy doses, taken regularly over an extended period of time, eventually poison the system and impede the patients' ability to cure themselves. Alice and I differed on how best to take care of our child. Alice, who was much more progressive in her thinking than me (possibly because she herself was a victim of the disease), was ready to try out radical and unconventional treatments. From time to time she came to me with suggestions about new and innovative treatments that she had read or heard about. At other times she suggested exploring the emotional sources of the illness, but, just like many of my contemporaries, I had little respect for psychology and did not believe it had the power to solve physical problems. I believed that the source of the disease was in the body, and I rejected the idea of a connection between body and mind. Alice asked me to take Ariela to Denver, Colorado in the US, where asthma patients were treated in an ideal climate at the best and most advanced clinic in the world. I refused. Why? Because of my lack of faith in American hospitals? Because of my inordinate confidence in Israeli doctors? And perhaps it was because I did not want to part from Ariela for such a long time, and my going to Denver with her would also have meant leaving Israel for an extended period, something I was reluctant to do.

Years would pass before I managed to shake off the agonizing feelings of guilt at my short-sightedness. Today, perhaps, I can pinpoint the reason for my tragic stubbornness: a kind of *hubris* that had been a part of my nature since my youth. I had always believed – and in time proved – that I could overcome any predicament I encountered by sheer willpower and effort and often with a bit of luck as well. When it came to Ariela's illness, out of sheer terror, I consciously denied the dreadful finality of her disease. I could not believe that I would lose the most important battle of my life: the battle for my daughter's survival.

There was something else – a matter of principle – that shaped my approach to the illness: I refused to allow Ariela to structure her life and personality around the fact that she was ill. I wanted my daughter to enjoy her life, to get the most out of every moment. I thought I was right, and I was convinced that Ariela was a winner. She was extraordinarily talented, bright and blessed with all the virtues a parent could wish for: an easygoing manner, intelligence, courage and a wonderful sense of humour. I remember watching her out of the corner of my eye one Saturday morning, as she took six of her friends on a 'guided tour' of the house. She stopped for a moment in front of a painting of a beautiful nude by a famous painter. 'Who's that?' one of the boys in the group asked. 'My mother,' she answered airily, and walked on. At the Galei Kinneret Hotel, a vacation spot on the Sea of Galilee favoured by many of the country's leaders, she moved easily among the celebrities of the time, asking them for their autographs. Abba Eban, Israel's famous Foreign Minister, chided her after she dared trade two of his autographs for one of Moshe Dayan's. In response, she simply looked sweetly up at him.

Constantly surrounded by friends, Ariela was active, ambitious, and loved by all. She always avoided making a fuss either of her achievements or of her privileges. She was fairly self-confident, sweet but not spoiled, and mature beyond her years. In the last winter of her life, we went for our first and only skiing vacation together. Ariela loved sports, and I was never quite sure whom she took after in that respect. With her natural verve and grace, she mastered the techniques of skiing very quickly. We were soon caught up in her enthusiasm, and in addition to the morning lessons at the ski school, we agreed to give her private lessons in the afternoon as well.

Every night before she went to sleep in the hotel we were staying at in St Moritz, I would sit with her and tell her about my day, listen to her describe the experiences of her day, then tuck her in all the way up to her eyes, and kiss her goodnight. At that time, prompted by my good friend and physician Dr Jacques Reisel, I had started writing my memoirs for the first time – a hedge against the failure of memory. Every evening I would read her a few of the pages I had written. One evening she was tired from her double dose of skiing training, and asked to eat in her room. After reading to her a few pages of what I had written that day, I asked what she thought of my writing. She refused to answer me directly, and promised, 'Keep on writing. I'll tell you in good time.'

That evening, sleepy yet still as alert as a small bird, she asked, 'Father, what was that I read in the paper: that you resigned from the bank and that Ab Vredenburg and Karl Reich are going to take your place, and you will continue as chairman of the board?'

'Yes,' I answered. 'In any case they always did all the professional work. They will go on doing what they know best, and I will have time to do those things that only I can do.' Ariela accepted my explanation, kissed me and fell asleep.

When I finished reading the forty or so pages of my autobiography that I had managed to write, I asked her once again to tell me what she thought of it.

In a thoroughly uncharacteristic manner, she once again sidestepped the question. 'I'll tell you tomorrow,' she promised finally, with little enthusiasm.

'*Nu*, Ariela, what do you have to say?' I asked her at the ski station the next day, as we waited for the lifts, looking somewhat ridiculous all bundled up in our ski clothes.

'It's no good, Father,' she finally said flatly.

'So what should I do, Ariela? Throw it all in the rubbish bin?' I asked.

'No! Why? Keep on writing, but do you remember what you explained to me about Ab Vredenburg, who understands professional banking stuff better than you do? So get someone, a professional, to do the writing for you. That's what you should do.'

And then came that terrible Pesach of 1972. The beginning of the holiday seemed filled with the promise of peace and tranquillity. On Jewish holidays and in the summer, we used to move to an apartment we had at the Sharon Hotel in Herzliya. That way we could enjoy the holidays and have a complete rest at the same time. Pinhas Sapir had lost his wife just six months earlier, and I asked him to join us for the Seder night at the hotel, even though I knew he would probably be invited by one of his three children. I was anxious to help him overcome his loneliness, so I invited him for a meal on the second night of Pesach. Dani and Matti Recanati joined us too, as well as the New York Recanatis, Raphael and Dina, who every year celebrated their Seder night with their family in Israel.

The meal was excellent. I was relaxed and happy, and apparently my good spirits were quite evident. 'What are you so happy about? Sapir asked, his heart still heavy with the sadness of his tragic loss.

'And why shouldn't I be happy?' I replied. 'You're here, Dani and Raphael are here – my best friends. And I have a wonderful family, and want for nothing. And besides, its springtime and a holiday: what more can a man ask?'

At eleven o'clock Ariela came in to the dining-room to say goodnight. She looked pale and tired. I wasn't worried; I knew that she had been at the beach for two hours that afternoon with two of her friends, and they had been watching television all evening. I kissed her, and all the rest of the guests kissed her goodnight and exchanged a few warm words with her. Sapir looked at his watch and asked me to take him home. He had to be up early the following morning for a tour of the industries in the Galilee, as far as the northernmost town of Metulla. I drove him to his modest apartment in Kfar Saba, where he had lived since his arrival in the country as a new immigrant. He hated – even feared – his loneliness. Every time I brought him home he asked me to wait until I was sure he had reached his door safely. This time too I waited, as usual, until I heard the door close behind him.

When I returned home I found Ariela in the throes of an asthma attack. 'Father, take me to the hospital,' she begged me. Her breath came and went with a sharp whistling sound. Alice was not unduly alarmed: we had been through more severe attacks than this one. I called Dr Bruderman, the specialist who had treated her at the Meir Hospital in Kfar Saba. I also called my daughter Judy, and my son-in-law Yitzhak came over immediately. By the time we got to the hospital, it was close to midnight, and Ariela was taken immediately to intensive care.

I suppressed the thought that this time her situation might be critical.

I paced back and forth in the corridor, measuring the distance from the end of the hallway to the closed door of the Intensive Care Unit. This is not the first time and it won't be the last, I tried to reassure myself. Ariela will have infusions for a day or two, and then she'll be sent home and recover quickly, just as she has always done. What I did not know was just how destructive her medication had been to her system. I did not know that her imminent death was in fact a foregone conclusion. At one o'clock I asked the doctor if my daughter was feeling better, and if I could go in and see her, just to kiss her goodnight and then go back home to Alice, who had stayed there on her own. The doctor looked at me with a strange expression on his face. 'Wait another quarter of an hour,' he said, trying to gain a little time before informing me that my daughter was no longer alive.

I had no idea how to break the news to Alice that our little daughter, the light of her life, was no longer with us.

My mother, my daughters and sons-in-law, my brother Zigi and his wife Leah stood by me throughout the ordeal. Dani and Matti Recanati came immediately, tears streaming down their faces. I almost felt that I had to comfort Dani, so overcome was he by the death of the child everyone had loved so much. When words of Ariela's death reached Sapir on his tour of the north, he immediately cut short his trip and came directly to our house, where Alice and I, the girls and their husbands wandered about the rooms numb with shock and grief, our souls shattered beneath the thin veneer of normal behaviour we tried to maintain.

The day before the funeral, I went to the cemetery to choose my daughter's plot, between the two plots I had purchased for myself and for Alice – who was to join Ariela sooner than any of us could have imagined. I walked about the cemetery – referred to in Hebrew as Beit Ha-Hayim, the House of Life (also: 'of the Living') – and I was surrounded by beggars. 'How much do you get on a regular day here?' I asked them. They quoted a sum. I doubled the amount, and asked them to join the funeral on the following day as *melavei mitzvah*, 'righteous mourners' in keeping with Jewish tradition. But no amount of charity and good deeds could do anything to bring back my Ariela.

The funeral took place on the third day of Hol Ha-Mo'ed, the intermediate days of the seven-day Passover holiday. On that day a meeting planned months in advance was scheduled to have been held at the Israel Corporation. Baron Edmond de Rothschild, the chairman of the company, cancelled the meeting, and he and all the other participants, who had come to Israel from the far corners of the earth, joined us at the funeral. Sapir, Dani and Edmond de Rothschild stood next to me through it all, giving me strength and supporting me. Relatives, friends and acquaintances paid their last respects to a four-teen-year-old child.

A few months before Ariela's death, a plan had been submitted to Pinhas Sapir and to the mayor of Tel Aviv, Yehoshua Rabinovitch, for the construction of a new municipal library for the city of Tel Aviv. The idea was to create a new, spacious and modern library that would bring together under one roof the five separate municipal libraries that were housed or stored in five different locations around town. In the early planning stages I had agreed to pay for the main reading-room, which was to be named after my parents. My father was a self-taught literary man, and a true bibliophile. In our house in Buenos Aires we had a superb private library, and whenever I wanted to talk to my father, I knew I would find him browsing among the shelves. During Ariela's funeral the thought suddenly came to me: I would donate the entire library and name it after Ariela. As I said this to myself, I could already imagine the many people, children and teenagers, sitting around the tables and paging through books at 'my daughter's library. These images were so vivid, so real, that they allowed me to forget for a fleeting moment the terrible finality of my daughter's death, which ravaged my very soul. 'You have to help me build this library,' I begged Sapir. 'I'll name it after Ariela.'

'Be quiet!' he whispered, almost angrily. 'This is not the time to talk about such things.'

But I pressed on, totally possessed by the idea, and only after Sapir promised to help me did I calm down, a little comforted.

The funeral was over. Since Jewish custom forbade mourning during the eight days of Passover we had to postpone the *shiva* – the traditional seven days of mourning after the death of a member of the family. I sorely missed the cleansing and the gradual acceptance that those seven days provide in times of grief. My close friends, my relatives, my brother

Ya'akov and his wife, who came from Holland, surrounded me almost constantly, but I was practically beside myself with grief. I wanted to have some form of ceremony with my family and close friends where I could remember Ariela. I asked my friend Dr Haim Gamzu, the Director-General of the Tel Aviv Museum, if he would allow me to use the hall that I had donated in memory of Alice's mother, and he readily agreed. He also asked if I would like to include an appropriate musical interlude during the event, and I accepted his offer. In the afternoon, after the funeral, everyone gathered in the auditorium. There was a large grand piano on the stage. And then Daniel Barenboim came out of the wings and sat down at the piano. His appearance was a total surprise for me. He played a piece by Bach with such gentle, heart-rending sadness that I wept as I listened. When he finished playing there was total silence in the hall. No one applauded. Barenboim left the hall quietly, so that I wouldn't need to thank him. I thank him now.

I was the only one who could rescue myself from the depths of my grief. In the days that followed Ariela's death, I was possessed by an uncontrollable burst of nervous energy. I had to be everywhere at once, become involved in endless projects. Just being active and getting things done made the pain more bearable, but it would reawaken with a vengeance when I was alone and idle once again. And then, when the next day came I would fill my hours once again with an endless round of activity in an agonizing vicious circle.

An important meeting of the ministerial committee for immigration, which had been planned long before, coincided with one of the days of my postponed *shiva*. I felt that the meeting was a crucial one and decided to attend. One of the members, a religious man, chastised me for coming. 'You shouldn't have come,' he said shaking his head. Another member of the committee said, 'I admire you for keeping things going like this!' Sapir smiled encouragingly and said, 'Shave your beard (the traditional sign of Jewish mourning that I observed), you look terrible.' When it was my turn to address the meeting I said what I needed to say about the work I had been doing. I knew that if only Ariela could have been there to advise me, if I could have asked her opinion as I had so loved to do when she was alive, she would have said, 'Of course you must go, Father; what a question!' I attended the cabinet meeting but didn't shave my beard for thirty days.

And yet, when I returned to my travels as roving ambassador, I could not avoid the heavy shadow of Ariela's death. I forced myself not to succumb to despair and kept up my usual pace, but I know that the people around me could sense my pain and desperation.

Loss of the kind we suffered can bring a bereaved couple closer together – or tear them apart. Time has not lessened the pain of our inability, Alice's and mine, to turn our tragedy into a force that would bind us together. Grief and loss struck both of us – but separately. Not long after the tragedy it became clear that our common journey, which had already begun to pull apart, was now going to lead us along separate paths.

That does not mean that we did not try, with all our strength, to support each other. Our relationship was strong, but something was slipping away, never to return. In her quiet, sensitive way, Alice tried not to trouble me, not to put any obstacles in my way. She understood better than me that the excess adrenaline flowing through my veins was a response to a terrifying emotional emptiness that was about to consume me. She made superhuman efforts not to be drawn into depression, and I, in my own meagre ways, tried to make her life happier. Even at the best of times it had been impossible to distract Alice with gifts and trifles. Now, in those terrible days of grief, this was all the more so.

Six months after the tragedy, I managed to persuade Alice to come with me to Buenos Aires. Unlike me, she did not like the city – her home for sixteen years – but, as was her custom, she tried to meet me halfway. We spent a few days there while I attended to my business. The visit was uneventful and we were rapidly approaching the time of our departure. On the very last day, Alice decided to visit her step-brother, her father's son. He was much younger than she was, and severely crippled. I tried to dissuade her from making the visit, mainly because I recalled that whenever she went to meet relatives from her father's side of the family she would almost inevitably return distraught and angry. But she was adamant. She felt she had to drink deeply of her cup of suffering. As a highly principled person, she could not cut herself off from her brother, even if she knew it might take a heavy toll in heartache and sadness. She refused to heed my warning and went to see him.

When she returned her face was dark with despair. All the way to the airport she was wrapped in a deep silence. I did not ask her what had happened. It was enough for me to see the tremor in her hands and the suffering in her eyes, which she kept carefully turned away from mine. We boarded the plane, and, within a few hours, the first signs of an asthma attack began. The attack grew steadily in intensity until soon it became a raging storm, worse than any she had ever had before. The pilot made an emergency landing at Dakar in Senegal, West Africa. A medical team was already waiting for us on the tarmac when we landed. A doctor ran up the stairs into the plane and gave Alice an injection that calmed the seizure, and the plane took off once again without us. The injection worked, and Alice soon felt much better, but I decided against flying on to our planned destination – Nice on the Côte d'Azur – wishing instead to take her to some place where she could receive proper medical attention. Five hours later we landed in Geneva, and it turned out that I had made the right decision: during the long flight to Switzerland her symptoms reappeared, more severely than before. It was unbearably hot in the city, and Alice seemed to be fighting for her life. I left our suitcases unattended at the airport, and the ambulance that I had ordered sped off in the direction of the hospital. Initially the doctors could not tell if Alice had just lost consciousness temporarily, or if it was too late to save her life. I asked Professor Alex Miller who was treating her whether I was about to lose my wife too. 'I'm not certain that your wife is going to make it,' he said gravely. 'She blames herself for Ariela's death, because Ariela inherited the vicious genes of the illness from her. Alice does not want to live, and people who do not wish to live – die.'

The hospital in Geneva was run with typical Swiss efficiency and order. The Intensive Care Unit was absolutely off limits to anyone, including even the closest family members. Doctors and nurses came and went, and I watched their every move, trying to glean some information from the expressions on their faces. I stood outside the door and peered in through the thick glass windows. Alice lay there, pale as a sheet, hooked up to tubes and wires, her face totally expressionless. I could only imagine the struggle raging inside her beneath that blank exterior. Did she know somehow, from deep within her coma, that I was there waiting outside? Could she in any way divine my thoughts? Had Bixie and Judy managed to pull her back from the abyss? After sixteen days in a coma, Alice opened her eyes and came back to us at the very moment that our physician, Professor André de Vries, arrived from Tel Aviv to see her.

15

IN ADVERSITY

The year following Ariela's death had yet another ordeal in store for me, one of the most difficult a man can endure, both as a businessman and as a private individual. When I embarked on what was intended to be a landmark financial project in Israel, no one could have imagined the horrendous fortunes that were to befall the prestigious Ha-Hevra Le-Yisrael – the Israel Corporation.

That was a time of euphoria following Israel's triumphant victory in the Six-Day War in 1967. The nationwide depression that had assailed the country during the severe recession that had preceded the war – with factories closing down, rampant unemployment and the tension of the 'Waiting Period' when most of the men in the country were in uniform – was replaced by an effervescent self-confidence proclaiming to the world that even the sky itself was not the limit. I myself refrained from joining the veritable orgy of celebrations. The multitude of victory albums that appeared in swift succession in the bookstores, the often insufferable arrogance of the military men, the messianic fervour of the extreme religious factions, a growing realization of the problems that might arise from the occupation of the West Bank and Gaza, the unification of Jerusalem – all these gave me little cause for rejoicing. I saw people such as Prime Minister Levi Eshkol as an isolated island of sanity in those heady days of rejoicing. I admired Eshkol's logical and rational approach to the problems at hand, and shared his abiding desire to strengthen Israel's economy.

Naturally Eshkol was happy about the illustrious military victory, but his was a moderate, balanced response. He was a pragmatic man, wholly devoted to the realization of Zionist ideals within a complex and very demanding socio-political reality. He felt that the Six-Day War, and the waves of euphoria that followed in its wake, had created a singular, once-in-a-lifetime opportunity to persuade the Jews of the Diaspora to come and live in Israel. That is what lay behind his initiative to set up a new company that was to be named Ha-Hevra Le-Yisrael – the Company for Israel or the Israel Corporation.

In the autumn of 1967, two months after war ended, Eshkol convened a meeting with a select group of sixty potential Jewish investors from around the world, myself included. At this preliminary gathering, the decision was made to convene a large-scale economic conference in 1968, and to persuade a thousand important investors to attend. In advance of the conference, I was asked to recruit the wealthiest Jews in South America for the project, even though I knew most of them were already involved in Clal. My task was to invite these potential investors on behalf of Prime Minister Eshkol. Once I had secured their assurances that they would attend the conference and might be prepared to invest, the Prime Minister sent them all personal invitations.

I set out on my mission. In the course of two trips throughout the Southern Hemisphere I managed to persuade over 120 entrepreneurs, businessmen and serious investors to attend the conference. Ultimately they all, among them top industrial leaders from Israel and around the world, attended the founding conference. The Israel Corporation was launched and I became a member of its Board of Directors.

Clal served as a good model for the Israel Corporation to emulate. At a preliminary meeting I gave a detailed description of the way we had created Clal and the reasons for its eventual success. However, whereas for Clal we had asked for a minimal investment of $10,000 per person (and most of the initial investments ran to $25,000), this time we set the mark very high indeed: $100,000 per investor. Our goal was to set up a seed capital of $100 million. Among the leading investors were, first of all, bankers such as Sir Sigmund Warburg of London, Hans Baer from Zurich and Baron Edmond de Rothschild. Among the leading Israeli names were Dr Yeshayahu Foerder, Ernst Yaphet, Ya'akov Levinson, Dani Recanati, Hilel Cohen, Abraham Friedman and myself. Sir Sigmund Warburg no doubt qualified as one of the most attractive of the investors. He was a German-born Jew, the co-owner of an important family-owned bank in Germany which he later transferred in part to England and to other countries. Sir Sigmund had also served as Winston Churchill's financial advisor. Another prestigious name was the Baron Edmond de Rothschild from France, grandson of the man, whose name he bore, who had become known in the early days of

Zionism as Ha-Nadiv Ha-Yadua – the 'Famous Philanthropist'. We counted on these two people to head the new company, since their names were our guarantee that the Israel Corporation would be regarded as a solid and serious concern, and that investors would feel they could count on making a profit on their investments as well as helping develop the state of Israel. The 'snob appeal' of these two men was a true asset. Wealthy people like to bask in the glow of publicity that surrounds famous international figures. The promises of meetings of the company's Board of Directors at Baron de Rothschild's Château Pregny near Geneva, or at his Paris offices, were music to the ears of many of the people we approached. To be able to tell one's friends, 'I just got back from a meeting with the baron at his residence in Paris or Geneva,' was a status symbol of the first order. I say all this without a trace of mockery for this forgivable human foible, and even as a salute to the baron, who was well aware of the role he was expected to play, and made every effort to shower the investors and directors with his charm and friendship.

Baron de Rothschild was no stranger to Israel. His grandfather, after all, was one of the greatest patrons of the Jewish Yishuv in Palestine, and one of the leading lights of practical Zionism. The baron was now following in his grandfather's large footsteps: he invested in the Ceasarea Development Company, and entered into partnership with the government in a number of factories and projects. He was also the first non-Israeli to set up a general-service bank in Israel, the General Bank of Israel. He owned a large part of the Eilat-Ashkelon Oil Pipeline Company, and served as chairman of its board until it closed down. He built a magnificent home for himself in the exclusive seaside residential area of Ceasarea.

Sir Sigmund Warburg was the most charismatic, and the most problematic, of the leading investors. He was nearing seventy at the time, and his German origins were evident both in his accent and in his inordinately serious approach to everything he dealt with. As a non-Zionist Jew, he found it difficult to accept the 'shortcuts' that we Zionist Jews often permitted ourselves. As he grew older he softened somewhat in this respect, and the unique historical circumstances of the time piqued his interest to the point where he was willing to enter into this adventure – a highly unusual step for him, given his track record in

Jewish affairs. Pragmatic to a fault, he believed that if major investors, Jews and non-Jews alike, could be persuaded to divert some of their resources to the young country, Israel could become a thriving financial centre on a par with Switzerland. As head of a banking empire with branches in England, the United States and Germany, he took it upon himself to harness his worldwide contacts for the benefit of the Israel Corporation, and turn it into a profitable international company based in Israel. Together with partners from top banking circles in Japan, Germany, Britain, the United States and Brazil, he believed he could succeed in helping to solve many of Israel's fundamental economic problems.

Things moved somewhat ponderously at first. The company's managers had been selected from among the upper echelons of the government bureaucracy, leading at times to problems of communication among people whose style and work habits were widely different. Sapir and the Israeli bankers regarded the Israel Corporation as a new, improved and updated version of Clal. Moreover, as they saw it, the company was no more than an economic arm of the state of Israel. The foreign investors, on the other hand, particularly Sir Sigmund Warburg, believed that the chief aim of the Israel Corporation was to do business, both in Israel and abroad, and that any benefits accruing to the state of Israel would be the natural consequence of good business. Was he naïve, or just overly optimistic? I too was filled with hope that his participation in the company would be a great benefit to everyone, but at the same time I was concerned that sooner or later there would be a rude awakening. This was the first time Sir Sigmund Warburg had shown any interest in Zionist and Israeli affairs, and I was afraid that any untoward behaviour on the part of anyone in the company would cause him to revert to his standoffish ways. Although it did not happen immediately, unfortunately my fears proved to be well founded.

At the time when the Israel Corporation was launched, the Israeli government was interested in privatizing several government-held companies, such as the Zim Shipping Lines and the Oil Refineries Company in Haifa. Consequently, the Israel Corporation purchased half of Zim's shares and a quarter of the shares of the Refineries. There was no great risk involved. As far as Zim was concerned, careful thought was given to the purchase of new ships: never too many ships of one kind or too few of another kind. The Oil Refineries also had a good rate of growth, particularly after it opened new refining installations in the southern port of Ashdod. The company had also made a wise decision to set up a petrochemical industry adjacent to the refineries. The implementation of all these decisions was closely monitored by a team of international experts, and ultimately they proved to be sound.

That was the situation from 1971 until 1973, at which time Michael Tsur was appointed managing director of the company. Following his appointment Tsur, who had been the Director-General of the Ministry of Commerce and Industry, now became the chairman of the board of Zim and the Oil Refineries. Tsur was regarded as a brilliant man, and was held in high esteem for his proven intelligence. Many very important people, such as Sapir, were totally won over by his talents, his brilliance and his charismatic personality. To our unutterable chagrin and profound shame, the man's term of office in the Israel Corporation was to end in disaster and became the source of almost unbearable embarrassment for the company and for the state of Israel.

I played a major role in uncovering the greatest financial deception in the history of the state, a scandal that to this day bears Michael Tsur's name. A great deal of pain, shame and rage are distilled into this chapter of my life, but I cannot avoid dealing with it here. Every agonizing detail of this dreadful affair is seared into my memory.

My suspicions were first aroused one day when I asked Tsur if I was supposed to attend a general meeting scheduled for that day. 'No, it won't be necessary, we'll only be discussing routine paperwork,' he said calmly. I soon discovered that Tsur had fired a number of directors – including myself – from the Board of Directors. Tsur apparently thought I would not object to this summary dismissal, since in any case I was there on a voluntary basis. But Sir Sigmund Warburg was not willing to let the incident go by without some response. When Baron de Rothschild convened the remaining members of the board for a meeting. Sir Sigmund flew into a rage over the changes Managing Director Tsur had made without consulting anyone. In his anger, he announced that he did not want to do any further business in Israel. Clearly this incident was not the English banker's main point of contention with the heads of the Israel Corporation. Sir Sigmund had entertained great expectations for the company, and had wanted to align it with powerful international financial institutions such as large banks and successful companies in Europe and the United States. However, before he managed to make a move, a number of partners were brought into the company behind his back. They were small or medium-sized German companies that had been awarded tax exemptions by the German government. Unlike Sir Sigmund, Baron de Rothschild found nothing wrong with the company's actions, and continued to support Tsur. After Sir Sigmund's resignation, the day-to-day activities of the company calmed down somewhat, but in retrospect, that meeting was the beginning of a long, hard fall.

One of the directors in the Israel Corporation was a Jewish-Hungarian banker by the name of Tibor Rosenbaum, who had several business interests in Israel. He had a reputation in the country, and it was not a terribly positive one. When the baron assumed the position of chairman of the board he asked for Rosenbaum's resignation. Rosenbaum lobbied his acquaintances among the directors, asking for their support in his efforts to remain on the board. I must admit I too was taken in by his pleading, and the baron eventually agreed to allow Rosenbaum to stay on for a year or two.

And then it happened. At that time, some unattached sums of money had accumulated in the company's account, and the managing director, Michael Tsur, deposited them in the company's name and reported on the interest they accrued. As long as these sums were deposited in respectable and reliable banks in Israel and abroad and in accordance with Israeli foreign currency regulations, everything seemed perfectly above board. Not a single person in the top echelons of the company took the slightest interest in finding out exactly where these funds had been deposited. Had anyone known that Tsur, without our approval or knowledge, had in fact deposited this money in a bank belonging to our fellow board member, Tibor Rosenbaum, there would have been a major outcry. Depositing money in a bank belonging to a member of the board, especially without the approval of the other members, went far beyond mere bad taste. Another enormous – and ultimately disastrous – aspect of this deposit was Tsur's strange decision to put all of his, or our, eggs in one basket, and a bottomless one at that: Tibor Rosenbaum's failing bank. Yet at the time we were not aware of any of this. We had such total faith in Michael Tsur that it never occurred to us to ask.

The first person to discover what had been done with funds belonging to the Israel Corporation – and to sound an alarm in a written document – was State Comptroller Dr Yitzhak Nebenzahl. However, instead of sending the letter to the highest authority in the company, the chairman of the board, Baron de Rothschild, Dr Nebenzahl sent the letter, a few months prior to our discovery of the entire affair, to none other than the managing director himself, Michael Tsur. I have no idea what Tsur did with that letter, but I learned of its existence only much later from the State Comptroller himself. I asked Dr Nebenzahl (whom I greatly respected and regarded as a friend), why he had not turned directly to the Executive Committee or to the chairman of the board, Baron de Rothschild. His reply was bizarre: 'You can bring a horse to water, but you can't make it drink.' Crushed and utterly frustrated, I muttered a few sharp words under my breath.

But that encounter took place long after the events I am describing here. In the meantime, rumours were spreading about the imminent collapse of Tibor Rosenbaum's International Credit Bank. I looked at all the information I had pieced together and realized that Rosenbaum was trying frantically to stabilize his bank, which had been shaky from the outset, with money from the Israel Corporation. All this happened in the autumn of 1974, shortly before Rosh Hashannah – the Jewish New Year. I had the feeling that the people involved in this affair, even government officials, were not telling me the whole truth about what was going on. With no help from these sources, I began checking the information on my own with the help of company clerks and whatever documents I could lay my hands on. And that was how I learned, for the first time and to my stunned amazement, about the deposits that had been made in Tibor Rosenbaum's nearly bankrupt bank, and about his bank's inability to honour its commitments.

When all these fragments of information finally formed into a coherent picture, I called Baron de Rothschild in Paris, and gave him a detailed account of my suspicions. 'Please look into it,' the baron instructed, his voice conveying caution as well as deep apprehension. 'Demand that Tsur shows you all the relevant documents. If what you say is true, try to find out the extent of the damage.'

I gathered all the necessary documents, locked myself into my office at the Israel Corporation, and began going through the papers as systematically as an accountant. For five days and nights I hardly left the desk, often falling asleep exhausted on the hard couch in the office, drinking unbelievable amounts of black coffee and chain-smoking cigars. Finally, nearly poisoned by the coffee, the cigars and an appalling lack of sleep, I could see the whole picture with brutal clarity: in the deals hatched between the two culprits, Michael Tsur and Tibor Rosenbaum, the Israel Corporation and its subsidiaries had lost a total of $40 million.

It was a catastrophe: a catastrophe for the state of Israel, for its reputation in the world, and for its resources. It was also, and no less so, a personal catastrophe for me. I felt as though my own credibility had been torn to shreds. Many of the investors had agreed to deposit their money with the Israel Corporation only because of assurances I had given them that their investments would be beneficial both to them and to Israel. They had also agreed to enter into these investments partly due to my personal powers of persuasion, and now they were about to find out that they had lost everything. It is hard to describe the depths of the shame I felt, for myself and for the country, that someone like Tsur represented us to the world.

But the worst was still to come. Contrary to what might have been expected in such a case, my findings did not result in any decisive action against Tsur or Rosenbaum. Instead of taking the prompt and drastic steps that my report virtually cried out for, the people involved embarked instead on a frenzy of activity 'to salvage the deposits'. A group of my colleagues in the company put together a broad-based support group, and came up with a number of proposals, chief among which was the idea of providing Rosenbaum's International Credit Bank with extremely generous government loans to save it from total collapse. Another suggestion was to fill Rosenbaum's empty coffers in Geneva by buying up worthless shares of one of his companies at their original price.

The Minister of Finance, Yehoshua Rabinovitch, resisted the enormous pressures that were brought to bear on him and rejected all of these suggestions. From his headquarters in Paris, Baron Edmond de Rothschild called a meeting of the Board of Directors at his offices.

Michael Tsur was asked to present his side of the story. And in the meanwhile, I was in for a harrowing ordeal.

A few days before the Paris meeting I asked to see the Prime Minister, Yitzhak Rabin. For over two hours I put my case to him as clearly as I could. He listened attentively, and said at last: 'But you know, Benno, I've spoken to a number of people about this matter, and most of them don't agree with you. I have to tell you – they don't think Tsur is guilty of any wrongdoing.'

I held my ground and insisted on my interpretation of the findings. Nevertheless, I had to ask Yitzhak Rabin one more question. 'Do you, as Prime Minister, believe that I will be causing damage if I pursue this matter in the direction that I have just described to you? Do you, like the others, think that I am doing an injustice to any one of the people involved, or to the state?' Rabin understood perfectly what I was implying. It was patently clear to both of us: if I insisted on proceeding according to my understanding of the events, it could lead in only one direction: to a full police investigation.

Rabin looked at me for a moment with his clear blue eyes. I detected a measure of sympathy in his gaze as well as guarded respect for my quixotic persistence. 'No. If you believe in what you are doing, Benno, then go ahead. Go ahead,' he repeated. 'Just try not to provoke Sapir.'

Rabin was absolutely right. One of the deepest scars that I bear from that affair is my loss of Sapir's support. At about that time I went to see him at his home that evening. I asked him to come with me to the board meeting in Paris. I desperately needed his backing, but he turned me down icily. There was a bitter taste in my mouth, and my heart hammered at my ribs. I restrained myself from revealing to him the depth of my pain, but inwardly I thought: if Sapir, a close personal friend, has turned his back on me, what must my colleagues think of me?

We did not quarrel openly over this affair, but for the first time in our long friendship a wall of strangeness and alienation sprang up between us. My heart was torn to pieces by this rift in our relationship, but there was no turning back. I had gone beyond the point of no return. And besides, I didn't feel there was any justification for turning back. I was convinced that Tsur had committed a heinous criminal act and that he should pay for it. Anger and despair wrought havoc with my soul. I wasn't consciously aware of it, but at that moment something deep inside me was being destroyed.

As the date of the board meeting approached, my physical and emotional condition deteriorated. I was in an unbearable state of stress, the result, no doubt, of sleepless nights, the strain of my lonely battle, Sapir's cold rebuff, and my pent-up feelings of rage and frustration. My physician, Dr Neufeld, insisted that I take a doctor along with me to the meeting.

I will never forget that fateful meeting of the Board of Directors of the Israel Corporation at the baron's offices in Paris. Tsur, a born actor, begged our indulgence: everything he had done, he claimed, had been for the good of the company. All he had wanted to do was to try and gain the highest possible interest on the unattached sums he had deposited. There was absolutely no personal gain involved. At the end of the meeting, the Baron de Rothschild notified Michael Tsur that he was to be suspended immediately from his position as managing director, and, almost in the same breath, told him: 'You had better find yourself a good lawyer.'

One day later I cracked. The doctor I had brought with me diagnosed the onset of a heart attack and ordered me to check into a hospital for observation. I chose to be hospitalized in Geneva under the care of Professor Miller, who had taken such wonderful care of Alice. Apart from the medical treatment, I was, apparently, in desperate need of some warm human affection. I spent a month in the hospital before finally recuperating. Newspaper editors sent senior reporters to the hospital to interview me, but the director of the hospital turned them all away, claiming that hospital regulations prohibited any press activity inside the building. Two weeks after I was hospitalized, I received a phone call from Gershom Shocken, the editor-in-chief and publisher of the prestigious Israeli daily *Ha-aretz*. 'I'm sending you the best interviewer in the country, Shabtai Teveth.' I told him I had no objection. And, in one of the two interviews I gave Teveth at the hospital, he gave me some indication of which way the wind was blowing when he asked me, among other things: 'Are you on some sort of crusade?' For the third interview, I was allowed out of the hospital. On the following day, during my fourth meeting with Teveth, Professor Miller came into the room and asked who my visitor was. 'A journalist from

Israel,' I replied. Like a stern school principal confiscating forbidden material, the professor immediately gathered up all the cassette tapes, and reiterated his unequivocal instructions that journalistic activities were absolutely forbidden inside the hospital. It was three years before I returned the tapes to the newspaper, but by that time the issue had faded from public – and personal – interest.

All these events took place in September and October of 1974, during the Days of Awe, as the days between Rosh Hashannah, the Jewish New Year, and Yom Kippur, the Day of Atonement, are known in Jewish tradition. Zim, the Oil Refineries and the Israel Corporation eventually pressed charges against Michael Tsur. A police investigation was launched some six months after the Paris meeting. Indeed, the dithering over how to deal with the main protagonists of the scandal went on for six months after I presented my initial, and well-documented, accusations. In the end, however, the findings were so damaging that they could no longer be either suppressed or ignored, and, at long last, Michael Tsur was arrested. At the end of a sensational trial he was sentenced to fifteen years in prison for fraud and embezzlement. After serving seven of his fifteen years he was granted clemency by the President of Israel, and released from prison. The Israel Corporation managed to curb the extent of the damage with the help of money that Tsur and Rosenbaum's International Credit Bank gave back to the company. But the Israel Corporation, which had come into the world with such fanfare and enthusiasm, was never able to regain its initial lustre and prestige. Today the company belongs to the family of the multi-millionaire businessman, Shaul Eisenberg.

A KISS FROM SAPIR

I have suffered two kinds of loss in my lifetime: one decreed by heaven, and the other the work of human beings. I managed to make peace with the personal tragedies I suffered, both of which were God's doing: the deaths of Ariela and Alice. Like everyone else who has experienced the loss of loved ones, I learned to live with the pain. But I could never reconcile myself to pain inflicted upon me by my fellow men. I have repeatedly asked myself how one deals with a friendship gone sour, or with a love that has turned to hate. Unfortunately, I have suffered several profound emotional disappointments in my life, and one of the worst was Sapir's attitude towards me during the Tsur affair in the Israel Corporation. In time we made up, Sapir and I, but our friendship was never the same. When, at the height of the affair, Sapir was asked for his opinion of me, he replied: 'Benno is ill now, and one doesn't talk about sick people.' Many months later we met in the United States. Sapir was then the chairman of the Jewish Agency, his last public position, and far from being commensurate with his abilities. He called me up and said, quite normally, for all the world as though nothing had happened, as though I hadn't suffered such prolonged agony, heartache and sorrow since our last conversation: 'Benno, I'm going to Connecticut for the UJA tomorrow. How about joining me?' Once again, I could not find it in my heart to refuse him.

We talked of many things on the way, both of us making an effort to behave as though nothing had changed. But beneath the flow of conversation, both of us were acutely aware of the almost insurmountable barrier that separated us. And then suddenly Sapir said, 'Benno, this black thing between us – we've got to get rid of it. Are you prepared to forgive me?'

I shrugged my shoulders, and struggled to hide the sudden lump in my throat.

'Can I give you a kiss?' Sapir asked. When he wanted to, he knew how to make amends.

'What's the matter with you? You and I were never enemies,' I replied in some embarrassment.

I forgave him. What else could I do? We shared too many good memories from the past: for example the Emergency Fund during the Six-Day War. I had met him at the airport in Rio de Janeiro at five in the morning, as he flew in from New York. 'What's new?' I asked him.

'I spoke to Eshkol before I left, and he said everything is quiet,' Sapir replied.

We were preparing to go to São Paulo and then to Buenos Aires, but first we went out to meet a group of people who were waiting for us. I left the airport to pick up some people who were supposed to join us at that meeting. One of them, a leader of the Jewish community in

Rio, told me he had just heard on the radio that war had broken out in Israel. As soon as I returned, I whispered the news in Sapir's ear. He continued his speech as though nothing had happened.

We decided then and there to change our plans. Instead of travelling overland, we flew to São Paulo, Montevideo, and Buenos Aires. Our mission took on a feverish energy. Our regular campaign turned into an emergency fundraising drive. Everywhere we went people waited for us with tremendous excitement. Thousands of Jews lined up patiently outside the embassy building, waiting their turn to demonstrate their support for Israel. They contributed everything, money, jewellery and personal effects. There were some people who even removed their wedding bands and gave them to us. I have a very clear memory of the long line of supporters that circled the entire embassy building in Buenos Aires. My father and I had been among those who helped purchase that beautiful building and donated it to the state of Israel. Forty years later it was reduced to rubble in a devilish terrorist act, whose perpetrators have not been found to this day.

We were joined on that trip by Major-General Orly, Commander of the IDF Paratroop Brigade, who had been on an advanced training course in the United States. He fielded all the questions on military issues. The contributors felt privileged to be given the latest news from the battlefront, and both Sapir and Orly knew how to give them first-hand information and a sense of belonging without, of course, revealing any military secrets. At two a.m., before the opening of the emergency convention of the UJA and Israel Bonds, the telex clattered out some last-minute information about the war, including the following message: 'Amos Sapir was wounded in action.' I tried to hide the news, but Sapir demanded to see all the messages that had come through, and took them all in at a glance. He carefully maintained his composure, giving no indication of the turmoil in his soul, then strode into the room where the major donors were gathered. He spoke, made jokes, cajoled and persuaded. Not one of them had any inkling that the war had struck so close to home. The meeting ended at five in the morning. Sapir had only one request: to be taken to La Cabana, the famous restaurant, which served steaks at all hours of the day or night.

The following morning, four and a half days after the outbreak of the war, Major-General Orly took all the telex reports we had received and tried to sketch out a map of the battles. What emerged was that the Egyptian air force had been totally destroyed on the ground, and the IDF had penetrated deep into the Sinai Peninsula. When Sapir awoke in his room at the embassy, we rushed in, in an effort to raise his spirits with our enthusiasm over the news. After much persuasion, he finally acceded to Ambassador Moshe Alon's request, and agreed to watch the news on television. 'All right. If it's so important to you, I'll watch it. But I want you to understand something: this victory is the tree they're going to hang us on.' When we returned home, Sapir shunned all the victory celebrations. Until the end of his days – barring two exceptions – he never crossed over into what became known as the Occupied Territories. The two exceptions were a meeting with the Military Governor of Judea and Samaria, Major-General Vardi, and a visit to Port Said in Sinai for a meeting with Arik Sharon. To this day I am still amazed by Sapir's prescience in relation to the larger, long-term ramifications of the Israel's stunning victory in the Six-Day War.

Years later, when Pinhas Sapir died, on 12 August 1975, his body lay in state at the entrance to the Binyanei Ha-Oomah convention centre in Jerusalem. I came to pay my last respects together with Dani and Raphael Recanati, and we stood with the general public. Sapir's family and members of the government stood close to the casket in an area that had been cordoned off. Just before the eulogies, Prime Minister Yitzhak Rabin and his wife Leah noticed me standing there. They both came over to me, moved the rope barrier aside, and said, 'This is a difficult day for you, we know, but you belong next to the coffin of your great friend, the late Pinhas Sapir.' It was an unforgettable gesture on their part.

HOW I DID NOT ESTABLISH A BANK

Prior to the Tsur affair, Sir Sigmund Warburg resigned from the board of the Israel Corporation, furious about the way it had been run. Nevertheless, he remained a shareholder and attended board meetings. One day he made me an offer that still makes me wonder what might have happened if I had accepted it.

In the autumn of 1972 the board met in Holland, in The Hague. In the middle of the meeting I went down to the men's room on the floor below the conference-room. A familiar voice with a heavy German accent surprised me there: 'What a boring meeting!' It was Sir Sigmund Warburg. Out of deference and courtesy to the banker, I nodded in agreement. 'Instead of going back to that boredom, why don't you come up and have some tea with me?' he suggested. I agreed and soon we were sitting in the elegant lobby of the hotel sipping tea. The somewhat stern-looking English banker did not leave me wondering for long what it was he wanted from me. 'I heard from friends and also read in the paper that you have started working for the government. I can't understand how a young and intelligent man like yourself can do such a thing!' He was referring of course to my appointment as roving ambassador.

It was a stunning opener, but I was not offended. I knew Sir Sigmund from my days as head of the investment division of the Discount Group. We had never engaged in any personal conversation, but I had learned then that while his attitude to Israel was not altogether patronizing, it was also not terribly empathetic. On occasion I was tempted to try and explain to him that building a country was not the same as setting up a company in a modern economy, and that it was a task that frequently defied the erudite theories of professors of economics. Once again, I felt this was neither the time nor the place to share my Zionist world-view with him. Instead I remarked quietly that it was an interesting job, that I felt I was doing some good for the country, that my efforts had borne fruit in some important respects, and, finally, that it was most definitely only a temporary appointment. 'Listen,' he went on. 'I have been looking for an opportunity to talk to you for a long time, but I didn't want to approach you as long as you were one of the heads of Discount Bank. I am not in the habit of stealing people away from other businesses.'

He had obviously done his homework! I felt a small twinge of pride. It was true that in order to become an officially approved roving ambassador on behalf of the state of Israel I had been required to resign from the bank. 'But,' he said, barrelling on without a pause, 'I have absolutely no compunction about taking you away from the government, since, in any case, your job there is temporary. What I am suggesting is that you resign from the government and come to work for me.'

I sat there, rooted to the spot with astonishment. When I finally recovered, I asked, 'And what is it that I would be doing for you?'

'A full partnership in everything: company business, board of directors, the lot. And to prove to you that I mean business, I want you to open a new bank, the best in Germany. If Germany doesn't suit you, it can be Switzerland. We'll call it the Warburg-Gitter Bank, or the other way around, if you prefer. My only condition is that you take full, personal responsibility for it.'

'I'm not sure I can leave my bank. I have a moral commitment to my partners,' I replied hesitantly.

'If you insist on going into partnership with an Israeli bank, then I would prefer doing it with Bank Leumi. I believe they can do better than Discount Bank,' he went, paying scant attention to my reservations.

'You'll have to give me some time to think about it,' I said. 'I would like you to meet Dani Recanati. Perhaps you'll change your mind.'

Sir Sigmund took out his diary. 'Where are the Recanati brothers right now?'

'In Geneva,' I replied.

'All right, come and have breakfast with me at the Richemont Hotel, just the four of us: you, the two Recanati brothers, and myself.'

'Yes, but you know, Sir Sigmund, I am a civil servant now. If you want this meeting to happen, I suggest that you speak with Sapir, my minister.'

Things moved very rapidly after that. Sapir called me from London, very excited. 'This is a wonderful thing for you, and for the country as well. Don't worry about it,' he tried wisely to reassure me. 'You'll live in Israel and travel to the bank. You've already done that sort of thing. Why are you so worried?'

Sir Sigmund Warburg kept up a rapid flow of added enticements, among them an offer to sell me some of his personal shares. And one day, when I asked him for more details about what I would actually be doing he replied expansively: 'You know the area like the back of your hand and speak the language, and you are also familiar with the local customs. If you complete your assignment there in less than six months, I'll ask you to go on to Japan. We have some major business interests there too,' he said. In one of our conversations, which took on a more personal tone, he told me he regretted not having any heirs to run his business and carry on from where he left off. Years later I learned from his biography that my hunch was right: Sir Sigmund was looking for an heir. There were several 'Crown Princes' that he had singled out and tried to nurture, but no one managed to remain really close to him for any length of time. He was a difficult, overbearing man. I am not at all sure we would have managed to work together productively over a long period, but at the time I was flattered that he had chosen me.

While all this was going on, I was invited to attend several meetings of the management of the S.G. Warburg Bank, and, I must admit, felt rather like Daniel in the lions' den. This was still the era of venerable, silver-haired bankers, and, even though I was fifty-three at the time, I felt like a youngster in their company. Warburg displayed admirable flexibility in his negotiations with me. After a number of discussions he finally agreed to set up a branch of the new bank in Israel, but on one condition: that I take on managerial responsibilities as a partner in his banking business in England.

Over breakfast with Dani and Raphael Recanati, we finalized all the details to everyone's satisfaction. The original ideas had undergone some changes: now we were talking about a new bank that would be set up in stages. Bank Leumi and Discount Bank would both own unequal shares in the bank, the larger part going to Leumi. Sir Sigmund made the partnership conditional upon my being appointed managing director.

Negotiating with my future partners was not easy. Ernst Yaphet, the head of Bank Leumi, demanded that his bank control fifty-one per cent of the shares. Since Warburg had a reputation as a 'bank swallower' – as indeed he was – our talks came to a dead end. Then bad luck entered the picture. Sir Sigmund, an avid reader of newspapers, discovered that the Israeli banking and financial community was in the throes of yet another scandal of enormous proportions: Yehoshua Ben Zion, the managing director of the Israel-British Bank, was thrown into jail for embezzling $47 million of the bank's money. And that, as far as Sir Sigmund was concerned, was the end of that. He decided that banking in Israel was not for him, and that he would limit his dealings with the country to visits with his daughter and grandchildren. Rumour had it that Sir Sigmund eventually brokered a merger between his business and a French bank involved in the oil business. It was also whispered in business circles that he bowed to the Arab boycott of companies doing business with Israel. Be that as it may, in the end nothing came of our grandiose plans.

Years passed and Sir Sigmund and I lost contact with each other. One day I received an invitation to come and visit him at his Swiss estate in Bloney near Lausanne. He very tactfully avoided any mention of the past, but I couldn't restrain myself. 'What a shame that our plans never got off the ground,' I remarked.

'Don't play games with me,' my host interrupted. 'You never meant it seriously. All you really wanted was to know how much you were worth.'

'You're absolutely right, Sigmund,' I replied and we both laughed.

After I dropped the formality of addressing him as 'Sir' the atmosphere became much more relaxed and unaffected, as though a barrier had been suddenly lifted. We both knew that he was right. I was never altogether serious about his plans for me. I was afraid that a partnership in an English bank would force me to leave Israel.

I cannot truly say I was totally aware of this as it was happening. Only a few months had passed since Ariela's death, and even though I invested enormous emotional energy in trying to prove that I was able to overcome the loss, even though I worked like a man possessed, I was on the verge of a total breakdown. I could not escape the thought that I had not done enough to save my daughter's life. Alice never once made any accusations on this score. As always, she tried to understand me as best she could, and even encouraged me to go my own way, giving me as much space as I felt I needed. I thought I might find some respite for my storm-tossed soul in the world of action I loved so, but somehow, the heart had gone out of it. Today I am ashamed of the importance I attributed at that time to success, to the respect and admiration of others, and to achievements that could be measured in numbers. Nevertheless, Sir Sigmund's offer was a timely compliment. At a period in my life when was I desperately in need of support, his offer was a balm to my soul.

That being the case, why did I allow this very serious offer – the most attractive I had ever received – to slip through my fingers? I think that under normal circumstances I would have mustered the strength and energy to take it on. Given the same opportunity at any other time in my life, I would have established a new bank in Israel even without Bank Leumi or Discount Bank. But I was at my lowest ebb, buffeted by destructive currents, caught up in a faltering spirit and an exaggerated sense of loyalty towards my associates.

HOW I MISSED A THIRD OPPORTUNITY TO HEAD A COMMERCIAL BANK

My relations with Baron Edmond de Rothschild had been extremely friendly since the first day we met. We first worked together in the company that ran the Eilat-Ashkelon oil pipeline, and our friendship grew stronger during the early days of the Israel Corporation. My wife and I were frequent visitors at the baron and baroness's estate at Pregny near Geneva, and at their homes in Paris and Ceasarea, and we often hosted them at our home in Tel Aviv. In appreciation of his many great achievements in support of the state of Israel, I proposed to the Senate of Tel Aviv University that he be awarded an Honorary Doctorate of Tel Aviv University, and the Senate agreed. The baron was deeply touched by the award, but since he was unable to come at the end of May that year to attend the awards ceremony, he asked to have the honour conferred on him separately at my home.

The members of the Senate approved this change in protocol, and the emotional ceremony, attended by over a hundred members of the Board of Governors, took place at my home, in the presence of the President of the University at that time, Professor Moshe Mani, the Rector, Professor Yoram Dinstein, and myself. Dressed in the traditional academic gowns, we spoke at length of the long-standing ties between the Rothschild family and the people of Israel. We stressed how the activities of the second Baron Edmond were an unequivocal affirmation of the continuity of the Rothschilds' commitment to philanthropy on Israel's behalf, and were the true realization of the Biblical injunction: 'The deeds of the fathers point the way for the sons.'

During the eighties I tried to bring Baron de Rothschild into closer contact with IDB, Discount Bank's investment company. Naturally I did so in cooperation with Dani Recanati, and managed to work out an agreement on a pooling of interests between the two companies.

Following the successful conclusion of this agreement, I was chosen to be the deputy chairman of ISROP, the baron's holding company in Israel. The baron himself was chairman of the company during the difficult period of the Tsur affair.

Everyone knew that in areas of common interest, the baron and I worked very closely together in complete coordination. We even had a motto that was indicative of our shared recognition of this business relationship: 'If I stay, you stay, and if I go, you go.'

While I was in hospital in Geneva, at the height of the Tsur affair, Baron Rothschild and the baroness came to visit me. 'Benno, you must rest, and not take all these things to heart,' they tried to comfort me. I had not fully recovered yet, and was still agonizing incessantly over the affair. The baron too was obsessed with the thought of how such a thing could have happened right under his nose, and was determined to find ways to repair the damage and bring Tsur to trial. Finally we went over the details of the events in painstaking detail, trying to assess their possible repercussions. One of the remedies we suggested was to strengthen ISROP and increase its major investments. In order to do so, we put together a circular deal that involved transferring the Israel Corporation's shares from IDB to ISROP, and giving ISROP shares to IDB in exchange.

ISROP was also the majority shareholder in the General Bank, the bank that Edmond de Rothschild had set up in Israel. Crushed by the Tsur affair, ISROP and IDB decided, with the consent of Baron de Rothschild, to sell off their stocks in the Israel Corporation to multi-millionaire businessman Shaul Eisenberg. The baron's position at ISROP was not affected in any way since he was the major shareholder. IDB also held a large percentage of ISROP shares. I was abroad when the contract was signed, though I was consulted at every stage.

On the day of the signing I was in London. The baron's cable reached me at my hotel there. He congratulated me for having thought up the transaction, planned every detail of its execution, and brought it to a successful conclusion. In his cable, he called me the architect of the Rothschild-IDB marriage. Years later, I was asked by Baron de Rothschild to take over as active chairman at the General Bank, and as the representative of the two main partners. Since there was a potential conflict of interest involved, the Bank of Israel was asked to approve the appointment. I was, after all, a member of the boards of Discount Bank and Barclays-Discount Bank. Dani Recanati agreed to my appointment on behalf of IDB, but the Supervisor of Banks in the Ministry of Finance, Galia Maor, informed us that she was unable to approve it.

Several years later, Dani Recanati passed away. The baron repeated his offer to me, stressing the fact that the bank needed a strong, active chairman. By that time I had lost interest in the Board of Directors of Discount Bank. Nevertheless, I still had to be given the green light by Raphael Recanati to take up the position at the General Bank, since, after Dani's death, he had taken over as head of the IDB Group.

I was about to go to New York to discuss the matter with Raphael in person. At the same time, eager to see the appointment go through, Baron de Rothschild was working behind the scenes to secure the necessary approval. He called Raphael personally and requested his permission to appoint me active chairman of the General Bank. As it turned out, that telephone call was not a good idea. Raphael was his own man, and shunned any kind of pressure, however slight – even if it came from the Baron de Rothschild.

I was in the middle of a meeting of Shimon Peres's task force in New York when a messenger came in to inform me that Raphael Recanati wanted to see me urgently. I replied that I would come to see him after the round of meetings scheduled for that day.

That evening I found 'the boss' in his room in a black mood. I sensed immediately that a storm was gathering that was about to be unleashed in my direction. 'How can you even think of resigning from our Board of Directors and going over to a much smaller bank? Is that all we mean to you? Some Rothschild shows up and you sever our ties, just like that?' he lashed out at me.

'I can't understand why you find this so surprising. There really is no problem. And besides, the General Bank belongs almost as much to Discount Bank as it does to Baron de Rothschild,' I replied. 'In any case I intended discussing the matter with the chairman of IDB.' As I saw it, there was nothing in this situation that could not be ironed out without any outside intervention and with a little goodwill on all sides.

Baron de Rothschild never asked me to resign from the board of his company, ISROP, not even in 1987. But Raphael and his aides were after my head.

And that was how I missed my third, and last, chance to become a top-flight banker: the first offer had come from IDB, the second from Sir Sigmund Warburg, and this was the third. None of them ever materialized – and I don't regret it in the least.

HOW I BOUGHT TWO INTERNATIONAL BANKS WITHOUT ANY REMUNERATION AND HOW I LOST CIGARS FOR LIFE

Around 1970 there were two major international banks in Israel, namely Barclays DCO branch of Barclays International, and Holland Bank Union, a branch of Hollandse Bank Unie (HBU), Amsterdam. There was another small Polish bank.

I was an old acquaintance of HBU which had a range of branches in South America (Argentina, Brazil, Uruguay). The general manager of the bank's branch in Argentina was Pieter Rost Onnes who lived in my neighbourhood in one of the suburbs of Buenos Aires. Both being members of the close-knit Dutch community we met frequently socially. His uncle, Nico E. Rost Onnes (nicknamed 'Nero' according to the initials of his name), who was one of the outstanding figures of the Dutch economy, headed the main office of HBU in Amsterdam for many years. I met him when he visited South America on several occasions. Pieter's brother headed the Brazilian operation.

Before the Second World War the major banks in Holland had a policy of not employing Jews. Nero, realizing that most of his good customers in South America were Jews, was smart enough to enrol a few Jews who were prominent banking intellects such as Mr Borchard in Amsterdam who was considered one of the master arbitrageurs (switchers) in Europe and Mr J. Baruch, the predecessor of Pieter Rost Onnes as head of the Argentine branches. Consequently, Jewish customers felt assured that HBU did not hate Jews.

Pieter Rost Onnes succeeded his uncle, Nico, after his death as the head of the HBU concern. He initiated merger negotiations with the then largest bank in Holland, Nederalandsche Handel MY, a bank in which the Royal House of Orange had a big stake. Before the Second World War it almost monopolized the trade with Netherlands East Indies (later known as Indonesia). The bank had never accepted a Jewish employee, with the exception of my cousin, Fritz Kaufmann, who was on a par with Mr Borchard, Europe's biggest arbitrageur. Perhaps the ABN (the bank changed its name to Algemene Bank Nederland prior to the merger with HBU) was not aware of my cousin's origin but when Fritz wanted to employ another Jew, Joop Voet, as his assistant the board told him plainly, 'One Jew is enough.'

The news about the merger was received with strong opposition from the Arabs who considered HBU as too friendly towards the Jews in view of its branches in Tel Aviv and Haifa. The ABN had too many interests in the oil world that could be jeopardized by the merger. In an article in an oil magazine, Pieter Rost Onnes wrote apologetically about the bank's involvement in Israel, stating that they had been trying for some time to sell the Israeli branches of the bank, which constituted a very limited part of the ABN/HBU's operations. When I read this I went to see Pieter in Holland and asked him about the many Jewish customers of the bank in South America and what they would say about the article. Pieter assured me that there was no change in their policy. He asked whether I would be interested in buying the bank as it had become a losing operation for them. I replied affirmatively that my bank (Israel Discount Bank) would pay only for the assets and not one penny more for goodwill, for all the above-mentioned reasons. That is how we closed the deal, taking over all the employees who agreed to stay with us at the Discount Bank.

Being a director of Israel Discount Bank and a deputy chairman of its mother company, IDB, I did not ask for any commission but I would have appreciated the flowers which never arrived.

Around 1970 and during his tenure of five years as the British ambassador to Israel, Sir John Barnes and his wife Cynthia became very good friends with Alice and me. We met frequently, almost two evenings a week in addition to standing invitations to all diplomatic dinners and receptions as well as the famous New Year parties in the residence of the British ambassador in Ramat Gan. One day Sir John called to ask me whether I was free that evening. I was a bit surprised since usually the ladies took care of our social calendar. He explained that he had an unexpected visit from the chairman of Barclays International Bank, Sir Anthony Tuke (the great-grandson of the founder of Barclays Bank), whom he wanted me to meet. During dinner, at the ambassador's residence, the conversation flowed easily with no reference to the bank or other matters concerning the UK and Israel. After dinner the ambassador excused us to the three ladies and invited Sir Anthony and me to his study, offering us cigars and coffee.

He said: 'Barclays DCO [Dominion Colonial Overseas] is the oldest bank in Israel and was the leading bank of the British government in Palestine at the time of the British Mandate. Sir Anthony Tuke has informed me that the board of Barclays International has decided to terminate its operations in Israel. The reason is not the Arab boycott but difficulties with other Moslem countries, not specifically Arab, and also Third World members. He explained that the bank, due to the necessity of a bilingual administration and the constant supervision from London, could not be competitive with the Israeli banks whose management was on hand to decide on the spot and consequently has incurred heavy losses.

'You will understand,' added Sir John, 'to Her Majesty's ambassador in Israel nothing worse could occur than the closure of the predominant British Bank in Israel: Barclays. Now,' he said, 'I am leaving you both, gentlemen, and request you not to leave my study before you reach an agreement. Then brandy and cigars are at your disposal and I shall see that the ladies arrive home safely.'

We were left to discuss the matter and after five hours of deliberations we signed a preliminary agreement in which Barclays Bank would be sold, fifty per cent to Israel Discount Bank and fifty per cent to Barclays International. It would be operated by Israel Discount Bank with a board consisting of half 'nominees of Barclays International' and half 'nominees of IDB'. As a prerequisite I named the chairman as Dani Recanati, while the chief manager of Barclays, Mr Mogford, would serve as his deputy. I signed the agreement subject to the approval of Dani and Raphael Recanati, to be obtained within the next few hours. Since Sir Anthony Tuke had a meeting with the governor of the Bank of Israel the next day he asked me to join him, provided the Recanatis approved the deal.

It was three thirty a.m. when I reached my home. I knew that Dani had to fly to Switzerland that same morning, so I called him right away. He could scarcely believe me but he promised to call Raphael in New York and give me their reply before his departure in half an hour. Twenty minutes later Dani called, confirming the deal and gave me a list of about a dozen requests to discuss with the governor of the Bank of Israel such as permission for both banks to open new branches wherever, as was the custom in Israel, two competing bank branches were situated next to or opposite each other.

I did not expect flowers for this deal which became one of the greatest and most lucrative in the annals of IDB. Nor did I anticipate then (1972) that fifteen years later I would be excluded from both banks on account of pure malice on the part of the surviving brother, Raphael.

I should have been accustomed to this attitude! The management of El-Yam tried to obtain a long-term shipping charter with the Israeli government through the Ministry of Trade and Industry. They approached me as their best bet for a successful negotiation of the contract with the Director-General of the Ministry of Trade and Industry, Gideon Lahav. Upon leaving Raphael's office on my way to that meeting I asked him for a cigar for the road. He replied: 'If you finalize this charter deal we shall supply you with cigars for all your life.' At that time I used to smoke ten cigars a day, and considering I am now celebrating my eightieth birthday I can calculate, as a former banker, how many cigars that would have cost Raphael Recanati...

But not to my surprise, even then, there were never flowers or cigars.

16

RIFT WITH THE RECANATI GROUP

Being betrayed is worse than enduring the tortures of hell. Anyone who has ever experienced a relationship that has soured knows the process: the shock, the anger, the endless picking at the open wound. I once asked the well-known Israeli painter Mané Katz why the figure of the Jew appears in every one of his paintings. 'Does it?' the artist asked with some surprise, and then shrugged. 'I really don't know. He just keeps popping up.' My relationship with the Recanatis keeps 'popping up' in exactly the same way: in my thoughts, in my conversations, and in this book.

Looking back now, I can trace the contours of my relationship with the Recanatis with much greater clarity. To this day I carry with me the feeling that the Recanati brothers exploited me, used my talents and my contacts, and in the end gave me a ringing slap in the face for my pains. The following is an example of one of the things I did for the Recanatis, which, like many others, counted for nothing in the day of reckoning. For many years the Bank of Israel has maintained a prestigious advisory committee comprising both public figures and political appointments, representing the balance of power in the Knesset. During The seventies this committee included major figures from the banking world such as Ya'akov Levinson and Dr Yeshayahu Foerder, to name but two. Dani Recanati very much wanted to become a member of this blue-ribbon committee. After all, he reasoned, Discount Bank was the second largest bank in the country, and there seemed to be no logical reason why it should be excluded from the forum of decision-makers and policy-makers. He regarded the fact that Discount Bank did not have a single representative on the Bank of Israel committee as a clearcut and scandalous case of discrimination. At the time, I thought his complaint was justified. Possibly because he was afraid that he himself would not be appointed in any case, he suggested that I speak to the Minister of Finance, Sapir, and suggest myself as Discount's representative on the committee. 'Under no circumstances,' I told him. 'I am not a commercial banker by profession. But,' I added when I saw the dejected look on his face, 'you're going abroad tomorrow, aren't you? I'll try to have the matter settled by the time you return.'

I went to talk to Sapir about this. 'What is this all about?' he asked Ya'akov Arnon, the Director-General of his ministry. Arnon explained that the governor of the Bank of Israel, David Horowitz, preferred to draw up the list of members of the committee by himself, and that indeed he – Arnon – had not seen Recanati's name on any of the lists up to that time. Listening to this convoluted answer, I thought to myself that perhaps Dani was not too far off the mark in his suspicions of discrimination. 'What do you mean?' Sapir said angrily. 'How is it possible that there is not a single representative of Discount Bank there? I am the Minister of Finance! Send a letter of appointment to Dani Recanati this week. He'll be an observer for a year, and then next year he'll be a full member. Gitter,' he concluded, 'consider it done.' And he was as good as his word, though during the weeks that followed I heard that Horowitz, in protest, studiously avoided any contact with Sapir. When Dani returned, he thanked me profusely for my lobbying on his behalf. Being a member of the Bank of Israel advisory committee brought him a great deal of personal satisfaction and prestige. It almost certainly had some important practical ramifications as well.

If everything was going so well, what was it that caused the first cracks to appear in the seemingly solid wall of our friendship? The answer is fundamentally very simple, even somewhat fatalistic. It had nothing to do with the nature of our relationship. It was rather part of the deep undercurrents within the Recanati family itself. As I try to reconstruct the events leading up to the collapse of my relationship with Dani and Raphael Recanati, it occurs to me that possibly, long before I had any inkling of the impending rift, they had already arrived at a decision to edge me out. As for myself, by the time I fully grasped the situation, it was far too late for me to fathom the true state of our relationship. It ultimately transpired that what seemed to me, at the time, to be a painful process of separation among friends had in fact been carefully planned.

I will never forget the evening, at the end of 1977, at the home of Amos Eran (Director-General of the Prime Minister's Office during

Yitzhak Rabin's first term as Prime Minister), when all the guests gathered to watch a televised interview I had given in response to the far-reaching economic reforms announced by the new Minister of Finance from the Likud, Simcha Ehrlich. In the interview I came out strongly and quite bluntly against the new economic measures. At eleven o'clock that night the phone rang at Eran's home. Dani Recanati was on the line, asking to speak to me. Never, in all the years we had known each other, had I heard him so angry. 'A banker should always keep quiet, particularly in matters pertaining to government policies,' he stormed. I am certain I paled visibly. Dani went on in the same accusatory tone: 'Raphael and I are deeply concerned. We haven't decided yet how to respond, but we certainly have no intention of just letting it go without comment.'

The people in the room watched me in silence, and must have been aware of the turmoil I was going through. For a brief moment I considered either playing it down with a show of indifference, or sidestepping the whole thing with a joke, but in the end my emotions dictated my response. I answered with barely concealed rage that there wasn't a shred of truth in what he had said, since there had been numerous precedents when his brother Raphael or other top officials of Discount Bank had publicly criticized government economic policies. 'I don't recall that their public statements ever elicited such sharp reactions from the bank, and I will not stand for this,' I raged. 'And I would please ask you to refrain from making any comments on my public statements in the future.'

This was the beginning of a new era in my relations with Dani, the Recanati family, and the entire IDB Group, an era marked by deep mistrust. Despite my foreboding, I preferred to look away and not see things as they really were. I drew strength from the support I received from many people, among them former Chief of Staff Haim Bar-Lev, who had been Minister of Commerce and Industry in Golda Meir's government, and was now serving as the Secretary-General of the Labour Party. We were not considered friends or close to each other in any way, but nevertheless he made a point of calling to express his full support.

Dani had been dear to me for many years. Ours was a very strong friendship that included our wives as well. Alice and Matti, Dani's wife, were close friends. It was a friendship that could not be destroyed just like that, at one stroke. We had shared each other's family events, both joyous and sad. The four of us had travelled the world together, to Switzerland, Italy, the United States, South America and the Far East. We had all stood next to Matti in the Japanese port of Kobe when she cut the ribbon and sent a champagne bottle swinging into the hull of a newly launched ship named after her. We had appeared together at innumerable ceremonies. When Dani invited people from the right-wing Herut Party and centrist Liberal Party to the second floor of his penthouse in Tel Aviv to discuss a possible merger between the two parties, he invited me as well, even though it was well known that my sympathies lay at the opposite side of the political spectrum. I attended the merger meetings of these two parties, meetings that were to have far-reaching effects on the future of our country. Dani knew I would listen and perhaps even offer an unbiased opinion. Not for a moment did he distrust me or consider my presence there an intrusion.

Indeed, our friendship was an honest and strong one, even though we didn't always see eye to eye on business affairs or government economic policies. We held opposing views about the new economic reforms, and about the role of the banker in these situations: should he keep his own counsel or take a stand? Dani was a very serious person, hardworking and totally dedicated, but it wasn't always possible to come to a mutually agreed upon – and final – decision with him on any issue. Even after he had made up his mind, chosen a course of action and notified me of his decision, he frequently changed his mind. And each time I would ask him with a smile, 'Whom did you talk to during the night?' Or: 'Where did you find Harry?' Dani's international telephone calls located Harry or Raphael anywhere in the world if necessary: Geneva, Paris, New York, or London.

As long as Harry was chief advisor, as had been the case in the early years, things continued more or less along their prescribed course. But when Harry withdrew from his position at the centre of the family business, everything turned upside down. I am deliberately using euphemisms to describe these events. The question of whether Harry had actually retired of his own free will, or was forced to do so, made the rounds of the business community for a long time, and I prefer not to elaborate on this subject here. In the case of the Recanatis, business and family affairs always went hand in hand, and, like good poker players, they held their secrets close to their chest.

To this day I am sorry that Harry left the group. For me he will always remain one of the best businessmen I have ever met, and I will be eternally grateful to him for his invitation, so many years ago, to become a partner in his business ventures. Alongside his great financial successes, Harry also worked to create centres for art and cultural affairs all over the world. I am proud that I was able to persuade him to build a most impressive private museum in Ceasarea, which belongs to the worldwide Rally museum network.

After Harry left, things appeared to become simpler. There was no longer any need, for instance, for me to speculate, guess or ask whom Dani talked to last before changing his mind about some decision he had already finalized – it was always Raphael. He became Dani's oracle, his only mentor, issuing his policy decisions from the Fifth Avenue tower where he had his offices. Raphael and I never shared anything like the wonderful friendship I enjoyed with Dani, or the profound mutual respect that characterized my relations with Harry.

Occasionally, I ask myself if my friendship with Dani ever truly removed all the barriers between us. And the painful conclusion I have reached is that there had always been a space that separated Dani and myself, a space filled by the looming presence of the Recanati family. Whenever one of the brothers called from abroad while I was with Dani, he never had to ask me to leave – I would get up of my own accord and leave the room. I truly believe that they might have even kept the great rift between them a secret from me had I not undergone yet another change in my life, this time in the form of another offer of an official government position. By nature I am not a secretive man, nor do I tend to resort to mystification or obfuscation to enhance the sense of my own importance. Moreover, I felt that Dani had every right, as my partner and friend, to be told about any significant changes that might occur in my life. Had I known that the appointment would never materialize I might not have mentioned it. As it was, I spoke about what I believed would be a definite change in my life. Dani's response to the news was quite unexpected: 'You can't do that to me just now,' he said. What did he mean by 'just now'? I wondered, and as hard as I tried, I could not come up with a satisfactory explanation. That evening I was given the answer when the three brothers phoned me and informed me that Harry was no longer going to be involved in the family business. They promised me that Harry's departure had been agreed upon amicably, that I had nothing to worry about, and that all this would have no adverse effects on the state of the bank or on their relationship with me.

But in fact, nothing was ever the same again. For the rest of my life I shall always be troubled by this nagging question: did my good friend Dani, the man that I so admired, actually take unfair advantage of my blind trust and betray me? After all, if Dani and Raphael had actually removed their brother, their own flesh and blood, from their inner circle, they would surely have no compunction whatsoever about getting rid of an outsider like myself. At that time, however, I did not have the slightest suspicion that this might be the case. To this day I find it difficult to come to terms with these fundamental questions of trust. Is it my ego that prevents me from seeing my mistakes? Or perhaps I dare not reopen the wound, for fear that I will have to go back and scrutinize every word, every deed, every meeting Dani and I ever had, and in the process totally erase close to thirty years of partnership and friendship. Today I am filled with remorse for my sin – the sin of excessive naïveté. I should have been more cautious and suspicious, and not given way to such unqualified loyalty.

These nagging suspicions have been reinforced by the perspective I have gained over the years concerning events that did not seem suspicious in any way at the time. Thus I remember, for example, how in 1963 Dani asked me to relinquish the founders' shares I held together with my group in the Development and Mortgage Bank. Had the Recanati family instructed him to do so? Had they already decided to get rid of me, take over my shares for next to nothing, and oust me from my position at the bank? The key to these suspicions may be found back in 1959, when I established the Development and Mortgage Bank together with Dani and Harry.

As you may recall, the Development and Mortgage Bank was established in Israel by the Discount group and by ARGEL, a company owned by a group of Jewish investors from South America. This company was headed by the Mirelman brothers, Simon and Yoseph, and by my brother Shimon and myself. Despite the fact that we had left Buenos Aires and moved to Israel, our contacts and influence in the Jewish community there were still strong, and as a result we could still get our friends in Argentina to commit themselves to contributions and investments in Israel. Our agreement was based on total cooperation and equality. The two sides, Discount Bank and ARGEL, had invested equal amounts of money in the new bank. According to the company's regulations, the two groups, which owned seventy-five per cent of the founders' shares, also controlled seventy-five per cent of the voting rights and of the right to elect directors to the board in equal numbers for each group. The remaining twenty-five per cent of founders' shares were sold to the public at large. It was impossible, therefore, to reach any decisions with regard to the bank without the agreement of the founding shareholders. At Discount Bank's insistence, it was agreed that I should be appointed managing director, and that I would commit myself, in a signed contract, to serve in that capacity for at least ten years.

The bank was an immediate success, far beyond anyone's expectations. During the early stages of its running-in period, whenever a deficit appeared, the two founding groups immediately covered it in equal shares. In its fourth year of operation, the bank's balance sheet showed a high turnover, an extraordinary achievement compared to the performance of other new banks that had been established in Israel.

In 1963, four years after the establishment of the bank, Dani Recanati asked me to transfer the founders' shares of my group to Discount. He explained that he needed the shares to prove Discount Bank's strength in the face of growing competition from Bank Hapoalim. At that time, Discount Bank was the second largest bank in the country (after Bank Leumi), and Bank Hapoalim was hard on its heels. In order to enhance Discount Bank's financial profile, Dani wanted to consolidate the balance sheets of the two 'family' banks, and in that way to shake off Bank Hapoalim's bid for supremacy. He explained that our status and involvement in the bank and its subsidiaries were so well entrenched that actual ownership of founders' shares had only symbolic value.

The majority of the ARGEL investors were vehemently opposed to the move. Simon Mirelman even threatened to resign at once if the transfer went through. Yoseph Mirelman and I, on the other hand, who were in daily contact with the bank, decided to agree to Dani Recanati's request in exchange for a promise that this would not affect the partnership in any way: we would retain the same number of directors on the board, the partnership would remain equal as originally stipulated, and so on.

Why did I agree to Dani's request about the shares? The answer has nothing to do with logic or economics. The truth is that, given the nature of our friendship, I simply couldn't refuse. I fully believed that this feeling was mutual, that our friendship was as dear to him as it was to me. In the end, all the founders' shares held by ARGEL were transferred to Discount Bank for the symbolic sum of less than one hundred dollars. In order to strengthen our connection with the bank, I personally bought some of its shares on the open market, along with another 100,000 Discount Bank shares.

Despite the wide-ranging financial implications of the share transfer, no written contract was ever drawn up to attest to the fact that, despite the official transfer to Discount Bank, ARGEL's founders' shares still belonged to their original owners. Everything was done on the basis of mutual trust and respect. During the initial stages of the share transfer, I asked Dani for a percentage of any future – even distant – profits that might accrue from the sale or cancellation of the founders' shares, but Dani replied that in any case the whole thing was a mere formality, and that Discount Bank would never sell or cancel founders' shares in one of its own banks. All this was agreed to verbally in a conversation between Dani and myself. Nevertheless, I asked him for a letter reiterating in writing his verbal promise to me that the share transfer was no more than a symbolic gesture, and that either they or their market value would be returned to us at no cost to the bank. Dani eventually provided me with a 'letter' to this effect – a handwritten note, couched in vague and general terms, in which he repeated his promise to me. The key sentence in the note was the following: 'This is as much as my lawyer will allow me to put in writing.' Warning bells should have started sounding in my head right away, but even then I still did not ask for a contract or a proper written agreement. I agreed to leave things as they were.

Later there was even more heartache in store for me. When the bank was established it was named the Development and Mortgage Bank of

Israel Ltd. One of the basic decisions made at that time was that the name would remain unchanged no matter what. Before Dani died, an attempt was made to change the name to Discount Mortgage Bank, and – how convenient – its abbreviation, DMB, would be the same. The people at Discount were so certain that the name change would go unnoticed that when they published the annual brochure in New York, detailing Discount Bank's performance for that year, the new name – Discount Mortgage Bank – actually appeared there, bold and bright, without any explanations. It was an out-and-out *fait accompli.* I protested, both out of respect for the South American investors, and because the original name was also a clearly stated commitment to the bank's primary goals as they had been stipulated from the outset: development and mortgages. The new name made no mention of this dual commitment, which I regarded as extremely significant. Dani was quite ill by that time, and ordered his family to honour my request and our mutual agreement from the past. This time my protest was heard loud and clear, and a new brochure with the original name in place was printed.

True to his word, Simon Mirelman resigned over the share transfer, and I was appointed to replace him as chairman of the Board of Directors. I filled both positions, chairman of the board and managing director, until 1972, the year I left the bank temporarily, at Sapir's behest, to become a roving ambassador. Up until the time of Dani's death in 1984, things remained more or less as they were. In other words, no one made any attempt to alter the balance of power on the board. After his death, new directors appeared who refused to acknowledge our previous understanding. On the pretext that they had been unable to find any written document to back up my claims, they demanded that Discount Bank's representation on the board be significantly increased, and that other investors' representation be reduced accordingly. In an attempt to counter their arguments, I said that the best proof of my claim was the fact that the original equal division of seats on the board had prevailed for over ten years after the transfer of the shares – but to no avail. I couldn't persuade a single one of them to see things my way.

The affair finally came to an end nine years later. Contrary to all the previous assurances I had been given, in 1994 Discount Bank decided to change the name of the bank that I had helped found. And while they were at it, the board also decided to annul the founders' shares. Gideon Lahav, the chairman of Discount Bank and a personal friend of mine, felt obliged to inform me of these developments. I asked him what Discount Bank would eventually get from the annulment of the founders' shares. Lahav replied that the company would allot the original shareholders 130,000 shares by way of compensation. It is important to note, in this context, that the Development and Mortgage Bank was never involved in any way in the infamous share-manipulation scandal that rocked Israel's banking world in the early eighties. As a result it was not eligible for inclusion in the compensation agreement worked out between the government and the other commercial banks that had been found guilty of manipulating their stocks. These new government-subsidized shares were a potential source of enormous profit for Discount Bank. I asked the chairman of the board of Discount Bank if he didn't think that the South American investors deserved half of these potential profits or some other mutually agreed-upon sum because, after all, the South American investors owned half of these founders' shares before they were improperly appropriated. Well aware of the deep-seated rancour from the past, I was not seeking any personal gain, but I did expect that the tremendous profits – or at least a portion of them – would be turned over to charitable causes. I should have known what the chairman's answer would be: 'It's impossible. There are no proofs of your claim.'

RAPHAEL RECANATI GOES WILD

For years after I permitted myself to speak out publicly against the economic reforms proposed by the Likud government, I could sense the Recanatis' barely contained anger. Their initial rage eventually turned into an icy coolness, but I continued to believe that it was only a minor upset, a fleeting crisis that would soon be over. Long after it became quite clear that there was no reason for me to do so, I continued to seek the good of the group in everything I did. One of the prime examples was the question of the management of IDB.

In the wake of the devastating share manipulation scandal of 1983, the bottom fell out of the Israeli stock market. Before this ill-fated balloon finally burst, most of the banks in Israel had been deeply involved, exploiting their dominant position in the stock market to pump up the value of their own shares artificially and rake in enormous profits in the process. The leaders of the banking industry during those years were held responsible for the catastrophe. At a meeting of the government on 13 July 1986 a decision was passed calling on the chairman of the board of Discount Bank, Raphael Recanati, to resign from all his duties at the bank owing to his involvement in the manipulation of bank shares on the stock market. I heard about this at five o'clock in the afternoon as I was on my way home to Herzliya.

As soon as I stepped into the house the phone rang. It was the governor of the Bank of Israel, Professor Michael Bruno. He asked me to use my influence to persuade Raphael Recanati to resign of his own free will. 'I expect him to hand in his resignation. If he doesn't do so immediately, we will have no choice but to suspend him within twenty-four hours,' Professor Bruno warned. 'I'm told by my people here at the Bank of Israel that you are the only one who can persuade him to take this step. I expect to find his letter of resignation on my desk by tomorrow morning at eleven o'clock.'

It was a most unpleasant situation. Knowing Raphael Recanati as I did, I was certain that he would not bow to the governor's demand. Pride and self-respect were among his most dominant traits. Moreover, given the state of our personal relationship at that time, I was not at all eager to be the harbinger of such bad news. In the end my sense of duty won out, and I agreed to discuss the matter with Raphael, but on one condition: 'You have to offer him something in return for his letter of resignation, otherwise we are all in for a great deal of unpleasantness,' I said.

'What kind of thing?' the governor asked, totally taken aback.

'Your agreement to allow him to stay on as chairman of IDB,' I replied.

'But that's absurd!' the governor exclaimed. 'The share manipulation scam was carried out with IDB stocks, Discount Bank's holding company.'

'I'm not a legal expert,' I countered. 'But to the best of my understanding IDB is not a banking company and is therefore not under the supervision of the Bank of Israel.'

The governor requested half an hour to consult with his experts, and then called me back to inform me that he was prepared to accept my condition. I asked him to announce his decision in the media immediately, and, once again, he was at first taken by surprise and then eventually agreed. I knew that only an official, public announcement that Raphael Recanati would be allowed to stay on as chairman of the board of IDB would enable him to swallow the bitter pill of resigning from the family bank.

At seven o'clock that evening, two hours after the government announced its decision demanding Raphael Recanati's immediate resignation, I was on my way to his home. When I came in I found Raphael and his family, as well as his assistant and right-hand man, Eli Cohen, and Yoseph Chechanover. Raphael went wild when he heard what I had come to tell him. He would never agree to such a humiliating ultimatum! He would not tender his resignation by eleven a.m. Clearly, I had not foreseen all the difficulties that might arise. I asked him how much time he needed, and he replied, 'Two or three days.' I promised to speak to the governor and ask him to postpone the deadline until the end of the following day.

'The governor is a very stubborn man,' Raphael said, attributing his own most distinctive trait to Professor Bruno. 'He won't grant a stay of even half an hour.'

At this point Raphael's family intervened, and begged him to allow me to talk to the governor. I called Professor Bruno from the Recanati house and asked for a postponement, to which he agreed.

The following day there was a meeting of Discount's board, in the course of which Raphael Recanati announced his resignation, and the resignation of his two sons, Udi and Leon, as well as that of his assistant Eli Cohen. He also announced the appointment of Yoseph Chechanover as chairman of the Board of Directors of Discount Bank, and Gideon Lahav as managing director.

I expressed my surprise over both decisions. His own resignation was unavoidable, but why did the others have to resign as well? He replied that they had done so of their own free will, under no pressure from him, as a gesture of solidarity. I also expressed my reservations about Chechanover's appointment. He was undoubtedly a man of integrity, but lacked practical experience in banking. 'This is a family decision, and it's final,' Recanati stated flatly, in the irate tone he usually reserved for me.

At five o'clock that afternoon, in Raphael Recanati's presence, I called the governor of the Bank of Israel and informed him of the resignations and the new appointments.

Thus it came about – through my direct intervention on his behalf – that Raphael Recanati retained his position at IDB. At the time, nothing could have led me to believe that one day this man, whose dignity and position I had saved, would strip me of my own position and status at IDB, a company that owed me almost as much as it owed him.

A few months later, in April 1987, Raphael Recanati called me from New York, asking me to meet with him during his upcoming visit to Israel. By that time our relations had already soured. He frequently complained that I hardly ever called him in New York. I had no idea what he wanted. Was he expecting me to report to him on every move I made, as Dani had done? I had my own way of working, and I called him whenever I felt it was necessary. 'Besides,' I said, 'a phone line usually has two phones, one at either end. I haven't noticed that you've been using yours all that often to call me.'

During this period, whenever Raphael came to Israel for his customary summer visits, I was under almost unbearable tension. Alice could see how much I was suffering, and suggested that I take a vacation somewhere outside Israel, but I absolutely refused to allow anyone, particularly Raphael Recanati, to influence my decisions. I stayed at home, my anxiety gnawing at my soul.

On this occasion I went to my meeting with Raphael with a sense of impending disaster. Nothing good could possibly come of it. And indeed, without any preamble or small talk, Raphael asked me to step down from all my duties at the IDB Group. His claim was very simple: ever since he had been forced to resign from the bank, he, the sons and Eli Cohen had been left with little to do. He spoke of all this as though he had been unfairly ousted from the bank – his family's principal asset – totally overlooking the part he had played in the share manipulation. Since, as he saw it, IDB was the bank's holding company, I should have understood the situation that had developed. If the government hadn't fired him, he stressed, he would not even have considered asking me to relinquish my position as deputy chairman of the Board of Directors, and the Executive Committee of the company. Throughout the conversation there was no mention of my resignation from any of the other companies that I had created and on whose board of directors I sat, such as Clal and its subsidiaries, Barclays Discount Bank, or the Development and Mortgage Bank.

I sat facing him, dark thoughts racing through my mind. That night was to be my first Seder night without Alice, and it was two days before the anniversary of Ariela's death. It was a particularly cruel time for our meeting. I knew that I would never forgive him for this.

'I have a letter you signed in which you agreed that in the event of a dispute between us, you will resign without argument,' I heard Recanati say as I weighed my answer to his demand.

The cat was out of the bag! After that television interview, which had all but disappeared from public memory, but not from the Recanatis' collective memory, I had promised them in writing that I would never agree to be interviewed like that again, and in the event of that or if there should ever be a dispute between us on matters of principle, I would have to resign from our partnership. And it was this document, which I had totally forgotten, that Raphael now produced. 'But what's the dispute between us?' I countered. Raphael looked embarrassed, smiled a cold smile, and our conversation ended there at a standoff.

I was devastated. Everything now pointed clearly to the inescapable fact that the Recanatis and I were about to part company, and yet Raphael's demand that I resign caused me profound anguish. After thirty years, during which I had devoted more time and effort to IDB than almost anyone else; after I had successfully negotiated on Raphael's behalf with the governor of the Bank of Israel, allowing him to stay on at IDB – after all that, I could hardly have imagined that this would be the way I would leave the company.

Not long after that, in May 1987, I was deeply involved in preparations for important meetings at the University of Tel Aviv. Since our fateful meeting, Raphael had done everything he could to pressure me into resigning of my own accord. The pressures, sorrow, frustration and anger all welled up in me to such a point that I ended up in the Intensive Care Unit at Ichilov Hospital. The diagnosis: a heart attack.

The following day, an enormous bouquet of flowers arrived in my room with a note from Raphael Recanati – from New York – wishing me a speedy recovery. I asked the nurses to remove the bouquet on the pretext that flowers should not be allowed in an Intensive Care Unit. I also refused to accept his call when he phoned me from New York. I think it was only then that I understood the depth of the torment and stress I had been subjected to over the preceding few months.

After I regained some of my strength, my hospital room was constantly humming with guests. Among them were several people from the management of the bank, including those who supported me in the dispute – or so at least I felt. After I recovered, Raphael Recanati told me, in one of our conversations, that a colleague of his in IDB had told him of a very cruel remark that I had allegedly made.

'What cruel remark?' I asked.

'You said that it was unfortunate that the wrong Recanati had died.'

In fact I remembered very well, as I do to this day, every one of my remarks on this entire issue. I also remembered whom I was speaking to when I had said, very cautiously and with no rancour, something that presumably was the source of this malicious piece of gossip. What I had said was that when Dani was still alive we had shared a common language and an unusually deep understanding. I told Raphael what I had said and totally rejected the possibility of any other version. Raphael listened attentively but gave no sign that he intended to let the matter rest.

Things went from bad to worse. The summer of 1987 was one of the darkest periods of my life. My relations with Raphael deteriorated even further. We were hardly on speaking terms. He communicated with me through Eli Cohen, in icily worded messages that sounded more like dictates.

I could no longer bear the situation, and when he arrived once again for his annual summer visit, I asked to meet with him. With his customary high-handedness, Raphael informed me that by 31 October I was to hand in my resignation from all my positions that had any connection with IDB. He went on to inform me that from that moment on he would refuse to cooperate with me, that I must leave any boards of directors I belonged to, that he did not want to see me in any meetings of the management or of any other forum, and that he would not participate in any meeting where I was present. 'You realize that your accusations are based totally on lies and rumours. I can't understand how you can take a stand and make decisions on the basis of false information,' I shot back at him.

Raphael looked at Eli Cohen, who was standing next to him, and suddenly broke down into heart-wrenching sobs. Tears poured down his cheeks. 'He, he,' he cried, pointing his finger at me like a child, 'he wants me dead . . .'

There was no point in talking to him any more. Besides the stinging sense of humiliation and the brutal and wanton trampling of the most sacred values of friendship and ethical conduct, we also had serious differences over some very concrete, practical matters, namely money or its equivalent. Raphael's tactics involved stripping me of my assets and my status in the Discount Group, and buying my shares in the El-Yam shipping company at far below their book value.

Thirty years before the split between us, Raphael had offered me a bundle of shares in El-Yam, after their previous owners had run into difficulties. I bought the shares for one of our family companies abroad. Now, after our relationship had run aground, Recanati was no longer willing that I should have a seat on the board of directors as long as I held onto the shares and as long as El-Yam remained a private company. Without any advance warning, my name was struck from the list of directors at El-Yam, and I was not invited to attend the meeting that had been called to elect new directors. I'm not even certain that the meeting ever took place, but I found out, after the fact, that new directors had been appointed, and that I had been removed from the board in disgrace. I learned about my ouster completely by accident: my secretary called the El-Yam offices to find out why I hadn't received a company diary for new year, as I had each year for thirty years. The answer she was given was that since I had been removed from the list of directors I was no longer entitled to receive one.

I have never been able to function in hostile surroundings. A negative atmosphere, filled with tension and hate, saps my strength. Under these circumstances, I refused to put up a fight and resigned as I had been asked to do from all those companies which I had founded and to which I had contributed so much for over thirty years. I was prepared to leave any position that connected me in any way to my past dealings with Raphael Recanati. At the end of a long and gruelling period of bargaining back and forth, I sold my El-Yam shares to them.

I cannot close this chapter without referring to the death of my friend Dani Recanati. The sordid affair with Raphael Recanati came to a conclusion two years after Dani died. I maintained my friendship with Dani even when that brilliant and widely respected man was wasting away. He knew that his end was near. I can only suppose that his illness and physical and spiritual deterioration accelerated the collapse of my relationship with his brother. Had Dani been alive and well, he would have no doubt prevented Raphael from treating me the way he did, of that I am certain.

I received word of Dani's death in September 1984 while I was in New York with Alice. I took the first available plane to Israel, and managed to arrive in time for the funeral. The plot had been cordoned off, and only the immediate family and close relatives were allowed to approach the grave. Eli Cohen eulogized Dani. I was sorry for Dani, sorry for Matti and the children, and sorry for myself. I remembered the brave young group we once were, and the deep friendship, our beautiful years together, and the wonderful experiences all four of us had shared. At the height of our friendship, he liked to call me 'My adopted brother, Benno'. Had I been given the opportunity, I would have spoken about Dani the way I remembered him – a warm, wise and truly generous man. But this was not to be: I was kept away from the graveside, just as I had been pushed out of his company in his lifetime. The family closed around him in his death as they had done in his lifetime, and he went to his grave, taking so many unanswered questions with him into that other world.

The years between 1960 and 1990 were the most fruitful of my entire life, and the clouds that darkened them now and again cannot in any way dull their memory. To the end of my days I shall always regard Dani as my closest and most beloved friend. Thanks to his intelligence and leadership I, too, devoted all my creative powers to the benefit of the country we both loved so much. Together we also honoured our desire to work for the greater good of the community, activities that we hope will serve as an example to our sons and daughters.

We were a happy foursome: Dani, Matti, Alice and me. Dani was the first to die, then Alice, and then Matti, Dani's charming wife, who died when she was only sixty. I am the only one of this wonderful quartet left, but despite everything that has happened over the past decade, my memories of them all will be with me for ever.

LEAVING CLAL

For thirty years I filled key positions in both business groups: IDB and Discount Investment Company, and Clal and its subsidiaries. These subsidiaries branched out from the various divisions, like Clal Trade, Clal Industries, and Clal Insurance (in which I was not involved in any way because of my directorship in the rival Phoenix Insurance Company). It was largely due to my efforts that IDB acquired partial control of the Clal group. The investment ventures that I led in both groups have since become 'smoother', with no fear of a conflict of interest. Over time, all these companies and most of their subsidiaries have gone public.

On a personal and parenthetical note, I would like to mention here that on occasion my family and I bought shares in Clal or its subsidiaries. These purchases, however, were never speculative and were strictly limited to shares of those business groups that I managed. The transactions were always carried out through the Tel Aviv Stock Exchange, and in that sense I was no different from any other Israeli buying shares on the stock market.

I have always opposed being given shares as part of my salary. In my opinion, this constitutes improper practice for anyone who is not actively and directly employed by the company involved. This was long before the Stock Market Committee in the Knesset came to a similar conclusion. When I was forced out of IDB I was no longer interested in owning their shares, and decided, therefore, to sell them through the Tel Aviv stock market. The shares that I owned in companies not listed on the TASE I sold privately.

In my worst nightmare I never dreamed that I, who had done so much to strengthen the ties between the two business groups, Clal and IDB, would suffer so grievously as a result. I was among the founders and leaders of both groups, as chairman, vice-chairman and then as deputy chairman. For three decades I had been on the Executive Committee of IDB and Discount Bank in Israel. In anything to do with IDB I acknowledged the Recanatis' pride of place in the hierarchy, and even if I had considered the possibility that one day I would have to relinquish my position there, I never imagined it would be accompanied by such acrimonious discord.

From my point of view, Clal was a different matter. After all, I was the founder and first managing director during the company's first three years of existence, and served for thirty years as head of its Executive Committee, and respectively as chairman of the board. It was I who brought IDB into this major economic concern, and carved out its pre-eminent position there. I was also the bridge between Bank Hapoalim and Discount Bank, which together controlled seventy-five per cent of Clal's shares. Without my help, IDB would never have attained the position of majority shareholder, which it enjoys to this day (the latter part of 1998).

For years I chaired all the weekly meetings in both companies, Discount Investment Company and Clal. The companies and industries belonging to IDB and Discount Investment Company required a great deal of attention and effort. They included some of Israel's flagship ventures: Iscar Nahariya and Iscar Blades, Elron in Haifa, the Hadera Paper Mills, Delek, Tambour, and Electrical Wires & Cables, all of which were on my daily agenda for decades.

In fact it all began much earlier, during the very first days of the state, when one thing led to another: ARPALSA's real-estate business led to the abortive Accadia venture, which in turn led to the establishment of the Development and Mortgage Bank. The contact with Discount Bank developed into my involvement with the IDB Investment Company and the Nechassim u-le-Binyan construction company. As a member of the IDB and Discount Bank group that worked through Clal, I helped start up many manufacturing firms and sat on their boards as chairman or active member.

From the very early stages of our joint ventures, in the bank and later in Clal, Dani Recanati and I agreed on a division of responsibilities between us. More to the point, it was Dani who suggested that I take upon myself the overall monitoring of the subsidiary factories and firms, so that he would be able to devote all his time to the development of the bank. I readily agreed: there is something fascinating and exciting in industrial activity, the pace, the momentum, the development, the products and the business results. Love for both these pursuits – banking and industry – flowed in my veins from a very early age.

Integrating these two spheres of interest was a natural outcome of my industrial experience in Holland and Argentina. Later, Dani wanted to appoint me chairman of Discount Investments, but I refused, because even though the offer constituted a strong affirmation of my status, I felt that someone from the family – preferably Dani himself – should hold that position. In the end, Dani agreed to participate in the meetings once a month, while we – general manager Dan Tolkowsky and myself – would continue our management meetings on a weekly basis, with me as chairman.

The list of firms I was involved in as part of my duties at Clal, IDB and the Development and Mortgage Bank is a long one: some two hundred firms. I will give a thumbnail sketch of some of them, and others I will mention only briefly.

MANY OF THE BUSINESSES I DEALT WITH WHILE AT CLAL

Kitan Dimona

Kitan Dimona was 'given' to me by Sapir. After a conversation in which he convinced me of the Zionist importance of setting up a firm in a development area of the Negev, I simply could not resist his arguments. With his encouragement, IDB invested a third of the firm's capital, while the rest was held by the Central Company, and by the original founders from the textile industry. After joining the Board of Directors, I served for eight years as chairman of the board.

Hadera Paper Mills

The old-timers at the paper mills often stake their claim to being the first to bring modern industrial technology to Israel. There are, no doubt, a few firms that might dispute this, but one fact is incontestable: the Hadera Paper Mills were the first Israeli company to sell shares on both the New York and the Tel Aviv Stock Exchanges.

To this day the paper mills occupy a very special place in my heart. Almost every one of us uses one or more of its products every day, and we take it for granted that an Israeli company produces and supplies us with such basic commodities. When I think of the book I am now writing which, in all likelihood, will be printed on paper manufactured at the mills, I take great pride in this firm, and long for the days when I was closely involved in its development.

However, despite the famous founders the company fell on hard times. The Astorre Maier family – known as the 'Jewish Medicis' – sold off all their shares and most of their other properties and assets, and Bob Mazer, the major investor from the United States, passed away. IDB eventually saved the company from an uncertain future by buying up more of the company's shares. On the heels of this move, I was appointed chairman, a position I thoroughly enjoyed. I was intimately acquainted with the daily life of the plant, and enjoyed the proximity to the inner workings of the company. Together with other members of the management team, we decided that if the plant was to survive it had to be expanded, and that new and more modern equipment must be purchased so as to streamline production and increase our productivity. This involved very large sums of money, and the best way we could do it was by making a public issue of new shares in New York. I had dealt in public stock offerings both in Israel and in America and was well acquainted with the procedures. This fascinating aspect of marketing – selling a company to potential stockholders – is known in the US as a 'roadshow', and I held quite a number of such 'roadshows' for people interested in buying shares in the Hadera Paper Mills. However, even after the successful offering, fluctuations in the international paper market forced us to postpone buying the new equipment.

In the meantime, Clal bought shares in the company and became an equal partner with IDB. Amos Mar-Haim joined the Board of Directors as the representative of Clal and became my deputy. I usually invited the heads of departments in the industry to join us in discussions relating to important decisions for the firm.

Over the years the company greatly expanded its range of products. Hogla, a company that converts paper into paper products, from disposable nappies to throwaway cups and plates, is a good example of modest beginnings that developed into a thriving business.

In the middle of 1996 the American paper giant Kimberly Clark bought up fifty per cent of the shares of Hogla. The shares went for a fair price, one that, as far as we were concerned, was also much higher than we dreamed of when the firm was established almost fifty years ago.

The years I spent at the Hadera Paper Mills were richly rewarding. And when I left IDB I turned down every suggestion to hold 'farewell celebrations' in my honour except one – from the paper mills. At the last meeting of the board I gave a detailed account of the state of the company, and sketched out plans for the future. I hoped that this would spare me the need to make a farewell speech at the dinner later that evening. The party itself was very moving, but some of my best colleagues whom I had expected to see there, did not show up. Some of them admitted to me privately that they had been 'ordered' to stay away. I was deeply hurt by this. I can't deny this very basic human emotion, or else perhaps I have never fully immunized myself against that kind of behaviour.

Elron

Elron, initially a producer of electronic components for high-tech industries, and today a holding company for a number of high-tech firms in the field of military and security equipment, was the brainchild of two highly talented men from the Haifa Technion, Israel's prestigious institute of technology. Their names are well known in Israel, and need no further introduction: Uzziya Galil and Moshe Arens (the latter served as Minister of Defence in Yitzhak Shamir's government). The two rented a small two-and-a-half-room flat in Haifa, and in those cramped quarters opened what amounted to a high-tech laboratory. Dani Recanati and I first heard about them from Dan Tolkowsky as we drove together to Haifa. Tolkowsky, former Commander of the Israeli air force, and deputy managing director of Discount Investments at the time, suggested that we look into setting up a partnership with these two men. As he saw it, the technological enterprise they were developing would lead to the growth of many similar enterprises. Just to make sure we did not go too far out on a limb, we decided to split the investment between IDB and the Development and Mortgage Bank (later we restricted ourselves at that bank more rigorously to mortgages, and transferred all our investments in industry to the investment company). The new company developed rapidly, and to our surprise, two of the Rockefeller brothers expressed an interest in it, and bought some of the company's shares through an investment company devoted to technology in developing countries. I will never forget a particularly pleasant incident that occurred at the end of March 1957. I was unable to attend the reception in honour of our new partners Lawrence and John D. Rockefeller, because on that same evening we were celebrating the Bat Mitzvah of our eldest daughter, Bixie. Towards the end of our party, the entire group from the Elron reception – including the Rockefellers – surprised us at our home.

However, this extraordinary partnership did not last long. Tax problems and internal complications in the Rockefeller's companies in the USA forced them to sell their shares in Elron. Although their departure weakened the company's financial structure, Elron managed to survive and flourish, and is today one of the leading high-tech companies in Israel.

In 1996 the Joint American-Israeli Commission awarded Dan Tolkowsky the Yitzhak Rabin prize for Science and Technology, for his pioneering role in the establishment of Israel's high-tech industry. The award was presented to him in the United States at the annual meeting of the commission, chaired by the US Secretary of Commerce and Industry, Mickey Kantor, and attended by the Israeli Minister of Commerce and Industry, Nathan Sharansky. Dan and I worked together, side by side, for thirty years, and I am proud to be able to say that he is as much a credit to the prize as the prize is to him.

Elscint

Elscint requires no introduction. One of the premier manufacturers of medical imaging systems in the world which, since 1969, has always been on the cutting edge of applied research in the field. The company occasionally ran into difficulties, but always managed to recover, due to the uniqueness of its products and its own inner vitality. I was a director of the firm from its inception. During his historical visit to Israel which was the real beginning of the peace negotiations not only between Israel and Egypt but for the whole Near East, President Anwar Saadat, and his wife Gian, visited Elscint. Being one of the hosts he said to me: 'When will you help us to build such wonderful plants in Egypt?!'

Elbit

My many and varied business affairs kept me from taking an active part in the running of this company, the flagship company of Elron Industries. I followed its growth through the quarterly reports it submitted to the parent company, Elron. This firm, too, expanded over the years and took under its wing a number of subsidiaries in the field of high tech for both defence and civilian use.

Scitex

I met Effie Arazi for the first time in 1968, before the big economic conference convened in Jerusalem in the wake of the Six-Day War. His vibrant energy and versatile talents struck me. He stood at the head of a large and successful company in the US, and it seemed very clear to me after our conversation that he was just waiting for someone to invite him to set up a similar company in Israel. In the course of our conversation I persuaded him to return to Israel. I regarded it as a very special honour to be able to announce to the five hundred delegates at its closing plenium session that Effie Arazi would be setting up a high-tech company with us in Israel – a promise that he indeed fulfilled, and fully justified, with the initial success of Scitex.

The innovative company that Arazi created had its big ups and downs. In the mid-eighties Arazi himself was forced to resign from the company. By that time I was no longer involved, but to the best of my knowledge the firm's partners bailed it out. Effie returned to the United States, and phoenix-like, rose from the ashes to set up a new company, Effie, in time one of the most successful high-tech companies in Silicon Valley.

Iscar

In the sixties Iscar was no more than a modest toolshop in the northern town of Nahariya. The founder of the small company was the charismatic and brilliantly talented Stef Wertheimer, whom I am proud to regard as one of my friends.

The company he runs, together with his son, Eitan (who is now the general manager), is a fantastic success story, leading from that small toolshop to an extraordinary reputation as a world leader in the field of propeller blades. The tiny firm that set out with no more than fifteen employees is now one of the largest single employers in the country.

A long time before the collapse of Tibor Rosenbaum's Credit Bank, contacts were established in Geneva between Rosenbaum and the young industrialist. Wertheimer, who had very healthy business instincts, wanted to pull out of this connection. That is where a childhood friend of mine from Holland, Yitzhak Klausner, the director of the small Yaphet Bank, stepped in. My friend tried to interest me in the young genius from Nahariya with the fascinating ideas, who needed seed money for his business.

I went up north with Dan Tolkowsky, and was immediately captivated by the prospect. I can't quite say what it was that captured my imagination: the fact that an Iscar subsidiary had recently been set up in Holland, or Stef Wertheimer himself who, dressed in blue overalls, looked like a cross between a labourer and a military man. For me, Stef was the true realization of the Zionist vision: an industrialist and a worker, a man of great aspirations that soar to great height but at the same time are totally within reach. I admired his self-confidence and his modesty. These two ostensibly contradictory qualities coexist in Stef's personality in perfect harmony. Those powerful initial impressions made my decision very easy. I weighed the possibilities before deciding to buy fifty per cent of the company's shares – at that time an investment of a few hundred thousand Israeli pounds. Twenty-five years later, Stef Wertheimer bought back some of its stock from IDB at over $20 million. Unquestionably, the big winner in the initiative that I had set in motion was IDB. Meanwhile, and before finishing this edition, the Wertheimers also repurchased the balance of the shares for an infinitely higher price.

Tambour

In the sixties PEC acquired part of the shares of Tambour, a paint company with headquarters in Akko (Acre). At that time, Tambour was one of three companies manufacturing paint in Israel. When the Discount Investment Company took over PEC, I joined the board of Tambour, and afterwards I was appointed chairman. Most of its shares, sixty per cent of them, were held by an industrial conglomerate in South Africa – one of the largest in that country. They had bought a company in South Africa that belonged to a Jewish family specializing in the paint business. The managing director, Uri Kelner, and I had maintained constant contact with the former owners who had remained on the board. They sold us all the know-how of the parent company. Next to the Tambour plant there was another, smaller, paint factory owned by the Histadrut's Hevrat Ha-Ovdim, and the two companies were in open competition. We decided to merge them and call the entire conglomerate Tambour. We didn't have a monopoly, and there were other smaller paint-producing firms as well as importers in the market, but the merger turned Tambour into the uncontested leading supplier of paints and paint products in Israel.

At some point, the parent company from South Africa notified us that for their own internal reasons they were forced to divest themselves of the paint company. A short time later, at the beginning of the eighties, they decided to put most of their shares up for sale. At the end of all these transactions, we were left holding over fifty per cent of the company's stock.

Tel-Ad

Long before the advent of Israel's commercial Second Channel, cable TV, with its 'ratings culture' and the glamorous icons of the new era, Uzi Peled set up a TV production company in Jerusalem that he named Tel-Ad. When the company was first created I was among the few who believed in its potential, and came out strongly in favour of making the investments needed to cover its deficits. Today the company is one of the leading TV production companies in Israel.

The Can Company

The stock of this thriving business had been divided in the past between its founders, Avraham Lev, the PEC group and others. After these companies merged with IDB, and I joined the board, I initiated negotiations to buy up the founders' shares. When I left the company, which produces, among other things, all the cans for Coca-Cola and most soft drinks in Israel, I could note with satisfaction the excellent business record that it has maintained to this day.

The Delek Company

Delek, the Israeli petroleum company (*delek* in Hebrew means 'fuel'), was created at the same time as the state, after the two foreign companies, Shell and Mobil, left the country. Delek was not the only Israeli energy company in the country. There were two other private companies as well: Paz, fifty per cent owned by Sir Isaac Wolfson, and Sonol, owned by the Sonneborn family and later by the Belfer group. Delek was regarded by successive governments as an economic resource of major national importance. The company drew its financial support from the Bank Hapoalim Group and IDB, both of which owned an equal amount of shares of its stock, and therefore had equal voting rights on its board. The government owned only one per cent of the company's shares, but maintained special privileges that endowed the company with its unique national status. Sir Charles Clore and the Nahmias family from France also had shares in the company.

Delek's importance was manifested in its appointments as well. Its first managing director was Emmanuel Racine, a French Jew with a Russian background, an expert in energy matters. Dr Eliezer Meron, a well-known figure in the Israeli economy, was appointed chairman of the board. Using his extensive experience in the Foreign Ministry and the Ministry of Commerce and Industry, Meron quickly consolidated his control over the company. After his sudden death, Dr Felix Shinar, another strong, authoritative executive, was appointed to replace him. Earlier Shinar had served in highly sensitive posts, among them as a member of the Israeli mission to the German Reparations talks, and later as Israel's first ambassador to Germany.

Delek's development was undoubtedly influenced by a great many elements, among them the ideological or party-political differences among its owners, as well as the personal biographies of its directors. When Felix Shinar fell ill and could no longer run the company, he called me in to take his place. Shinar was regarded as the government's representative in the company, but there was another tough and important representative who made his presence felt: Asher Yadlin, the Director-General of Hevrat Ha-Ovdim (The Workers' Company), the company that managed all the industries belonging to the powerful Histadrut – the General Federation of Labour. Yadlin suggested that we share the position of chairman of the board on a two-year rotation. The idea was that he would serve as chairman of the Board for the first two years while I served as head of the Executive Committee. We worked out all the details of the agreement, and then the Secretary-General of the Histadrut, Yitzhak Ben Aharon, notified us bluntly, in his typically plain-spoken manner, that under no circumstances would he allow 'a company that stinks of capitalism like Delek does' – sharp words that I quote here verbatim – 'to be represented by a Director-General from Hevrat Ha-Ovdim.'

This pronouncement by the moral and ideological oracle of the Labour Party exploded with a loud bang in our home court without any prior warning. Not long afterwards, the Labour Party was plunged into a battle royal when this same Asher Yadlin was indicted and convicted for massive embezzlement of Histadrut funds. When the dust settled, I was appointed sole chairman of the board of Delek, a position I retained for twelve years. A colleague named Naftali Ushpiz replaced Yadlin as representative of Hevrat Ha-Ovdim on the board, and we worked together amicably for many years.

In the meanwhile, Emmanuel Racine retired, and was replaced by Avraham Agmon, who had been Director-General of the Ministry of Finance. We were very close friends and had known each other since Sapir's days in the ministry. With sad irony I might add that our friendship lasted to the very last moment: at a festive dinner at the home of Professor Yoram Dinstein, President of Tel Aviv University, Agmon and I were sitting next to each other when he suddenly collapsed and died.

The Delek Foundation

Many large companies these days are involved in social, cultural and humanitarian enterprises. It is considered the thing to do to donate and contribute in areas of public interest, and to display a heightened social and ecological consciousness, as well as occasionally providing direct financial assistance in case of dire need that touch the hearts of the public at large. All this points to a new way of thinking on the part of the wealthy, and to a heightened awareness of their collective responsibility. Does it mean that a new form of capitalism is emerging right under our noses? Are we witnessing the belated rise of an ideology of mutual responsibility – 'one for all and all for one' – now that old-time Socialism has run its course? Are these new winds, new perspectives? I am not certain. What is abundantly clear is that our society is ready to accept – and truly needs – the involvement of the privileged classes. Governments and establishments, as I have already said, do not do enough for the general good and for humanitarian causes. Peace, the war on disease, violence and racism, the battle for the environment and a better quality of life – all these should unite not only governments but humanity as a whole in a common purpose.

In the seventies and eighties however, it still required a large measure of stubborn naïveté on my part to champion 'non-economic' goals in my business environment. I had been brought up by my parents to believe in the value of charity and public service.

One of my initiatives in this regard is connected to Delek, and looking back on it now gives me great satisfaction: the establishment of the Delek Foundation for students and young scientists. When I was in the process of setting it up, I discussed the matter with Sapir in order to secure his approval for government-provided matching funds. I am a great believer in the 'matching' system in public funding. Its beauty lies in the fact that on the one hand it automatically doubles any contribution to a worthy cause, and on the other, it cuts in half the amount the government needs to allocate from its budget for a cause that it intends to support in any case.

As a great believer in applied science, I have no doubt that some of the research projects carried out by recipients of Delek Foundation grants were extremely beneficial to society as a whole, and helped further important scientific initiatives. The annual scholarships were awarded for excellence in academic research into oil, energy, geology and ecology.

The success of the Delek Foundation gave me a deep sense of personal satisfaction. I don't think there is another company in Israel that has earmarked such large amounts of money for research fellowships. Every year I had the honour of awarding the scholarships to outstanding students from the seven universities in Israel.

In the wake of the events that I have described above, and over which I had no control, the time came when I was forced to resign from Delek. I was not looking forward to my farewell party. It was only due to the wonderful wisdom and graciousness of my good friends Avraham Agmon and of Ya'akov Hefetz (Agmon's colleague) that the party turned into an unforgettably moving experience. First of all there was the awards ceremony, and the heads of all the universities in the country made a point of being there in my honour. The pleasurable glow provided by that moment lingered with me for a long time afterwards. Conceivably, some of the people who came to say their farewells had actually come to 'pay their respects' to me, people who thought that once out of the business world I would flounder like a beached whale. In fact, their farewell was carefully prepared by my late unforgettable colleague, Agmon, next to the farewell from the Israel American Paper Mills organized by my other great friend, Shmuel Rotem, its managing director and his excellent successor, Jacky Yerushalmi compensated much of that time of 'dire adieu c'est mourir un peu' (to say 'goodbye' is like a little bit to die.) That was not my style. Instead of grieving over my enforced retirement from the hectic world of business, I was filled with anticipation at the prospect of a new beginning: this time as chairman of the Board of Governors of Tel Aviv University.

El-Yam

This private shipping company in Haifa had been run by the youngest of the Recanati brothers, Ya'akov. I became acquainted with the company when one of the partners resigned and had to sell his holdings. Thirty years ago I bought his shares, and replaced him on the Board of Directors, a position I held for twenty-five years. I was not too deeply involved in the day-to-day business of the company, and also had a few differences of opinion with the management concerning its running. I was not an expert in shipping, but I did agree to Raphael Recanati's request to lead the negotiations with the Ministry of Commerce and Industry about renewing the company's long time part in the transport of grains. Across from me at the negotiating table sat the Director-General of the ministry, Gideon Lahav, and we conducted the negotiations with a great deal of mutual respect. We were pleased with the outcome of our talks, which set the course for the company for years to come.

My friendship with the Recanati family, and particularly with Dani and his wife, was more like a family relationship. I recall two events from the time I joined the board of El-Yam that were typical of the wonderful bond we shared. My wife Alice was asked to launch one of the company's large bulk carriers, *Har Adir*, a gesture that was considered a great honour. The second event was the ceremony in Japan launching the tanker *Ariela G.* named after our daughter who had died a short while before. For political reasons we were asked not to attend the actual launching, but we threw a party for our friends in Israel in honour of the event. When the tanker sailed into Eilat for the first time a few months later, we went to meet it with our good friends Dani and Matti Recanati.

Hevra Le-Nechassim u-le-Binyan (Property and Building Company)

At the beginning of the sixties Harry Recanati pointed out that the IDB group was involved in real estate only indirectly, and suggested that we proceed to develop this area by means of a new company with the help of the Development and Mortgage Bank. On his initiative, we set up a new company called Hevra Le-Nechassim u-le-Binyan. I was to be appointed deputy chairman in return for five per cent of the company's profits. I didn't ask for that arrangement, but I did agree to it when it was proposed to me.

The managing director Dov Tadmor and I cooperated closely on the development of the company, and within a very short time Tadmor had guided Hevra Le-Nechassim to almost instant success. Based on the excellent performance of the company in its early stages, we decided to go public. The partners asked me to stay on but to forgo any profit sharing, and I agreed.

Clal Israel

Clal, which was and remains today the largest privately owned conglomerate in Israel, has derived much of its success from the endless efforts it has invested in developing Israeli industries. Clal laid the foundations for Israel's high-tech industry, an industry that has propelled Israel far into the future. Clal understood the changes that had begun to transform the world of technology, and helped set up 'sophisticated industries' which would enable Israel to utilize its most precious natural resource -Jewish brainpower – so as to compete successfully with the natural and financial resources of other larger and richer countries. Scitex, E.C.I. and other such companies were controlled by Clal. It was through both the Discount Investment Company and Clal that I entered into the area of high-tech companies.

Not long after Clal went public in 1966, and some of its companies encountered hard times, IDB became one of its senior partners, the other one being Hevrat Ha-Ovdim.

The recession that crippled Israel's economy in 1965–6, and the failure of a number of companies that until then had been run from afar by remote control, as it were, caused many of the absentee shareholders to put their shares on the market. Clal bought some of these shares through its subsidiaries, but Clal itself could absorb only so much of its stockholders' shares.

When the situation worsened, we decided to suggest to the three major banks that they buy up the shares of the Latin-American shareholders. It was a delicate situation that required very careful handling. As chairman of the board of Clal and of Discount Investments, I had to avoid to be accused of using insider information to push through a lucrative transaction. I asked Sapir for his advice, and he approved our plan of action. Aharon Dovrat and I decided to put the proposal to the three big banks: first to Bank Leumi, the largest bank in Israel, then to Bank Hapoalim and only afterward to Discount Bank. I asked Dovrat to discuss the offer with Dr Foerder, the chairman of Bank Leumi. A few days passed and no answer was forthcoming. Ten more days passed, and not a word was heard from Avraham Zabarsky, the chairman of Bank Hapoalim, either. I understood their silence to mean that they were not interested in the offer. It was only then, when it seemed as though there was no other alternative in sight, that we offered the shares to the Discount Group.

The purchase sparked a huge outcry. Companies and shareholders took exception to the fact that Discount Bank had taken the lead in this affair. It was not too difficult to allay the shareholders' fears: after all, if their shares had been purchased by a bank they must be worth something, and they did increase in value.

It was precisely then that Avraham Zabarsky stepped down from his position as chairman of the board of Bank Hapoalim, and a rising young star appeared: Ya'akov Levinson. Levinson expressed his dissatisfaction with the fact that Bank Hapoalim was left out of the share purchase.

Levinson, so it was rumoured, had more influence over the government than some of the cabinet ministers. I was not surprised when, once the situation had calmed down somewhat, Sapir advised me to work out a new agreement with the three large banks concerning Clal's stocks. After making the rounds once again, the situation resolved itself as follows: Bank Leumi contented itself with five per cent of the shares (in the meanwhile Ernst Yaphet had replaced Yeshayahu Foerder as chairman of the board of Bank Leumi), while Bank Hapoalim and Discount Bank initially wanted to split the rest of the shares equally between them. But Levinson was insatiable and arranged to purchase additional stock through other Histadrut-owned companies. In the end Bank Hapoalim held a total of forty per cent of the absentee stock, while Bank Discount had 'only' thirty per cent and both banks became joint owners and chief stockholders of Clal.

During the years I was at Clal, I had an excellent working relationship with the managing director of Bank Hapoalim, although Ya'akov Levinson, who was a very powerful person, hinted on a number of occasions that I would retain my position as chairman of the board of Clal only as long as I 'behaved myself'. He would suffer my existence there as long as I did not make waves...

Levinson, one of the brightest stars in Israel's economic firmament, came to a tragic end a few years after these events, when he took his own life. Some time after his sensational suicide I was ousted from my position as chairman of the board at Clal. It was a strange twist of irony that the people who forced me out were not the 'competition' – Ya'akov Levinson or his successor at Bank Hapoalim, Amiram Sivan – but the people at IDB, 'my' company, the one that I had co-founded and directed successfully for thirty years.

A final word on the Business Chapter of my Life

Throughout my years at Clal I was deeply and intensely involved in the company's Executive Committee, the monitoring body that oversaw all the giant concern's activities. The committee generally met at least once a week. When in time subsidiaries from the various sectors went public in their own right, I became the chairman of the Board of Directors of Clal Industries, of the Meniv financial company, of Hevra Merkazit, of the Azorim construction company and others.

In contrast to my deep involvement in IDB, I reduced my activities in the Clal conglomerate because it was physically and technically impossible. I was the focal point for the boards of all the firms, and we are speaking of 200 large and highly complex companies. The task of checking all the balance sheets and figures – even superficially – as I did, demanded an enormous amount of time and effort.

All of this would not have been possible if it hadn't been for the enduring, easygoing and mutually respectful friendship between Aharon Dovrat and myself. I first met him when he was a young student in Buenos Aires, and I was very impressed by him. And indeed, he became a superb managing director. In an area where misunderstandings and acrimonious disputes are always just around the corner, Dovrat brought to his work a cultivated approach and a sympathetic disposition. We are no longer involved in any joint business ventures, but our friendship and the memories of the times we worked together will endure for ever.

When completing the English translation of my book destiny has brought Aharon Dovrat back to my life and our long-standing friendship is taking a new turn.

Due to personal circumstances, Aharon Dovrat has retired, in December 1998, from a well reputable investment company he founded less than a decade ago. After several talks we both decided to establish a new partnership along with two good friends from South America. The purpose of this partnership is similar to that at Clal where we worked together for almost thirty years. Our intention is to fortify Isal Amlat Investment Company, a daughter company of Isal BV since June 1998, registered and quoted at the Tel Aviv Stock Exchange developing it to one of the leading investment companies in Israel, as we both did with Clal thirty years ago.

As one of the leading financial newspapers in Israel reported, 'It is especially remarkable that Gitter (79), who about 10 years ago vowed never to invest in Israel any more is performing a come-back at his age.' The reporter did not quote my answer that according to the Talmud a Jew can repent until the day of his death. Since I soon hope to celebrate my eightieth birthday and have no intentions of dying I have the fervent hope that my partnership with these brilliant friends will last for many years. It is also gratifying that Aharon Dovrat appointed his son, Shlomo as his successor in this venture while I chose my grandson, Boaz to succeed me when my time is up.

AHARON DOVRAT AND 'BOSSITO'

At the beginning of the sixties the government-owned industries in the economy were offset by private industries run by a handful of families – Recanati, Hakhmi, Carasso and others. These families were in no way connected to any of the Histadrut-owned firms.

My role was quite unique since I was the one who nurtured the contacts between shareholders and the management of the companies I was involved in. The shareholders had given me the authority to represent them, as far as the management was concerned, I was 'the

Boss', or, as Aharon Dovrat liked to call me, 'Bossito'. Our special relationship was based on the Argentine background we shared and our common facility with the Spanish language. I felt a strong sense of responsibility towards the shareholders, and maintained constant contact with them. I had no desire to become an active manager in the company. I therefore carefully maintained the necessary distinction between the daily running of the business and the Board of Directors, i.e. the owners.

In the early seventies Hevra Merkazit merged with Clal. This company was actually larger than Clal itself, and included several of Israel's largest industrial, financial and real estate enterprises. It is highly doubtful that a managing director would have been able to manage so complex a business through a traditional Board of Directors. There were twenty-five shareholders in Hevra Merkazit and forty directors at Clal. In the course of one Shabbat, Dani Recanati, Aharon Dovrat and I arrived at the decision to take over the company.

We had already discussed the possible purchase of Hevra Merkazit a year earlier, and originally the package had included the Swiss-Israel Bank. At that time I had hesitated about going ahead with it because I did not want to enter into competition with the major shareholders in Clal – the three large banks. We therefore decided to go about the purchase slowly and carefully. A short time later, the Swiss-Israel Bank was sold to a Latin American investor, and it was at that point that we decided to go ahead and purchase Hevra Merkazit. The Executive Committee approved the transaction after Aharon Dovrat and I put together a detailed proposal. The Board of Directors of Clal, which gave the Executive Committee its authority, retained the sole right to decide on declaring dividends. The Executive Committee consisted of fifteen members, while the Board of Directors had fifty.

As I have already mentioned – and it is important to repeat it here – the wonderfully harmonious relations that prevailed between Aharon Dovrat and myself reflected both towards the management and the owners, and to the shareholders.

17

LOSS, MIXING WITH THE FAMOUS, AND PHILANTHROPY

On 31 July 1986 Alice died, following a devastating attack of asthma. She was sixty-two years old.

Throughout her life Alice made every effort to ensure that her illness would not hamper me in any way. Looking back now on our life together, I regret that I did not know how to relent, to slow down my pace for her sake, a pace that would have worn down a much healthier woman than Alice. I find some consolation in the thought that the forty-one years of our marriage had many moments of happiness. She made the most of what her life with me could offer: trips around the world, participating in historic events, meeting fascinating people, security and wealth. We were both born into merchant families, and we shared a basically cosmopolitan outlook on life – we lived in many places but the world was our home. The many languages we spoke enhanced this feeling. We loved travelling the world with our daughters, driven by the desire to give them a sense of space and unlimited possibilities.

Over the years Alice developed her own areas of interest. I accompanied her to museums and galleries all over the world. Alice shunned the trappings of wealth. Although she was born into a wealthy family, money and what it could provide never impressed her. Her ascetic personality allowed only one exception: an avid passion for art. Under her tutelage I learned how to acquire unique works by fine painters, and thus we developed a common interest that gave us both pleasure and excitement, and created another bond between us.

It was Alice, too, who discovered Tel Aviv University. Long before I had any connection with the university, she created her own contacts there. She began as a regular student, wishing simply to add to her knowledge in the areas she loved: English, literature, philosophy and Jewish history. Later, she began to take part in fundraising on behalf of the university. With her innate personal charm and her many contacts, she persuaded friends from abroad to donate money and give their time and take up key voluntary positions with the university framework. She dedicated herself whole-heartedly to the aim of helping the Tel Aviv University in many different ways.

Alice abhorred the machinations of false friendship. She had many friends, people who loved and respected her modesty, gentleness and integrity. She had three close personal friends with whom she shared a profound relationship. One was Tin Gompen, the wife of my best friend, Jaap. Jaap and I had been close friends since childhood and as we grew older we maintained our friendship and had active business contacts through our mutual involvement in the leather business. Alice and I were among the matchmakers who brought Tin and Jaap together when they returned from the concentration camps. Jaap came from Bergen-Belsen while Tin spent one horrible year in the camp of Vught, one week in Auschwitz and ten months in various concentration camps in Germany. Thanks to the Philips Company which had employed many Jews and provided them even in the camps with protection from the Nazis, she survived the terrible ordeal. But the three years in the camps exacted a heavy price and they could not have children. They decided instead to adopt two children and did so at the same time as we became parents. They always treated our daughters as their own, and their children called us Uncle and Aunt. I will never forget how Tin came from Amsterdam to be with Alice after Ariela's death. My friend Jaap did the same for me after Alice died.

Alice's second close friend was Miriam Shneerson, the wife of my friend Mordechai from the embassy in Buenos Aires. Miriam accompanied her husband on all his diplomatic postings, while never concealing for a moment her loathing for what she felt was the emptiness of diplomatic life. She became friendly with Alice while they were in Argentina, and their friendship remained steadfast until Miriam's death.

Alice also had a close personal relationship with Dr Henriette Wijzenbeek, with whom she shared not only memories of their youth in Rotterdam, but also their common thirst for studies, the development of their families, and, not least, their support for Tel Aviv University.

Time goes by, and I find myself saying goodbye to old friends with increasing frequency: Mordechai Shneerson, a great intellectual and translator of classical masterpieces, died. His wife, Miriam, who loved her job – nursing terminal patients – more than anything else in her life, herself died of cancer. And my friend Jaap Gompen too is no longer among the living.

SIMCHA EHRLICH RACED AHEAD

My life and business interests brought me into contact with the leaders of the country during many different periods of our history. Time plays havoc with our memory of names, but some of them remain clearly etched in our minds, often because of certain anecdotes, or moving, annoying, or sometimes absurd and comic events. Some of these have already appeared in this narrative at various points, such as Sapir's sudden kiss intended at healing the rift between us. Those that I have chosen to describe here cover a broad expanse of time, and their very distance in time gives them a special nostalgic aura.

In 1964 I hosted a group of contributors from Latin America who had been invited to meet with the Prime Minister, David Ben Gurion. We waited in his office for a few minutes, and then he entered with his usual buoyant step, his entire being exuding vital energy. He looked at the group and said, 'Is there a Paul Antebi among you?'

A sixty-year-old man whom I knew to be an industrialist from Mexico rose and said, 'I am Paul Antebi, Mr Prime Minister.'

'Come here,' Ben Gurion ordered.

The man approached the Prime Minister slowly, leaning on a stick – a memento from an accident that occurred in his youth – and stood before Ben Gurion, somewhat embarrassed. Ben Gurion, who was exactly the same height as Antebi, grabbed the man's face in his hands, and kissed him on both cheeks.

We were all quite taken aback, but Ben Gurion soon provided us with an explanation for his extraordinary gesture. 'You probably all think I kissed Antebi because of his wealth and his contributions, don't you?' Ben Gurion said with a smile. 'No, I kissed him because of a legacy, and I'll tell you the story. In 1914, when Palestine was still under Ottoman rule, I was thrown into prison by the Turks for supposedly having been involved in subversive nationalistic activities. The President of Israel, Yitzhak Ben Zvi, was in another cell at the same prison. I heard some terrifying rumours from the jailers: the Turks intended to hang all the leaders of nationalist movements in Palestine who were being held in the prison. First the Arabs, and then, one week later, the Jews. We had no contact with the outside world. I was in solitary confinement, and tried as best I could to listen carefully to everything that went on in the jail. Every creaking of a cell door might prove the rumours to be true. And then, suddenly, my cell door opened, and in walked a tall, impressive-looking man who introduced himself as the representative of the Alliance Israelite in Jerusalem. 'Don't worry, David, we'll get you out of here,' he said with absolute confidence. 'No harm will come to you and you will be able to get out and continue your work,' he announced resolutely. From that moment on I felt totally confident. I knew that our release was just a matter of time, as indeed it turned out to be. Now do you understand why I kissed Antebi's son,' Ben Gurion said, beaming, and then added: 'Even though he was born here in this country and should have been living here like his father did, and not in Mexico!'

At one of the most difficult moments in my life, a short time after Ariela's death, I received an invitation from the Minister of Defence, Moshe Dayan, to come and meet him privately. I was somewhat surprised by the invitation, since up until then I had not had any significant contact with him. We had met informally once or twice at his house at parties I attended with my colleague and his old friend, the former Commander of the Israeli air force, Dan Tolkowsky.

What could Dayan possibly want from me? I asked myself on the way to the Ministry of Defence. Dayan received me very warmly, and then for two hours proceeded to talk to me as a friend about matters pertaining to defence and security, about problems and possible solutions. Here and there I nodded in assent, once in a while I commented on one thing or another, and, since I agreed with most of his assessments, we had no cause to argue about any of the issues he raised. It was a friendly conversation, but surely that was not the reason I had been invited. We weren't even friends.

When at last I thought the conversation had run its course, even though I was still in the dark as to the real agenda of our meeting,

Dayan suddenly said, 'I have one more question to ask you. Are you involved in tourism and construction?'

'That's one area that I failed in,' I admitted quickly. 'I built a hotel – but there were no tourists. But what do you have in mind? I'd be interested to hear about it.'

Dayan opened a drawer and took out some maps. 'You see, in order to strengthen the southern part of the country I want to build a new city here,' he said, his finger pointing at an area in the northern part of the Sinai Peninsula. 'And to ensure its success, I want to set up a tourist infrastructure in the area as well.'

'If you're talking about a trailer camp, I'd be more than willing to participate,' I said. 'But I am not prepared to have anything to do with permanent buildings of any kind there, because I hope we won't remain there for ever. I have no desire to do anything with this piece of land, either for national or commercial purposes.'

Dayan, who had broached the subject quite unexpectedly, dropped it with equal alacrity. We never spoke of it again, not even after the signing of the Camp David Accords when the city of Yamit in northern Sinai, which had been the subject of our meeting, was razed to the ground in advance of the Israeli pullback from Sinai.

One week after the change of government in 1977, when Menachem Begin's Likud Party came into power after decades of Labour rule, I met Simcha Ehrlich, Begin's new Minister of Finance, in the lobby of the Mann Auditorium in Tel Aviv. I introduced myself and congratulated him on his appointment. Ehrlich smiled broadly at me, and just as he was about to say something to me, a Likud Party member interrupted our conversation and said, quite vehemently, 'Simcha! Don't talk to him. Gitter is a died-in-the-wood Mapainik [Mapai was the acronym of the ruling left-wing party – Mifleget Poalei Eretz Yisrael]. He was the most vocal of my opponents and worked for Rabinovitch in the Tel Aviv municipal elections.'

Ehrlich was unfazed. 'You don't have to tell me who Benno is. We haven't had a chance to get to know each other up until now,' he said, turning back to me, 'but I would like to get to know him better.' That evening we arranged for our first meeting for later that week.

As our friendship grew, I began to realize the strange contradiction in my attitude towards him. On a purely personal level he was a very pleasant person. I liked his decency, his sense of humour and his liberal views. This in itself was not surprising; after all he had come from the same liberal school of thought as my former mentor, Peretz Bernstein. He was even somewhat naïve and overly decent. Ehrlich was one of the few ministers in the new government who did not immediately fire ministry officials from the previous administration as soon as he took office. As far as he was concerned, anyone could stay on, regardless of his or her political affiliation, as long as they proved themselves capable of doing their jobs satisfactorily. Looking at the issue dispassionately, I didn't agree with him. It is impossible, I said to him, for you to count on people to carry out policies they don't support. Those who were brought up on the ideals of Socialist economics will have a difficult time getting used to an open-market economy, and vice versa.

My first conversation with Ehrlich was very pleasant and frank. He told me about his plans to liberalize foreign currency regulations in the country. According to his proposed reforms, the citizens of Israel would be allowed to bring in to the country and take out unrestricted sums of money. I was appalled at the thought that the Minister of Finance was about to make the same mistake that many other people, older and wiser than he, had made elsewhere in the past. I tried to prove to him that even Sapir and Eshkol's so-called Socialist economy did not toe the purist Socialist line, but rather operated in accordance with the country's true needs. I was very forthright, and told him that changing the existing foreign currency regulations at that point in time would cause havoc in the country. Even well-established and much richer countries like Britain, I argued, had not deregulated foreign currency. I tried to warn him of the grave consequences of such a move in a country in which economic growth, immigrant absorption and, of course, security and education, were at the top of the national agenda.

Try as I might, I could not convince him of the dangers inherent in his plan. Ehrlich raced forward on his own chosen path. The day before the implementation of the reforms Dr Ono Ruding, a Dutch economic expert with the International Monetary Fund in Washington, responsible for Israel and four other small countries at the IMF, arrived in Israel to monitor the implementation of the proposed reforms. Ruding was a member of the Christian-Democratic Party in Holland, and a man of far-reaching liberal persuasions. As an old friend, who was well aware of my position and activities in the Israeli economy, he wanted to know what I thought of Ehrlich's reforms. We arranged to meet for an hour to discuss the matter. I explained to him that I could foresee the imminent development of a dangerous inflationary spiral. I tried to describe to him the structure of the Israeli economy, but my powers of persuasion failed me even in my own native tongue. The meeting lasted well into the small hours of the morning. He stood firm by his liberal views, and I by my conservative ones.

The following morning Eli Kushnir, a leading economic commentator on Israel TV, asked me to participate in a panel discussion dealing with the new economic plan. My views on the subject were fairly well known in a general way, and I assumed I had been invited to represent those opposed to the reforms. The other participants were supposed to be industrialists and economists who were favourably disposed to the plan. In the end, the programme was not recorded as a panel discussion, and each participant was interviewed separately in his home (it was this interview that caused the angry quarrel between the Recanatis and myself). One of the participants was the Director-General of the Ministry of Finance, Amiram Sivan, and another was Eitan Sheshinsky, an economics professor from the Hebrew University in Jerusalem who later became the chairman of the board of Koor Industries. The interviewers asked questions and I responded. I hardly referred to the actual reform itself, but offered my opinion on the basis of a similar liberalization of foreign currency regulations that had been implemented in South America. Based on the disastrous outcome of that experience, I warned listeners and interviewers alike that we were heading for an economic catastrophe: hyper-inflation of thousands of percentage points annually, wholesale bankruptcies of companies and factories, the economic ruin of families and individuals, wild profiteering by stock market and currency speculators, and the creation of a select group of 'winners' who would make vast profits by beating the system.

That evening I was invited to a reception at the home of Amos Eran, who had been Director-General of the Prime Minister's Office during Yitzhak Rabin's first term as Prime Minister. The guests at Eran's house that evening were known, for the most part, as 'decision-makers'. We all gathered in front of the television as the broadcast, which included my interview, began. Not all the people there were acquaintances or friends of mine, so it was both strange and refreshing to observe their very mixed reactions at first hand without the filters of good manners or hypocrisy. Some of the Labour Party people there agreed with me, but others, such as the late Noah Moses, pooh-poohed my ideas saying, '*Nu*, as usual, Benno likes to come across as an armchair Communist.' Many were critical of my appearance on television. 'Why did you agree to give that interview? Was your ego in need of a boost?' These reactions proved to me once again how difficult it was for some people to believe that others might be motivated by decent, objective – even idealistic – goals.

Begin himself joined the supporters of the economic reform, and in a television interview said, among other things: 'We did it in order to enable all those Jews sitting on their suitcases in Brazil and Argentina to come on *aliya* to Israel.' This was an infuriating statement, and I sat down that night to compose a letter of protest to Mr Begin. 'Dear Mr Prime Minister,' I wrote. 'On what basis do you claim that the Jews of South America are sitting on their suitcases? To the best of my knowledge, they are living very satisfying lives in their own countries, and can leave at any time they see fit. Irresponsible statements of the kind you just made tonight can cause them serious damage.'

To my amazement, I was called in for a meeting with Minister Ehrlich. He had only one complaint: 'Why didn't you tell me a week ago what you thought of my plan? Why did you have to broadcast your opinion on television?'

'With all due respect, Simcha, I did give you my opinion in our previous conversation! I understood then that I hadn't convinced you, but I didn't realize you had gone so far ahead with the plans for implementing these reforms. Surely you must be aware of the fact that my opinion carries no weight in this government.'

'Well, here you are; now you have influence,' he said with his genial smile.

Despite the unpleasant circumstances that brought us together again after a year during which we had not had any contact, Ehrlich did not bear a grudge. 'I want to suggest to you that you find a way to advise me just as you did for the previous governments,' he proposed. 'And I am willing to give you the same position Sapir gave you: roving ambassador and personal advisor.'

'I am very grateful to you for the honour, and I am fully prepared to be at your service whenever you wish, but not in any official capacity,' I responded. 'When I was an ambassador, I had to resign from all sorts of other positions I held. I am not willing to go through all that again. It's too complicated, and not worth either the cost or the effort.'

Ehrlich respected my position, and asked me to become his personal advisor. Up until the time he resigned from the Ministry of Finance and moved to the Ministry of Agriculture, he frequently asked for my advice. I continued to perform the same service for his successor, Yigal Horowitz, at his request.

However, the damage had already been done, and, just as I predicted, inflation spiralled almost out of control, causing immeasurable damage to the financial stability of the country. Israel's economy was to pay the heavy price of that tragic mistake for many years to come. It was only seven years later, in 1985, that Prime Minister Shimon Peres, and his Minister of Finance, Yitzhak Moda'i, with infinite patience and wisdom, managed to extricate the country from its economic woes.

'... AND I IGNORED HIS OUTSTRETCHED HAND'

Here and there in the course of my recollections, I have mentioned the royal house of Holland. The following story is about Queen Juliana of Holland and the old age home in Herzliya that bears her name.

The story begins during the time of the German Occupation of Holland, and perhaps even a little earlier, in the carefree days before the war when the Lipman-Rosenthal Bank was one of the more important banks in Holland. The Lipman-Rosenthal family was regarded as one of the richest and most respected families in the Jewish community of Holland. The heads of the family were famous for their extensive collections of Judaica, which they eventually donated to the University of Amsterdam. Titles of nobility were only very rarely conferred in Holland, and members of the Lipman-Rosenthal family were among the select few who received such an honour and joined the very small ranks of Jewish nobility.

After the German Occupation of the country, the Lipman-Rosenthal Bank of Holland was forced to merge with the Mendelsohn Bank of

Berlin. This was one of the first acts the Germans carried out after conquering the country, but as usual, the Jews refused to read the writing on the wall. 'It's nothing,' they nodded with naïve confidence. 'After all, the Mendelsohn Bank is also a Jewish bank!' What they did not know, or did not want to know, was that the Mendelsohn Bank had been incorporated *in toto* by the Dresden Bank – the official bank of the SS. The Germans left the name Mendelsohn Bank in order to deceive the Jews into believing it was still a safe place for their deposits.

A few months after the beginning of the Occupation, the edicts began appearing slowly but surely. I have already described how the Jews were systematically – and devilishly – stripped of their basic freedoms: no sitting on public benches, ostensibly a minor annoyance, but an intensely humiliating one none the less; a curfew in effect from eight in the evening, a regulation that turned our social lives upside down; no riding on trains, and many other similar restrictions. One of the edicts from that time caused us severe distress: we were ordered to bring all our gold and silver possessions, and deposit them in the Lipman-Rosenthal Bank. Naturally, everyone complied with the draconian demand: a Dutch Jew simply does not violate the law, even if that law is the brainchild of an evil régime. The Gitter family had never totally internalized all the Dutch traits, and in this case, instead of depositing our precious possessions in the bank as required, we hid part of our money and our valuables. And indeed, as I have already described, we managed to survive our break for freedom largely due to the money we kept hidden in the soles of our shoes. But most of the Jews of Amsterdam duly queued up to hand over their valuables. The optimists were certain that everything would be returned to them after the war.

To everyone's total amazement, nothing ever happened to the valuables deposited at the Lipman-Rosenthal Bank. Most of treasure was forgotten in a vault, and discovered intact after the war. The Dutch papers published large ads calling on the owners of the gold and silver to come and claim their possessions, but since only fifteen per cent of the Jewish community of Holland survived the war, there were hardly any claimants. Most of them had died, while others had left the country for Israel or elsewhere.

After the establishment of the state, the issue was taken up by Dr Ya'akov Arnon, the Director-General of the Ministry of Finance and a native-born Dutchman like myself. Pinhas Sapir asked me to go to Amsterdam to meet with the mixed – Jewish and non-Jewish – committee that had been set up by the Dutch authorities to deal with the recovered property. To my surprise, some of the Jewish members on the committee suggested that the entire collection of religious articles and *objets d'art* be donated for cultural purposes in Holland. The non-Jews suggested selling the items and giving the proceeds to Israel, which they regarded as the natural heir of property belonging to Jews murdered in the Holocaust. As I listened to the discussion, I put together my proposal: 'There are elderly Jews in Holland who have relatives in Israel,' I told the committee finally. 'There are also Dutch Jews in Israel who, in their old age, would like to live together with people who speak their language, and to enjoy the benefits of good medical care and safe housing. I suggest that we use the proceeds of the entire treasure in the bank vault to build old-age homes for former Dutch citizens now living in Israel. This would both relieve old-age homes in Holland from some of the crowding, and help bring families together in Israel.'

My proposal was accepted. A plot of land near Haifa had previously been selected, and all that was needed now was to start building. A second home was planned for Herzliya. Two years later, it turned out that the money allocated for the project had run out before construction was completed, and I was asked to contribute the remainder. I could not refuse: the request came just six months after my mother's death, and the members of the building committee offered to name the building after her.

It was a beautiful summer day in St Moritz. Alice and I were taking a walk, and suddenly I was overwhelmed by a kind of superstitious fear. I felt that I didn't want to name the old-age home after my mother. Her name already graced other institutions around the country. I felt that we should avoid any further exposure of our family name and the gossip it might arouse. 'Well, do you have any ideas about whom you would like to name it after?' Alice asked. She knew me well, and understood that I did not like to leave problems half solved.

'Yes, of course. You won't believe this, but I want to ask Queen Juliana if she would agree to have it named after her: the Queen Juliana Parents' Home – how does that sound to you?'

Alice was very excited, and I immediately placed a call to the Queen's secretary, Mr Van der Hoeven, whom I knew. I told him of my idea, and asked him to make an appointment for me to see the Queen. A couple of hours later he called me at my hotel and set a date for two days later. I flew to Amsterdam, and continued on from there to Soestdyk, the Queen's residence not far from the city.

The Queen received me graciously. My heart was pounding with excitement. No matter how many citizenships I had added to my collection over the years; no matter how many myths and beliefs I had debunked; no matter how much of a democrat I was, or how profoundly convinced I was of the equality of all men; for me this elderly, plain-looking woman was a queen and I was her subject. It was as though no time at all had passed since I fled Holland. She said, with a radiant smile, '*Menhir Hitter* ['Mr Gitter' in Dutch], my secretary informed me of your request. Please explain to me why you choose to name an old-age home in Israel after me.'

I thought for a minute and then replied, 'Your Majesty, I cannot forget the centuries-old connection between the House of Orange and the Jews. Those ties became even stronger when your mother, Queen Wilhelmina, fled from the Nazi Occupation. I heard her speaking on Free Dutch Radio, encouraging us, giving us strength, and I felt that in spite of everything I am still a Dutchman. But my children and grandchildren no longer know Dutch, no longer have the same sense of belonging that I feel towards my homeland. Is it too much to ask that in one place in Israel the Israeli and Dutch flags should fly side by side?'

I watched the Queen's expression carefully. I could sense that she was touched by my words. After considering my explanation briefly, she graciously agreed to my request, and expressed her appreciation for the honour I was about to bestow on her. I asked if she would honour us with her presence at the opening. 'I cannot promise that,' she said, explaining that her government would not approve of her visit to such a tense region of the world. 'But,' she promised, 'as soon as I hand over the throne to my daughter Beatrix, I shall be as free as a bird. I will come for a visit, just wait and see.'

The building was completed to my total satisfaction. Every detail was living proof of the meticulous planning that had gone into providing maximum comfort for the elderly. The rooms were pretty, and simply but tastefully furnished. I had demanded that the small windows of the original plans be replaced by larger ones that would let in more light. Whenever I visit the home, as I do from time to time, I enjoy the sight of the beautiful dining-room, and the spacious rooms and corridors. My brother Shimon saw to all the medical aspects of the building. On 8 May 1979, my sixtieth birthday, the Queen Juliana Parents' Home was inaugurated at an impressive ceremony.

Three years later the Queen kept her promise. One of Queen Juliana's most wonderful traits was her natural, unaffected simplicity. She rode up with me in the elevator to the third floor to visit the department for ambulatory care; went down to the living accommodation, and then we walked over to the dining-room. The residents of the home sat excitedly at round tables that had been lavishly set for them. A head table had been prepared at one end of the room. 'Do you really think I'm going to sit there?' the Queen asked with a smile. Instead, she went from one table to the next – some thirty or forty altogether – sat with the residents and talked to them, reminiscing and finding her own connections to their home towns in different regions of Holland. She brought so much happiness to everyone there on that day.

I told Queen Juliana a story about my father who, years ago, was asked to propose a toast to Queen Wilhelmina. He was extremely nervous and made every effort to prepare himself properly for the visit, fearing that he would forget how to address the Queen, when to say 'Your Majesty' and what was permitted or forbidden according to the rules of protocol. 'Did it all go well?' we asked him later at home. 'You didn't forget to say "Your Majesty" did you?'

'There was no time,' my father replied. 'All I had to say was the Jewish blessing, "He who bestowed His honour on flesh and blood". So I took out my *kippa*, made the blessing, translated it into Dutch and the visit was over.'

And when I finished telling Queen Juliana the story I did the same: I took out a *kippa* and gave the ritual Jewish blessing my father had recited for God and royalty.

There are a few other memorable anecdotes from that visit, but the most important incident that I recall is a conversation I had with the Queen at a reception which I gave in her honour at the Hilton Hotel in Tel Aviv. 'Mr Gitter,' she said. 'What did you think of Ascher and Cohen, the two leaders of the *Judenrat* in Amsterdam? I never liked them.'

'When they began, they did good work, Your Majesty, helping refugees who came from Central and Eastern Europe, but gradually they became the Germans' lackeys. In my opinion they should have either run away or committed suicide when they realized what was really happening,' I replied, trying to salvage the honour of those two very controversial and unfortunate men.

'You know,' the Queen recalled, 'shortly after the war Queen Elizabeth of Great Britain came on a visit to Holland. Her itinerary originally included a visit to Ascher's diamond works where the famous Koh-i-Nor diamond, which graces the British crown, was cut and polished. I informed my Prime Minister that I would not attend the event, and that I had no interest in meeting Mr Ascher. In my opinion, he did not do enough to protect his people, and may even have been a collaborator.

'You have nothing to worry about,' my Prime Minister promised me. 'He won't be there. He's an old man now and the diamond works don't belong to him any more.'

'I arrived at the factory, and who do you think was the first person to greet us? Ascher! "It is a great honour for me to shake your hand, Your Majesty," he said to me. I turned around and ignored his outstretched hand.'

The Queen of Holland could afford to be unequivocal in her feelings towards Ascher and Cohen, but the Jewish community struggled with an unrelenting sense of ambivalence towards them. After the war, the Queen allowed the Jews to resolve the issue of prosecuting Jews suspected of collaboration or unseemly behaviour during the war. The trials went on interminably, and in fact never arrived at a conclusion. The entire issue of Jewish collaboration with the Germans was left open and unresolved. The Dutch indicted a number of collaborators and then let them off with light sentences. By the end of the forties the issue had been virtually forgotten.

In our own company in Holland we had a non-Jewish employee who served in a fairly senior position. When I learned that this man had been a member of the WA (the Dutch SS), I tried to have him brought to trial. A friend of mine, a Dutch Jewish legal expert, advised me not to press charges since the matter had already been dealt with through legal channels. I had no choice but to accept his advice in the matter.

BEIT ARIELA

As I have mentioned earlier, my father did not approve of the lifestyle I adopted in Israel. Because our last conversation before his death focused on this issue, I regarded what he said to me then as a kind of last will and testament. It was from my father that I inherited my inclination towards philanthropy. He served as a role model for me in all his charitable deeds both in Holland and in Argentina. This was his legacy, one that was no less significant than the personal example he set for me as a businessman. Did I, in the final analysis, make him proud of me? I do not know. But of one thing I am certain: that the charitable enterprises which I built in his memory are worthy of his everlasting soul.

Of all these enterprises, the one dearest to my heart is the Tel Aviv municipal library, Beit Ariela (Ariela House).

Before the building was initiated, I lost my beloved daughter. I have already mentioned how I talked to Sapir about the library at her funeral. He chastised me for raising the issue during the burial ceremony, and he was right, of course. But it was at those agonizing moments that I promised myself that I would devote time and money to doing good deeds in her memory, and that I would begin at once. Ariela loved to read, and in her brief life did not have the time to read all the books she might have read had she lived longer. While she did not live long enough to read everything she wanted to, today, thanks to her blessed memory, youngsters and adults can find all the books they could wish for in the ample reading-rooms of the library.

The construction of the library took a great deal longer than we expected. It took us a long time to find the right architect, draw up the plans, and have them approved by all the required planning commissions. Alice, who was a member of the committee overseeing the tenders for the work, spent a great deal of time, and more energy than she really should have, on the project. But all these efforts proved invaluable in the end: the completed building fulfilled all our expectations in its beauty and the perfection of its design. All the major municipal libraries were brought in under its roof: the Central Library, the Shar'ar Zion Library, the Ahad Ha'am Library, the Rambam Library, the Newspaper Library, and the Children's Library.

After Alice's death, I donated her private library to Beit Ariela. It was a wonderful collection that perfectly reflected her personality: books on philosophy and Jewish history in Hebrew, French and German, and books on English literature. The books in Dutch I donated to the library at the Queen Juliana Parents' Home. Many of the books had handwritten comments she had scribbled in the margins.

On the second floor of Beit Ariela, in the Ahad Ha'am Library, there is a special collection that is particularly dear to me. It includes first-edition copies of French and German philosophers, among them Hegel and Kant. They were donated to the library by the widow of Dr Cohen, a Jewish doctor who lived in the town of Ijbergen in the eastern part of Holland. Some time before he passed away, the National Library in Jerusalem learned of the existence of his unique collection and expressed an interest in purchasing these rare books. After his death, his widow did indeed try to find an appropriate place for them, yet somehow negotiations with the National Library fell through. I heard about this rare collection after Dr Cohen's death from an old friend, Dr Jacques Reisel. During the German Occupation of Holland, Jacques had been caught by the Nazis after a confrontation between the SS and Jewish youths in the Jewish quarter. From among the hundreds of Jews arrested in the streets in that incident, all of whom were sent to their deaths at Mauthausen, Jacques Reisel was the only one released by the SS. No one knew how or why he was spared. It is possible that some high-ranking Dutchman, perhaps even the mayor of Amsterdam, Voute, used his influence to obtain his release. Like many other Dutch Jews, he spent most of the war in hiding.

A few years after the war Reisel, fearing a Communist takeover of Europe, decided to leave Holland. I helped him get to Curaçao together with his large family – his wife and seven children. After a few years on the island, where he worked in his profession, his intense fear of Communism abated, and he returned to Holland. Whenever I came on one of my frequent visits to Amsterdam I made a habit of spending at least one evening, sometimes even a whole day, with him. He was very critical of my eating habits, and suggested that I follow his example: eat brown rice, watch my cholesterol level, and engage in some form of sport. I always admired his strong, lean physique. And yet, for all his care, my dear friend Jacques Reisel died of a heart attack at the age of sixty-five.

It was Reisel, then, who told me about the eighty-seven-year-old Dr Cohen, a Holocaust survivor who had lost his three sons, and whose precious book collection had miraculously survived the war intact. Jacques, who looked after the elderly doctor at the end of his days, asked me if we could find an appropriate place for the books in our library, and ensure their proper storage and display. The thought of enriching the library, which was in the first stages of its development, with such a wonderful collection was very exciting. I notified Shlomo Lahat, the mayor of Tel Aviv, and he enthusiastically supported the idea and said he would send an expert to evaluate the collection. The expert returned thrilled by what he had seen; Jacques Reisel had apparently not exaggerated in the least when he described its value.

Now the negotiations for the acquisition of the books went into high gear. After only a few meetings, the widow's representative signed a contract with the management of Beit Ariela donating the collection to the library. When everything was signed and sealed, and the collection was on its way to Israel, I asked Shlomo Lahat to write a letter of thanks to the doctor's widow. He agreed and asked me to write the letter in Dutch. I did so, and Lahat sent it out from the mayor's office on his official letterhead.

A week later, I sat down to write a personal note of thanks to the doctor's widow. I had waited those few days in order to allow the official letter from the mayor to arrive first. Had I known that I would be too late I would have set aside those petty calculations. The reply I received was from a notary public in the village, who informed me that Mrs Cohen was no longer alive. After the deaths of all her loved ones, and totally at peace with herself, she had chosen to bring her life to an end. The notary added that the widow had been very touched by the letter from the mayor of Tel Aviv, and was very happy to learn that a proper home had been found for her precious collection in Beit Ariela.

I myself chose the location for the Cohen collection: the first row, in the middle. A special plaque was affixed to the shelves introducing the collection to the public. I hope that many people appreciate the value of this rare collection. Whenever I visit the library I pass by the Cohen books, and feel very close to them, as though the silent pages were the repository of dear souls.

Another unique collection in Beit Ariela is the legal library of the late Judge Zeltner. I purchased it on the advice of the lawyers Amnon Goldenberg, head of the Israel Bar Association. He pointed out to me how valuable such a library might be for students, lawyers and judges. Those books in the collection that were more purely academic I gave to the library of the Law Faculty of Tel Aviv University.

In order to make certain that these law books would be well cared for, a few changes had to be made in the library building. Baron Edmond de Rothschild informed Amnon Goldenberg and me of his willingness to undertake the costs of making these changes, and I am proud of the partnership that also developed in Beit Ariela between the Baron and myself. At my request, the municipality agreed to hire a special librarian for this important collection, which serves such a large public. The fact that Beit Ariela is literally a stone's throw from the Tel Aviv courthouse makes the location of the collection all the more useful and attractive.

Despite my special feelings for Beit Ariela, I did not automatically agree to every request for assistance. For example, as a matter of principle, I refused to take upon myself the cost of maintaining the building, because I believed that to be the responsibility of the municipality. However, I did propose to use the proceeds from another fund to buy more books than were originally budgeted. At the same time I established a scholarship fund for high school students of Ariela's age. There were people who believed that since secondary education in Israel is free and compulsory, there was no need for such scholarships for children of high school age. But I insisted. After looking into the issue carefully, I discovered that many parents found it difficult to pay for many of the extra-curricular expenses of high school education, and that many teenagers from lower-income families dropped out of school for that very reason. I made a point of stipulating that some of the scholarships be awarded not only on the basis of need, but also on the basis of excellence. In this way, I wanted to promote the education of uniquely gifted children. For over twenty years some one hundred and eighty scholarships were awarded from this fund each year. The warm letters of thanks that I received from the recipients warmed my heart. Many students wrote to tell me that their scholarships had literally made it possible for them to continue their secondary education, and had boosted their self-confidence. The beautiful and moving ceremonies always took place on the third day of the Pesach week, the anniversary of Ariela's death, with the participation of officials from the municipality, the recipients and their families, the management of Beit Ariela, my family and myself. The speakers at these ceremonies spoke glowingly about Ariela, paying her deeply moving tribute.

Nevertheless, after twenty-one years I brought this scholarship project to an end. Ariela's death seemed to be receding further and further into the past, and while it is true that she seems for ever frozen in time at an age close to that of the recipients, for them she was nothing but a vague, ethereal name. I looked for new ways to refresh our way of remembering her. Initially, I increased my donations for the acquisition of new books, and later I connected Beit Ariela to all the large libraries in Israel through a sophisticated computer system – a very important tool for readers and librarians alike.

Despite their variety, all these activities did not engage me in anything radically new, and my desire for action still had to find an outlet. When someone suggested that I contribute towards the creation of a music library, I immediately took to the idea. Throughout her life Alice, whose name graces the library, was a lover of art, literature and music. I am certain that she would have been delighted to take part in the creation of such a library and to enjoy its many services. Like everyone else who visits the library, she would no doubt have been very impressed by the enormous investment and the attention to detail. The library is equipped with listening and recording posts, computers and TV screens, and houses thousands of CDs. Special attention was paid to the interior design: comfortable chairs, handsome furniture, soft, pleasant lighting. I purchased a wall-hanging for the library created by one of Israel's greatest artists, the world-renowned Mordechai Ardon. This piece, completed by the artist not long before he died at the grand old age of ninety-five, added a special beauty and artistic sensitivity to the library.

I was never blessed with an ear for music, but I was brought up to love it, and it is for that reason too that this unique library gives me so much pride and satisfaction. Every time I visit Beit Ariela I go into the music library and once again enjoy the unique atmosphere that attracts so many students and music lovers of all ages.

As I have said, I sought to commemorate my father as well through a fund I established after his death. For over thirty years the fund contributed to the following enterprises: a day-care unit for diabetic children at Beilinson Hospital (now renamed the Yitzhak Rabin Medical Centre), a hall in the Tel Aviv Museum named after Mali Kaufmann and Alice Gitter; students' housing at the AMIT boarding school at Kfar Batya named after my parents, Jenny and Natan Gitter; a respiratory intensive care unit at Schneider Children's Hospital; an intensive care unit for asthma patients at Meir Hospital in Kfar Saba named after the Gitter family; a surgical wing and doctors' lounge at Ichilov Hospital in Tel Aviv named after Alice Gitter, in honour of the late director of the department, Professor Theo Vishnitzer; a dining-room and part of the shelter for retarded youth at the Lewzeller Institute in Herzliya; a dormitory at the Haifa Technion, named after Alice, and a dormitory at the Ben Shemen boarding school, named after Ariela; the Queen Juliana Parents' Home in Herzliya; a community centre named after my father at his synagogue, Ichud Shivat Zion, in Tel Aviv; annual scholarships for students at the Hebrew University in Jerusalem, the Weizman Institute in Rehovoth; an academic chair at the Technion in Haifa, and the scholarships at the universities of Haifa, Tel Aviv and Beersheba; participation in a chair for Talmudic Law at Bar-Ilan University, in memory of my friend Herman Hollander; the Technological High School at Tel Aviv University; a youth hostel in Eilat named after Ariela; and contributions to the Israel Philharmonic Orchestra, the 'Bimartef' Hall experimental stage at Habima, the National Theatre, a hall in the Habima theatre, and most of the major museums in the country. Together with friends of mine from South America I helped fund the construction of a number of buildings on the campus of Tel Aviv University. It was a special pleasure for me to join the Smolarz family, good friends from Argentina, in building the multiple-storey Gitter-Smolarz Library of Life Sciences and Medicine.

A few months before Ariela's death I was asked to make a contribution to the Tel Aviv Museum. I knew Alice would derive great satisfaction from having a hall in the museum named after her mother, Mali Kaufmann. Alice had been very close to her mother, who died at a relatively young age and never had the privilege of visiting Israel. As I have mentioned, Alice was a true patron of the arts, and as a result was very pleased by our family's connection to Tel Aviv Museum. A year later, Alice too died, and I began thinking of ways to keep her memory alive. A few years ago I donated money for extensive renovations in the Mali Kaufmann Hall at Tel Aviv Museum, and renamed it the Kaufmann-Gitter Hall.

'TELL HIM THAT I LOVE HIM'

Beatrix, Queen Juliana's daughter and the present Queen of Holland, visited Israel with her husband in 1976. At that time she was still Crown Princess, and my brother, Professor Shimon Gitter, was Dean of the Medical School at Tel Aviv University. A floor at the medical school was donated by friends and admirers of his from Holland, and named after the Princess. The inauguration of the building was an excellent opportunity to invite the Princess to attend the event.

Without any formal invitation from the Israeli government, the Princess landed at Ben Gurion Airport. The fact that the visit was private raised some eyebrows, and elicited criticism from within government circles. Nevertheless, we held a festive luncheon in her honour at Prime Minister Yitzhak Rabin's home, and many senior government officials were invited, among them the Speaker of the Knesset, Kadish Luz. If I am not mistaken, Alice and I were the only guests invited to the event simply because we were Dutch, and not because of any official position that we held. I was presented to the Princess, and she immediately spoke to me in Dutch, displaying a remarkable familiarity with the names of the guests and their occupations. 'If I am not mistaken, you are a banker, Mr Gitter, are you not?' she asked me.

'Yes, Your Highness,' I replied.

'Are you by any chance a relative of Professor Gitter?' she continued, with a smile that reminded me of her mother, Queen Juliana.

'I am his brother,' I affirmed.

'Then why are you smiling?' she asked. 'Did I say something I shouldn't have?'

'No, Your Highness. I am indeed a banker, and Professor Gitter's brother, and both things make me very proud, but that is not why I am smiling. I am thinking about what my late father would have said if he could have seen me like this, sitting in the home of the Prime Minister of a country that is very dear to me and talking to the Crown Princess of another country that is equally close to my heart.'

'I can understand that,' she said, nodding.

But could she really? Naturally, I could not confide in the Princess and share with her my conflicting feelings about my adopted homeland. On the one hand I could not, and did not wish to, deny my profound sense of gratitude to Holland for the life it allowed us to lead, and the safe haven it provided for its Jews for over three hundred and fifty years. My family too had a great deal to be grateful for. After all, it was in Holland that I grew up to be what I am: a proud Jew with no sense of inferiority. On the other hand, it was hard to forget the attitude of a great many Dutch people towards the Jews of Holland during the war. I consoled myself with the thought that the Princess's parents had proved their opposition to the Nazis publicly and bravely. Beatrix's father, a German by birth, took great pains to establish his anti-Nazi credentials. The entire royal household exiled itself to England and from there to Canada, and, throughout the war, continued to support and encourage the Dutch resistance fighters.

Twelve years after that first meeting with Beatrix, I had the privilege of meeting her once again, this time when she was Queen of Holland. The event was one that aroused great excitement throughout Europe: the inauguration of the new theatre and opera house complex in the very heart of the former Jewish quarter in Amsterdam. Before the Second World War five synagogues had stood on that very site, side by side with a number of *heders* – schools of religious studies for youngsters. During the war years these buildings were severely damaged, and their beautiful wooden interiors were broken up for firewood during the freezing weather of 1944–5 – of one of the worst winters in many years. Only the Portuguese synagogue – the Esnoga – escaped intact. Even the German vandals decided not to touch this extraordinary edifice and treated it as a national treasure that had to be protected. After the war, what was left of the Jewish community of Amsterdam found itself in dire financial straits, and offered to sell much of its property to the municipality, on condition that the community would have a say in any decision relating to reconstruction plans for the site. It took the Jewish community and the municipality of Amsterdam thirty years finally to come to an agreement, and in the meantime the ruined synagogues remained just as they were at the end of the war.

At long last, a Jewish mayor of Amsterdam, Van Tijn, proposed a plan that met with the community's approval. The synagogues were renovated, and a museum was created in the women's section, filled with historical artifacts documenting the life of the Jewish community before the German Occupation. In the area of the famous Jewish market, which used to be held every Sunday not a hundred metres from the synagogues and just in front of the Moses and Aaron Catholic Church, the city put up an impressive cultural complex that includes a theatre and opera house.

The Dutch authorities regarded the reconstruction of the area as an important event in the life of the Jewish community of Amsterdam, and of the city at large, and invited a glittering list of guests from all over the European Community for the inaugural ceremony. Israel was given pride of place at the ceremony: the famous Israeli composer Noam Sherif was asked to compose a cantata in honour of the occasion, and to perform it with the Israel Philharmonic Orchestra. As chairman of the Philharmonic Orchestra Foundation, I accompanied the orchestra to the gala event in my home town.

There was considerable tension at that time between the governments of Israel and of Austria. The Israeli government had recalled its ambassador from Vienna in protest over the election of Kurt Waldheim – who was accused of having been involved in the Holocaust – as President of Austria. The Austrian government did not retaliate by recalling its own ambassador from Israel, but, in a kind of delayed reaction, it decided not to extend its ambassador's appointment to Israel at the end of his term of office.

Before I left for Amsterdam with the orchestra I was approached by officials from the Israeli Foreign Ministry, which was headed by Shimon Peres at the time, and asked to undertake a diplomatic mission on behalf of the state: to meet with the Austrian Chancellor – who was supposed to attend the event in Amsterdam – and try to persuade him not to recall their ambassador. For our part, I was to promise that as soon as Waldheim stepped down we would reinstate full diplomatic channels of communication with Austria.

My meeting with the Austrian Chancellor, Franz Vranitzky, took place on Saturday in The Hague. The Chancellor was very open and friendly, but said that he was unable to agree to my request. 'In any case,' he explained, 'our ambassador has been in Israel for over five years – a long period of time by any reckoning. Clearly,' he went on, 'under these circumstances we cannot send a new ambassador: countries with diplomatic relations must maintain a certain symmetry in the exchange of ambassadors. How can you expect us to send you a new ambassador, if you refuse to send us an official of the same rank and function?' No amount of persuasion could help, and I left with a sense of having failed in my mission.

The following day was the inaugural ceremony of the Jewish Museum and the gala concert of the Israel Philharmonic Orchestra. The event was very exciting and, at the same time, fraught with emotion. Walking among the display cabinets, I once again came face to face with the twenty-three years of my life that I spent in Amsterdam: letters, photographs, souvenirs, places, events, meetings, plays, festivities, and most of all, beloved faces that evoked intense feelings of longing, pain and guilt. Here they were, those who had departed never to return. Here was the photograph of Rabbi Frank, who had gone from house to house bringing the terrible news of the death of loved ones, comforting and encouraging the bereaved parents and relatives. Here was a postcard from Bergen-Belsen: 'Don't give up! Lift your heads up proudly!' My feelings for this museum go very deep, and every time I return to visit it again, I am choked by tears that I cannot hold back.

The cantata *Mechayeh Ha-Meitim* ('The Resurrector of the Dead' – a line from a Jewish prayer), was the high point of the inauguration festivities of the new complex. At the end of the ceremony, Queen Beatrix and her husband held a reception for a limited number of invited guests. I waited my turn to go up to the small podium where the Queen was receiving her guests. The Chief of Protocol introduced me by name and position: 'Benno Gitter, chairman of the Israel Philharmonic Orchestra Foundation', and the Queen was about to shake my hand. Suddenly she looked at me closely, and said to her Chief of Protocol: 'No! Why did you introduce him like that? This is Benno Gitter, the chairman of Tel Aviv University! How are you, *Menhir Hitter*? How good it is to see you.'

I admit I was taken aback, even stunned by the Queen's attention. Her extraordinary memory flattered me. I descended from the podium in a daze, so much so that for a moment I did not recognize the handsome man who addressed me in German as I came down from the stage. 'Don't you recognize me?' he asked. 'We had lunch together yesterday!' It was Chancellor Vranitzky.

'I apologize,' I said, extremely embarrassed. 'Apparently, deep inside, I am still truly Dutch, and the exchange with the Queen threw me off balance.'

'May I have a word with you?' the Chancellor said. We stood off to one side and proceeded to engage in a conversation that was in total contrast to the official, buttoned-up talk we had held the day before. He was deeply moved by the story of the Jewish community of Amsterdam as it had been presented that day.

'Mr Chancellor,' I said. 'If *you* are moved by this day's events, what should I say? I was born not two hundred metres away from here, and lived in a house just eight hundred metres down the road. I know every paving stone. When I was a child I used to skip all the way to our synagogue – the same one you visited today. Each time I skipped I covered forty centimetres, and when I grew older – sixty centimetres. So I know how to calculate the distance from my house to the synagogue right down to the last centimetre. In my youth I was intimately acquainted with the entire neighbourhood, and with all of its residents. Today, of the 1,800 invited guests I recognized only three of my former acquaintances: one came here from New York, the other from Israel, and only one lives here in Holland.'

Vranitzky listened attentively, and seemed to be deep in thought. 'When are you going back to Israel?' he asked, seeming to stray from the subject of our conversation.

'Tomorrow,' I replied.

'And you will be seeing Shimon [Peres]?'

'Of course I will be seeing him. After all, I have to report to him on my failure!'

'Please don't tell Shimon anything for now, all right? Or rather, yes, tell him that I love him very much.'

My diplomatic mission, turned out to be a great success: the Austrian ambassador remained in Israel for a total of nine years, an unheard-of length of time for a diplomatic posting. Whenever we met at a reception or any other official function, he would bow slightly and say, with a tiny smile playing on his lips, 'Hello, Mr Gitter! Thank you, Mr Gitter!'

Tel Aviv University proposed conferring an honorary doctorate on the Austrian Chancellor, Vranitzky. He agreed in principle, but asked that we postpone the ceremony 'until the old fool' – as he called Waldheim – 'leaves Schönbrunn Palace.' Waldheim's term of office came to an end and he left Schönbrunn, but our plans of awarding Vranitzky an honorary doctorate never materialized. Instead, Chancellor Vranitzky accepted an invitation from the Hebrew University in Jerusalem to receive an honorary doctorate there. There were, evidently, political reasons for this change of plans, and I completely understood – and accepted – the decision.

THE STUDENT CANTOR AND FIDEL CASTRO

One day in 1961 I was sitting at my desk at the Development and Mortgage Bank when my secretary handed me a very elegant-looking visiting card: 'Dr Ricardo Subirana y Lobo, Havana, Cuba', it said in Spanish. I had barely managed to glance at the card when its owner strode in to the office. He was a good-looking man in his late sixties, with grey hair, and, naturally, spoke perfect Spanish. We were both delighted to converse in our common language. He told me that he had met Simon Mirelman aboard a ship they had both taken from Brazil to Italy. They had struck up a friendship over the bridge games they played to while away the time during the long voyage. They spoke at length about Israel, about the Accadia Hotel, and about Simon's Israeli brother, Yoseph. My name too came up in their conversations, and, when he arrived in Israel and discovered that Yoseph was out of the country, he contacted me instead.

I received him warmly, and wondered aloud how a German-born Jew had become a Cuban citizen. My guest seemed very eager to tell me his story and grew increasingly excited as he related it. He was the eldest of twelve children born to the Wolf family in Hamburg. His father had been the chief *hazzan* (cantor) in the Hanover synagogue. Having discovered that his son was possessed of an excellent singing voice, the *hazzan* selected the young boy to be his successor. The young Wolf accepted the future his father had chosen for him, but fate intervened: one day his baby brother fell from a third-floor window into a rainwater cistern and miraculously survived the fall. As a token of his gratitude for the miracle that saved their baby's life, the elder Mr Wolf allowed the older brother to plan his life any way he wished, and chose the baby to follow in his footsteps as *hazzan*.

I don't recall the details of how Dr Subirana arrived in Cuba fifty years earlier, but I do remember what he told me of his life in Cuba under Castro. 'Life under his régime is very good,' he assured me. 'Perhaps especially so for me. Fidel's father and I have been neighbours for years, and we are very close. He calls me "Uncle Ricardo".' The relations between Dr Subirana y Lobo (Wolf) and Fidel Castro were indeed very close. The Jewish doctor had been one of the Cuban dictator's first supporters, and when Fidel Castro set out on his campaign to overthrow the corrupt rule of Fulgencio Batista, Lobo gave Castro a contribution of $50,000.

About two weeks after our first meeting, Dr Subirana invited me to dinner at the Accadia Hotel, where he was staying with his wife, a daughter of the last Spanish governor of Cuba. In the course of the evening, the lady told us that Pablo Casals, the world-famous cellist, was her cousin. As for herself, she was the daughter of the last Spanish from Spain before Cuba's independence in 1905 and the tennis world champion at the Olympic Games in Paris in 1920. As is accepted practice in Cuba, my new friend had added his wife's name – Subirana – to his own. The hotel staff, who recognized me as their former 'boss', reported to me with great excitement: 'There's someone in the hotel who receives telegrams from Fidel Castro every day!'

'I know,' I said nonchalantly, as though making the acquaintance of friends of a much-maligned Communist dictator was something I did every day before breakfast.

At that time my parents were also staying at the Accadia. Whenever I entered the hotel I felt an impossible combination of happiness and failure. But my meeting with Dr Subirana y Lobo Wolf had an element of the unexpected. It was about to lead me into an interesting adventure: not only for me personally, but for the state of Israel as a whole.

After dinner, my host sat down across from me at the table, offered me a fine Havana cigar, and began telling me the story of his life. He had made a fortune from the invention of a steel forging process that he had patented. One of the largest steel companies in the United States bought the rights to his patent. 'They offered me either a lump sum, permission to use the patent myself, or a lifetime pension – whether they actually used the patent or not. I chose the last opinion,' he said with a smile. His gamble eventually paid off: he lived in the lap of luxury for the rest of his life, dying at the ripe old age of ninety-three.

'Do you believe in dreams?' he suddenly asked me. Fragments of my 'cigar dream' floated back into my consciousness, but I put aside this unpleasant association. Dr Subirana did not notice the expression that must have crossed my face at the thought, and went on: 'I dreamed about my mother. She appeared to me on her *yahrzeit* [Yiddish for the anniversary of her death] and said to me, "What are you doing, son?" And I answered, "I'm in the land of my forefathers, and I feel very good here." And then she said, "Stay where you are, but don't forget the country that made you what you are." The following day,' Dr Subirana went on, 'a telegram arrived from Fidel Castro in reply to a telegram I had sent him earlier, wishing him well after he survived an attempt on his life: "Thank you for your good wishes. Glad that you love your historic country. What about representing your present homeland in the land of your forefathers? Reply immediately!"'

Dr Subirana gazed at me for all the world as though I were the Oracle of Delphi. 'What do you think?' he asked imploringly.

'What do I think? If the Israel government agrees, you are on the brink of a brilliant diplomatic career in the service of both countries!' In 1961 Israel had no diplomatic ties with Cuba, but at the same time was engaged in strenuous efforts to increase the number of its embassies around the world, in order to gain support for its case in international forums.

'And how will I know?' Dr Subirana went on to ask.

'I will consult with Ya'akov Tsur. He is the Director-General of the

Foreign Ministry and a good friend of mine from the time when he was ambassador in Argentina. I will let you know if there are any developments.'

Tsur had absolutely no idea what I was talking about. 'We have not received any indications whatsoever from Cuba about sending us an ambassador. If a country wishes to establish diplomatic ties, we must first receive a document known in diplomatic circles as a *placet* [document of agreement], which is, in effect, a request for the host country to approve the appointment of a new ambassador. As of this moment we have not received any such document from Cuba.'

The following day, Tsur called me: 'How did you know?' he asked, nonplussed. 'We just received, via Mexico, a request from Cuba for a *placet* for one Dr Ricardo Subirana y Lobo (Wolf). Is this the man you were talking about?'

And thus it came about that the doctor of many names, the German-born Jew, the first-born son of a *hazzan*, and a personal friend of Fidel Castro, became the first Cuban ambassador in Israel. He lived to a ripe old age in the house he built for himself in Herzliya. He wanted to bequeath this magnificent house to the state of Israel and turn it into a kind of summer residence for Israel's presidents, but eventually donated it to his cultural foundation. Even after he retired from diplomacy he lived in the house for most of the year. And throughout our acquaintance he also continued to supply me with incomparable Cuban cigars – my one great addiction.

That, however, was not the end of the story. During his term as ambassador, Dr Wolf was approached by Pinhas Sapir, the tireless patron of Israel's universities, and by myself, to leave his considerable fortune to educational and welfare institutions in Israel, particularly the universities. He graciously and gladly agreed.

One night, a few years later, the phone rang at my home. Dr Subirana was on the line. 'Benno, come at once! I must talk to you!' he said excitedly. My protests about the lateness of the hour made no impression on him – he simply refused to take no for an answer. By the time I arrived at his house, it was four thirty in the morning.

'I had a dream,' he began excitedly. 'My mother appeared to me and said, "What will you do with your money, son, after you die? Have you thought about that?"

"Of course Mother. Most of the money will go to the universities and to other educational enterprises in Israel. Everything's been arranged."

"That's fine, son," she said in her determined way, "but those institutions that you agreed to support are – above all – the responsibility of the state of Israel. Who will remember that it was you who gave the money? You have no children, and when you die your family name will die with you. You must do something to commemorate our name, son!" '

Between the time he called me and my arrival at his home, Dr Wolf had already come up with a plan. He would leave a small amount to charity, as he had promised, but the bulk of his estate would go into the creation of a highly prestigious international prize bearing his name, to be awarded for achievements in a variety of scientific fields and in the arts. Although it was not an out-and-out imitation, the Wolf Prize, which was to be awarded to scientists from all over the world, was no doubt inspired by the Nobel Prize.

I was not keen on the idea. Israeli academic circles, too, closed ranks in their opposition to the prize. A senior professor told me that he was against special Knesset legislation for the prize, particularly since the chances that any Israeli scientists might be among the winners of the prize were very slim due to their limited presence in the world scientific community. To my utter surprise, Sapir welcomed the idea, and once again proved the breadth of his vision. 'Whatever you wish, Mr Subirana,' he said to the former Cuban doctor. 'It's your money, your will, and we will do everything we can to cooperate with you to your complete satisfaction.'

A few years later, Israeli scientists made their peace with the prestigious international prize, and began honouring the prize-giving ceremonies with their presence. To this day I am ambivalent about the real value of this prize to Israel. On the one hand, the fact that Israel administers the Wolf Prize and is associated with it undoubtedly enhances the country's stature in international scientific circles. On the other hand, it still seems to me too grandiose, too large a prize for a country the size of ours, especially with all the enormous problems we still have to contend with. But most of all, I was saddened by the fact that during the twenty-five years of its existence only two Israeli scientists have ever won the award, and one of them shared it with a scientist from abroad. However, with the presentation of the English edition of my book, I am glad to note that with this year's award there are now five Israeli recipients, among them intimate friends of mine.

18

THE PAST REVISITED

In the spring of 1989, the 'Glasnost Spring', I joined a delegation of Jewish leaders on a visit to the USSR. For me this meant, among other things, a singular opportunity to visit Stanislawow, my mother's birthplace, and Horodenka, my father's birthplace, thirty kilometres away from Stanislawow. While my father was growing up there, Horodenka was considered part of Galicia, and was ruled by the Austro-Hungarian Empire. With the break-up of the empire shortly before the First World War, Horodenka was incorporated into Poland, and later became a part of the Ukraine and the USSR. The city is still there today, a part of the newly independent Ukrainian Republic. For years after the war no visitors from the West were allowed into that area because of its proximity to secret military installations, but as I prepared for my trip, I discovered that the region had been opened up to tourists from all over the world.

A dilapidated old aircraft, which reminded me more of a farm wagon than a modern passenger plane, brought me to Stanislawow, the dismal, grey city that my parents had told me so much about in my youth. Today the city is called Franko-Ivanov, after a famous Ukrainian poet, and is considered primarily an industrial town. However, any resemblance to what we in the West might refer to as an 'industrial town' is totally in the realm of fantasy ...

I did not know much about the life my relatives had led in Stanislawow, and even less about how they had met their deaths. The brief visit I paid them in 1939 made all these people real for me, rather than just disembodied names in my parents' stories. And I did make an effort to save them then by trying to persuade them that they were in dire and immediate danger, and that they should flee the impending catastrophe before it was too late. Over the years I suffered great anguish over their deaths which I failed – through no fault of my own – to prevent, and now I wanted to try and piece together as much as I could about the way in which they died, and take leave of them properly.

All I knew about my father's sister, Dina, was that she was a childless widow, she had lived in a two-and-a-half-room flat in the heart of the Jewish quarter. She was afraid to live alone, and always had relatives staying with her. When the Germans turned that area into a ghetto, some forty people crowded into her tiny apartment, including Lonek, my mother's brother from Hungary, his wife, son and daughter, even though they were not Dina's blood relatives.

The old Jewish cemetery of Stanislawow is at the far end of the ghetto, beyond the old site of the tanning works that belonged to the Margoshes family – distant relatives of ours. The Nazis gathered the Jews from the nearby ghetto and marched them to an area near the cemetery. Eleven deep ditches awaited them there. The Ukrainian guards ordered the Jews, men, women and children, to undress and stand facing the grave-ditches. Then they shot them all in the back. What were my relatives thinking of before they died? I asked myself. What were they feeling? Maybe they felt nothing, because even before their deaths they were already dead. Perhaps it was hopelessness that killed them.

When I arrived at the site of the massacres, I was appalled. The desolation and neglect broke my heart. No stone marked the ditches that had become mass graves. Near the entrance there was a small plaque with the following words in Ukrainian: 'Between 1941 and 1944, 220,000 Ukrainians were murdered here.' Grief and anger filled my heart. Only Jews were buried in those eleven pits beneath the ground I was standing on, Jews who had been brought there from the entire region to be murdered. Ten thousand of them were Hungarian Jews, like my Uncle Lonek and his family. They were all annihilated within a few days, and not over a period of three years as claimed in the plaque.

The ditches had been covered over, but the ground had never been levelled. Where were my relatives buried? Had they been murdered together and thrown into the same ditch, or were they separated in death? The answers to these questions were really not important. Each and every one of the 220,000 people buried there was my blood brother. I went from one ditch to the next, prayed for their souls and recited the prayer for the dead: *Kadish*. When I finished saying the *Kadish* over all eleven ditches, I spoke to them, straight from my heart. Somehow, without even noticing it, I shifted into Dutch, my mother tongue. Into this belated eulogy I poured the boiling lava of my pain, my heartfelt longing, and my terrible feelings of guilt for having survived. As I had innumerable times before, I saw them all walking to their deaths: mothers with their children, teenagers and elderly people. Tears coursed down my cheeks, as though it had all happened yesterday and not fifty years before.

'Sir, we must go – you'll miss your plane,' my guide said, tugging gently at my sleeve. I looked at my watch. I thought I had been talking for five minutes, when in fact I had been talking without a break for over an hour!

Four hundred Jews survived the war in Stanislawow. Most of them left the Ukraine and came to Israel. Before I left this grim, depressing town, I met a few representatives of the local Jewish community. I left them a sum of money in dollars to set up a memorial chapel at the cemetery. I have never been back since, and have no idea if my request was ever carried out.

The day before my visit to Stanislawow, I went to Horodenka. The pastoral view was nearly perfect: spectacular mountain scenery equalling the best Switzerland has to offer; clear springs bubbling down the slopes and, not far from there, the Jewish cemetery. The headstones had either been destroyed by vandals, or eroded by the sun, wind and rain.

I do not know if the mayor of Horodenka, my father's birthplace, honoured my request to plant trees and flowers in the cemetery. I have no intention of going back there to see what was actually done with the contribution I made for this purpose. The sense of relief I felt at the time was enough for me. The mayor told me that before the war the city had numbered 11,000 inhabitants, of whom 6,000 were Jewish. There were now 12,000 inhabitants – and only one Jew. I asked to meet him, but the mayor said, 'No, you can't, he's blind and deaf.'

MY MOTHER

'I have no daughters and I'm lonely as a dog,' my mother used to say, half-jokingly. I remember those words well. My brothers and I tried to be good, devoted sons, but my mother may have had a point. Daughters can probably give their mothers more warmth and support than sons. As for myself, my mother felt that our relationship was not nearly as strong as my bond with my father. With him I had a very strong sense of partnership and an almost telepathic affinity, while I felt none of that towards my mother. I don't know the reason for this disparity, but there is one thing of which I am absolutely certain: my love for her was in no way less than my love for my father.

My mother was a very energetic, active person. She ran our households in Amsterdam and in Buenos Aires, and did so with an iron hand. From our point of view, at that time, nothing could have been more natural. Today, however, I have second thoughts and feel a sense of regret and a need to ask her forgiveness. Although we were always impressed by her ability to manage the household, and by her boundless energy, we – her husband and her sons – stood in her way on too many occasions. When she expressed a desire to learn how to drive, we protested: how could a woman of her advanced age (fifty!) possibly sit behind a steering wheel? Ostensibly we wanted to protect her after all she had been through during the war, but the truth is we simply did not want her driving around on the roads. Today I am acutely aware of how much – and how needlessly – we curbed her freedom, for reasons that we couldn't really explain even to ourselves. In the same way we frustrated her desire to take an active part in the family business. And thus my mother, who on the face of it lacked nothing in her life, was forced to accept the vetoes the family imposed on her deepest desires.

I have nothing to say in our defence except to offer the poor excuse of the prevailing custom of that time and place. Civil rights were never Argentina's strong suit, and giving women equality was at the very bottom of that country's order of priorities. Women from the upper middle classes were unaware of such concepts as feminism, personal fulfilment, or the pursuit of independent careers. Ostensibly it was all for their own good, but it was, in fact, just another manifestation of South American *machismo*.

Since we hadn't allowed her to fulfil her aspirations in other areas, my mother devoted all her energies towards raising money for Kfar Batya, a youth village near Ra'anana established by the Mizrahi women. Here she came into her own: quite suddenly she was discovered by the community as a gifted fundraiser. Without the slightest hesitation, and with enormous charm, she turned her circle of friends and acquaintances into a pool of donors. Even our business competitors could not find it in their hearts to refuse her, not to mention people who generally objected to anything to do with religious institutions (Mizrahi is a right-wing religious party). Years later, when I returned to Argentina to raise money for education, welfare or investments in Israel, I was hardly ever turned down. And there were two reasons for that: the fact that I had left the easy life of Argentina and gone on *aliya* to Israel, and the fact that I was my mother's son.

Had it been up to my mother, my parents would have come to Israel years earlier; but my father simply could not bear to relinquish the business he cared about so passionately, and feared that he would never be able to find similar satisfaction in Israel. That being the case, my parents never spoke of *aliya*. During their last visit, Mother – like Father – was overjoyed at the prospect of beginning a new chapter in their lives in a new house in their new country, close to their sons and grandchildren. But sadly, this chapter ended even before it began when my father suddenly passed away.

During the *shiva* (the traditional first seven days of Jewish mourning), my mother was a tower of strength. Despite her profound grief, she helped organize everything throughout the long days. It was during that week that she decided to remain in Israel. For a few years she took turns living with Zigi and with my brother Ya'akov in Argentina. After the Six-Day War she decided to live in Israel all year round, in a very beautiful apartment she bought for herself not far from my home. Those were good years. Mother enjoyed being close to her sons and grandchildren. She loved to cook, and we adored her incomparable Jewish cusine. Zigi, of course, watched over the state of her health at all times.

We celebrated her eightieth birthday by building a students' dormitory that we named after her. The gesture gave her inordinate happiness. She complained that we had actually added a year to her real age: she had always claimed that her mother had changed the date on her birth certificate so that she could study in the same class as her sister. At that time, she was living in the Golden Age Home in Kfar Shmaryahu, a very pleasant place where she felt well taken care of. I visited her often.

Bixie's daughter Yif'at, my eldest granddaughter, often accompanied me on these visits and brought extra joy to my mother's heart.

As long as she was healthy, she enjoyed life to the full. Towards the end of her life, she fell ill, and suffered a great deal. She died on 30 June 1977, fifteen years after my father.

TO THE UNIVERSITY – AT LAST

Ever since my childhood, the university had always been the real world for me. I never forgot what my mother had said when I was a child, and so accurately predicted our future: 'Zigi will be a professor, and Benno will go into business.' At that moment I had the feeling – and it remained with me for years – that my brother's mission in life was somehow more exalted than mine, more deserving of respect and admiration. I felt that whatever role I might play in life – even if I were hugely successful – it would always be somehow inferior.

None the less, I never truly envied those lucky people who had the good fortune to work in the halls of academe. In fact, it was only a twist of fate – or history – that deflected me from the path to scholarship. On the day after the Germans occupied Holland I received my long-awaited Certificate of Immigration to Palestine, enabling me to take up the place I had been offered in the Department of Economics at the Hebrew University in Jerusalem. But by that time it was too late: I was no longer allowed to leave Holland. I therefore learned economics in the real world of business, without the benefit of academic theory.

Did I ever have the feeling that somehow, somewhere, I would find my way back to the longed-for world of the university? Perhaps. But in the meanwhile, life propelled me in a different direction altogether. My regret over the opportunity that had been stolen from me by the Germans left me with a longing, a kind of weakness for everything to do with higher education. In time, this longing turned into an obsession: if I couldn't actually study at the university, I could at least try to help the students and the universities throughout the country. And that was how the longest affair of my life began.

As early as 1944 I was already a member of the Friends of the Hebrew University in Argentina. Four years later, when the Administrative Director of the Weizman Institute, Meir Weisgal, came to South

America on behalf of the first President of Israel, Haim Weizman, I was among the first to join the newly formed Friends of the Weizman Institute. The institute was in its very early years, and I supported it enthusiastically. How wonderful it is today to see the institute's magnificent achievements over the years, achievements we never dreamed of in those early days. At about the same time, the Haifa Technion began its fundraising activities in Argentina. Apart from my usual support for their fundraising efforts, I also gave the Friends of the Technion in Argentina free use of two rooms in the company's offices. In 1994 the Technion awarded me an honorary doctorate in engineering. I had no connection whatsoever to the profession, but the gesture was very heartwarming. I received it in recognition of my contribution over several decades to the advancement of higher education in Israel, and to the Technion in particular.

With the establishment of the other universities in Israel – Haifa, Bar Ilan in Ramat Gan, and Ben Gurion in Beersheba – and after my emigration to Israel, I became a member of the Board of Governors of all of them. At the Hebrew University I served as deputy chairman of the Board of Governors and of the Executive Committee. That was the case until 1963, when Tel Aviv University gradually began moving to its permanent site in Ramat Aviv. It was then that I began devoting most of my time and energy to this institution. In the university's first years it was no more than a branch of the Hebrew University in Tel Aviv, with the addition of the School for Life Sciences and Economics that was housed in a few dilapidated prefab huts at Abu Kabir in Jaffa, and one building, the Trubovitch Building, on the present site of the Tel Aviv University campus.

By that time I had already met Dr George Wise, a man of prodigious talents who had contributed a great deal of his time, money and academic abilities to the Hebrew University in Jerusalem. His one ambition was to become the President of the Hebrew University, but this was not to be. At the same time, Tel Aviv University was taking its first small steps from the periphery on to the centre stage of academic life in Israel. In order to expand and to be able to meet the needs of higher education in the centre of the country, the university needed someone of Dr Wise's calibre to provide it with the leadership and vision required to make this momentous transformation. My good friend Yoseph Mirelman, who had come to know Wise well from his work in Mexico, was the one who brought his great potential to my attention. Yoseph spoke to my brother, Professor Shimon Gitter, and they decided to discuss the matter further with a few other people, among them the Rector of the minuscule Tel Aviv University at Abu Kabir, Professor Klopstock, and Professor André de Vries, a childhood friend of ours from Holland. Dr Wise was invited to this meeting, and plans were discussed to transform the university from a small local institution of higher education into a major autonomous university, that would include every branch of scholarship in its curriculum and research. I did not attend that meeting, but at the participants' request I agreed to discuss the idea with Sapir. I raised the issue at a lunch Sapir invited me to at the Samuel Hotel, together with the Minister of Finance, Levi Eshkol, and the major of Tel Aviv, Mordechai Namir.

My lobbying was successful. With warm recommendations from Eshkol, Sapir and Namir, Dr George Wise was appointed President of Tel Aviv University. Once we were given the green light to go ahead with the appointment, I invited all the people involved to a meeting at my house: Dr Wise, my brother, Shimon, Professor de Vries, Dr Yoseph Mirelman and Dani Recanati. At that meeting, landmark guidelines were set out for the future development of the university. I take personal credit for bringing Dani Recanati into the founding team. Over the years his involvement proved to be extremely beneficial to the university. One could say that Professor André de Vries, my brother Professor Shimon Gitter and, most certainly, Pinhas Sapir and Mordechai Namir were responsible for the establishment of the Tel Aviv University Faculty of Medicine on the site where it exists to this day.

As I predicted, Dr Wise brought Tel Aviv University a very long way from its humble beginnings in the huts at Abu Kabir, turning it, within a few years, into the largest and most important university in the country. Dr Wise raised money, saw to the construction of major faculty buildings, brought back Israeli academics who had left Israel during the 'brain drain' of the sixties, created a superb academic faculty, helped establish top-flight academic programmes, and much, much more. For a short while George Wise and I were at loggerheads (among other things because of our mutual interests in Clal), but in time things were smoothed out between us, and to this day I am on excellent terms with his widow, Florence, who lives in Miami. Not long before he died, Dr Wise was elected Chancellor of the University.

Professor de Vries was the first Dean of the Medical School, and when he was appointed Rector, my brother was elected to replace him as Dean. Professor de Vries, who was for many years a close personal friend of both my brother and myself, passed away shortly before I finished writing this book.

Even though we never discussed it formally at any time in our lives, my brother and I had a tacit agreement never to intervene in each other's spheres of work. After my initial involvement in building up the university campus in Ramat Aviv, I distanced myself from the university, and for years followed its development from afar. In 1979 the President of the university at that time, Professor Haim Ben Shachar, invited me to become the chairman of the Executive Council, I was aware of the large responsibility involved and it took much thought before I accepted.

Two prominent figures held this position before. The first one was Mordechai Namir, the mayor of the city of Tel Aviv who co-founded the university. His successor in this position, Yehoshua Rabinovitch, was also his successor as mayor of Tel Aviv. Rabinovitch later became Minister of Finance and I felt it would be a hard act to follow in their footsteps. Thus I was quite relieved when during the first meeting in which I had to be elected, the dean of the Faculty of Law, Professor Dinstein objected on the ground that only the Board of Governors, supposed to convene in nine months' time, can elect the chairman of the Executive Council. This period in which I officiated as acting chairman provided me with the time to consider a permanent nomination that eventually extended to nine years through three successive nominations.

During these years I worked very closely with the outstanding presidents of the university – Professor Youval Neeman, the leading physicist, Professor Haim Ben Shachar and Professor Moshe Mani. When completing my fourth term as chairman of the executive council I was nominated to chair the International Board of Governors of the University. After nine years and two elections I still hold the lay leading office. This period coincided with the presidency of Professor Yoram Dinstein and the rectors Professor Itamar Rabinovich, Professor Dan

Amir and Professor Nili Cohen. The reason for the succession of the rectors is due to Professor Rabinovich's nomination by the Rabin government to head the peace talks with Syria and thereafter his nomination as ambassador of Israel to the government of President Bill Clinton. Since retiring from the diplomatic service Professor Rabinovich resumed his teaching activities at the university. The nomination committee that I chair chose, in August 1998, Professor Rabinovich, unanimously, to be formally elected the next president during the forthcoming meeting of the Board of Governors in May 1999.

For seven years Professor Dinstein and I worked in full understanding and our cooperation was very effective and agreeable, resulting in most efficient drives mainly abroad and in Israel. During that period our yearly fundraising income more than doubled. Together we organized regular regional meetings for members of the Board of Governors and friends of the university in Switzerland, The French Riviera, Canada, USA, and Spain as well as regular events in Buenos Aires and Punta del Este. The last two, which are under Dr Ilana Ben Ami's brinkmanship have already taken place for thirteen years.

With the very capable rector, Professor Nili Cohen, at the side of the next president of the University, Professor Itamar Rabinovich, I feel confident that my investment of twenty years of intensive work on behalf of the Tel Aviv University will usher us successfully into the twenty-first century.

As chairman of the Executive Council, my duty was to oversee the day-to-day affairs of the university from one annual meeting of the Board of Governors to the next. In fact, there is no truly substantial difference between the two positions, as long as there is good cooperation between myself and the top echelons of the university – the President, the Rector, and the chairman of the Executive Council.

In my capacity as chairman of the Board of Governors, I may participate in all committee meetings in the university, and I do so whenever I believe it is necessary or beneficial. I chair all important meetings that deal with our representatives abroad, as well as all the sessions of the annual meeting of the Board of Governors.

It is a well-known fact that the university cannot be maintained solely on tuition fees (despite the many complaints on this score, tuition fees in Israel are still relatively low). The universities manage to function with the help of government appropriations for higher education, funnelled through the Planning and Budget Committee of the Council for Higher Education in Israel. The funds that truly help the universities grow and develop, above and beyond this government subsidy, are the private contributions raised by the institutions themselves. It is no exaggeration to say that there is a direct correlation between the level of these contributions and the success of any particular university. It is the donations that construct buildings, pay for much-needed equipment, stock the libraries, fund research, and much, much more.

My predecessor chairpersons at Tel Aviv University, all of whom resided abroad, did not always regard fundraising as part of their obligation to the university. However, I regard it as the most important task of all, and as a natural continuation of my many years of activity on the university's behalf. I have no problem with meeting potential donors, first of all because I am a benefactor of the university myself, and second – and this is the most important thing – because I believe that only those Jews who are deeply involved and display a fundamental sense of responsibility towards their people are deserving of 'membership' in the Jewish people. And what could possibly be more important than donations for education, welfare and health?

At about the same time that I began working on behalf of the university in 1979, Ilana Ben Ami joined the staff of university fundraisers, and, in her capacity as deputy chairperson for Latin American countries, took responsibility for fundraising efforts in these countries. She began her work for the university at a difficult time, when both Argentina and Uruguay were reeling under highly unstable governments. Nevertheless, she proved to be extraordinarily capable in her work. Her extensive social contacts, her native knowledge of Spanish and her talent for public relations all added to her success. I gradually withdrew from my own long-term involvement in these countries, and she eventually took sole responsibility for all the work being done there. While all the Israeli universities are more or less successful in their fundraising efforts in Europe and the United States, South America has become virtually the exclusive province of Tel Aviv University in this respect. Much of this success is the result of Ilana's tireless efforts, boundless dedication and both hers and mine manifold intimate relations with the members of those communities and their leadership.

Some time ago I concluded a good meeting with a big donor from California. The man had committed himself to setting up an important new project in the university. As we parted, he said to me, 'You know, Benno, Tel Aviv University should be very happy that they have someone like you.'

I was touched by the compliment, but I saw things somewhat differently, and immediately replied, 'Believe me, you're right,' I said. 'But the way I see it, it is I who should be happy to have the university.'

And indeed, when I look back on the many careers I have pursued – merchant, industrialist, banker – I know for certain that I wouldn't exchange what I am doing now for any of them. The profound satisfaction that I find in this field of endeavour is greater than any I have ever known. Working for the university, I am totally immersed in what I love most of all and believe in deeply. I use my talents, my contacts, live a very full life, and, most important of all, my efforts benefit other people. My gratitude for having had this privilege is immeasurable. It is difficult for me to put into words the deep attraction I have felt, since childhood, for the academic world.

When I ended my term of office as chairman of the Executive Council of the university, the President, Professor Moshe Mani, gave me a very special gift: an annual lecture bearing my name to be given each year on my birthday. I was awarded the privilege of inviting the speaker, either from Israel or from abroad, and naming the topic. Based on the way I see my life, I cannot think of any other gift that could give me more pleasure. The first speaker I chose for the annual Benno Gitter Lecture was Dr Ono Ruding who, despite his relatively young age, was an old friend of mine from Holland. For seven years he served as Minister of Finance in Holland, and at the age of fifty decided to go into private business. Because of upcoming elections in Holland and his own private schedule we set the date of the lecture for 14 January 1991 rather than on my birthday in May. Never in our wildest dreams could we have imagined that on that very day Israel would be facing the outbreak of a major war in the region: the Gulf War. Despite the tension, Dr Ruding refused to cancel his trip. The lecture – an overview of the European economy – was fascinating, and the compliments he showered on me before he began his talk were almost embarrassing. I moved the time of the lecture forward to the early evening because we were all eager to hurry home and watch the television news at nine, and to finish taping up our windows in anticipation of a possible Iraqi rocket attack on Israel.

The subsequent Gitter lectures took place under much less dramatic circumstances. In 1992 my good friend Professor Ya'akov Frenkel, governor of the Bank of Israel, gave the second B.G.-lecture on the Israeli economy, and in 1994, on my seventy-fifth birthday, I was honoured by Prime Minister Yitzhak Rabin who gave his Benno Gitter lecture at a meeting of the Board of Governors in May. He began his talk in the accepted manner, with congratulations for my birthday and praise for the work I had done over the years. To this day it moves me to recall his warm words at the opening of that session. He then proceeded to discuss the political situation in the region and the chances for peace. After his assassination, his remarks acquired a new dimension, and the videotaped recording of that lecture is now a treasured personal possession of mine.

The 1995 B.G. Lecture, by the Speaker of the Knesset, Professor Shevach Weiss, was an unforgettable experience. Because my birthday coincides with the anniversary of the victory over Nazi Germany, and since 1995 was the fiftieth anniversary of that event, I sought some way to connect the lecture to that historic date. I had almost given up hope of finding an appropriate lecturer when I attended a reception for Queen Beatrix of Holland in the Knesset and heard a brilliant talk given by Professor Weiss, himself a survivor of the Holocaust. At that moment I said to myself, 'That's it, I've found him!' I was very pleased when Professor Weiss accepted my invitation, and his wonderful lecture surpassed all my expectations. I took the unusual step of requesting permission to thank the speaker and to add a few words of my own. I reminded the audience of three particular instances when my birthday had intersected with events in my life in highly significant ways. The first of these was in 1939, when I travelled to Poland and met my relatives and many other Jews who were soon to be annihilated by the Germans; the second was in 1940 when, two days after my birthday, Holland fell to the Germans; and the third in 1945, when the war finally ended.

YITZHAK RABIN: I SIMPLY LOVED THE MAN

I started writing this book more than five years ago, and reached these final chapters during the *shloshim* (the thirty-day mourning period in Jewish tradition) of the late Yitzhak Rabin. Despite the seemingly random timing, I have been searching for some kind of significance that might serve as a source of meaning or strength, and perhaps help me contend with the new reality that came crashing down on us following the assassination.

When I returned from Argentina, during the *shiva* (week of intense mourning) for the late Prime Minister, I found it extremely difficult to sift out the true and honest sentiments from among the surfeit of words, pictures and events that popped up everywhere in connection with Yitzhak Rabin. At times I felt that some people's need to use his name, or to try to establish some kind of connection with him, took precedence over their desire simply to remember the man and honour his memory. When I sift out from my life story the occasions on which I stood side by side with Yitzhak Rabin I know that I, too, must tread carefully, and yet at the same time I must be totally frank.

I had the privilege of being counted among his friends. The death of Yitzhak, the soldier, the statesman, the friend, was a terrible blow to the entire people of Israel. I am not a native-born Israeli, nor had I served in the Palmach (the élite infantry unit before and during the War of Independence), or on the General Staff of the IDF. What is more, during my first few years in Israel, Rabin and I did not have too many occasions to get to know each other very well. I first met Yitzhak through Sapir, who greatly respected him. It was through Sapir that I too came to admire the young Chief of Staff. At that time Sapir often said to me: 'Just wait and see, Rabin will be a great national leader.' I accepted his prediction without any reservations. Later I discovered the many ways in which Rabin proved his decision-making abilities, his wisdom and his leadership.

I followed Yitzhak Rabin's career as ambassador to the United States and as Prime Minister with great admiration. For a while after he returned to Israel from his diplomatic posting to Washington he had no clearly defined job, either in the army or in politics. And it was then, of all times, during that period of uncertainty, that we became close friends, once again through the good offices of Pinhas Sapir. With his keen political instincts, Sapir could not reconcile himself to the fact that a man of Rabin's calibre and talents was not given something meaningful to do for the country. It was a critical time – the beginning of the Yom Kippur War – and Sapir suggested to Rabin that he take over the running of the Voluntary War Loan – an immense economic enterprise that needed a person like himself with a worldwide reputation and extensive personal contacts. Rabin seemed to Sapir to be the perfect candidate, but Rabin himself was not at all enthusiastic. Somewhat embarrassed, he said to Sapir, 'This is not really for me.' Sapir promised him all the expert counsel he would need, and recommended among others Zalman Susayev, a member of Knesset, a former Deputy Minister from the Liberal Party, and a top economic expert. I was also asked by Sapir to join the economic forum that was being put together to assist Rabin.

In the following months we sat together, Rabin, Susayev and me, in a room in the offices of the Ministry of Finance in Tel Aviv, not far from Sapir's office. Whenever we encountered a difficult 'client', I would press a hidden button, and the secretary would call Sapir in to bring the power of his personality and authority to bear on the issue until it was resolved. But the greatest surprise of all was Yitzhak Rabin himself. This reserved, even bashful, man met with people from all sectors of the economy, and seemed to impress them even in the field of economics, in which he was not an expert. His very presence there had a powerful impact both on ordinary people and top political leaders, leading them all to open their wallets and buy the loan bonds. He did not need to make any special effort to convince them. In this unheralded chapter of Rabin's career, I found great nobility, inner strength and dignity.

During the Yom Kippur War, I could read the pain in his face when no one turned to him for help or advice. Other reserve generals ran from one battlefront to another, while his uniform remained neatly ironed in the closet. He never complained, and continued doing his work with a constant smile on his face, even though the dissonance between his outer demeanour and his inner feelings became more and more apparent. He paced the office like a caged lion. One day Henry

Kissinger arrived for secret talks on a possible peace agreement. Rabin didn't have to say anything, I simply knew how he felt. 'Go to the Prime Minister's Office,' I told him. 'What can possibly happen? Do you honestly think anyone will throw you out?' He went, but I never asked him how Golda Meir received him.

When my good friend Ono Ruding, the former Dutch Minister of Finance, visited the country for the first annual Benno Gitter lecture, I asked him if he would be interested in having lunch with a former Prime Minister and Chief of Staff. He readily agreed, as did Rabin. The following day we met at the Olympia Restaurant in Tel Aviv. I introduced them to each other. 'This is the former and future Prime Minister,' I said of Rabin. 'And this is the former Minister of Finance and future Prime Minister of Holland.' I was right about Rabin, but wrong about Ruding, who at the age of fifty changed his profession, and in a short time because one of America's leading bankers.

On 4 November 1995, when Prime Minister Yitzhak Rabin was assassinated, I was in Argentina at a joint academic session of Tel Aviv University and the University of Buenos Aires. I was there with the heads of the university, among them the President, Professor Yoram Dinstein, and Ilana Ben Ami who had organized the conference. All of us were unutterably shocked and horrified by the news. Not quite certain about how we should proceed, we tried to regroup and decide on a course of action in the light of the tragic event. We postponed the academic part of the conference until after the funeral, which we all watched on CNN. At the opening session of the conference we stood in silence in Rabin's memory. The words uttered in Hebrew by President Clinton -'*Shalom Haver*' – became the motto of my personal eulogy for the slain Prime Minister. I refused to accept the fact that my last meeting with him was now going to become part of a storehouse of memories associated with Rabin. Less than two weeks had passed since I had attended an important event in Washington where President Bill Clinton and Prime Minister Yitzhak Rabin were the guests of honour and the keynote speakers. Like almost everyone else there, I could sense the warm bond of friendship that characterized their relationship, and affected everyone present. I had thought at the time that this moment was the pinnacle of the Prime Minister's career. As always, my all-too human short-sightedness made it impossible for me to foresee a higher peak, albeit an infinitely more tragic one, from which he would depart this life as a symbol of hope and peace.

Now that he has left us, I frequently think of Rabin. Occasionally on a weekend Yitzhak would answer our phone personally and respond to the caller warmly, displaying neither the affectation nor the self-importance of a Prime Minister. That's the way he was. Quite simply – I loved the man.

EPILOGUE

I have tried to avoid taking an overt political stand in this book. I have never been involved in politics, and I see no reason to change my habits at this late stage in my life. Nevertheless, it would be hard to say that I ever kept my political opinions hidden from view. Here and there they have appeared in this narrative directly or indirectly through the people I have been close to in my life. But now, after two fateful gunshots irrevocably changed the face of Israeli history, I cannot avoid taking a stand.

Over the thirty years that I knew Shimon Peres and the late Yitzhak Rabin I was an avid supporter of both of these impressive men. I had many opportunities to get to know their strengths and their wisdom. They were very different from each other, and under normal circumstances it might have been impossible to reconcile their differences. Many mutual friends, myself included, tried to bridge the gaps, but it was all in vain. And yet, in times of crisis, times when truly crucial decisions had to be made, they worked well together, and, one might even say, complemented each other. That is how the Oslo Accords were born, and that is how the two leaders cooperated with each other throughout the negotiations for peace.

Like Moses, who led his people through the wilderness for forty years and was not allowed to enter into the Promised Land, Rabin did not live to see the fulfilment of his dream. In the history of the state of Israel over the last forty years it is hard to find anyone who did more for peace, for the future of the people of Israel – and thus the future of the Jewish people as a whole – than Yitzhak Rabin. But the promised peace, the lasting peace, is still out of reach. A majority – a very slim majority – denied Shimon Peres the possibility of completing the mission which he and Yitzhak Rabin began together in Oslo, and which led them to become the joint recipients of the highest recognition given by the civilized world to people involved in such endeavours: the Nobel Prize for Peace.

As I write these lines, and observe the direction in which my country is moving, my heart is filled with trepidation. I am convinced that in the end, when all is said and done, peace is our only option. I am afraid, and regret very deeply, that the people of my generation, myself included, will not be here to witness the peace when it does eventually arrive.

My book is nearing its end. The process of writing has given me a unique opportunity to examine my life methodically, and to return to some of the experiences of my childhood. I remember the world of games and fantasies that my friends and I created in the charred remains of the Paleis voor Volkslijt, the popular palace of culture that housed a theatre before it was destroyed by fire. I had a wonderful and secure childhood. When did it end?

As I look back, I can point with some certainty to the moment when I became an adult. It was when I was fourteen years old, an instructor in the Zichron Jacob youth movement, and I stood with my friends on the platform of the Amsterdam railway station waiting for Jewish refugees from Germany whom we had been asked to meet and help integrate into Dutch society. They stepped down on to the platform – fearful, persecuted, hopeless. Their desolation was the first scratch on the protective shield of my being. I had never experienced persecution of any kind, but at that moment I felt a deep and painful empathy for these refugees. For the first time in my life I understood the meaning of the term 'the fate of the Jewish people', and at that very moment it was branded deeply and indelibly into my soul.

By the time I reached Argentina at the age of twenty-three, I had completed a very compressed, accelerated process of growing up. The gruelling experiences I had endured prior to my arrival in that safe haven could have provided material for an entire biography: my year in Hungary, my travels to Vienna and Poland, the German conquest of Holland, and my family's harrowing escape from the Nazis. I was born into a family of émigrés, and I too was destined to grow up as an émigré. And even after I had fully settled and created a life for myself in my adopted country, Argentina, I picked up my roots once again and moved to yet another country – my home: Israel. Every such process of uprooting involves a descent from a level of financial security and personal self-confidence and comfort to a lower level, of instability and uncertainty. But if there was a descent involved in our decision to move to Israel, it was, in fact, a prelude to an ascent: making *aliya* to the land of our forefathers (*aliya* – 'going up' to Israel – means 'ascent' in Hebrew). For ten years after our *aliya*, I still ran the family business in Argentina. As the situation in that country worsened in the sixties, my partners and I decided to sell the business to good friends and sever that connection to Argentina.

Forty-five years after my arrival in Israel, I am proud of the name I have made for myself here, and the status I have achieved. I have been very active in Israeli society, promoting industry and fostering the development of economic life, and to this day I have not cut myself off from these pursuits altogether. Ten years ago I created ISAL, a company devoted to the promotion of Latin American investments in Israel. The birth of ISAL was a direct outcome – albeit somewhat belatedly – of the fortunes of Clal. As I have mentioned, despite the fact that the great majority – some eighty per cent – of the original shareholders in Clal were Jews from South America, the situation changed within a few years of the creation of the company. During the recession of the sixties many of the original investors began to fear for their investments and divested themselves of their holdings in Clal. Their shares were eventually taken up by the three major banks: Discount, Hapoalim and Leumi. In order to revive the close, even familial, ties these South American Jews had with the state of Israel, Aharon Dovrat and I decided to set up a new company which would, on the one hand, use Clal's success as a model and, on the other, bring these people together again in a common purpose, giving them a sense of belonging and of being involved in the life of the country.

In an effort to emphasize the continuity of the new company with Clal, we held the founding meeting in Miami in May 1986: the same place and the same month where Clal was established twenty-four years earlier. We invited 120 entrepreneurs, Jewish investors from all over Latin America. Among them there were, no doubt, some people who had witnessed the birth of Clal, but most of them were representatives of a new, young generation of businessmen. They were all interested in investing in Israel, and a few score of them eventually became share-holders in ISAL. The company's investments cover a broad spectrum of interests, from industry to construction and services. Among the companies in the group are the cable company Kavlei Zion, the packaging company Kargal, Chemipal, Poster Media, and Schnapp. I am the chairman of the Board of Directors and of the Executive Committee, and the managing director is Dr Hugo Chaufan. I go to my offices in the Clal building in Tel Aviv almost every day, and enjoy working with the devoted, highly skilled and loyal team that I have assembled there.

After my almost total break from activity in one sphere, business and banking, I have had the rare privilege of being welcomed in to a different realm of activity, one that combines spirit and action, culture and art. I devoted an entire chapter to the university. I shall devote only a few lines to all my other activities, even though they will not suffice to convey the deep satisfaction all these activities have given me over the years. I am referring to the Israel Philharmonic Orchestra, the Tel Aviv Museum, and a large number of institutions and projects with which I have been connected for three or four decades. I have mentioned Beit Ariela a number of times, and I return to this superb institution once again – the jewel in the crown of all the cultural enterprises I have established in memory of my loved ones. When my daughter Ariela died, very few people had ever heard of her. Today there is hardly a person in Tel Aviv who has not hear of Beit Ariela. This knowledge contains a difficult paradox: on the one hand providing a measure of consolation, and on the other emphasizing the finality of my loss.

Thanks to my father, I have never known what it means to want for anything. I have related at length stories of danger, flight, sorrow and loss, but I have hardly ever experienced poverty. I have lived my entire life surrounded by people who dealt with money. I have often been asked about my attitude to money, and my answer is rather banal: making money is a good thing. However, only making money, without the added value of a spiritual content or higher purpose, is meaningless. For years I have set aside a part of my wealth for goals I felt were important: health, education, welfare, culture and the arts. I have derived a double pleasure from all this, being both contributor and fundraiser, and I have managed to infect others with my philanthropy. In many cases I offered to match contributions given by potential donors. I set no store by the name given to any particular project, be it someone else's name, the names of my family members whose memory I want to enshrine, or a combination of both. I have always felt that the donor and the fundraiser are equally important.

I have written at length about the strong spiritual grounding I was given by my father. In these very days, as I write the final pages of this book, the most fundamental problems of our country are rising to the surface: religion and the state, universal values as opposed to adherence to Jewish tradition and belief. Does strict, self-imposed enclosure within the world of Torah and Talmud constitute true Judaism? Am I obliged to be tolerant and open-minded about my spiritual heritage, even though I am sorely tempted to disassociate myself from everything that is included today under the banner of 'religion'?

My parents' home was a model of religious tolerance. My father, a truly, profoundly observant Jew, and my mother, a deeply religious woman, never imposed their beliefs on us, and never forced us to do anything against our will. Wearing a *kippa* outside the house, for example, was never regarded as absolutely necessary. My parents saw to it that side by side with our comprehensive Jewish education we also acquired a more universal upbringing. We never felt that there was, in any sense, a conflict between these twin foundations of our education. Eventually, I grew up and chose my own way of life, and, after coming to Israel, I gave up the observant lifestyle that I had maintained for many years. Despite my anger over what I feel are distortions of the sense of Jewish religious beliefs that characterize the various religious factions in Israel, I am convinced that the way my parents brought us up, and the educational milieu that we enjoyed, including the religious Zionist youth movement, gave us a strong basis and a clear direction in life. Every one of our actions, every form of conduct, is rooted in our family background. I am very happy to have had this kind of upbringing, and I would be happy, too, if the same kind of integration between Jewish, Zionist and universal values could be inculcated into a new generation of Israelis. Unfortunately, I have grave misgivings about future trends in Israeli society, which appears to be moving inexorably towards destructive manifestations of extremism.

The sum total of my life experiences has shaped my attitude towards religion and belief into a simple statement: 'Religion and I maintain separate households.'

Writing an autobiography has turned out to be a much more difficult task than I had imagined. I have tried to take hold of my past and trace a coherent pattern through the events, in a manner that would be at once moving and humorous. But will the events I think are important, historical, painful or funny be the same in the eyes and minds of my readers? I do not have the answer to that question. Whenever I have been called upon to make a speech, I have always done so without notes, from memory alone, basing my presentation on my thoughts and my reading of the audience's receptiveness. My memoirs, however, I have written using only my highly selective, subjective memory, without resorting to historical research or referring to books or written documents of any kind. Historians are now aware of the presumptuousness involved in supposedly objective writing. There is no writing of any kind that is not totally defined by the personal point of view of the author.

It is very difficult to write an autobiography without taking refuge behind a kind of protective mask. George Orwell once said: 'An autobiography should be written in such a way that the author should have grounds for a libel suit against himself.' Orwell also had this to say on the same subject: 'An autobiography that does not say something derogatory about its author, cannot be deemed a good one.' I hope I have said truthful things about myself. As for whether these things are good or bad – that will be left for my readers to decide.

I have made strenuous efforts to reconstruct the past from a critical vantage point. I have been particularly helped in this by my companion, Ilana Ben Ami, with whom I have shared many of my activities over the past decade. Argentine-born Ilana, a lawyer by profession, has been the head of the Latin American desk at Tel Aviv University for over sixteen years, during which time she has proven herself many times over. She has brought Tel Aviv University into pre-eminence among all the universities in Israel in everything to do with contacts in South America. I have cooperated with her in creating contacts in Latin America, and she has done the same for me in Israel and other places abroad. Our numerous mutual contacts and combined interests have turned our home into a warm open house for all the friends of the university. In this, as in many other things, it is Ilana who assumed the initiative and the responsibility.

As a former banker, I have become used to submitting quarterly reports, and giving a full annual report once a year. Now that I have reached the latter years of my life, I feel the need to submit a balance sheet, an accounting, to myself and to society at large. On the debit side, I entered a number of mistakes I have made. On the credit side, I am deeply satisfied with the strong ties I have had with the seven institutes of higher learning in Israel, and on whose boards I served, particularly Tel Aviv University. Another one of my goals was to support thousands of students at all seven universities, and at least the same number of high school students in Tel Aviv, through the Natan Ben Shimshon Foundation which I established in my father's name. Beit Ariela, with which I am involved to this day, and other institutes for education, medicine, welfare and culture, continue to benefit the people of Israel from all walks of life. In all of these, and in my relations with the management of all the institutions I have mentioned, I have found a great deal of personal satisfaction and great appreciation for what I have been able to contribute.

From the vantage point of the present, and weighing the myriad ups and downs, joys and disasters that have made up the fabric of my personal history, my life has been – and still is – a good one. I do not for a moment forget that this good life was given to me as a gift. For years my conscience troubled me for having survived while others perished. I shall never be able to shake off the question of: why me? why am I alive while the lives of others, more deserving than myself, were so cruelly cut short? I have no answer, no explanation. And perhaps I have been trying all my life to give myself – and the world – the answer through my deeds.

In these golden years, I am naturally concerned with the quality of my life, and my health. I try to maintain both at a high standard, and to continue to work creatively with the same intensity that has characterized everything I have done in the past. Should there be an epilogue to the story of my life, I promise to include it in the next edition . . .

INDEX